W9-CAV-776

Your Wish
Is My Command
Programming by
Example

The Morgan Kaufmann Series in Interactive Technologies

Series Editors:

- Stuart Card, Xerox PARC
- Jonathan Grudin, Microsoft
- Jakob Nielsen, Nielsen Norman Group
- Tim Skelly, Design Happy

Your Wish is My Command: Programming by Example
    Edited by Henry Lieberman

GUI Bloopers: Don'ts and Do's for Software Developers and Web Designers
    Jeff Johnson

Information Visualization: Perception for Design
    Colin Ware

Robots for Kids: Exploring New Technologies for Learning
    Edited by Allison Druin and James Hendler

Information Appliances and Beyond: Interaction Design for Consumer Products
    Edited by Eric Bergman

Readings in Information Visualization: Using Vision to Think
    Written and edited by Stuart K. Card, Jock D. Mackinlay, and Ben Shneiderman

The Design of Children's Technology
    Edited by Allison Druin

The Usability Engineering Lifecycle: A Practitioner's Handbook for User Interface Design
    Deborah J. Mayhew

Contextual Design: Defining Customer-Centered Systems
    Hugh Beyer and Karen Holtzblatt

Human-Computer Interface Design: Success Stories, Emerging Methods, and Real World Context
    Edited by Marianne Rudisill, Clayton Lewis, Peter P. Polson, and Timothy D. McKay

Your Wish Is My Command
Programming by Example

Edited by
Henry Lieberman

Media Lab
Massachusetts Institute of Technology

MORGAN KAUFMANN PUBLISHERS

AN IMPRINT OF ACADEMIC PRESS
A Harcourt Science and Technology Company

SAN FRANCISCO   SAN DIEGO   NEW YORK   BOSTON
LONDON   SYDNEY   TOKYO

Executive Editor   Diane D. Cerra
Assistant Developmental Editor   Marilyn Alan
Publishing Services Manager   Scott Norton
Production Editor   Howard Severson
Editorial Assistant   Mona Buehler
Cover Design   Yvo Riezebos
Cover Image   Kazuo Kawai / Photonica; Back photo: © 2000 by Webb Chappell
Text Design   Rebecca Evans & Associates
Copyeditor   Laura Larson
Proofreader   Ruth Stevens
Composition & Illustration   Technologies 'N Typography
Indexer   Steve Rath
Printer   Courier Corporation

The following material is reprinted with permission from *Communications of the ACM,* March 2000, Vol. 43(3): Smith, D. C., Cypher, A., and Tesler, L. "Novice Programming Comes of Age," 75–81; Myers, B. A., McDaniel, R., and Wolber, D. "Intelligence in Demonstrational Interfaces," fig. 3; Repenning, A. and Perrone, C. "Programming by Analogous Examples," figs. 3, 4, and 5; St. Amant, R., Lieberman, H., Potter, R., and Zettlemoyer, L. "Visual Generalization in Programming by Example," figs. 3 and 4.

Designations used by companies to distinguish their products are often claimed as trademarks or registered trademarks. In all instances where Morgan Kaufmann Publishers is aware of a claim, the product names appear in initial capital or all capital letters. Readers, however, should contact the appropriate companies for more complete information regarding trademarks and registration.

ACADEMIC PRESS
A Harcourt Science and Technology Company
525 B Street, Suite 1900, San Diego, CA 92101-4495, USA
http://www.academicpress.com

Academic Press
Harcourt Place, 32 Jamestown Road, London NW1 7BY, United Kingdom
http://www.academicpress.com

Morgan Kaufmann Publishers
340 Pine Street, Sixth Floor, San Francisco, CA 94104-3205, USA
http://www.mkp.com

© 2001 by Academic Press
All rights reserved
Printed in the United States of America

05 04 03 02 01   5 4 3 2 1

No part of this publication may be reproduced, stored in a retrieval system, or transmitted in any form or by any means—electronic, mechanical, photocopying, recording, or otherwise—without the prior written permission of the publisher.

Library of Congress Cataloging-in-Publication Data

Your wish is my command : programming by example / Henry Lieberman, editor.
    p. cm.
    Includes index.
    ISBN 1-55860-688-2
        1. Computer programming. I. Lieberman, Henry.
QA76.6.Y63 2001
005.2—dc21   00-069638

This book has been printed on acid-free paper.

Foreword

Ben Shneiderman
University of Maryland

Setting an alarm clock is probably the most common form of programming. Users set a time and then put the clock in alarm mode. Older twelve-hour mechanical clocks usually had a special alarm hand that could be moved to the time for the alarm to ring, and then the users turned the alarm switch on. A nice form of direct manipulation programming—easy to learn and use.

Direct manipulation is a term I coined in 1981 to describe the visual world of action in many successful graphical user interfaces such as video games, air traffic control, and what-you-see-is-what-you-get word processors. The principles were to

- represent the objects and actions visually,

- replace typing with pointing and dragging,

- provide rapid, incremental and reversible actions, and

- offer immediate and continuous feedback to users.

These principles can lead to interfaces that help novices and experts, prevent or at least reduce errors, and encourage exploration because reversibility is supported. Designers continue to refine and extend direct manipulation, but critics complain that direct manipulation only works for limited tasks. They often ignore the possibility of direct manipulation programming, which was part of the original conception (Shneiderman 1982, 1983).

To explore the possibilities, we built a direct manipulation programming tool in 1984–85 that enables users to create macros for MS DOS. This tool, Direct Manipulation DOS (DMDOS) (Iseki 1986), enabled users to record and view their actions, and then store and replay macros. We were motivated by successful macro facilities for Unix, word processors, and spreadsheets. These early keyboard-oriented systems led us to joke that "those who ignore history are destined to retype it." We were also inspired by innovative programming by demonstration in David Canfield Smith's (1977) Pygmalion, graphical macro facilities in Dan Halbert's (1984) SmallStar, and Alan MacDonald's (1982) early call for visual programming. These pioneers and other innovators believed in the goal of empowering users to create useful programs, extend existing interfaces, and build small just-in-time programs that automated daily tasks.

This important volume carries forward the agenda of making direct manipulation programming (or programming by example, programming by demonstration, end-user programming, programming in the user interface, etc.) a reality. While there have been successes in the intervening years, such as programmable machine tools, visual programming languages, and a variety of macro-building programs, widespread adoption is still elusive. Henry Lieberman deserves credit for his long devotion to this topic and for collecting the diverse strategies and application domains in this volume. He and the contributors to this volume remind us all of the breadth of opportunities and depth of ambition.

The allure of direct manipulation programming is its capacity to empower users, while minimizing learning of programming concepts. Researchers continue to seek simple cognitive models for programming that are in harmony with the cognitive model of the existing user interface. Just as the programmable mechanical alarm clock is tied to the familiar model of clock hands, researchers have wanted to build on the visual nature of graphical user interfaces.

This fundamental human-computer interaction challenge has inspired a generation of designers, who have come up with innovative strategies for supporting iteration, conditionals, parameter passing, modular design, pattern matching, and data representation. This treasure chest of strategies is likely to pay off in multiple solutions for direct manipulation programming and related problems. A successful strategy would not only be easy to learn but also support rapid composition of common programs. Then it would also be easy to invoke, with comprehensible feedback about successful and unsuccessful executions.

One strategy represented in this book is to develop software that recognizes familiar patterns of action and infers a useful program. There may be some opportunities along this path, but I prefer the second path of special tools for users to create a program, just as they move the special hand of an alarm clock to set the wake-up time.

A third path, also well represented in this book, is visual programming languages in which the users set out to write a program, but visually instead of textually. Visual programming languages may have a simple basis such as dragging items from a relational table to a screen-based form to create a report program. More elaborate visual programming languages have graphic symbols to represent objects, actions, conditionals, loops, and pattern matching.

A fourth path might be to add history capture environments for every interface. Unix command line interfaces had a history log that allowed users to conveniently review and reuse commands. World Wide Web browsers support history keeping of page visits with relatively easy review and reuse. Microsoft Word captures a history of actions to support undo operations, but users cannot review the history or save it. Adobe Photoshop 5.0 added a nice history feature for graphic designers, demonstrating that even in complex environments, rich history support is possible.

Our current efforts with Simulation Processes in a Learning Environment have emphasized history keeping, enabling users to review their work, replay it, annotate it, and send it to peers or mentors for advice (Plaisant 1999). An immediate payoff was that faculty could run the simulation in exemplary or inappropriate ways and store the histories for students to use as a training aid.

The story of this field and this book is that there is magic and power in creating programs by direct manipulation activities, as opposed to writing code. The potential for users to take control of technology, customize their experiences, and creatively extend their software tools is compelling.

Eighteenth-century scientists, such as Ben Franklin, experimented with electricity and found its properties quite amazing. Franklin, Michael Faraday, James Clerk Maxwell, and others laid the foundation for Thomas Edison's diverse applications, such as refinements of telegraphy, generators, and electric lighting. This book brings reports from many Franklins, Faradays, and Maxwells who are laying the foundation for the Thomas Edisons still to come. It is difficult to tell which idea will trigger broad dissemination or whose insight will spark a new industry. However, the excitement is electric.

References

Halbert, Daniel. 1984. Programming by example. Ph.D. diss. University of California, Berkeley. (Available as Xerox Report OSD-T8402, Palo Alto, CA, 1984.)

Iseki, O. and B. Shneiderman. 1986. Applying direct manipulation concepts: Direct Manipulation Disk Operating System (DMDOS). *ACM SIGSOFT Software Engineering Notes* 11, no. 2 (April): 22–26.

MacDonald, Alan. 1982. Visual programming. *Datamation* 28, no. 11 (October): 132–140.

Plaisant, C., A. Rose, G. Rubloff, R. Salter, and B. Shneiderman. The design of history mechanisms and their use in collaborative educational simulations. In *Proceedings of the Computer Supported Collaborative Learning Conference* (December 1999).

Shneiderman, B. The future of interactive systems and the emergence of direct manipulation. *Behaviour and Information Technology* 1, no. 3 (1982) 237–256.

———— 1983. Direct manipulation: A step beyond programming languages. *IEEE Computer* 16, no. 8 (August 1983): 57–69.

Smith, D. C. 1977. *Pygmalion: A computer program to model and stimulate creative thought.* Basel: Birkhauser.

Contents

Foreword   **v**

Ben Shneiderman

Color Plates   **following page 192**

Introduction   **1**

Henry Lieberman

Chapter 1   Novice Programming Comes of Age   **7**

David Canfield Smith, Allen Cypher, and Larry Tesler

        Abstract 8

  1.1   Introduction 8
  1.2   Programming without a Textual Programming Language 9
  1.3   Theoretical Foundations 11
        1.3.1   Sloman's Approach 13
        1.3.2   Bruner's Approach 15
  1.4   Empirical Evidence 16
  1.5   Conclusion 18
        References 19

Chapter 2   Generalizing by Removing Detail: How Any Program Can Be Created by Working with Examples   **21**

Ken Kahn

        Abstract 22

  2.1   Introduction 22
  2.2   A Brief Introduction to ToonTalk 24
  2.3   An Example of Programming by Example 26

2.4   Discussion   40
2.5   Conclusion   42
      Acknowledgements   43
      References   43

Chapter 3   Demonstrational Interfaces: Sometimes
                You Need a Little Intelligence, Sometimes
                You Need a Lot   **45**

Brad A. Myers and Richard McDaniel

      Abstract   46
3.1   Introduction   46
3.2   Our Demonstrational Systems   47
3.3   Level of Intelligence   49
      3.3.1   No Inferencing   50
      3.3.2   Simple Rule-Based Inferencing   50
      3.3.3   Sophisticated AI Algorithms   52
3.4   Feedback   54
3.5   Conclusion   57
      Acknowledgements   58
      References   58

Chapter 4   Web Browsing by Example   **61**

Atsushi Sugiura

      Abstract   62
4.1   Introduction   62
4.2   Underlying Problems of PBE   63
      4.2.1   Problem of Inferring User Intent   63
      4.2.2   Problem of Accessing Internal Data of
              Applications   64
4.3   Web Browsing: Good Domain for PBE   64
4.4   Internet Scrapbook   65
      4.4.1   Overview of Internet Scrapbook   66
      4.4.2   Generating Matching Patterns   67
      4.4.3   Extracting Data from Web Pages   70
      4.4.4   Evaluation   71
4.5   SmallBrowse: Web-Browsing Interface for Small-
      Screen Computers   73

4.5.1   Overview of SmallBrowse   74

4.5.2   Tip Help   80

4.5.3   Informal Experiments   80

4.6   Discussion   81

4.7   Conclusion   83

Appendix: Copying HTML Data from Web Browser to Scrapbook   84

References   85

Chapter 5   Trainable Information Agents for the Web   **87**

Mathias Bauer, Dietmar Dengler, and Gabriele Paul

Abstract   88

5.1   Introduction   88

5.2   An Application Scenario   89

5.3   The HyQL Query Language   91

5.3.1   The Construction of Wrappers   94

5.4   The Training Dialogue   96

5.4.1   Wrapper Generation and Assessment   98

5.4.2   Suggesting an Action   100

5.4.3   Executing an Action   101

5.4.4   A Simple Training Dialogue   102

5.5   Lessons Learned   104

5.6   The Communication Problem   105

5.7   Another Application Scenario   109

5.8   Related Work (Non-PBE)   110

5.9   Conclusion   112

Acknowledgments   112

References   113

Chapter 6   End Users and GIS: A Demonstration Is Worth a Thousand Words   **115**

Carol Traynor and Marian G. Williams

Abstract   116

6.1   Introduction   116

6.2   A Story of End Users and GIS   116

6.3   Why Is GIS Software So Hard to Use?   118

6.4   Are Things Improving for GIS Users?   120

6.5   How Can Programming by Demonstration
        Help?   121
6.6   A Programming-by-Demonstration Approach for GIS:
        C-SPRL   123
6.7   Conclusion   132
        Acknowledgements   132
        References   132

Chapter 7   Bringing Programming by Demonstration
                 to CAD Users   **135**

                 Patrick Girard

                 Abstract   136

7.1   Introduction   136
7.2   PBD and CAD   137
        7.2.1   CAD: A Suitable Area for PBD   137
        7.2.2   Variational and Parametric Solutions   140
        7.2.3   Requirements for PBD in CAD   142
7.3   Toward a Complete Solution   143
        7.3.1   Classical 2D CAD Systems   143
        7.3.2   Specificity and Naming in CAD   145
        7.3.3   Expressiveness   149
7.4   True Explicit PBD Solutions   155
        7.4.1   Fully Integrated PBD Systems   155
        7.4.2   An Actual Programming Environment,
                 but for Users...   157
7.5   Conclusion   159
        References   160

Chapter 8   Demonstrating the Hidden Features that
                 Make an Application Work   **163**

                 Richard McDaniel

                 Abstract   164

8.1   Introduction   164
8.2   The Perils of Plain Demonstration   165
8.3   Who Is Actually Programming?   166
8.4   Giving the System Hints   167
        8.4.1   Creating Special Objects   167
        8.4.2   Selecting the Right Behaviors   170

8.5   The Programming Environment Matters   171
8.6   Conclusion   172
      References   174

Chapter 9   A Reporting Tool Using Programming by
               Example for Format Designation   **175**
               Tetsuya Masuishi and Nobuo Takahashi
               Abstract   176
9.1   Introduction   176
9.2   System Overview   178
      9.2.1   System Configuration   178
9.3   User Interface of Format Editor   179
      9.3.1   Window Configuration   179
      9.3.2   Specifying Iteration   180
      9.3.3   Adjustment   182
9.4   Extracting Formatting Rules   182
9.5   Generating Reports   183
9.6   Example of the Process   183
9.7   Evaluation   187
9.8   Conclusion   190
      References   190

Chapter 10   Composition by Example   **191**
                Toshiyuki Masui
                Abstract   192
10.1   Introduction   192
10.2   PBE-Based Text Editing Systems   193
10.3   Dynamic Macro: A PBE-Based Text Editing
       System   193
10.4   POBox: A PBE-Based Text Input System   197
       10.4.1   Various Text Input Techniques   197
       10.4.2   POBox Architecture   200
       10.4.3   POBox for Pen-Based Computers   202
       10.4.4   Using POBox on a Cellular Phone   204
       10.4.5   POBox Server on the Internet   206
10.5   Conclusion   207
       References   207

Chapter 11   Learning Repetitive Text-Editing Procedures with SMARTedit   209

Tessa Lau, Steven A. Wolfman, Pedro Domingos, and Daniel S. Weld

Abstract   210

11.1 Introduction   210
11.2 The SMARTedit User Interface   212
11.3 The Smarts behind SMARTedit   215
11.4 Choosing the Most Likely Action   219
11.5 Making SMARTedit a More Intelligent Student   221
11.6 Other Directions for SMARTedit   223
11.7 Comparison with Other Text-Editing PBD Systems   223
11.8 Conclusion   224
        References   225

Chapter 12   Training Agents to Recognize Text by Example   227

Henry Lieberman, Bonnie A. Nardi, and David J. Wright

Abstract   228

12.1 Text Recognition Agents   228
12.2 Writing Conventional Grammars as Text   230
12.3 Programming Grammars by Example for More Accessibility   231
12.4 Grammex: A Demonstrational Interface for Grammar Definition   232
12.5 An Example: Defining a Grammar for Email Addresses   233
        12.5.1 Top-Down Definition   234
12.6 Rule Definitions from Multiple Examples   236
        12.6.1 Definition of Recursive Grammar Rules   236
        12.6.2 Managing Sets of Rule Definitions   238
        12.6.3 Complexity and Scalability   239
        12.6.4 Defining Actions by Example   240
12.7 Future Work: Using Grammar Induction to Speed Up the Definition Process   241
12.8 Related Work   242

12.9   Conclusion   243
         Acknowledgements   243
         References   243

Chapter 13   SWYN: A Visual Representation for Regular
                  Expressions   **245**
                  Alan F. Blackwell

         Abstract   246

13.1   Introduction   246
         13.1.1   Factors in the Usability of PBE Systems   247
         13.1.2   A Test Case for Visibility in PBE   248
         13.1.3   Summary of Objectives   249
13.2   Other PBE Systems for Inferring Regular
         Expressions   250
13.3   A User Interface for Creating Regular Expressions
         from Examples   251
13.4   A Heuristic Algorithm for Regular Expression
         Inference   255
         13.4.1   Probabilistic Algorithm   256
13.5   A Visual Notation for Regular Expressions   258
         13.5.1   Experiment: Evaluation of Alternative
                  Representations   259
         13.5.2   Method   261
         13.5.3   Results   263
         13.5.4   Discussion   264
13.6   An Integrated Facility for Regular Expression
         Creation   265
         13.6.1   Visual Integration with Data   265
         13.6.2   Modification of the Regular Expression   266
13.7   Conclusion   267
         Acknowledgements   268
         References   268

Chapter 14   Learning Users' Habits to Automate
                  Repetitive Tasks   **271**
                  Jean-David Ruvini and Christophe Dony

         Abstract   272

14.1   Introduction   272

14.2   Overview of APE   274

    14.2.1   The Observer   276

    14.2.2   The Apprentice   277

    14.2.3   The Assistant   278

14.3   Illustrative Examples   279

    14.3.1   Example 1   279

    14.3.2   Example 2   281

    14.3.3   Example 3   281

    14.3.4   Example 4   284

14.4   Detecting Repetitive Tasks   284

    14.4.1   Repetitive Sequences of Actions   284

    14.4.2   Loops   284

    14.4.3   Writing of Repetitive Pieces of Code   286

    14.4.4   Repetitive Corrections of (Simple)
          Programming Errors   286

14.5   Learning a User's Habits   286

    14.5.1   What Makes the Problem Difficult?   287

    14.5.2   Which Algorithms?   288

    14.5.3   A New Algorithm   289

14.6   Use and Experimental Results   290

14.7   Conclusion   293

    References   294

Chapter 15   **Domain-Independent Programming by
Demonstration in Existing Applications**   **297**

Gordon W. Paynter and Ian H. Witten

    Abstract   298

15.1   Introduction   298

15.2   What Familiar Does   300

    15.2.1   Arranging Files   301

    15.2.2   When Errors Occur   304

    15.2.3   Sorting Files   306

    15.2.4   Converting Images   309

15.3   Platform Requirements   311

15.4   AppleScript: A Commercial Platform   313

    15.4.1   High-Level Event Architectures   313

    15.4.2   Deficiencies of the Language   314

    15.4.3   Deficiencies of AppleScript
          Implementations   316

15.4.4 Learning from AppleScript's
Shortcomings   317

15.5 Conclusion   318
References   319

Chapter 16   Stimulus-Response PBD: Demonstrating
"When" as well as "What"   **321**

David W. Wolber and Brad A. Myers

Abstract   322

16.1 Introduction   322
16.1.1 PBD: An Elaboration of Macro
Recording   322
16.1.2 PBD Macro Invocation   323
16.1.3 Augmenting the Capabilities of Traditional
Interface Builders   324
16.1.4 A Quick Example   324
16.1.5 Wait a Second!   326
16.2 The Syntax of Stimulus-Response   326
16.2.1 Eliminating Modes   327
16.2.2 Demonstrating Stimuli   328
16.2.3 Demonstrating Responses   334
16.2.4 Demonstrating Aids: Guide Objects and
Ghost Marks   334
16.3 The Semantics of Stimulus-Response   336
16.3.1 Object Descriptor Problem   337
16.3.2 Response Parameter Descriptors   338
16.3.3 Linear Proportions   339
16.3.4 Complex Parameters   340
16.4 Feedback and Editing   340
16.4.1 Storyboards   341
16.4.2 The Stimulus-Response Score   341
16.5 Conclusion   342
References   343

Chapter 17   Pavlov: Where PBD Meets Macromedia's
Director   **345**

David Wolber

Abstract   346

17.1 Introduction 346

17.2 Example 346

17.3 Objects that React Asynchronously to Events 347

17.4 Conclusion 349

     References 350

Chapter 18   Programming by Analogous Examples   **351**

Alexander Repenning and Corrina Perrone

     Abstract 352

18.1 Introduction 352

18.2 The GUI to Program Chasm 354

18.3 Programming by Analogous Examples 356

    18.3.1 Making Cars Move Like Trains: An
            Analogy 357

18.4 Discussion 360

    18.4.1 Beyond Syntactic Rewrite Rules 360

    18.4.2 From Substitutions to Analogies 363

    18.4.3 Reuse through Inheritance 366

18.5 Conclusion 367

     Acknowledgements 368

     References 368

Chapter 19   Visual Generalization in Programming
by Example   **371**

*Robert St. Amant, Henry Lieberman, Richard Potter, and
Luke Zettlemoyer*

     Abstract 372

19.1 If You Can See It, You Should Be Able to
     Program It 372

19.2 What Does Visual Generalization Buy Us? 374

19.3 Low-Level Visual Generalization 376

19.4 High-Level Visual Generalization 378

19.5 Introducing Novel Generalizations:
     Generalizing on Grids 381

19.6 Conclusion 383

     References 384

Your Wish
Is My Command
Programming by Example

Introduction

HENRY LIEBERMAN

Media Laboratory
Massachusetts Institute of Technology

When I first started to learn about programming (many more years ago than I care to think about), my idea of how it should work was that it should be like teaching someone how to perform a task. After all, isn't the goal of programming to get the computer to learn some new behavior? And what better way to teach than by example?

So I imagined that what you would do would be to show the computer an example of what you wanted it to do, go through it step by step, have the computer remember all the steps, and then have it try to apply what you showed it in some new example. I guessed that you'd have to learn some special instructions that would tell it what would change from example to example and what would remain the same. But basically, I imagined it would work by remembering examples you showed it and replaying remembered procedures.

Imagine my shock when I found out how most computer programmers actually did their work. It wasn't like that at all. There were these things called "programming languages" that didn't have much to do with what you were actually working on. You had to write out all the instructions for the program in advance, without being able to see what any of them did. How could you know whether they did what you wanted? If you didn't get the syntax exactly right (and who could?), nothing would work. Once you had the program and you tried it out, if something went wrong, you couldn't see what was going on in the program. How could you tell which part of the program was wrong? Wait a second, I thought, this approach to programming couldn't possibly work!

I'm still trying to fix it.

Over the years, a small but dedicated group of researchers who felt the same way developed a radically different approach to programming, called *programming by example* (PBE) or sometimes *programming by demonstration* (the user demonstrates examples to the computer). In this approach, a software agent records the interactions between the user and a conventional "direct-manipulation" interface and writes a program that corresponds to the user's actions. The agent can then generalize the program so that it can work in other situations similar to, but not necessarily exactly the same as, the examples on which it is taught.

It is this generalization capability that makes PBE like macros on steroids. Conventional macros are limited to playing back exactly the steps recorded and so are brittle because if even the slightest detail of the context changes, the macro will cease to work. Generalization is the central problem of PBE and, ultimately, should enable PBE to completely replace conventional programming.

Significantly, the first real commercial market for PBE systems might be children. Children are not "spoiled" by conventional ideas of programming, and usability and immediacy of systems for them are paramount. We'll present two systems that have been recently brought to market and are enjoying enthusiastic reception from their initial users. David Smith, Allen Cypher, and Larry Tesler's Stagecast Creator, evolved from Apple's Cocoa/ KidSim, brings rule-based programming by example to a graphical grid world. Ken Kahn's ToonTalk, a programming system that is itself a video game, uses a radically different programming model as well as a radical user interface. The crucial problem of generalizing examples gets solved in a simple, almost obvious way—if you remove detail from a program, it becomes more general. Later in the book, we'll see Alexander Repenning and Corrina Perrone-Smith's AgentSheets, which operates in a similar domain and for a similar audience.

One way in which PBE departs from conventional software is by applying new techniques from artificial intelligence (AI) and machine learning. This approach opens up both a tremendous opportunity and also some new risks. Brad Myers and Rich McDaniel treat the thorny issue of "How much intelligence?" from their wide experience in building a variety of PBE systems.

Of course, we can't convince people about the value of programming by example unless we have some good examples of application areas for it! Next, we move to some application areas that show how PBE can really make a difference. Everybody's current favorite application area is the Web. The Web is a great area for PBE because of the accessibility of a wealth of knowledge, along with the pressing need for helping the user in organizing, retrieving, and browsing it. The emerging developments in intelligent agents can help—but only if users can communicate their requirements and control the behavior of the agent. PBE is ideal.

Atsushi Sugiura's Internet Scrapbook automates assembling Web pages from other Web sources, and he also explores Web browsers on small handheld devices. Mathias Bauer, Dietmar Dengler, and Gabriele Paul present a mixed initiative system: at each step, either the user or the agent can take action, cooperating to arrive at a "wrapper" that describes the format of Web pages.

Carol Traynor and Marian Williams point out the suitability of PBE for domains that are inherently graphical, such as Geographic Information Systems. If you can see it and point to it, you should be able to program it. PBE lets users see what they are doing, unlike conventional programming languages, in which graphical data can only be referenced in a program by file names and numbers. They illustrate the utility of PBE for "user-programmers"—those who specialize in the use of a particular application but also, at least occasionally, have the need to resort to programming. Patrick Girard embeds a PBE system in an industrial-strength computer-aided design (CAD) application. Designers of mechanical, electrical, manufacturing, or architectural systems can see the objects they are trying to design directly. Rich McDaniel moves from static graphics to the dynamic world of computer games, showing how interaction techniques can also demonstrate "hidden features" of applications that are not directly reflected in the graphics that the user will eventually see but are nevertheless crucial.

PBE can automate many common but mundane tasks that tend to consume a frustratingly large fraction of people's time. Text editing remains the application that people spend the greatest amount of time in, and so text editing applications are the target of the next set of PBE systems we'll look at. Tetsuya Masuishi and Nobuo Takahashi use PBE successfully for the common editing task of generating reports. Toshiyuki Masui's Dynamic Macro and PoBox systems use loop detection and a predictive interface to automate repetitive typing and editing, which can be especially important in minimizing typing in small handheld devices or for users with disabilities. The systems of Masuishi, Masui, and Sugiura have all been distributed to a large user community in Japan. Tessa Lau, Steve Wolfman, Pedro Domingos, and Dan Weld use the time-honored AI technique of version spaces to maintain a space of hypotheses about user actions, illustrating the synergy between work in machine learning and PBE.

Bonnie Nardi, David Wright, and I also put PBE to work for user convenience, in training text recognition agents to recognize by example common patterns of data that occur in the midst of unstructured information. Their PBE system for developing text recognition grammars, Grammex, was the first interactive interface of any kind to make the powerful grammar and parsing technology accessible to end users. Alan Blackwell adds to this general approach a visual syntax for the grammar rules, which he shows increases user comprehension of the resulting programs.

We shouldn't forget programming environments themselves as a domain for PBE, even if the programming is done in a conventional write-a-file-and-compile-it programming environment. Jean-David Ruvini and Christophe Dony take advantage of the truism that people are creatures of habit. They have a software agent detect habitual patterns in a conventional programming language environment, Smalltalk, and automate those patterns.

Well, if PBE is so great, how come everybody isn't using it? It's our hope that they soon will. But we realize that PBE represents such a radical departure from what we now know as "programming" that it is inevitably going to take a while before it becomes widespread. Despite the existence of many systems showing the feasibility of PBE in a wide variety of domains, conservatism of the programming community still seems the biggest obstacle.

Signs are growing, however, that PBE might just be beginning to catch on. Commercial PBE environments are beginning to appear, such as the children's PBE environments cited earlier that are now on the market. But it also makes sense to view more conventional user-programming facilities, such as so-called "interface builders," macros, and scripting systems, as the "poor man's programming by example." Some of these facilities are beginning to evolve in directions that may incorporate elements of the PBE approach. We also will need conventional applications to become more "PBE-friendly" so that PBE systems can use the conventional applications as tools in the same way that a user would operate them manually. Gordon Paynter and Ian Witten show how we might be able to leverage scripting language and macro capabilities that are already present or on the way for applications into full-blown PBE systems. This might facilitate an adoption path for PBE.

In programming, as in theater, timing is everything. Much of the work in PBE is involved with demonstrating how to do something, but equally important is when to do it. David Wolber and Brad Myers explore what they call "stimulus-response" PBE, in which we generalize on time and user input, to assure that PBE-programmed procedures are invoked at just the right time. Wolber also compares his PBE animation system to a conventional animation editor/scripting system, Macromind Director, which brings the similarities and differences of PBE versus conventional applications into sharp focus.

We then move on to explore some directions where PBE might be heading in the future. Alexander Repenning and Corinna Perrone-Smith show how we can take PBE a step further, using another important intuitive cognitive mechanism—analogy. We often explain new examples by way of analogy with things we already know, thus allowing us to transfer and reuse old knowledge. Repenning and Perrone-Smith show how we can use analogy mechanisms to edit programs by example as well as create them from scratch.

Robert St. Amant, Luke Zettlemoyer, Richard Potter, and I explore what at first might seem like a crazy approach. We actually have the computer simulate the user's visual system in interpreting images on the screen rather than accessing the underlying data. Though it may seem inefficient, it neatly sidesteps one of the thorniest problems for PBE: coexistence with conventional applications. The approach enables "visual generalization"—generalizing on how things appear on the screen, as well as properties of the data.

Programming by example is one of the few technologies that holds the potential of breaking down the wall that now separates programmers from users. It can give ordinary users the ability to write programs while still operating in the familiar user interface. Users are now at the mercy of software providers who deliver shrink-wrapped, one-size-fits-all, unmodifiable "applications." With PBE, users could create personalized solutions to one-of-a-kind problems, modifying existing programs and creating new ones, without going through the arcane voodoo that characterizes conventional programming. In this collection of articles, we hope that the diversity of systems presented, compelling user scenarios, and promising directions for the future of PBE will convincingly demonstrate the power and potential of this exciting technology.

Acknowledgements

I'd like to give special thanks to Andy Rosenbloom at ACM for giving me the impetus to get started on this project. Diane Cerra, Marilyn Alan, and Howard Severson at Morgan Kauffman were helpful throughout the publication process.

I'd also like to extend personal thanks to Christopher Fry, Suzanne Hanser, Walt Lieberman, Cindy Mason, Pattie Maes, Joanie Morris, Liz Rosenzweig, Sybil Shearin, Ted Selker, and Jim Youll. And a special thanks to the contributors to this book, who are all terrific examples of friends and colleagues.

About the Web Site

Some of the book's color figures appear in the color insert following page 192. You can also view all of the book's full-color figures at Morgan Kaufmann's *Your Wish Is My Command* Web site at *http://www.mkp.com/your_wish/*.

CHAPTER 1

Novice Programming Comes of Age

DAVID CANFIELD SMITH

Stagecast Software, Inc.

ALLEN CYPHER

Stagecast Software, Inc.

LARRY TESLER

Stagecast Software, Inc.

Abstract

Since the late 1960s, programming language designers have been trying to develop approaches to programming computers that would succeed with novices. None has gained widespread acceptance. We have taken a different approach. We eliminate traditional programming languages in favor of a combination of two other technologies: programming by demonstration (PBD) and visual before-after rules. Our approach is now available as a product named Stagecast Creator, which was introduced in March 1999. It is one of the first commercial uses of PBD. Stagecast Creator enables even children to create their own interactive stories, games, and simulations. Here, we describe our approach, offer independent evidence that it works for novices, and discuss why it works when other approaches haven't and, more important, can't.

1.1 Introduction

The computer is the most powerful tool ever devised for processing information, promising to make people's lives richer (in several senses). But much of this potential is unrealized. Today, the only way most people are able to interact with computers is through programs (applications) written by other people. This limited interaction represents a myopic and procrustean view of computers, like Alice looking at the garden in Wonderland through a keyhole. Until people can program computers themselves, they'll be able to exploit only a fraction of a computer's power.

The limits of conventional interaction have long motivated researchers in end-user programming. An *end user* in this context uses a computer but has never taken a programming class—a definition describing the vast majority of computer users. We use the term *novice programmer* to describe end users who want to program computers. Is novice programmer an oxymoron? Is it a reasonable goal? Certainly there are "novice document writers," "novice spreadsheet modelers," and even "novice Internet surfers." But in more than thirty years of trying, no one has come up with an approach that enables novices to program computers. Elliot Soloway, director of the Highly Interactive Computing Project at the University of Michigan, estimates that even for novices who do take a programming class, less than 1 percent continue to program when the class ends. We'll explore the reasons for this, but first we explore our own new approach to programming that seems to work for novices.

Stagecast Creator, a novice programming system for constructing simulations from Stagecast Software, Inc., founded by the authors and others in 1997, is the culmination of a seven-year research and development effort, the first five at Apple Computer (Smith, Cypher, and Spohrer 1994; Cypher and Smith 1995; Smith and Cypher 1995; Smith, Cypher, and Schmucker 1996). The project, initially called KidSim, was later renamed Cocoa, and finally became Creator. The goal was to make computers more useful in education. The co-inventors of Creator—the authors Smith and Cypher—decided to focus on simulations because simulations are a powerful teaching tool. They can make abstract ideas concrete and understandable. Interaction with them is unstructured and explanatory in nature. Students can conduct experiments. They can formulate hypotheses as to what will happen, then run a simulation and observe the results (the scientific method). When their hypotheses are refuted, students really get engaged. They lean toward the monitor and begin talking animatedly with each other. Even better, with Creator children learn by *building* simulations, encouraging the constructivist approach to learning. Children learn sequential, causal reasoning. In view of this potential, the goal of the Creator project evolved into empowering end users (teachers and students) to construct and modify simulations through programming.

Our initial approach was much like that of other language developers: to invent a programming language that would be acceptable to end users. We tried a variety of syntaxes; all failed dismally. That experience, together with the history of programming languages during the past thirty years—from Basic to Pascal, from Logo to Smalltalk, from HyperTalk to Lingo—convinced us we could never come up with a language that would work for novices.

Our first insight was that language itself is the problem and that any textual computer language represents an inherent barrier to user understanding. Learning a new language is difficult for most people. Consider the years of study required to learn a foreign language, and such languages are natural languages. A programming language is an artificial language that deals with the arcane world of algorithms and data structures. We concluded that no conventional programming language would ever be widely accepted by end users.

1.2 Programming without a Textual Programming Language

How can a computer be programmed without a textual programming language? Our solution combined two existing techniques: PBD and visual before-after rules. In PBD, users demonstrate algorithms to the computer by operating the computer's interface just as they would if they weren't programming. The computer records the user's actions and can reexecute them later on different inputs. PBD's most important characteristic is that everyone can do it. PBD is not much different from or more difficult than using the computer normally. This characteristic led us to consider PBD as an alternative approach to syntactic languages.

A problem with PBD has always been how to represent a recorded program to users. It's no good allowing users to create a program easily and then require them to learn a difficult syntactic language to view and modify it, as with most PBD systems. In Creator, we first sought to show the recorded program by representing each step in some form, either graphically or textually. Some of the representations were, in our opinion, elegant, but all tested terribly. Children would almost visibly shrink from their complexity. We eventually concluded that no one wanted to see all the steps; they were just too complicated.

Our second insight was not to represent each step in a program; instead, Creator displays only the beginning and ending states. Creator does in fact have a syntax—the lists of tests and actions in a rule—but people can create programs for a long time without even being aware of this syntax. This feature is dramatically different from conventional languages, in which users must know whether a routine is called "move" or "go," the order of the parameters, and where all the various quotation marks, semicolons, and parentheses belong.

As an example of the Creator approach, suppose we want the engine of a train simulation to move to the right. We move the engine by defining a visual before-after rule for the engine. Rules are the Creator equivalent of subroutines in other languages. Each rule represents an arbitrary number of primitive operations, or statements in other languages. Visually, Creator shows a picture of a small portion of the simulation on the left, then an arrow, and then a picture of what we want the simulation to look like after the rule executes. Figure 1.1 shows the interactive, visual process of creating a rule by demonstration.

First, we define the initial rule. Notice that the left and right sides start out the same; all rules begin as identity transformations. Users define the behavior of the rule by demonstrating changes to the right side. Here, we grab the engine with the mouse and drag it to the right. When we drop the engine, it snaps to the grid square it is over. That's all there is to it. Nowhere did we type `begin-end`, `if-then-else`, semicolons, parentheses, or any other language syntax. The rule we just created may be read as follows:

FIGURE **1.1**

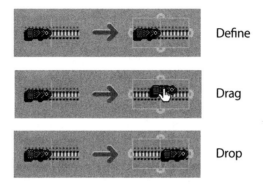

Define

Drag

Drop

Defining a rule by demonstration.

If the engine is on a piece of straight track and there is straight track to its right, then move the engine to the right.

Notice that programming is kept in domain terms, such as *engines* and *track,* rather than in computer terms, such as *arrays* and *vectors.* Also, instead of dealing with objects indirectly through coordinates, users program them by manipulating them directly; that is PBD (see Table 1.1).

Since a rule in Creator may not show all the steps involved, just their beginning and ending states, it is not a representation for the steps, suggesting instead the *effect* of the rule. The rule acts as a memory jogger for users. This turned out to be the key technique in Creator for helping users understand recorded programs, even those written by others.

A similar commercial software development system called AgentSheets, developed by Alexander Repenning (1993) at the University of Colorado in Boulder, also uses visual before-after rules (see Chapter 18, "Programming by Analogous Examples," which also gives an example using a train). A delightful system, it is the closest to Creator of any software system we know of.

1.3 Theoretical Foundations

Why does Creator's approach to programming apparently work where syntactic languages don't? We hinted at the answer earlier. An essential

TABLE **1.1**

Examples of the kinds of operations that can be recorded by demonstration.

Operation	What the user does	What the computer records
Move	Drag an object with the mouse	Move <object> to <location>
Create	Drag an object from the Character Drawer into the rule	Create <object> at <location>
Delete	Select an object by clicking on it and press the Delete key	Delete <object>
Set Variable	Double-click on an object to display its variables, select a variable's value, and type a new value	Put <value> into <object>'s <variable>

ingredient is certainly the PBD technique, which eliminates the need for any syntactic language during program construction. The technique of using visual before-after rules finishes the job, eliminating the need for any syntactic language for program representation. But why would these two techniques be acceptable to the typical novice programmer? The answer is interesting, illustrating why traditional approaches haven't and, more important, *can't* work.

The main problem novice programmers have when programming computers is the gap between the representations the brain uses when thinking about a problem and the representations a computer will accept. "For novices, this gap is as wide as the Grand Canyon," as Don Norman documented in his 1986 book *User Centered System Design* (see Figure 1.2). He argued that there are only two ways to bridge the gap: move the user closer to the system or move the system closer to the user. Programming classes try to do the former. Students are asked to learn to think like a computer. This radical refocusing of the mind's eye is difficult for most people. Even if they learn to do it, they don't like where they end up. They don't want to think like a computer; they want to use computers to accomplish tasks they consider meaningful.

In Creator, we've tried to do the opposite of what programming classes do—we want to bring the system closer to the user. We did this by making the representations used when programming the computer more like the representations used in the human brain. To do this, we needed a theory of the brain's representations that would be helpful to us. We found two: one developed by Aaron Sloman, the other by Jerome Bruner.

FIGURE **1.2**

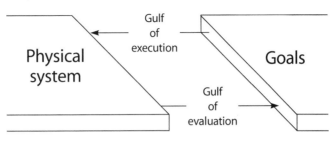

The "Grand Canyon" gap between human and computer.

1.3.1   Sloman's Approach

In 1971, Aaron Sloman divided representations into two general types: analogical and "Fregean," after Gottlob Frege, the inventor of predicate calculus. In an analogical representation, Sloman wrote, "the structure of the representation gives information about the structure of what is represented" (Sloman 1971, 273). A map is an example; from a map, one can tell the relationships between streets, the distance between two points, the locations of landmarks, and which way to turn when one comes to an intersection.

By contrast, Sloman (1971) wrote:

> In a Fregean system there is basically only one type of "expressive" relation between parts of a configuration, namely the relation between "function-signs" and "argument-signs." . . . The structure of such a configuration need not correspond to the structure of what it represents or denotes. (p. 273)

We can, for example, represent some of the information in a map through predicate calculus statements, such as

```
g:  "Gravesend"
u:  "UnionVille"
m:  "Manhattan Beach"
s:  "Sheepshead Bay"
East(g, u)
EastSouthEast(s, g)
South(m, s)
```

Sloman goes on to say:

> The generality of Fregean systems may account for the extraordinary rich-
> ness of human thought. . . . It may also account for our ability to think and
> reason about complex states of affairs involving many different kinds of ob-
> jects and relations at once. The price of this generality is the need to invent
> complex heuristic procedures for dealing efficiently with specific problem-
> domains. It seems, therefore, that for a frequently encountered problem do-
> main, it may be advantageous to use a more specialized mode of representa-
> tion richer in problem-solving power. (Sloman 1971, 274)

Most programming languages use Fregean representations, aiming to be
general and powerful. Creator emphasizes ease of use over generality and
power, and so it has adopted analogical representations. Although Creator
is "Turing-equivalent," meaning it can compute anything, it addresses only
the specialized problem domain of visual simulations. It doesn't try to do
everything well but is very good at what it does. A better way to describe it
than Turing-equivalent may be "PacMan-equivalent." Creator is powerful
enough to let kids program the game PacMan. That's all we're trying to do.

Creator uses analogical representations in its rules. For example, a rule
for moving a train engine, as shown in Figure 1.1, can do the same thing as
Fregean HyperTalk code, which can include dozens of arcane commands,
as in the following list which goes on for another seventy lines. It is obvious
which is easier to understand.

```
on runTrain
   global AutoSwitch,BtnIconName,PrevBtnIconName
   global Dir,PrevDir,LastLoc,PrevLocs,LookAhead,
          TheNextMove
   global LastMoveTime,SoundOff,MoveWait,Staging,
          TheStage,TheEngine
   global TheMoves,Choices,Counter,EngineIcon,XLoc
   —This routine is long.
   —Most of the code is inline for acceptable speed
   lock screen
   setupTrain
   unlock screen
     repeat
     —check user action often
        if the mouseClick then checkOnThings the clickLoc
     —get iconName of current position
```

```
put iconName(icon of cd btn LookAhead) into
    BtnIconName
if the number of items in BtnIconName > 1 then
  put "True" into Staging
  if TheStage = 0 then put BtnIconName into
    PrevBtnIconName
  if BtnIconName contains "roadXing" then put
    LookAhead into XLoc
  if BtnIconName contains "Rotatetrain" then put 1
    into TheStage
end if
if the mouseClick then checkOnThings the clickLoc
put LastLoc & return before PrevLocs
put LookAhead into LastLoc
put Dir & return before PrevDir
if the mouseClick then checkOnThings the clickLoc
add 1 to Counter
.  .  .
```

1.3.2 Bruner's Approach

In 1966, the educational psychologist Jerome Bruner (1966) asserted that any domain of knowledge can be represented in three ways:

- "By a set of actions appropriate for achieving a certain result ('enactive' representation). We know many things for which we have no imagery and no words, and they are very hard to teach to anybody by the use of either words or diagrams and pictures." For example, you can't learn to swim by reading a book.

- "By a set of summary images or graphics that stand for a concept without defining it fully ('iconic' representation)." For example, children learn what a horse is by seeing pictures of horses or actual living horses.

- "By a set of symbolic or logical propositions drawn from a symbolic system that is governed by rules or laws for forming and transforming propositions ('symbolic' representation)."

The first two ways are analogical representations; the third is Fregean. Jean Piaget, the noted Swiss psychologist best known for his work in the developmental stages of children, believed that children grow out of their early enactive and iconic mentalities and that becoming an adult means learning to think symbolically. By contrast, Bruner recommends encouraging children to retain and use all three mentalities—enactive, iconic, and symbolic—when solving problems. All three are valuable in creative thinking.

Creator seeks to involve all three mentalities in programming. The enactive mentality is involved in PBD when users manipulate images directly; drag-and-drop functions are enactive. The iconic mentality is involved in visual before-after rules and the domain of visual simulations. Finally, the symbolic mentality is involved in Creator's use of variables, which can help model deeper semantics in simulations. For example, predator-prey-type simulations can be modeled through variables.

1.4 Empirical Evidence

We've also gathered evidence that the Creator approach to programming works with novices. This evidence has taken three forms: informal observation, formal user studies, and anecdotal user reports.

Teachers and parents have used versions of Creator for years. We and our associates conducted hundreds of hours of direct tests on children and adults for the past five years, most on children ages six to twelve in school settings.

We implemented three computer prototypes of Creator, each smaller and faster and closer to product quality than the previous one, testing each on progressively larger audiences of novice users, and the final prototype—Cocoa—to an audience of hundreds of novice users. We distributed Cocoa through the Internet, just as we have with Creator, but our most important source of information was longitudinal studies in several elementary school classrooms in California. Teachers integrated the prototypes into year-long curriculums designed to improve their students' problem-solving skills. They contrived problems that required programming for their solutions; for example, one had her class program ocean science simulations. Our most gratifying success was when in June the students in one class asked to extend the school year so they could continue to work on their simulations. For the first six weeks of vacation, a third of the class continued to come to school once a week to program. The surprising thing is not that two-thirds of the children decided not to participate but that *any* of them wanted to keep coming to school during summer vacation. These kids did not find programming an onerous task.

FIGURE **1.3**

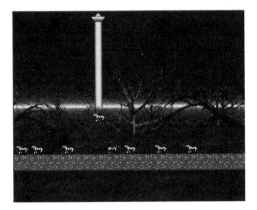

Alien Abduction.

Independent researchers at several universities in the United States and England conducted formal user studies of the Creator prototypes KidSim and Cocoa (Gilmore et al. 1995; Brand and Rader 1996; Sharples 1996; Rader, Brand, and Lewis 1997). While each identified areas for improvement, all answered affirmatively what we consider the two most important questions: Can kids program with this approach? Do they enjoy it?

The studies found that within fifteen minutes, most novice-user children were able to create running simulations with moving interacting objects. The studies found no gender bias: girls and boys enjoy Creator equally. The studies also suggest that the technology is usable by novices and is flexible enough for implementing a variety of ideas.

One of our early concerns was whether Creator would have enduring interest for children. We've now heard from some users and their parents and teachers that it does. For example, in Cedar Rapids, Iowa, Steve Strong, who teaches computer programming to students ages fourteen to seventeen, lets each one choose the language he or she would like to learn, including C, Java, and Creator. Since adding Creator to the curriculum, he reports that as many girls as boys now take his course; students who use Creator have well-developed projects to show at the end of the class, whereas those using traditional languages typically have only a small part of their project implemented. Moreover, students learning Creator first and other languages later are better programmers than those who go directly to a traditional language.

FIGURE **1.4**

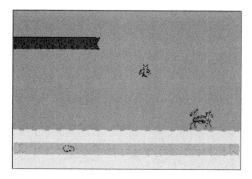

Olivia's Owl.

Figure 1.3 shows a hilarious game created by a twelve-year-old boy in which a spaceship beams up cows. A user controls the ship's direction with the arrow keys and the beam with the space bar. The goal is to beam up all the cows. Because of the high-level nature of the Creator rules, this game required only thirteen rules to implement.

Figure 1.4 shows a model created by an eleven-year-old girl of the way owls hunt mice in winter, when mice dig tunnels under the snow. But the owl had better watch out, because a wolf wants to eat it. The player controls the owl with the keyboard's arrow keys. The trick is to drop the owl on the mouse just as it passes under its claws. The goal is to catch five mice without getting eaten yourself. This game (actually two games in one) required fifty-seven rules.

1.5 Conclusion

Early evidence suggests the approach to programming being pioneered by Creator is more acceptable to novice programmers than traditional approaches. Creator uses PBD, which is inherently enactive and iconic, for program construction. It also uses an analogical representation—visual before-after rules—for its programs. The programming domain is limited to visual simulations, helping Creator bring the system closer to the user. In summary, Creator shifts the language design emphasis from computer science to human factors.

References

Brand, C., and C. Rader. 1996. How does a visual simulation program support students creating science models? In *Proceedings of IEEE Symposium on Visual Languages* (Boulder, Colo., Sept. 3–6). Los Alamitos, Calif.: IEEE Computer Society Press.

Bruner, J. 1966. *Toward a theory of instruction.* Cambridge: Harvard University Press.

Cypher, A., and D. Smith. 1995. KidSim: End user programming of simulations. In *Proceedings of CHI'95* (Denver, Colo., May 7–11). New York: ACM Press.

Gilmore, D., K. Pheasey, J. Underwood, and G. Underwood. 1995. Learning graphical programming: An evaluation of KidSim. In *Proceedings of Interact'95* (Lillehammer, Norway, June 25–30). London: Chapman & Hall.

Norman, D. 1986. Cognitive engineering. In *User centered system design: New perspectives on human-computer interaction,* ed. D. Norman and S. Draper. Hillsdale, N.J.: Erlbaum.

Rader, C., C. Brand, and C. Lewis. 1997. Degrees of comprehension: Children's mental models of a visual programming environment. In *Proceedings of CHI'97* (Atlanta, Ga.). New York: ACM Press.

Repenning, A. 1993. AgentSheets: A tool for building domain-oriented dynamic visual environments. Ph.D. diss. University of Colorado, Boulder; see www.agentsheets.com.

Sharples, M. 1996. How far does KidSim meet its designers' objectives of allowing children of all ages to construct and modify symbolic simulation? Report of the School of Cognitive and Computing Sciences, University of Sussex, Falmer, Brighton, England.

Sloman, A. 1971. Interactions between philosophy and artificial intelligence: The role of intuition and non-logical reasoning in intelligence. In *Proceedings of the 2nd International Joint Conference on Artificial Intelligence (London)*. San Francisco: Morgan Kaufmann.

Smith, D., and A. Cypher. 1995. KidSim: Child-constructible simulations. In *Proceedings of Imagina '95* (Monte Carlo, Feb. 1–3). Institut National de l'Audiovisuel.

Smith, D., A. Cypher, and K. Schmucker. 1996. Making programming easier for children. In *The design of children's technology,* ed. A. Druin. San Francisco: Morgan Kaufmann. See also *Interactions of ACM* 3, no. 5 (September–October 1996): 58–67.

Smith, D., A. Cypher, and J. Spohrer. 1994. KidSim: Programming agents without a programming language. *Common. ACM* 37, no. 7 (July): 54–67.

CHAPTER 2

Generalizing by Removing Detail:

How Any Program Can Be Created by Working with Examples

KEN KAHN

Animated Programs

Abstract

A long-standing goal of the programming by demonstration research community is to enable people to construct programs by showing how the desired programs should work on sample inputs. A major challenge is how to make the programs general. Heuristics and inference can generalize recorded actions on sample data in narrow domains but have yet to be much help in general-purpose programming. This chapter describes a programming system called ToonTalk (Kahn 1996, 2001) that takes a different approach. In ToonTalk the programmer generalizes recorded actions by explicitly removing details. Children as young as six have constructed a wide variety of programs in this manner (Playground 2001).

2.1   Introduction

There is a very important interplay between the way in which programs are created and generalized in ToonTalk and the underlying model of computation. A program is executed as a collection of autonomous processes that communicate asynchronously in which the behavior of a process is specified by a set of guarded clauses. A clause is constructed by performing operations on a single sample data structure. To make the clause capable of operating on other data structures, the programmer needs only to remove details from the guard or conditional part of the clause.

ToonTalk is built on the idea of *animated programming.* Animated programs are not constructed by typing text or by constructing diagrams or stringing icons together. Instead, the programmer is a character in an animated virtual world where programming abstractions are replaced by tangible analogs (see Figure 2.1). A *data structure,* for example, is a box whose holes can be filled with number or text pads, other boxes, birds, nests, and robots. *Birds* and *nests* are concrete analogs of send and receive capabilities on communication channels. A *robot* is a guarded clause that has been trained by the programmer to take actions when given a box. The thought bubble of a robot displays the guard or conditions that need to be satisfied before the robot will run. To generalize a robot, a programmer needs only to use an animated vacuum to remove details from the box inside the robot's thought bubble.

Figure **2.1**

Computational Abstraction	ToonTalk Concretization
Computation	City 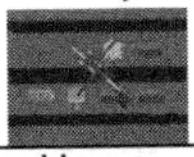
Actor Process Concurrent object	House 
Method Clause	Robot 
Guard Method preconditions	Contents of thought bubble 
Method actions Body	Actions taught to a robot
Message Array Vector	Box  4 2
Comparison test	Set of scales 
Process spawning	Loaded truck 
Process termination	Bomb 
Constants	Numbers, text, pictures, etc.  1997 ToonTalk
Channel transmit capability Message sending	Bird 
Channel receive capability Message receiving	Nest 
Persistent storage File	Notebook  Pictures 1 Sally 2

Computer science terms and ToonTalk equivalents.

2.2   A Brief Introduction to ToonTalk

After thirty years of mixed results, many educators today question the value of teaching programming to children. It is difficult, and children can do so many other things with computers. Proponents of teaching programming argue that programming can provide a very fertile ground for discovering and mastering powerful ideas and thinking skills (Papert 1980). Furthermore, programming can be a very empowering and creative experience. Children who can program can turn computers into electronic games, simulators, art or music generators, databases, animations, robot controllers, and the multitude of other things that professional programmers have turned computers into.

Why do we rarely see these wonderful results from teaching children to program computers? The answer seems to be that programming is hard—hard to learn and hard to do. ToonTalk started with the idea that perhaps animation and computer game technology might make programming easier to learn and do (and more fun). Instead of typing textual programs into a computer, or even using a mouse to construct pictorial programs, ToonTalk allows real, advanced programming to be done from inside a virtual animated interactive world.

The ToonTalk world resembles a twentieth-century city. There are helicopters, trucks, houses, streets, bike pumps, toolboxes, handheld vacuums, boxes, and robots. Wildlife is limited to birds and their nests. This is just one of many consistent themes that could underlie a programming system like ToonTalk. A space theme with shuttlecraft, teleporters, and so on, would work as well, as would a medieval magical theme or an Alice in Wonderland theme.

The user of ToonTalk is a character in an animated world. She starts off flying a helicopter over the city. After landing she controls an on-screen persona. The persona is followed by a doglike toolbox full of useful things.

An entire ToonTalk computation is a city. Most of the action in ToonTalk takes place in houses. Homing pigeonlike birds provide communication between houses. Birds are given things, fly to their nest, leave them there, and fly back. Typically, houses contain robots that have been trained to accomplish some small task. A robot is trained by entering his "thought bubble" and showing him what to do. This chapter focuses on how robots remember actions in a manner that can easily be generalized so they can be applied in a wide variety of contexts.

A robot behaves exactly as the programmer trained him. This training corresponds in computer science terms to defining the body of a method in

FIGURE **2.2**

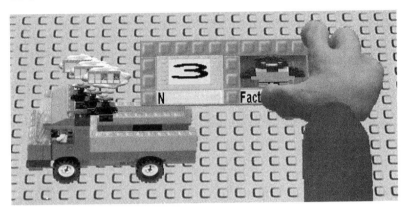

A truck being loaded with robots and a box.

an object-oriented programming language such as Java or Smalltalk. A robot can be trained to

- send a message by giving a box or pad to a bird;

- spawn a new process by dropping a box and a team of robots into a truck (which drives off to build a new house);

- perform simple primitive operations such as addition or multiplication by building a stack of numbers (which are combined by a small mouse with a big hammer);

- copy an item by using a magician's wand;

- change a data structure by taking items out of a box and dropping in new ones; or

- terminate a process by setting off a bomb.

The fundamental idea behind ToonTalk is to replace computational abstractions by concrete familiar objects. Even young children quickly learn the behavior of objects in ToonTalk. A truck, for example, can be loaded with a box and some robots (see Figure 2.2). The truck will then drive off, and the crew inside will build a house. The robots will be put in the new house and given the box to work on. This is how children understand trucks. Computer scientists understand trucks as a way of expressing the creation of computational processes or tasks.

2.3 An Example of Programming by Example

The ideal way to convey how a programming by demonstration system works is to demonstrate it. While a live demo would be easier to follow, I'll present two detailed examples here on paper. (A dynamic replay of these examples is available from *www.toontalk.com/English/wishes.htm.*) The first example is very simple. The benefits of a general-purpose programming with examples system are most apparent, however, with nontrivial examples. Hence, the second example is complex. While a complex example is hard to follow, it has the advantage that readers probably will need to think to figure out how to construct an equivalent program in their favorite programming language. Because the example requires some thinking, I hope that it shows how it really helps to program in a concrete fashion.

As our first example, let's imagine that Sue is a six-year-old girl who is fascinated by powers of 2. Sometimes in bed she repeatedly doubles numbers in her head before falling asleep. In ToonTalk she's discovered that she can use the magic wand to copy a number and then drop the copy on the original. Bammer, a small mouse with a big hammer, runs out and smashes the two numbers together. She starts with 1 and after ten doublings has 1,024 (see Figure 2.3).

FIGURE **2.3**

Bammer smashing
numbers together

Sue holding
the magic wand

Manually doubling numbers by copying.

She gets tired of repeated copying and dropping and decides to train a robot to do this for her. Since robots only work on things in boxes, she takes out a box and drops a 1 in it. She takes out a fresh robot and gives the box to the robot (Figure 2.4[a]).

She finds herself in the robot's thought bubble, and as she moves the computer's mouse, the robot moves. She trains the robot to pick up the magic wand and copy the 1 and drop it on the 1 in the box (Figure 2.4[b]). Bammer smashes them so that a 2 is now in the box. Sue indicates that she's finished training the robot and leaves his thoughts.

To try out her robot, Sue gives him the box with the 1 in it again (Figure 2.4[c]). This time the robot knows what to do. Sue watches as he copies the 1 and drops the copy on it. But the robot stops. He won't work on a box with a 2 in it. Sue knows that this is because his thought bubble contains a box with a 1 in it, so the robot will only accept a box with a 1 in it. He's just too fussy.

So Sue picks up Dusty the Vacuum and uses him to erase the 1 in the robot's thought bubble (Figure 2.5[a]). Her robot is now thinking about a box with any number in it. She has generalized her program by removing detail—in this case by erasing the 1.

Now she gives the box with a 2 in it to the robot (Figure 2.5[b]), and he copies the 2 and drops it, resulting in a 4. He then repeats since the result still matches his thought bubble (Figure 2.5[c]). Sue sits back, smiles, and watches as the number doubles over and over again.

Sally, Sue's twelve-year-old sister, is building a card game in ToonTalk. She has come to a point where she wants to sort the cards in a player's hand by rank. Without thinking very deeply about how to go about this, she creates a box with five numbers—[3 9 6 4 2]—and gives it to a robot. She then proceeds to train the robot to rearrange the numbers until she has [2 3 4 6 9]. When she gives the box to the robot, he repeats the recorded actions and sorts the box. She then creates another example box [4 8 2 3 1] and gives it to the robot, who rejects it because his thought bubble contains a copy of the original box [3 9 6 4 2] and this new box doesn't match. She then calls for Dusty the Vacuum and erases the numbers in the box in the robot's thought bubble. When she gives him the box [4 8 2 3 1] once again, she watches as the robot rearranges the box into [1 4 3 2 8]. A bit confused, she then gives the robot the box [1 2 3 4 5] and watches the robot turn it into [2 5 4 3 1]. While she thought she was training a robot to sort the numbers, she now realizes she had only trained a robot to permute five numbers so that the first number becomes the second number, the second one the fifth number, and so on.

ToonTalk does not contain program generalization heuristics. It does not try to solve the "data description problem" of figuring out what users mean

FIGURE **2.4**

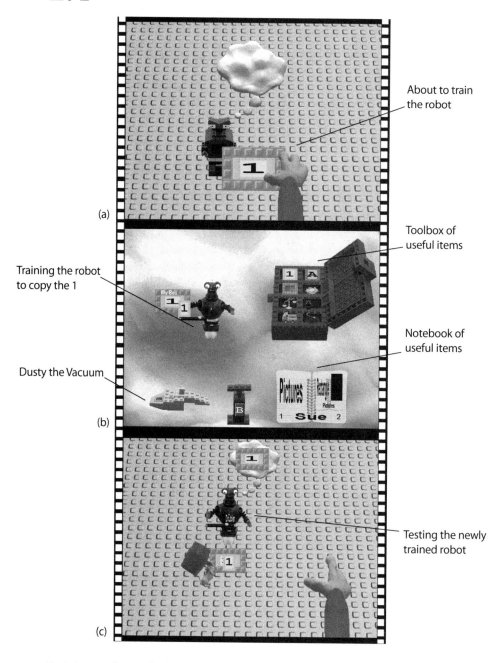

(a) About to train the robot

(b) Toolbox of useful items
Training the robot to copy the 1
Notebook of useful items
Dusty the Vacuum

(c) Testing the newly trained robot

Training a robot to double numbers: (a) giving an untrained robot a box to initiate his training; (b) training the robot to copy the contents of the box; and (c) testing the newly trained robot.

FIGURE **2.5**

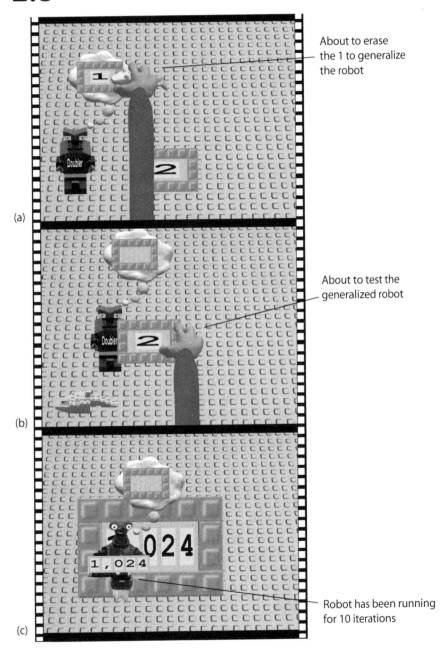

Generalizing and testing the robot: (a) erasing the number in the robot's thought bubble with Dusty the Vacuum; (b) testing the newly generalized robot; and (c) observing the robot's tenth iteration.

TABLE **2.1**

Programmer's actions and how the robot remembers them.

Programmer's actions	Robot's recording of the actions
Took the 3 out of the box	Pick up what is in the *first* hole of the box
Set it down	Set it down
Picked up the 2	Pick up what is in the *fifth* hole
Dropped it in the hole where the 3 was	Drop it in the *first* hole
Picked up the 9	Pick up what is in the *second* hole
Dropped it in the hole where the 2 was	Drop it in the *fifth* hole
Picked up the 3	Pick up the *first thing set down* (in step 2)
Put it where the 9 was	Drop it in the *second* hole
And so on until the numbers were sorted	And so on

when they manipulate objects on the screen. Instead, it has a small number of very simple rules of generalization, and it leaves the task of weakening the guard conditions to the programmer. As the programmer trains a robot, the robot moves around, picks things up, drops things, and uses tools to copy or remove things. Robots remember the actions they were trained to do based on the history of objects and their location in boxes. Robots ignore the path and timing of actions, labels (they are like comments in textual languages), and other details.

When Sally trained the robot to permute the box of five elements, she took the actions on the left side of Table 2.1. The robot recorded those actions as described on the right side of Table 2.1.

When she completed training the robot, his guard was the condition that his input be exactly the box [3 9 6 4 2]. After she erased the numbers, the guard only checked that the box contained exactly five numbers; the numbers could have any value. Clearly, relaxing the conditions didn't get her any closer to having a sort program. She could have trained 13!/8! robots to create a team that could have sorted any hand of five cards. The resulting program would only work with hands of exactly five cards. Instead, some other approach is needed.

She then thinks that maybe this is a job for recursion. If she could split the cards into two piles and sort those two piles somehow, she could merge the two piles by repeatedly taking the card from the pile that is showing the lower ranking card and putting the card down on a new stack. (In this scenario we'll see how she implements sorting by using the Merge Sort algorithm, but we could, of course, have seen her implement Quick Sort, Bubble

Sort, or other algorithms instead. Also, we'll see her work with arrays when she could equally well have used lists or other data structures.)

Sally figures that the first thing she'll need to do is split the box of numbers in half. She might have been misled by working with concrete examples and thought she had to train a robot to break the box with five holes into a piece with three holes and a remainder with two holes. But then on the recursive calls she would have to train another robot to break up the box with three holes into boxes with two and one holes and also train yet another robot to break a box with two holes. By removing details, she'll be able to make each of these robots work for any numbers but the team will only be able to sort boxes with five, three, or two holes. Because ToonTalk is incapable of generalizing one of these robots into one that breaks boxes in half, she needs to train the robot to compute the size of the box, divide the size by 2, and use the result to break the box in half.

Sally knows that in ToonTalk you can find out the number of holes a box has by dropping the box on a blank number. (This is an instance of a general facility that uses blank or erased data types to express data type coercion.) She also knows that if she drops a box on a number, the box is broken into two pieces where the number of holes of one piece is equal to the number underneath. She now has a plan for how to train the robot to break the box into two equal parts.

She'll need a robot that returns the sorted version of a box of numbers (see Figure 2.6[a]). So she constructs a box whose first element is her first sample box [3 9 6 4 2] and whose second element is a bird who will be given the sorted version of the box when the computation terminates. Sally knows that the bird will then take the box to her nest. Since the Sort robots will need the help of Merge robots, she takes out a fresh robot and places it in the third hole. She plans to later replace that robot with the team of Merge robots after she has trained them. By placing a dummy robot in the hole, the Sort robots can now refer to the yet-to-be defined Merge robots. She takes out a fresh robot and gives him the box.

She enters the robot's thought bubble and trains the robot to create a blank number by taking out a number, erasing it, and dropping the list of numbers on it (Figure 2.6[b]). The blank number changes to the size of the box. She then has the robot divide the resulting size by 2. (ToonTalk currently only supports integer arithmetic.) When she makes the robot drop the box on the number, the box splits into a part with two holes [3 9] and the remainder [6 4 2] (Figure 2.6[c]).

Sally now removes the bird from the box and then makes a copy of the input box and puts the [6 4 2] box in the copy. She puts the [3 9] box in the original input box. She creates a box for the Merge process and puts the bird

FIGURE **2.6**

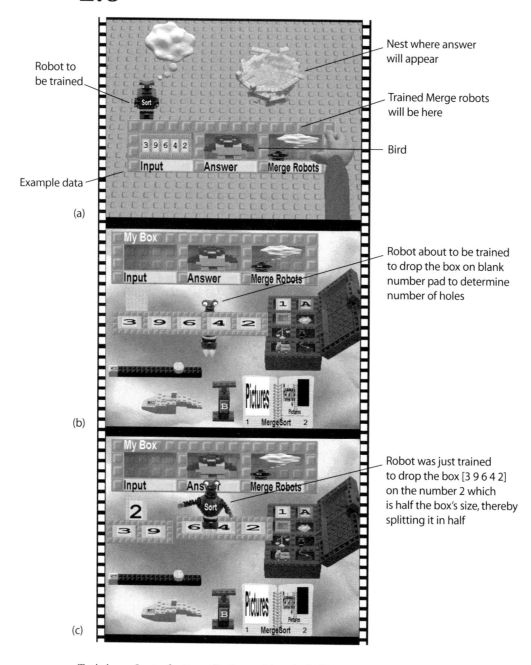

Training a Sort robot to split the problem in half: (a) initiating the training of a robot who will sort by splitting the problem in half; (b) preparing to train the robot to determine the number of compartments in the box he is holding; and (c) splitting the box being sorted into roughly two equal parts.

in it since the Merge process will produce the final result of the computation. She takes out two new nests and waits for eggs in the nests to hatch into birds. She puts the birds in the holes labeled "Answer" in the Sort boxes. The nests she puts in the holes labeled "Sorted1" and "Sorted2" in the Merge box (Figure 2.7[a]).

She trains the robot to take out a truck and use the magic wand to copy himself (and any future teammates), and to load the truck with his copy and the Sort box with [6 4 2] in it. She knows that when the robot repeats this, the crew in the truck will build a new house where the robots will work on the box—in other words, this will spawn a new process. She watches the truck drive off and takes out another truck. She puts a copy of the robot in the hole labeled "Merge" and the Merge box in the truck (Figure 2.7[b]). She is now finished training the Sort robot and exits the thought bubble. The robot has now been trained to iteratively split the box in half, spawn another Sort process to work on the second half of the box, and spawn a Merge process to combine the results from the two Sort processes.

Sally is now ready to try out her sorting robot (Figure 2.7[c]). She knows that she still needs to train more robots but wants to see this one work. She takes Dusty the Vacuum and uses him to erase the box in the hole labeled "Input" in the newly trained robot's thought bubble. By doing so the robot's "guard" is relaxed so that he'll accept any box whose first hole contains a box, second hole contains a bird, and third hole contains one or more robots.

Sally trained her robot to spawn a new Sort process to sort [6 4 2]. The robot then iteratively sorts [3 9]. She could have chosen to spawn two new Sort processes and let the current robot terminate instead. But there would be no advantage to doing so since iteration is tail recursion. In ToonTalk terms, the only difference is whether the team of robots continues to work in the same house (iteration) or a new house is built and the robots and box are moved there (tail recursion). She also trained her robot to spawn a Merge process to combine the results from the two Sort processes. Sally also needs to arrange for communication between these new processes so that the two Sort processes send their results to the Merge process. That is why she trained her robot to put a bird in the box used by each Sort process and the nests of the birds to be in the box used by the Merge process.

When Sally filled a truck with a box and a robot, the truck drove off. Since she was in the robot's thoughts, nothing was "returned" from these recursive calls. This ensures the generality of what the robot is being trained to do since it will not depend on the computation of any other program fragment.

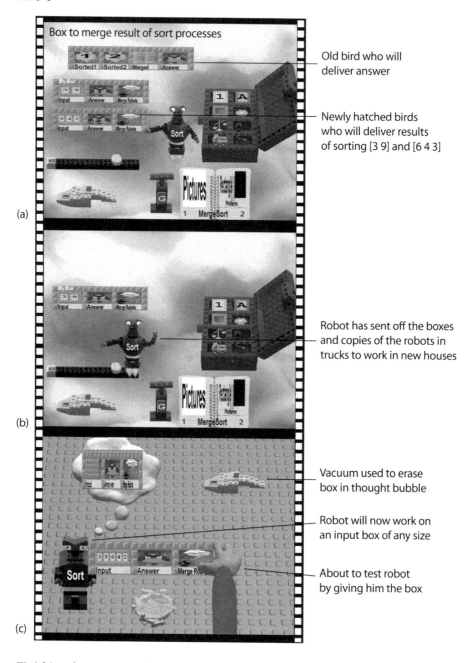

FIGURE **2.7**

Finishing the training of the Sort robot and generalizing it: (a) The robot has been trained to create boxes for sorting the two halves of the input box and a box for the Merge robot to use to combine the results; (b) the robot has been trained to generate a process to compute the sorting of the second half of the input box and a process to merge the results leaving the sorting of the first half of the box for himself; and (c) testing the newly trained and generalized robot.

One may be concerned that this scenario is complex—the robot is doing quite a large number of steps, and some are rather sophisticated. The alternative is even more difficult for most people: entering a symbolic encoding of Merge Sort with variables and parameters names. Here, the equivalent structures and actions are concrete and tangible, thereby reducing the cognitive load for most people.

ToonTalk programmers generalize robots by erasing and removing things from their thought bubbles. The simplicity of this process relies on the fact that all conditionals in ToonTalk are depicted as a visual matching process. The story one might tell a student learning ToonTalk is that the robot's thought bubble displays the kind of box he's willing to work on. If he is given a box that differs from that, he'll pass the box along to another team member. But if he is given a box with more detail than he is "thinking about," then that is fine, and he'll accept the box. If a number pad, for example, is erased, then he'll be happy with any number in the corresponding location of the box he is given. This part of the conditional is simply a type test. If the number pad is removed, then he'll accept anything in that location. Comparisons of numbers and text are handled by pictorially matching with the tilt of a set of scales that indicates the relationship between the objects on its sides. If a robot expects an item in the box and sees a nest, he'll wait for a bird to put something on the nest. This is the essence of how processes synchronize.

Returning to our example, Sally gives the robot the box and watches him correctly reenact her actions. She watches as he splits off the [6 4 2] box and loads trucks to spawn the other processes. Her robot then iterates on the remaining [3 9] box. She watches the robot split the box and give the [9] part to a recursive process. But when she watches the robot try to sort the [3] box, she watches as he stupidly splits it into [] and [3] and then proceeds to work on the [] part. He then stupidly splits that into [] and []. Sally realizes that she'll need more robots to help her robot with the easy problem of sorting one thing. She grabs her robot to stop him, sets him down, and takes out a fresh robot. She takes the box and replaces the [] box with a [3] box (see Figure 2.8[a]).

This new robot just takes the contents of the "Input" hole and gives it to the bird since the input is already sorted (Figure 2.8[b]). Sally then remembers that in ToonTalk it is good to be tidy and to destroy houses when a team of robots is finished. So she trains the robot to then pick up a bomb and set it off. This ends the robot's training. It also will stop the recursive process.

She now has a robot that will work with a box containing a 3 and another robot that will work on any box (but incorrectly if the box has only one hole). She calls for Dusty the Vacuum and erases the 3 in the box in the

FIGURE **2.8**

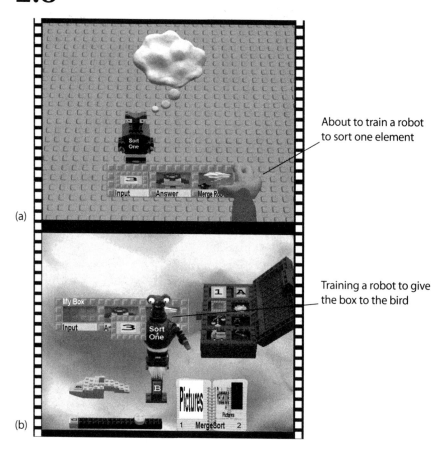

About to train a robot
to sort one element

(a)

Training a robot to give
the box to the bird

(b)

*(a) About to train the robot to sort boxes with one hole and (b) training the robot
for the base case of the recursion.*

robot's thought bubble. By erasing the 3, she has generalized the robot to
work on any box containing a single number. If, instead, she had removed
the 3 completely, then the robot would work with any box containing a single element regardless of its type.

Sally drops the robot that will work on any size box on top of this new robot. The robot then moves behind the new robot, forming a team. If a box
with one hole is being worked on, then the first robot will take care of it;
otherwise, the second robot will do the work. She has now completed programming the Sort process robots and has only the Merge process robots
left to do.

The training of the Merge robots illustrates an important programming technique of programming by demonstration—the use of derivative examples. Sally has run the Sort robots on an example, and they have created houses where dummy Merge robots have been given boxes to work on. These boxes are new examples that were generated by the Sort robots. Sally can go to one of these houses and start training a robot with the example box there. Then when a robot has been trained to do some of the processing on that box, she can run the robot until he stops. The robot has now generated another example box for training yet another robot.

She walks out of the house into a nearby new house where she sees a Merge box and a dummy robot. This is one of many houses that the Sort robots created by loading trucks. She wants to work on an example that covers lots of cases and modifies the box to become [[4 6] [3 6 7] [1 2] bird]. This represents the merging of the sorted records [4 6] and [3 6 7], where the partial answer [1 2] has already been produced. The advantage of working with such an example is that in the process of training robots to accomplish this task, nearly all the different cases will be covered. It can be done with the same number of robots as clauses in a traditional programming language and system.

She wants to train a robot to transform [[4 6] [3 6 7] [1 2] bird]] into [[4 6] [6 7] [1 2 3] bird]. But she knows that if she trained a robot to take the first element of the second box and move it to the end of the third box, the robot would do this regardless of the relationships between the numbers. Somehow she must make it clear why she is moving the 3 and not the 4.

Sally knows she can use a set of ToonTalk scales to compare numbers. If the number on the left of a scale is larger than the one on the right, the scale tilts toward the left. Since she wants to compare the first numbers of each list, she realizes she'll have to put a scale between copies of those numbers. (Instead of copying, she could move the numbers and then move them back.)

She takes out a fresh robot and gives him the box she made (Figure 2.9[a]). She trains the robot to add three new holes to the box, place a scale in the middle hole, and use the Magic Wand to copy the 4 and put the copy to the left of the scale and put a copy of the 3 to the right (Figure 2.9[b]). She watches as the scale tilts to the right. Her plan is to have another robot, whose guard (i.e., thought bubble) will check that the scale is tilted to the right and will move the 3 in that case. So she stops training this robot.

Sally gives the box to her new robot and watches him reenact her actions. She then takes out a fresh robot and gives him the resulting box: [[4 6] [3 6 7] [1 2] bird 4 > 3]. She trains this robot to break the [3 6 7] into [3]and [6 7]. She puts the [6 7] box back and takes out the [1 2] box, joins the [3]

FIGURE **2.9**

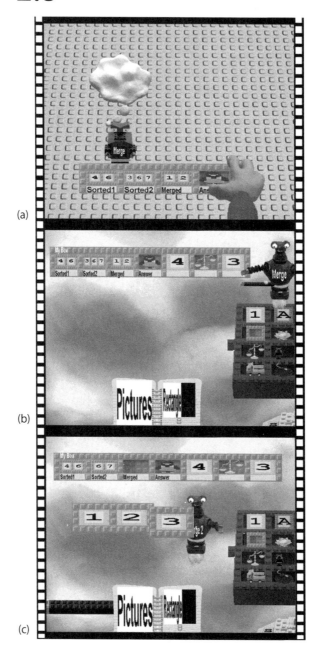

(a)

(b)

(c)

(a) About to train the first Merge robot; (b) training the robot to add the three new holes on the right; and (c) training the robot to add the first part of the box in "Sorted2" to the end of the box in "Merged".

FIGURE **2.10**

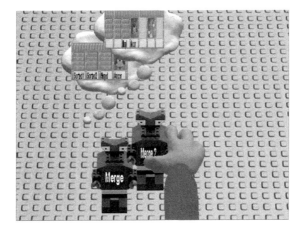

Joining the robots into a team after generalizing them.

box on the right, and puts the [1 2 3] box back (Figure 2.9[c]). This robot then removes the three temporary extra holes to restore the box for further processing.

Sally decides it is now time to generalize her two new robots. She decides the first robot should work with any three boxes followed by a bird and erases accordingly. The second robot should work with any three boxes, followed by a bird, followed by a number, a scale tilted to the right, and a number. She joins the robots into a team (Figure 2.10).

She gives the [[4 6] [6 7] [1 2 3] bird] box to the Merge team. The box is transformed to [[4 6] [6 7] [1 2 3] bird 4 < 6], and then the robots stop because the scale is tilted the other way so it doesn't match. She gives the box to a fresh robot and trains him very much like the previous robot. This robot differs only in that he moves the first number of the second, rather than first, box to the end of the third box. She generalizes him like the other robot and joins him to the team. The box is transformed to [[6] [6 7] [1 2 3 4] bird] and then to [[6] [6 7] [1 2 3 4] bird 6 = 6], and then the team stops because the scale is balanced and none of the robots can match a balanced scale. Sally trains a robot to move both numbers to the end, generalizes him, and joins him to the team. The box is then transformed to [[] [7] [1 2 3 4 6 6] bird]. When the team iterates, the robot that adds the numbers and scale to the end of the box triggers an error message. Marty, the personification of the error system, appears and gives her the warning that the Merge robot stopped because he was looking for a hole that a box didn't have. A robot needs to be trained to handle the case where the first hole contains a box without any holes. This robot needs to take the [7] and add it to the end of [1 2 3 4 6 6], give the result to the bird, and then set off a bomb because the task is completed.

After training this robot, Sally mistakenly believes she's finished and puts the teams in the correct holes and tries sorting some boxes. She tries [3 2 1] and she sees a bird fly to the nest with [1 2 3]—the right answer. But then when she tries [3 9 6 4 2 1 2], Marty appears and gives the same error message as before. To see what the problem is, she gets up, goes outside, and gets into her helicopter. She flies up and sees four extra houses. She lands near one and goes inside. She sees [[2] [] [1] bird] on the floor and realizes the problem is just that she didn't train a robot for the case where the second hole has a box with no holes. She trains a new robot much like the previous robot and adds him to the team.

Sally tries out her program again, and this time flies her helicopter over the city as it is running. She feels proud as she watches trucks driving to empty lots, houses being constructed, birds leaving some houses before they explode, while more trucks emerge from others. Sally has successfully constructed, tested, and debugged a parallel Merge Sort program.

2.4 Discussion

It might seem to be easier for Sally just to type in a parallel Merge Sort program in some textual language using variables rather than go through the process described here. One way to discover if ToonTalk is easier is to study real people using it and compare them with people using conventional programming tools. The Playground (2001) research project has begun such a study of children six to eight years old, and preliminary results are encouraging. Based on informal observations of about a hundred fourth-grade students and feedback from many hundreds of beta testers and customers, we are confident that studies such as this will show a dramatic advantage to programming by example.

Program development is much easier in ToonTalk for several reasons. As many researchers in the field of programming by demonstration (Cypher 1993) have pointed out, people are generally better at working with examples than abstractions. Pygmalion (Smith 1993) and Tinker (Lieberman 1993) are two pioneering systems to support general-purpose programming by example. These systems were not able to eliminate abstractions completely, however. The need for a conditional test in Tinker, for example, was automatically discovered, but then the programmer needed to provide the predicate expression. When faced with multiple examples, both systems needed help from the programmer. Tinker asks the user which previous example is closest to the current one, for example. In Pygmalion, conditionals need to be introduced early in the process of demonstrating a program. In contrast, each ToonTalk clause (i.e., robot) is a self-contained unit whose conditional test is automatically generated by the system and relaxed by the programmer.

The task of supporting programming by demonstration is greatly simplified by the use of an appropriate computation model. ToonTalk has no nested conditionals, no complex conditionals (i.e., deep guards), no non-local variables, and no subroutine calls. It is nonetheless a very expressive high-level programming language. Each of these widespread programming abstractions interferes with the process of programming by example. Much of the power and simplicity of ToonTalk comes from the fact that once a robot starts working, it is just executing "straight-line" code without conditionals or procedure calls (though this straight-line code often includes process spawning and interprocess communication). In addition, any "variable references" are resolved to either the box that the robot was given or some local temporary variables that are concretized as something placed on the floor. Procedure calls interfere with a top-down programming style. If the subroutines aren't defined yet, then the system must, like Tinker, introduce descriptions of data to represent the return values. These descriptions are not part of the programming language and add cognitive complexity. Procedures that modify data structures are even harder to handle. In ToonTalk, a procedure call is just a particular pattern of spawning processes and using communication channels to return results. A ToonTalk programmer frequently creates pairs of birds and nests and uses the birds to deliver computed values to nests. The nest, when used like this, is a "promise" or "future" value (Lieberman 1987). If a ToonTalk programmer needs to compute something before proceeding, then she splits the task between two robots, one to spawn the process that computes something and the other to use the result after it is received.

Pygmalion made the task of programming more concrete by letting the programmer manipulate iconic representations of programs and sample data. Tinker made things more concrete by letting the programmer manipulate sample data and descriptions of computations. ToonTalk makes the process of programming even more tangible by avoiding icons and descriptions and by providing concrete animated analogs of every computational abstraction. Everything in ToonTalk can be seen, picked up, and manipulated. Even operations like copying or deleting data structures are expressed by using animated tools like the Magic Wand and Dusty the Vacuum.

Stagecast Creator is the only other programming by demonstration system designed for children. Creator relies upon analogical representations. "Programming is kept in domain terms, such as engines and track, rather than in computer terms, such as arrays and vectors" (Smith, Cypher, and Tesler 2000, 78). In contrast, ToonTalk is programmed in computer terms, except those terms have "translated" to familiar and tangible objects such as boxes, birds, and robots. Consequently, ToonTalk is general and powerful, whereas "Creator emphasizes ease of use over generality and power" (Smith et al. 2000).

Special-purpose programming by demonstration systems derive much of their advantage from the fact that the task of extending or automating tasks in an application is very similar to the task of performing the task directly in the user interface. While ToonTalk is a general-purpose programming system, it also has this property. The same objects and tools used when training robots are also used by the programmer directly to accomplish tasks. Direct manipulation and recording are distinguished visually by whether the programmer is controlling a programmer persona (hand or person) or a robot. Furthermore, when controlling a robot the system displays the robot's thought bubble as the background instead of the usual floor. The same skills and way of thinking can be used in both modes.

2.5 Conclusion

According to Smith (1993), "The biggest weakness of Pygmalion, and all the programming by demonstration systems that have followed it to date, is that it is a toy system." ToonTalk is the first system in widespread use that enables programmers to construct general-purpose programs by demonstrating how the program should work on examples. Unlike its predecessors Pygmalion and Tinker, ToonTalk was not designed for computer scientists (Smith 1993) but for children and adults with no prior programming experience. Thousands of children have successfully used ToonTalk to construct a wide variety of programs, including computer games (Playground 2001), math and word manipulation programs, and animations.

Programming, however, is a cognitively challenging task. A programmer needs to design the program's architecture, break large tasks into manageable pieces, choose wisely among a range of data structures and algorithms, and track down and fix the all too common bugs once the program is constructed. Enabling the programmer to do these tasks while manipulating concrete data and sample input helps reduce some of the complexity. But the hard fun (Papert 1996) remains.

Acknowledgements

Thanks to all those who gave comments to earlier versions of this chapter. In particular, Mary Dalrymple, Henry Lieberman, and Gordon Paynter deserve special thanks.

References

Cypher, A., ed. 1993. *Watch what I do: Programming by demonstration.* Cambridge, Mass.: MIT Press.

Kahn, K. 1996. ToonTalk—An animated programming environment for children. *Journal of Visual Languages and Computing* (June).

———. 2001. ToonTalk Web site: www.toontalk.com.

Lieberman, H. 1987. Concurrent object oriented programming in Act 1. In *Object oriented concurrent programming*, ed. Aki Yonezawa and Mario Tokoro. Cambridge, Mass.: MIT Press.

———. 1993. A programming by demonstration system for beginning programmers. In *Watch what I do: Programming by demonstration*, ed. A. Cypher. Cambridge, Mass.: MIT Press.

Papert, S. 1980. Mindstorms: Children, computers, and powerful ideas. New York: Basic Books.

———. 1996. The connected family: Bridging the digital generation gap. Longstreet.

Playground Research Project. 2001. Web site: www.ioe.ac.uk/playground.

Smith, D. C. 1993. Pygmalion: An executable electronic blackboard.

Smith, D. C., A. Cypher, and L. Tesler. 2000. Novice programming comes of age. *CACM* 43, no. 3 (March). (See also Chapter 1 of this book.)

CHAPTER 3

Demonstrational Interfaces:

Sometimes You Need a Little Intelligence, Sometimes You Need a Lot

BRAD A. MYERS

Human Computer Interaction Institute
Carnegie Mellon University

RICHARD MCDANIEL

Siemens Technology to Business Center

Abstract

Over the last fifteen years, we have built over a dozen different applications in many domains where the user can define behaviors by demonstration. In some of these, the system uses sophisticated artificial intelligence (AI) algorithms so that complex behavior can be inferred from a few examples. In other systems, the user must provide the full specification, and the examples are primarily used to help the user understand the situation. This chapter discusses our findings about which situations require increased intelligence in the system, what AI algorithms have proven useful for demonstrational interfaces, and how we cope with the well-known usability issues of intelligent interfaces such as knowing what the system can do and what it is doing.

3.1   Introduction

Demonstrational interfaces allow the user to perform actions on concrete example objects (often by direct manipulation), but the examples represent a more general class of objects. This can allow the user to create parameterized procedures and objects without requiring the user to learn a programming language. The term *demonstrational* is used because the user is *demonstrating* the desired result using example values. Significant differences exist among demonstrational systems along many dimensions. Some demonstrational interfaces use *inferencing,* in which the system guesses the generalization from the examples using heuristics. Other systems do not try to infer the generalizations and therefore require the user to tell the system explicitly what properties of the examples should be generalized. One way to distinguish whether a system uses inferencing is that if it does, it can perform an incorrect action even when the user makes no mistakes. A noninferencing system will always do the correct action if the user is correct (assuming there are no bugs in the software, of course), but the user is required to make all the decisions.

The use of inferencing comes under the general category of *intelligent interfaces.* This category entails any user interface that has some "intelligent" or artificial intelligence (AI) component, including demonstrational interfaces with inferencing but also other interfaces such as those using natural language. Systems with inferencing are often said to be "guessing" what the user wants. Another term is *heuristics,* which refers to rules that the system uses to try to determine what the user means. The rules in most demonstrational systems are defined when the software is created and are often quite specialized. (For another discussion of the strategies used by demonstrational systems and other intelligent interfaces, see Chapter 3 of Maulsby 1994.)

Over the past fifteen years, the Demonstrational Interfaces group at Carnegie Mellon University has created over a dozen demonstrational systems that use varying amounts of inferencing. Some systems have none and just create an exact transcript of what the user has performed so it can be replayed identically. Most provide a small number of heuristics that try to help users perform their tasks. Our most recent system, Gamut, employs sophisticated AI algorithms such as plan recognition and decision tree learning to infer sophisticated behaviors from a small number of examples. (Gamut is described in more detail in Chapter 8 of this book.)

This chapter discusses our experience with using various levels of "intelligence" in the interfaces. Some have criticized the whole area of intelligent interfaces because users may lose control. We strive to overcome this problem by keeping users "in the loop" with adequate feedback so they know what is happening and opportunities to review what the system is doing and to make corrections. However, this is still an unsolved area of research, and reviewing the different trade-offs in different systems can be instructive.

First, we provide an overview of the demonstrational systems we have created, followed by a discussion of systems that have no inferencing, simple rule-based inferencing, and sophisticated AI algorithms. Finally, we discuss the issue of feedback, which is important to keep the user informed about what the system is doing.

3.2 Our Demonstrational Systems

The Demonstrational Interfaces group at Carnegie Mellon University has created a wide variety of demonstrational systems over the last fifteen years. This section summarizes our systems.

- *Peridot* (Myers and Buxton 1986; Myers 1990): One of the first demonstrational systems to use inferencing, it allows users to create widgets such as menus and scroll bars entirely by demonstration. It uses extensive heuristic, rule-based inferencing from single examples and, for each rule that matches, asks the user to confirm the inference.

- *Lapidary* (Myers, Vander Zanden, and Dannenberg 1989; Vander Zanden and Myers 1995): It allows application-specific graphical objects, such as the prototypes for node and arc diagrams, to be created interactively. Lapidary uses simple heuristics from a single example.

- *Jade* (Vander Zanden and Myers 1990): It automatically creates dialogue boxes from a specification. Some of the parameters of the layout could be specified by demonstration.

- *Gilt* (Myers 1991b): This is an interface builder where the parameters to the callbacks attached to the widgets can be demonstrated by example. A callback that sets some widget's value based on others can be eliminated by demonstrating its behavior. Gilt uses simple heuristics from single examples.

- *Tourmaline* (Myers 1991c; Werth and Myers 1993): It uses rule-based inferencing of text structures and styles from one example. When an example contains more than one kind of formatting, the system tries to infer the role of each part and its formatting. For example, if a conference heading is selected, the system tries to infer the separate formatting of the author, title, affiliation, and so forth.

- *C32* (Myers 1991a): It provides a spreadsheet-like display for defining and debugging constraints. The constraints can be generalized by giving an example.

- *Pursuit* (Modugno, Corbett, and Myers 1997; Modugno and Myers 1997b): It creates scripts for automating "visual shell" (desktop) tasks on files. Focuses on providing a visible record of the inferred program in a graphical "comic book"–style visual language. Generalizes the objects on which to operate based on the properties of a single example.

- *Gold* (Myers, Goldstein, and Goldberg 1994): It creates business charts and graphs given an example of one or two elements of the chart and the desired data. It generalizes from the example marks to match the format of the data, and the results of the inferences are immediately shown in the chart.

- *Marquise* (Myers, McDaniel, and Kosbie 1993): It creates drawing editors by showing examples of what the end user would do, and then what the system would do in response. Built-in heuristics and widgets help with palettes that control modes and parameters. Feedback to the user is provided using an English-like presentation of the inferred code, where choices in the code are pop-up menus.

- *Katie* (Kosbie and Myers 1993, 1994): It records high-level events (e.g., "delete object-A") as well as low-level events (e.g., mouse-move) and allows macros to use any level. Katie proposes that macros could also be invoked when low- or high-level events occur.

- *Turquoise* (Miller and Myers 1997): It creates composite Web pages from examples of what they should contain. The demonstration is performed by copying and pasting content from the source Web pages.

- *Topaz* (Myers 1998): It creates scripts in a graphical editor, in a way analogous to macros in textual editors such as Emacs. Generalizations of parameters to operations are available in dialogue boxes. The generated script is shown in an editing window.

- *Gamut* (McDaniel and Myers 1998, 1999; see also Chapter 8): Sophisticated inferencing mechanisms allow the creation of complete applications from multiple examples, both positive and negative. Novel interaction techniques make specifying the behaviors easier.

3.3 Level of Intelligence

Many of our systems, and most of the PBD systems by others, have used fairly simple inferencing techniques. The hope has been that since these systems are interactive, the user will be "in the loop," helping the system when it cannot infer the correct behavior. Furthermore, many of the PBD system developers have not been AI researchers, so they have been reticent to apply unproven AI algorithms. Finally, a number of human-computer interface (HCI) researchers (e.g., Shneiderman 1995) have argued against "intelligent" user interfaces, claiming that this will mislead the user and remove the necessary control. On the other hand, experience with the many PBD systems shows that users continually expect the system to make more and more sophisticated generalizations from the examples, and the PBD researchers want their systems to be able to create more complex behaviors. Therefore, there is pressure to make the systems ever more "intelligent." In our own systems, we have explored systems at both ends of the spectrum and many points in between.

3.3.1 No Inferencing

Our Topaz system for creating macros or scripts of actions in a video editor requires the user to explicitly generalize the parameters of the operations using dialogue boxes (Myers 1998). For example, Figure 3.1(a) shows a script window (in the background) with a pop-up dialogue box that can be used to generalize the references to objects in the recorded script. The script was created using specific example objects, but the user could generalize these objects in various ways. Among the choices in the dialogue box are that the run-time object should be whatever object is selected at run time, the objects that result of a previous command, and so forth. The only heuristic built into Topaz is that when a script creates objects and then operates on the created objects, the default generalization for the latter operations is that they operate on the dynamically created objects each time the script executes. This heuristic is almost never wrong, so there is little chance of the system guessing incorrectly in this case.

Since there is little inferencing, the system never makes mistakes, and the user has complete control. However, the user must figure out how to get the desired actions to occur, which often requires clever use of special Topaz features, such as searching for objects by their properties and the different ways to generalize parameters.

Many other PBD systems take the no-inferencing approach, including the seminal Pygmalion (Smith 1977) and SmallStar (Halbert 1993) systems.

3.3.2 Simple Rule-Based Inferencing

Most of our systems have used simple rule-based heuristic inferencing for their generalizations. For example, the early Peridot system (Myers 1990) used about fifty hand-coded rules to infer the graphical layout of the objects from the examples. Each rule had a test part, a feedback part, and an action part. The test part checked the graphical objects to see whether they matched the rule. For example, the test part for a rule that aligned the centers of two rectangles would check whether the centers of the example rectangles were approximately equal. Because the rules allowed some sloppiness in the drawing, and because multiple rules might apply, the feedback part of the rule was used to ask the user if the rule should be applied. For example, Peridot would ask something like, "Do you want the selected rectangle to be centered inside the other selected rectangle?" If the user answered yes, then the action part of the rule generated the code to maintain the constraint.

FIGURE **3.1**

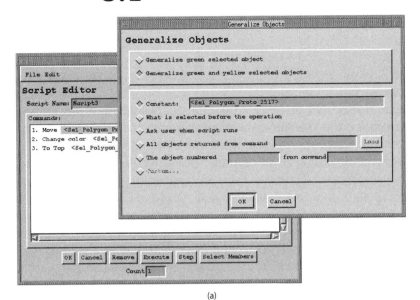

(a)

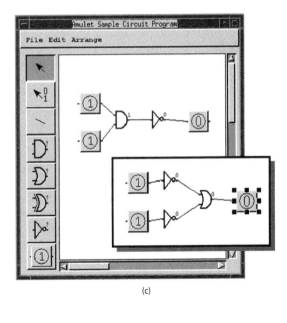

(b)

(c)

(a) The dialogue box for generalizing objects in Topaz, with the script window in the background. The user must select which generalizations to apply. Using such dialogue boxes, sophisticated scripts can be created, such as (b) a script to create a "Sierpinski Gasket" and (c) a script that applies DeMorgan's law by changing an And gate and a Not gate into two Not gates and an Or gate and reconnects the wires.

Subsequent systems have used similar mechanisms, although often without the explicit list of rules used by Peridot. For example, Tourmaline contained rules that tried to determine the role of different parts of a header, such as the section number, title, author, and affiliation, and the formatting associated with each part (Werth and Myers 1993). The results were displayed in a dialogue box for the user to inspect and correct. Many other PBD systems use the rule-based approach from single examples, including Mondrian (Lieberman 1992) and Pavlov (Wolber 1997).

An important advantage of using such rule-based heuristics that generalize from a single example is that it is much easier to implement. No sophisticated AI algorithms are required, and the developer can hand-code the rules and adjust their parameters. It is also easier for the user to understand what the system is doing, and eventually users may internalize the full set of rules. The disadvantages are that only a limited form of behavior can be generalized, since the system can only base its guess on a single example. More complex behaviors either are not available or must be created by editing the code generated by the PBD system. Since predetermined behaviors are all that are available, some argue that these behaviors might instead be made available in a direct-manipulation way, such as a menu, to avoid the problems of inferencing.

Another interesting issue with rule-based systems is whether the end user can change the rules. Most existing PBD systems have used a fixed set of rules created by the designer. In many cases, the users might have a better idea of the rules that would be appropriate for the applications they would like to build, so it would be useful for the end user to be able to specify new rules. However, if users could write the code for the rules, then they would probably not need PBD support. No one has produced a system that allows new rules to be entered into the system using PBD, which is an interesting metaproblem.

3.3.3 Sophisticated AI Algorithms

Recognizing the limitations of single-example, rule-based approaches, and wanting to create more sophisticated behaviors, the Gamut system infers behaviors from multiple examples (McDaniel and Myers 1999).

Gamut begins building a new behavior in much the same way as the single-example systems. However, each time the developer refines the behavior by adding a new example, Gamut uses metrics to compare the new example with the current behavior and choose how the behavior should be changed. For example, if Gamut sees that parts of the code that were previously executed are no longer being used in the new example, it will enclose that code in an if-then statement. If Gamut sees that an object is being set with a different value, it will use the new value along with heuristics to select changes to the code that produces that value. Gamut also uses a *decision tree* algorithm to generate code that could not be generated from rules alone. For example, Gamut uses decision trees to represent the predicates of if-then statements.

Gamut uses interaction techniques to support its algorithms. For example, the developer can create "guide" objects to represent the state of the application that is not part of its visible interface. These are visible at design time but disappear at run time. The developer can also highlight objects in order to give the system hints. The hints guide Gamut's heuristic algorithms when they select relationships to put into a behavior. Gamut can also request that the developer highlight objects when its algorithms reach an impasse and can no longer infer code without the developer's help.

Other PBD systems have worked from multiple examples. Some script-based systems, such as MetaMouse (Maulsby and Witten 1989) and Eager (Cypher 1991), compare multiple executions of commands to look for possible macros that the system might create automatically for the user. From the matches, these systems generalize the parameters to the operations, using simple heuristics such as the next item in a sequence, or offset by a constant factor. InferenceBear can generate more sophisticated behaviors by supporting linear equations to compute the parameters and letting the user provide negative examples to show when behaviors should not occur (Frank 1994).

When inferring from multiple examples, the system must be able to recognize both positive and negative examples. In the simplest case, a positive example demonstrates a condition when a behavior should occur; a negative example shows when the behavior should not occur. Without negative examples, a system cannot infer many behaviors, such as ones that use a Boolean-OR. In Gamut, the developer can use either the Do Something or Stop That button to create a new example. These choices roughly correspond to creating a positive or negative example. In some other systems, negative examples are recognized implicitly. For instance, when MetaMouse detects that a behavior is repeating, the actions that are not repeated in the current iteration act as a negative example. This will signal to the system that a conditional branch is required. InferenceBear required users to note negative examples explicitly, which proved difficult for users to understand.

The primary advantage of using more sophisticated techniques is that the system can infer more complex behaviors. The disadvantages include that the systems are much more difficult to implement, and they still may not infer correctly. There is a "slippery slope" for all intelligent interfaces, including PBD systems: once the system shows a little intelligence, people may expect it to be able to infer as much as a human would, which is well beyond the state of the art. It is still an open problem to balance the sophistication of the system with the expectations of users.

3.4 Feedback

In user studies of the Eager system, users were reticent to let the system automate their tasks because it provided no feedback about what the stopping criteria were (Cypher 1991). Another important issue is how can users edit the program if they change their minds about what it should do?

Clearly some form of representation of the inferred program is desirable. But since users of PBD are generally considered to be nonprogrammers, it seems inappropriate to require them to read and understand code. If they could understand the code, they might be able to write it in the first place, so no PBD would be needed. In some cases, however, the goal of the PBD is to help the user get started with the language. Since it is easier for people to recognize than to recall, seeing the code generated from the examples may help people learn the language and give them a start on their programs. This is an important motivation for adding the record mode for creating macros by example in spreadsheets and other programs. However, much evidence indicates that people have great difficulty understanding the generated code and modifying it when it isn't exactly correct. Therefore, an important challenge for PBD systems is how to let the user understand and edit the program without obviating the benefits that PBD provides.

Peridot (Myers 1990) used question-and-answer dialogues to confirm each inference, which proved to be problematic because people tended to simply answer yes to every question, apparently assuming that the computer knew what it was doing. Peridot also had no visible representation of the code after it was created, so there was no way to check or edit the resulting program.

Our Pursuit system (Modugno and Myers 1997) focused on studying the issue of feedback. It used a novel graphical presentation that showed before and after states, based on a "comic strip" metaphor. The domain was the manipulation of files in a "visual shell" or desktop, and the visual presentation showed examples of files icons before and after each operation. Figure 3.2 shows an example of a relatively complex program in Pursuit. The same

FIGURE **3.2**

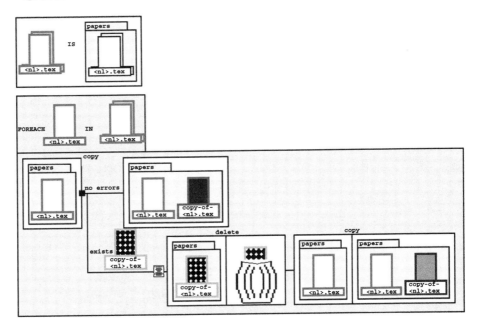

A program represented in Pursuit that looks for all the files in the papers directory that match ".tex" and, for each of these, tries to copy the file. If an error occurs during copying because the resulting file already exists (lowest branch), then the program deletes the old file and does the copy again.*

visual language was used to allow users to confirm and repair inferences by the system (e.g., how to identify the set of files to operate on) and to enable editing of programs later (e.g., if the user wanted a slightly different program for a new task). User studies with Pursuit showed that people could more easily create correct programs using the graphical language than with an equivalent textual representation and that they could make relatively complex programs containing conditionals and iterations.

Marquise (Myers et al. 1993) generated a textual representation of the program, as shown in Figure 3.3. The evolving program was represented as sentences, with each choice represented by a button embedded in the sentence. Clicking on a button would provide alternate options, and changing the option might also change the subsequent parts of the sentence.

Experience with this form of feedback showed that it had a number of problems. The implementers found it very difficult to design the sentences

FIGURE **3.3**

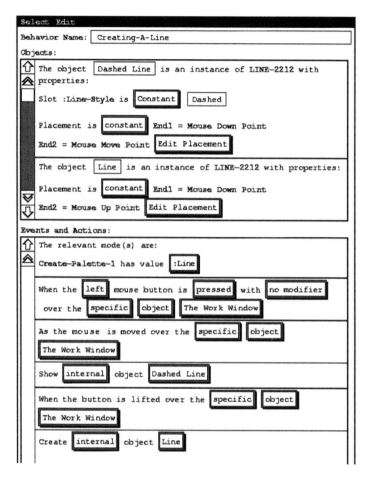

This behavior, shown in the feedback window of Marquise, controls the drawing of a line. When the Create palette is in the line mode, a dashed line follows the mouse, and when the mouse button is lifted, a solid line is drawn. The embedded buttons represent options that can be used to edit the behavior.

so they were readable and still contain the correct options. When users wanted to change the behavior in significant ways, it was often difficult to figure out which button to use.

The Topaz system (Myers 1998) used a relatively straightforward representation of the program (see Figure 3.1[a]). The operation name shown in the script was often the same as the menu item that the user selected (e.g., To Top), and the parameters started off constant and could be changed using dialogue boxes. All the usual editing operations are supported for the script, such as Cut, Copy, and Paste. Clicking on a parameter would bring up the dialogue box used to generalize that type of parameter. The result is that this representation seems easy to understand and edit.

Like Eager, Gamut has no visible presentation of the inferred program, and user studies with Gamut report that one would be desirable (McDaniel and Myers 1999). Gamut gets around the editing problem by allowing users to supply new examples at any time that will modify the existing behaviors, so it is never necessary to edit code directly.

Many other systems have researched different presentations of the generated program. Most use custom languages designed specifically to match the PBD system. SmallStar (Halbert 1993) provides a textual representation of the program created from the examples, and the user has to explicitly edit the program to generalize parameters and add control structures. InferenceBear (Frank and Foley 1994) uses a novel form of event language as its representation called *Elements, Events & Transitions* (EET) in which the actions and their parameters are represented as event handlers. This relatively complex language is probably not accessible to nonprogrammers. Mondrian (Lieberman 1992) provides a comic strip–style visual program, similar to Pursuit. Pavlov (Wolber 1997) tries to make the program accessible to nonprogrammers by using a time line–based view, in the style of MacroMedia's Director but based on an event-based model. This makes the language more appropriate for describing graphical applications since they are primarily event based (using the keyboard and mouse generates events that are handled by the application).

3.5 Conclusion

Designing the heuristics for a PBD system is a very difficult task. The more sophisticated the inferencing mechanism, the more complex the behaviors that can be handled, and, hopefully, the more likely it is that the system will infer correctly. On the other hand, sophisticated inferencing mechanisms often bring with them more elaborate user interfaces to control the inferencing, and these systems are much more difficult to implement. In any kind of PBD system, it is important that there be a well-designed feedback mechanism so that users can understand and control what the system is doing and change the program later. Much more research is needed on the appropriate level of intelligence and the forms of feedback in PBD systems.

Acknowledgements

The systems reported here were developed under many research grants, with support from the National Science Foundation under grants IRI-9020089 and IRI-9319969, DARPA under Contract No. N66001–94-C-6037, Arpa Order No. B326, and others. The views and conclusions contained in this document are those of the authors and should not be interpreted as representing the official policies, either expressed or implied, of the U.S. government.

References

Cypher, A. 1991. Eager: Programming Repetitive Tasks by Example. In *Proceedings of CHI'91*, ACM, New Orleans, pp. 33–39.

Frank, M. R., and J. D. Foley. 1994. A pure reasoning engine for programming by demonstration. In *ACM SIGGRAPH symposium on user interface software and technology* (Marina del Rey, Calif., November): 95–101.

Halbert, D. C. 1993. SmallStar: Programming by demonstration in the desktop metaphor. In *Watch what I do: Programming by demonstration,* ed. A. Cypher. Cambridge, Mass.: MIT Press, 102–123.

Kosbie, D. S., and B. A. Myers. 1993. A system-wide macro facility based on aggregate events: A proposal. In *Watch what I do: Programming by demonstration,* ed. A. Cypher. Cambridge, Mass.: MIT Press, 433–444.

———. 1994. Extending programming by demonstration with hierarchical event histories. In *Human-computer interaction: 4th International Conference EWHCI'94. Lecture Notes in Computer Science, Vol. 876.* Berlin: Springer, 128–139.

Lieberman, H. 1992. Dominos and storyboards: Beyond icons on strings. In *1992 IEEE Workshop on visual languages* (Seattle, Wash., September): 65–71.

Maulsby, D. 1994. *Instructible agents.* Ph.D. diss. University of Calgary, Alberta, Canada.

Maulsby, D L., and I. H. Witten. 1989. Inducing procedures in a direct-manipulation environment. In *Human factors in computing systems* (Austin, Tex., April). ACM CHI'89 Proceedings: 57–62.

McDaniel, R. G., and B. A. Myers. 1998. Building applications using only demonstration. In *1998 International Conference on Intelligent User Interfaces* (San Francisco, January). ACM: 109–116.

———. 1999. Getting more out of programming-by-demonstration. In *Human factors in computing systems* (Pittsburgh, Pa., May 15–20). ACM CHI'99 Proceedings: 442–449.

Miller, R. C., and B. A. Myers. 1997. Creating dynamic World Wide Web pages by demonstration. Carnegie Mellon University School of Computer Science, CMU-CS-97-131 and CMU-HCII-97-101.

Modugno, F., A. T. Corbett, and B. A. Myers. 1997. Graphical representation of programs in a demonstrational visual shell—An empirical evaluation. *ACM Transactions on Computer-Human Interaction* 4, no. 3: 276–308.

Modugno, F., and B. A. Myers. 1997. Visual programming in a visual shell—A unified approach. *Journal of Visual Languages and Computing* 8, no. 5/6: 276–308.

Myers, B. A. 1990. Creating user interfaces using programming-by-example, visual programming, and constraints. *ACM Transactions on Programming Languages and Systems* 12, no. 2: 143–177.

———. 1991a. Graphical techniques in a spreadsheet for specifying user interfaces. In *Proceedings of CHI'91*, ACM, New Orleans, 1991, pp. 243–249.

———. 1991b. Separating application code from toolkits: Eliminating the spaghetti of call-backs. In *ACM SIGGRAPH symposium on user interface software and technology* (Hilton Head, S.C., November): 211–220.

———. 1991c. Text formatting by demonstration. In *Human factors in computing systems, ACM CHI'91 Proceedings:* 251–256.

———. 1998. Scripting graphical applications by demonstration. In *Human factors in computing systems, ACM CHI'98 Proceedings* (Los Angeles, April): 534–541.

Myers, B. A., and W. Buxton. 1986. Creating highly interactive and graphical user interfaces by demonstration. In *Computer graphics, ACM SIGGRAPH'86 Proceedings* (Dallas, Tex., August).

Myers, B. A., J. Goldstein, and M. A. Goldberg. 1994. Creating charts by demonstration. In *Human factors in computing systems* (Boston, April): 106–111.

Myers, B. A., R. G. McDaniel, and D. S. Kosbie. 1993. Marquise: Creating complete user interfaces by demonstration. In *Human factors in computing systems, ACM CHI'93 Proceedings* (Amsterdam, April): 293–300.

Myers, B. A., B. Vander Zanden, and R. B. Dannenberg. 1989. Creating graphical interactive application objects by demonstration. In *ACM SIGGRAPH Symposium on user interface software and technology* (Williamsburg, Va., November): 95–104.

Shneiderman, Ben. 1995. Looking for the bright side of user interface agents. *ACM Interactions* 2, no. 1: 13–15.

Smith, D. Canfield. 1977. *Pygmalion: A computer program to model and stimulate creative thought.* Basel: Birkhauser.

Vander Zanden, B., and B. A. Myers. 1990. Automatic, look-and-feel independent dialog creation for graphical user interfaces. In *Human factors in computing systems, ACM CHI'90 Proceedings* (Seattle, Wash., April): 27–34.

———. 1995. Demonstrational and constraint-based techniques for pictorially specifying application objects and behaviors. *ACM Transactions on Computer-Human Interaction* 2, no. 4: 308–356.

Werth, A. J., and B. A. Myers. 1993. Tourmaline: Macrostyles by example. In *Human factors in computing systems, ACM CHI'93 Proceedings* (Amsterdam, April): 532.

Wolber, D. 1997. An interface builder for designing animated interfaces. *ACM Transactions on Computer-Human Interaction* 4, no. 4: 347–386.

CHAPTER 4

Web Browsing by Example

ATSUSHI SUGIURA

Human Media Research Laboratories
NEC Corporation

Abstract

This chapter describes programming by example (PBE) techniques to automate daily Web-browsing tasks. A number of research efforts have tried to solve two major problems of PBE: difficulties in inferring user intent behind examples and insufficient accessibility to applications' internal data. However, these problems can be avoided in the Web-browsing domain, and practical PBE systems can be developed. Internet Scrapbook and Small-Browse are presented here as two examples of such practical systems.

4.1 Introduction

Web browsing is a highly repetitive task. We have many Web pages to visit every day, seeking such information as news, sports results, and weather forecasts. Users of a Web browser are forced to repeatedly perform the same sequence of operations: going to the same Web pages, scrolling to the same positions where users' desired information would appear in those pages, and following the same hyperlinks.

One way to automate Web-browsing tasks is to write programs. For example, a user could avoid repetitive accesses and scrolling operations by writing a program for generating personalized pages—that is, dynamically collecting articles that he or she usually browses from multiple pages and merging them into a single page. However, most Web users are nonprogrammers, and even for expert programmers, it is tedious to make programs that can handle various types of Web documents with different formats.

Programming by example (PBE) is one of the possible solutions to this problem. PBE is a technique that creates an executable program from example data and/or a sequence of example operations given by the user. This PBE framework allows users with little programming skill to automate repetitive tasks without learning any complicated programming languages.

In spite of this great advantage, only a few PBE systems have been of practical use to date. One of the main reasons is that PBE systems cannot always infer the user intent behind the given examples. As long as it is not guaranteed that the system will generate a program as the user desired, no user would make a program with PBE. Another reason is that, in general, a PBE component cannot be attached to existing applications with which the user is familiar. Although many approaches have been taken to these problems (Cypher 1993), one important topic in the discussion was lacking: application domains. Since the degree of difficulty in solving these problems depends on the application domains (text editing, graphical editing, Web browsing, or others), we should further discuss this issue.

This chapter will first explain the general problems of PBE and show how they can be avoided to some extent in the Web-browsing domain. Then, two PBE systems for Web browsing will be described, *Internet Scrapbook* and *SmallBrowse,* followed by a concluding discussion of their strategies and feasible applications.

Internet Scrapbook (referred to simply as "Scrapbook") automates the repetitive operations in daily Web-browsing activities. It allows a user to create a single personal page by copying only the necessary data from multiple Web documents, and it automatically updates itself by extracting the user-specified portions from the latest Web pages. SmallBrowse predicts the hyperlinks that a user would next follow based on that person's browsing history and generates shortcut links to avoid searching a Web page for links. While Scrapbook is designed for Web browsing using desktop computers, SmallBrowse is aimed at facilitating the Web-browsing tasks in handheld computers with small screens.

Scrapbook is one of the first PBE systems that is being marketed commercially. It has been shipped in Japan since July 1997.

4.2 Underlying Problems of PBE

There are two major problems in PBE: how the system can infer user intent behind the given examples and how the PBE component can work with existing applications by accessing their internal data.

4.2.1 Problem of Inferring User Intent

PBE systems are required to convert examples/demonstrations into generalized programs as the user desired. This means that systems have to infer the user intent behind these examples/demonstrations. However, such inference systems sometimes guess wrong. The users would not willingly use the PBE systems without guarantees that the program will operate as desired.

It is difficult to solve this problem as long as the inference relies only on the given examples. Therefore, many PBE systems have an interaction session, in addition to a demonstration session, to get more information necessary for the inference. For example, Peridot (Myers 1993) asks the user whether it is applying appropriate rules for the correct inference. MetaMouse (Maulsby and Witten 1993) has the user teach important relationships between graphical objects. Although such interactions are useful for making the proper generalizations, they impose additional burdens on the user. If the cost of program definition is more expensive than that of simply repeating a sequence of operations, users would not use PBE facilities.

4.2.2 Problem of Accessing Internal Data of Applications

Users prefer adding the PBE component on existing applications that they are usually using, rather than replacing their familiar applications with unfamiliar ones in which the basic functions of the application plus PBE functions are embedded.

However, adding the PBE component is not easy. To make the add-on framework available, the external PBE component has to record user operations on the target application and display the program execution results in the application's window. However, ordinary commercial applications do not provide application program interfaces (APIs) that allow external processes to access their internal data or user interface events.

Therefore, PBE systems have to be developed from scratch, including the user interface and the basic functions of applications. Since it is difficult to develop a sophisticated user interface and functions, PBE systems that have been developed in laboratories have not replaced commercial products.

4.3 Web Browsing: Good Domain for PBE

It is difficult to find general solutions to the problems explained in the previous section, but it can be done in specific application domains. One such domain is Web browsing, which is a relatively new domain. Many PBE systems only supported editing tasks, such as text and graphical editing, but the appearance of the Web sharply increased the need for repetitive browsing tasks.

A good feature of the Web-browsing domain is that users do not suffer so much from the system's wrong guesses. In the case of editing tasks, wrong guesses may result in important data being missed and/or destroyed, whereas PBE systems for browsing tasks never destroy a user's data. Therefore, the inference engine does not need to be as sophisticated as the engine for the editing tasks.

The data access problem can also be avoided. By tapping into the http stream like a proxy, the PBE component can know the URLs that the user requested and also what the user inputted into HTML forms. It can also add the results of program executions into the original Web pages. This framework can be used in SmallBrowse. (However, in the current implementation of SmallBrowse, PBE functionality is embedded into a browser whose source code is available.)

Another way of capturing user operations is to use the browser's APIs. Fortunately, the widely used Web browsers, Microsoft Internet Explorer and Netscape Navigator, offer various APIs for the external processes. By using these APIs, the external PBE components can identify even the portion of the Web page where the user highlights on the browser window by using the mouse (see the appendix for details). Scrapbook operates by relying on the browser's APIs.

By taking advantage of these features of the Web-browsing domain, Scrapbook and SmallBrowse are able to be practical PBE systems.

4.4 Internet Scrapbook

World Wide Web (WWW) browsers allow users to access Internet information sources easily. While the operation of these browsers is simple, users need to spend much time and care in their daily access to the Web information they desire for the following reasons:

- The information that users need is usually distributed across several different pages. In cases where users need to obtain a weather forecast, computer news, and sports results from different pages, for example, they have to access all the necessary pages by repeatedly specifying URLs or by selecting them from bookmarks.

- Users often need to browse only a portion of a Web page. On a nationwide weather forecast page, for example, users probably want the forecast only for the area where they live. Consequently, they are often required to search the page for the desired information either by looking or by using the string search function provided by the browser.

If users' target pages are frequently updated, it is a heavy burden for the users to keep up with the latest information by repeating these Web-browsing operations.

4.4.1   Overview of Internet Scrapbook

Internet Scrapbook is a PBE system for automating daily Web-browsing tasks. It clips portions of multiple Web pages and merges the clipped data into a single page so that the user can browse all of his or her necessary information without repeatedly specifying URLs and scrolling to the position where the user's target information would appear.

One characteristic of Scrapbook is its ease of use. The user's main task in Scrapbook is to demonstrate his or her desired information by using actual Web pages. Specifically, the user creates a personal Scrapbook page by repeatedly selecting data in a Web browser (Figure 4.1[a]) and copying it to the Scrapbook page (Figure 4.1[b]). The selected data can be copied simply by clicking the Scrapbook's Copy button. Once the personal Scrapbook page is created, the user has only to click the Update button to browse the latest Web information. The system updates the Scrapbook page reflecting the modifications of the source Web pages (Figure 4.1[c]).

An important design aspect is that Scrapbook is designed so that Web data can be copied directly from the most commonly used Web browsers—Netscape Navigator 3.0, Microsoft Internet Explorer 3.0, and their newer versions for Windows95/NT3.51—rather than forcing users to use a special browser only for Scrapbook. This can be done using the browser's APIs and Windows' APIs. (The details are given in the appendix.)

Figure 4.2 shows the PBE process in Scrapbook. In the demonstration phase, given a single example of a user selection in the Web browser (Figure 4.2[a]), Scrapbook infers a matching pattern to identify the selected region in the source Web page (Figure 4.2[b]).

In the execution phase, Scrapbook updates the user's Scrapbook page by using the generated patterns. It downloads the latest Web page (Figure 4.2[c]), extracts portions that match the patterns from newly downloaded Web pages, and reconstructs the Scrapbook page with the extracted data. However, a portion that *completely* matches the pattern cannot necessarily be found in the modified version of the Web page. When there is no complete match, the system performs partial matching to find possible candidates for extraction (Figure 4.2[d]) and selects the most plausible one by applying heuristics (Figure 4.2[e]).

FIGURE **4.1**

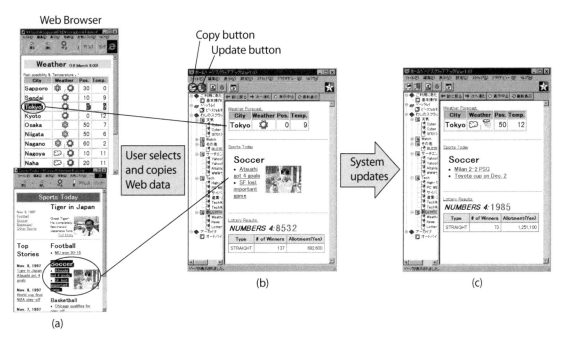

Overview of Scrapbook: (a) User selection in Web browsers; (b) Scrapbook page created by the user; and (c) page updated by the system.

A major challenge here is how Scrapbook can extract specific portions from frequently modified Web pages in the example-based framework. The system has to find the correct portions on many types of Web pages, using only a single example. To do this, Scrapbook uses a heuristic method based on certain regularities observed in frequently modified Web pages (i.e., that article headings and positions in the Web pages are rarely changed).

4.4.2 Generating Matching Patterns

As mentioned, Scrapbook generates a matching pattern at demonstration time and uses it to extract the user-desired portion from the *future* versions of the page. Therefore, patterns must be described using information that is expected to remain constant even after the page has been modified.

FIGURE **4.2**

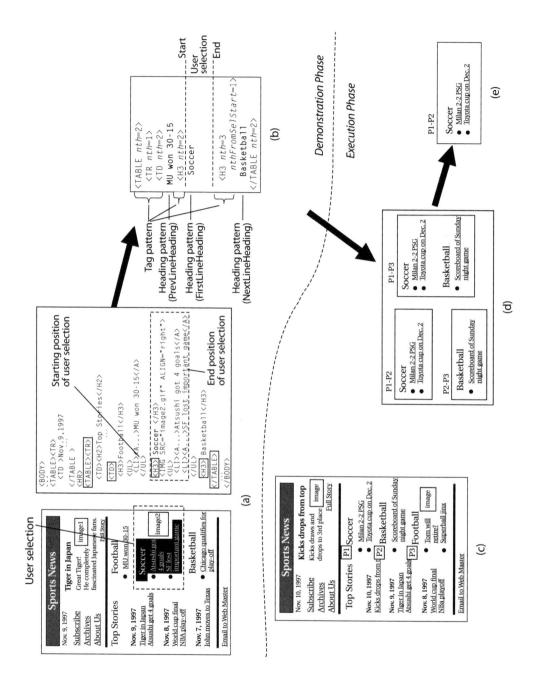

According to our observations, there are certain regularities in modifications to Web pages, and two kinds of information are likely to persist over these modifications: the heading of an article and the position of an article. In the Web page shown in Figure 4.2(a), for example, the heading of the selected region "soccer" would not be changed. Also, the top news would always be at the top of that page. Therefore, the system includes descriptions of both the article headings and positions in the matching pattern. These descriptions are called the *heading pattern* and the *tag pattern,* respectively.

Heading Pattern

The heading pattern consists of text that the system regards as the heading of the user-selected article (data). Scrapbook simply infers that headings are likely to be in the lines *previous* to, *first* in, and *following* the user selection. For example, if the user selects the data as shown in Figure 4.2(a), the system generates the heading pattern shown by the bold text in Figure 4.2(b). This heading pattern gives an abstract interpretation of a user selecting the region from "Soccer" (the first line of the selection), whose previous line is "MU won 30–15," to just before "Basketball" (the text following the selection).

This inference is based on some characteristic of the regions selected by users. Users usually select the whole article from the beginning to the end. They do not start in the middle of the article. Since many articles in Web pages are preceded by headings that explain the contents or the category of each article, there is a high probability that the first line of the user selection is a heading.[1] The line previous to the selection may become a heading because of slight variations in the selected region—users sometimes select articles without including the heading. In many cases, the heading of the next article appears in the next line after the user-selected article. The text in that line would be useful for determining the end position of data to be extracted.

Tag Pattern

The tag pattern represents the position of selected data in a Web page. It consists of HTML elements, each of which has an *nth* parameter. The *nth* parameter represents the appearance order of the HTML element counted

---

1. The system might be able to find headings more precisely if it relied on H1-H6 elements. Since, however, headings are not necessarily tagged by H1-H6 elements (instead FONT and B are often used), we currently employ the simple method of relying on the selected region.

from the document top. For example, the *nth* parameters of the tag pattern
in Figure 4.2(b) indicate a region from the second H3 to the third H3 em-
bodied in the second cell (the second TD in the first TR) of the second
TABLE.

To identify the starting position of the user-specified portion, the tag
pattern contains all HTML elements that mark up the starting position.
Only layout elements that affect the page layout, such as TABLE, TR, TD,
UL, LI, H1-H6, P, and HR, are included in the pattern, while font style elements, such as FONT and B, are not considered. Since the tag pattern has
the nested structure of the HTML elements, the *nth* parameters are hierarchically counted from their parent elements.

To identify the ending position, the *nthFromSelStart* parameter is used
in addition to the *nth* parameter. It represents the position relative to the
starting position of the user selection, such as the first appearance of an H3
element after the starting position. It is set to the number of elements
counted from the starting position.

4.4.3   Extracting Data from Web Pages

Scrapbook extracts the user's target portions from the latest Web pages by
using a matching pattern described by the headings and positions of a user-
specified article. However, there is no guarantee that both the headings and
the positions will remain unchanged, and the pattern might not completely
match any portion of the page. For example, if the Web page in Figure 4.2(a)
is modified to that in Figure 4.2(c), the pattern in Figure 4.2(b) does not
completely match any portion of the page because the position of the "Soccer" section has moved up.

To deal with the various modifications of Web pages, the data extraction
process consists of two steps: (1) finding candidate portions of the extraction result by *partial* matching and (2) choosing the correct one among a
number of possible candidates by applying heuristics.

Generating Candidate Portions by Partial Matching

Scrapbook finds candidates of starting positions and those of ending positions separately. The candidate regions are generated from all combinations
of the starting positions and the ending positions.

If the pattern of Figure 4.2(b) is applied to the Web page shown in Figure
4.2(c), for example, P1 and P2 would be the candidates of the starting position. P1 is the position where the text "Soccer" of the heading pattern exists,

and P2 is the position where the tag pattern matches; that is, the user-specified data originally appeared in the document of Figure 4.2(a). Likewise, P2 and P3 would be the candidates of the ending position. They are listed by the heading pattern and the tag pattern, respectively. Combining these candidate positions, Scrapbook makes the list of candidate portions to be extracted: P1-P2, P1-P3, and P2-P3 (Figure 4.2[d]).

Choosing One Candidate Using Heuristics

Scrapbook chooses one portion from the generated candidates using a set of sophisticated heuristics. Basically, the system prefers portions identified by a heading pattern to those found by a tag pattern. This is because the headings are expected to reflect the user intent in the selection and explain the contents of articles more clearly than the article position. Based on this idea, the region P1-P2, found by the headings "Soccer" and "Basketball," is selected in Figure 4.2(e).

However, things are not quite as simple as this. Imagine the Web page where articles are chronologically ordered with the newest one added to the top, as shown in Figure 4.3. In this case, a portion found by a tag pattern (the article at the top of the page) should be chosen as the extraction result. If the heading pattern is used, the same data from "98.4.14" to "98.4.13" would always be extracted. To handle such a case, Scrapbook has a rule to choose the tag-pattern portion when the heading pattern extracts exactly the same data as before the update. Scrapbook has several other rules to handle various types of Web pages. For more details, see Sugiura and Koseki 1998.

4.4.4 Evaluation

I asked eighteen subjects to create their own Scrapbook pages by selecting portions of their favorite Web pages, and then update the Scrapbook pages for two weeks. In the experiment, 155 portions were selected and copied to Scrapbook pages by all subjects. They were selected mainly from news sites (any kinds of news, such as general, weather, sports, technical news, etc.), some from company homepages, a music CD sales-ranking page, and novels written in a personal homepage. None of the subjects selected portions starting in the middle of articles.

During the experimental period, a total of 887 updates were made, and 92.1 percent of the updates were successfully made as the subjects desired. According to our observation and the subjects' own views, most of the

4.3

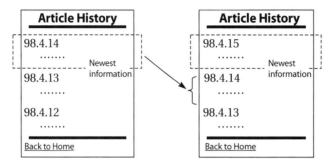

A Web page where the articles are chronologically ordered.

subjects could easily determine whether the update results were appropriate without displaying the whole source of the Web pages for comparison.

This result shows that the headings and positions of articles are very useful for finding the specific portions of Web pages. Although the system could not properly update 8 percent of the selected portions, many of them were trivial failures, such as extracting one line more than expected. We believe that our data extraction method can be of practical use.

We speculate that there are two reasons that the article headings and positions are preserved. First, changing the structure of Web pages is a heavy burden for information providers as well as costly. Second, Web sites must ensure the readability of their Web pages. If the document structure is changed often, readers cannot easily find their target information.

The robustness of the data extraction method against the various ways of modifying Web pages is supported mainly by the partial matching process for generating candidates of the extraction. The partial matching allows the system to generate a matching pattern without precisely predicting the future modifications of a Web page and to find some candidates for extraction as long as the Web page keeps either the same heading or position of the user-specified article.

Scrapbook fails to extract the user's target portion if partial matching cannot find any candidate portions in the latest Web page or if the candidate list generated by the partial matching does not contain the user-desired portion. Finding no candidate portions means that neither the headings nor the positions of the article selected in the user demonstration are preserved. Typically, such cases occur when Web pages are totally rewritten.

A typical case of no user-desired portion is observed in schedule-result pages where the schedules are replaced with the results one by one (Figure

FIGURE **4.4**

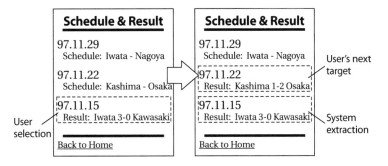

Schedule and result pages.

4.4). Since both the heading and the position of the newest result (target information) keep changing, the system can never extract the portion that the user needs.

4.5 SmallBrowse: Web-Browsing Interface for Small-Screen Computers

Recently, palm-top computers and handheld PCs, such as Palm V, have come into wide use. However, document browsing in those computers is not an easy task due to their limited screen size. It is especially difficult to search a document for target data with scrolling, because a user is required to recognize that the data have appeared in the small screen area and immediately stop scrolling before it disappears. In Web browsing, such scroll operations are often required to display a hyperlink to be followed, which is a heavy burden for users. Although bookmarks allow users to jump directly to their target Web pages, they cannot be a solution for the following reasons:

- When many URLs are registered as bookmarks, scrolling operations become necessary again to select one from a long list of bookmarks.

- Bookmarks are effective for recording the pairs of static URLs and page titles, but they are not appropriate in the case where the URL and title of a target page are dynamically changed. Imagine a serial column page where each column has a unique serial number, as shown in Figure 4.5.

FIGURE **4.5**

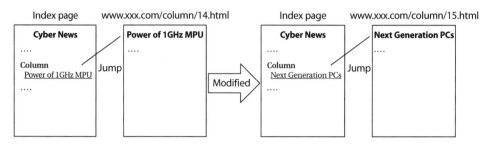

A URL and a page title dynamically changed.

In this case, a bookmark saved at some time point will not be useful next time. News sites often have such dynamic URLs and titles in daily articles. For pages with dynamic URLs, the user actually has to follow a link from an index page to reach the target page. Not only a URL but also an anchor text is important. Since the anchor text is often the same as the title of the referred page, the user needs to see it to determine whether he or she should follow the link.

4.5.1 Overview of SmallBrowse

The bookmark problem suggests requirements of a Web-browsing user interface in small-screen computers. That is, only the low number of links that the user is most likely to follow should be shown in the small screen, and at the same time their destination URLs and anchor texts should be refreshed to the newest ones.

Based on this idea, I have developed a PBE component, called *Small-Browse*, that facilitates Web-browsing tasks in small-screen computers. Using the user's Web-browsing history, SmallBrowse predicts hyperlinks that a user would next follow. Specifically, it chooses three links from the newest version of Web pages and inserts those three predicted links[2] (we refer to them as *p-links*) at both the top and bottom of an original Web page

---

2. The number of p-links should be determined according to the screen size. SmallBrowse currently assumes a 360×180 resolution.

FIGURE **4.6**

Screen snapshot of SmallBrowse.

(Figure 4.6). Since p-links are extracted from the latest Web pages, their destination URLs and anchor texts are also the newest ones.

The user can use the p-links when the Web page is first displayed in the browser and/or when the user finishes reading the page and jumps to other pages without scrolling. When one of the p-links is focused, SmallBrowse displays a "tip help" to show the data around the original link. This helps the user determine whether he or she should actually follow the link.

Example Task

This section explains an example task on SmallBrowse. The user browses the same news site, which is updated every day, repeatedly on different days. Figures 4.7(a) and (b) show the first and the second browsing session, respectively.

Since the hyperlink prediction relies on a user's Web-browsing history, p-links are not inserted in the first browsing session. So the user normally follows links. In the index page, the user first scrolls down to the position of the Weather link and follows it. Next, in the weather page, she again scrolls to the Seattle link and follows it. After browsing the Seattle weather, she then goes back to the index page using the Back command of the Web browser. Likewise, she follows the link of the column and one of the links of sports articles. The upper portion of Figure 4.8 depicts the sequence of URLs that SmallBrowse recorded through the first session.

In the second session, p-links are inserted based on the recorded history. As shown in Figure 4.7(b), many of the scrolling operations can be eliminated using the p-links. In the index page, for example, Weather, Seattle, and the column links are selected as the p-links because the user followed in the first session these three links just after the index page. Note that the Seattle link can be a p-link for the index page although it is not originally contained in the index page.

Another feature of SmallBrowse's prediction can be seen in the prediction of the column link. The destination URL of column link is continuously changed, and the newest one at the second session (. . . /column/24.html) differs from the one when the user had followed the column link at the first session (. . . /column/23.html). Nevertheless, the column link is selected as a p-link. SmallBrowse judges /column/23.html and /column/24.html as the identical URL by using some heuristics (details in "Predicting p-links" section below). This allows the system to handle the continuously changing links.

When multiple links that can be regarded as identical to the old URL are found, SmallBrowse creates a p-link to scroll to the position of the first link found. This can be seen in the p-link inserted into the column page. The p-link Sports leads users to the position of sports articles on the index page.

In the third or subsequent sessions, the Weather link will not be selected as a p-link because it is followed only once in the first session and the user will never visit the weather page. The links followed more frequently, such as the Seattle link and the column link, will be selected as p-links.

Recording a History

As shown in Figure 4.8, SmallBrowse records pairs of two URLs, called *R-URL* (Requested URL) and *S-URL* (link source URL). R-URL is a URL that the user requested, and S-URL is the latest requested URL of a Web page that contains an R-URL. In other words, the S-URL represents a Web page from which the user jumped to the page of the R-URL. Note that Web pages displayed by using the Back command are not recorded in a history.

Predicting p-links

Predicting a p-link means determining a pair of its destination URL and anchor text. So the prediction process consists of two steps: determining the URL of a p-link and finding in the latest version of a Web page an anchor text to be associated with the predicted URL.

FIGURE **4.7**

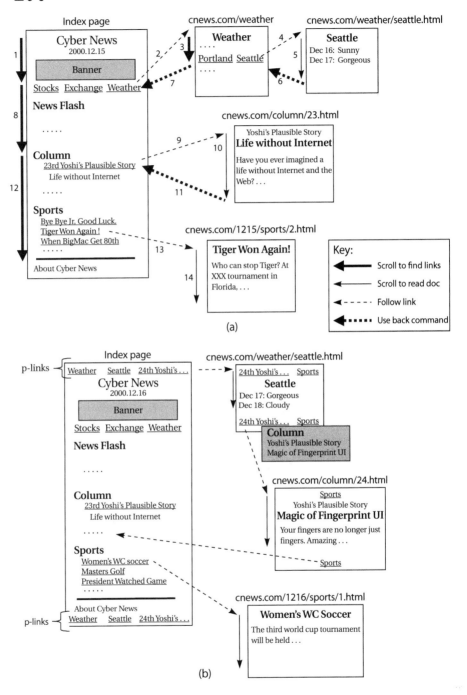

Web browsing on SmallBrowse: (a) the first browsing session and (b) the second browsing session.

FIGURE **4.8**

Web pages that a user browsed	Web pages that had been containing the browsed URLs	
http://www.cnews.com/ http://www.cnews.com/weather/ http://www.cnews.com/weather/seattle.html http://www.cnews.com/column/23.html http://www.cnews.com/1215/sports/2.html	N/A (specified from bookmark) http://www.cnews.com/ http://www.cnews.com/weather/ http://www.cnews.com/ http://www.cnews.com/	First session
http://www.cnews.com/ http://www.cnews.com/weather/seattle.html http://www.cnews.com/column/24.html http://www.cnews.com/1216/sports/1.html	N/A (specified from bookmark) http://www.cnews.com/weather http://www.cnews.com/ http://www.cnews.com/	Second session

Web-browsing history.

In the first step, a URL is predicted only by a sequence of R-URLs in the history. In the second step, the anchor text is extracted from S-URL pages. Since some URLs are continuously changing, however, the second step is also used to refresh the predicted URL (URL selected from the R-URL history) to the newest one. To do this, SmallBrowse performs pattern matching by using an abstracted description of the URL.

Determining URLs from a History   To insert p-links into a Web page of a URL U0, SmallBrowse selects as URLs of those p-links the most frequently requested URLs after U0. Specifically, the system first finds U0 in the R-URL history, then picks up the next three URLs, and counts the occurrences of each URL. The URLs with the top three occurrences are selected for the URLs of the p-links. Consider a case, for example, where the R-URL history is as follows:

U0 *U1 U2 U3* U4 U5 U0 *U2 U3 U4* U5 U0 *U1 U3 U5* . . .

In this case, U3 (three occurrences), U1 (two occurrences), and U2 (two occurrences) are selected as the URLs of p-links that are inserted into the Web page of U0.

However, URLs of some Web pages are changing continuously. In the example task, a URL of the column page contains a serial number, and the URL for the newest one is different from any of the recorded R-URLs.

Therefore, the column link would never be chosen as a p-link if the system counted the occurrence of URLs by simply comparing their strings.

To solve this problem, SmallBrowse uses simple heuristics about formats of URLs of periodically updated articles. Such URLs are likely to contain decimal numbers that represent year, month, day, and/or a serial number. For example, URLs for the newest columns might be changed as follows:

http://www.cnews.com/column/<u>23</u>.html (the 23rd column)
http://www.cnews.com/column/<u>24</u>.html (the 24th column)

SmallBrowse regards two URLs as identical when the differences between them are only decimal-number parts. In other words, SmallBrowse compares URLs at an abstract level. In the case of the column page, both of the above two URLs can be generalized into "www.cnews.com/column/\ d*.html," and they are dealt with as the same one. The occurrences are also counted based on the abstract patterns of URLs.

Finding the Newest URL and Anchor Text   The next task is to find anchor texts to be associated with the predicted URLs. To reflect the current state of an anchor text, SmallBrowse looks through the latest version of the C-URL page corresponding to the predicted URL (the one selected from the R-URL history) and extracts a link whose destination URL matches the abstract pattern of the R-URL. Note that through this process the URL as well as the anchor text are refreshed from the old state URL, recorded in R-URL history, to the newest one.

Imagine a case where the system is predicting p-links in the second browsing session based on the R-URL history recorded in the first session (Figure 4.8), and it selected "www.cnews.com/column/23.html" as a URL of a p-link. In this case, the system searches the current "www.cnews.com/" page (S-URL corresponding to the selected R-URL ". . . /column/23.html") for links that match the generalized pattern of ". . . /column/\d*.html." As a result, ". . . /column/24.html" matches the pattern. That newest URL and its anchor text will be used in a p-link.

One special treatment takes place when there are multiple URLs that match the abstracted pattern. In this case, the system generates a URL to scroll to the position of the first matched URL in the C-URL page (using <A> NAME property) and assigns as its anchor text a heading text just before the first matched URL. The heading is identified using some heuristics about font size, font color, horizontal rule, and so forth.

Such multiple matching cases often take place when the articles of the same category are listed. In the example task, this can be seen in sports articles of the index page. The system inserts a p-link to directly jump to the position of a list of sports articles and sets its anchor text to "Sports," which is the heading of those articles. Such p-links give the user a chance to select from the list of the articles the ones that the user wants to read.

4.5.2 Tip Help

In some cases, an anchor text does not explain the content of the reference. In the column link in the example task, the format of its anchor text is "n-th Yoshi's Plausible Story." The content of the referred document is explained in the next line of that link (Figure 4.7).

SmallBrowse shows data that seem related to the content of the reference with a tip help. The system identifies headings just before and after the link and extracts text between two identified headings. This feature would be helpful for users.

4.5.3 Informal Experiments

The author conducted informal experiments to confirm the effectiveness of the prediction method of SmallBrowse. Unfortunately, the current version of SmallBrowse is not sufficiently sophisticated to be used for user study. Therefore, I simulated the prediction process using access logs recorded by a proxy and estimated the accuracy of p-links' URLs. That is, I predicted three URLs (destination URLs of p-links) that the user would next access for

FIGURE **4.9**

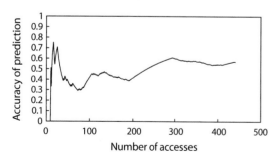
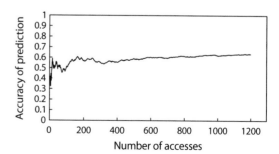

Warning curves for accuracy of predictions of two subjects.

each URL in the access log and examined whether one of the three pre-dicted URLs was the one that the user actually requested next.

In the experiments, access logs of six subjects over twenty-eight days were used, and the accuracy was calculated for each subject. During the ex-periments, 7,350 accesses were made in total (one subject accessed about forty-four pages per day on average), and 50.2% of URLs were requested more than once. The predictions were done on these repeatedly requested URLs. Using the access histories for twenty-eight days, the accuracy of pre-dictions for each user was 31.7%, 40.5%, 42.9%, 56.8%, 63.3%, and 64.2%. Figure 4.9 shows the typical learning curves of two subjects.

4.6 Discussion

Although the application domain of Scrapbook and SmallBrowse is the same, the strategies they use to achieve a practical level are different. The Scrapbook module has its own user interface (it can also be used in combi-nation with Netscape Navigator or Internet Explorer) and requires users to give examples explicitly through the demonstration session. This means that some cost for learning how to use the system and for instructing the system is imposed on users, although the operations in Scrapbook are sim-ple. To compensate for this, Scrapbook pursues high accuracy in extracted user-specified portions from the newest Web pages (about 92 percent).

In SmallBrowse, the accuracy in predicting hyperlinks is at most 64 percent. However, it does not require users to do anything special to use the prediction results. Namely, since the prediction is based on the user's Web-browsing history, the user does not have to invoke special commands for recording the user's browsing actions. Also, the prediction results are in-serted into Web pages as p-links that can be used in the same way as the or-dinary links. That is, the users do not have to learn anything about how to use SmallBrowse. They have simply to click the p-links to jump to other pages just as when clicking ordinary links. Because of this advantage of SmallBrowse, we could expect that users would be generous when it comes to the system's failures.

No matter which strategy is taken, users do not seriously suffer from the systems' (Scrapbook's and SmallBrowse's) wrong guesses. As mentioned in the Scrapbook section, even in the case in which Scrapbook cannot exactly extract portions of Web pages as the user desired, many of the failures are trivial, such as extracting one line more than expected. Even when the sys-tem cannot find any portion to be extracted, it displays a message as shown

4.10

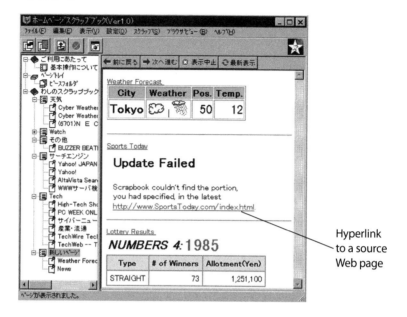

Hyperlink to a source Web page

Message for failure of data extraction.

in Figure 4.10 so that users can immediately access the source Web page by clicking the hyperlink. In SmallBrowse, users simply have to perform browsing operations as usual even when the system fails to predict appropriate links.

I believe that both Scrapbook and SmallBrowse are or will be operational on a practical level. Even after the experiments on Scrapbook had finished, some of the subjects continued using Scrapbook. In fact, Scrapbook is being preinstalled in NEC PCs and is in use by many end users. As for SmallBrowse, user studies have not been done yet, but I think that the framework of SmallBrowse, which does not impose any burdens on end users, is acceptable for many users.

Since the invention of the Web, many researchers studying PBE, autonomous software agents, artificial intelligence, and so forth, have focused their application domain on the Web.

The research area to which Scrapbook is the most relevant is wrapper induction for extracting a specific portion from a Web page. Trainable information assistants (TrIAs) (Bauer and Dengler 1999) are software agents that use a PBE technique to create wrappers. They are aimed at very accurately extracting a small piece of information, such as the price of a specific airline ticket. To make this possible, TrIAs employ an interactive session, in addition to a demonstration session, to obtain information necessary for generalization through various types of dialogues with a user.

Scrapbook, on the other hand, is designed to extract a relatively large block of Web data such as one whole line or article or a whole list of hyperlinks. Another feature distinguishing Scrapbook from TrIAs is that Scrapbook does not have an interactive session because users do not prefer additional tasks. Actually, Scrapbook used to have an interactive session (Sugiura and Koseki 1998), but only a few users were willing to use the interactive learning framework. So we decided not to include it in our commercial version of Scrapbook. It is, of course, critical to be able to extract the user-specified portions exactly. However, more important things are ease of use and simplicity of operations.

The concept and architecture of SmallBrowse are similar to that of Letizia (Lieberman 1995) and WBI (Barret, Maglio, and Kellem 1997), which are autonomous interface agents that assist Web browsing based on the user's past Web-browsing history. Letizia records the URLs chosen by the user and reads the pages to learn the user's interests. The interest is represented by pairs of terms and their frequencies. When the user is browsing the Web, Letizia recommends a Web page that is the most likely to match the user's interests by searching "nearby" the user's current position (a set of pages linked from the current page). Since Letizia needs a large screen area to display its recommendation, however, it is not suitable for browsing on small screens. WBI inserts shortcut links by analyzing the user's usual browsing pattern. Unlike SmallBrowse, however, WBI does not have a function to refresh URLs and anchor texts for the shortcut links.

4.7 Conclusion

This chapter described two PBE systems for Web browsing. Web browsing is a good application domain of PBE because of its highly repetitive nature. PBE can clearly offer an advantage to a wide range of users of Web browsers. Furthermore, the failures of inferences cause only minor inconvenience, compared with other tasks, such as text editing and user interface construction.

PBE has been applied to desktop applications so far. However, I believe that a wide variety of application domains are good for PBE. One example is the small-screen, portable computer domain, which SmallBrowse is targeting. Another possibility is the wearable computer domain. Such environments have a natural need for intelligent support from a PBE component.

Appendix: Copying HTML Data from Web Browser to Scrapbook

In Scrapbook, Web data can be copied directly from Netscape Navigator and Microsoft Internet Explorer to a user's Scrapbook page, as shown in Figure 4.1(a) and (b). When HTML data are copied, not only the text selected in the Web browser but also the HTML elements that affect that text need to be copied. However, the system can only get the selected text through a cut buffer (Windows clipboard). Scrapbook copies the related HTML elements in the following fashion:

1. Get the text, which the user selected in the browser, via the cut buffer.

2. Get the complete source of the HTML document through the API provided by the browser.

3. Find the starting and ending position of the user selection in the source document obtained in step 2 by searching the source document for the selected text of step 1. In this search, HTML elements in the source document are not considered.

4. Parse the HTML of the source document, and pick up the HTML elements that affect the region identified in step 3.

5. Copy the text and the HTML elements within the region found in step 3, together with the related HTML elements picked up in step 4.

In step 5, all HTML elements within the region selected by the user are copied into Scrapbook. This means that objects, such as inline images, Java applets, plug-ins, and ActiveX controls, can be copied if the user selects text surrounding those objects, although the objects themselves are not selected in the browsers.

References

Barret, R., P. P. Maglio, and D. C. Kellem. 1997. How to personalize the Web. In *Proceedings of CHI'97*.

Bauer, M., and D. Dengler. 1999. TrIAs: Trainable information assistants for cooperative problem solving. In *Proceedings of the 1999 International Conference on Autonomous Agents* (Agents).

Cypher, A., ed. 1993. *Watch what I do: Programming by demonstration*. Cambridge, Mass.: MIT Press.

Lieberman, H. 1995. Letizia: An agent that assists Web browsing. Paper presented at the International Joint Conference on Artificial Intelligence, Montreal, August.

Maulsby, D., and I. H. Witten. 1993. MetaMouse: An instructible agent for programming by demonstration. In *Watch what I do: Programming by demonstration*, ed. A. Cypher. Cambridge, Mass.: MIT Press.

Myers, B. A. 1993. Peridot: Creating user interfaces by demonstration. In *Watch what I do: Programming by demonstration*, ed. A. Cypher. Cambridge, Mass.: MIT Press.

Sugiura, A., and Y. Koseki. 1998. Internet Scrapbook: Automating Web browsing tasks by demonstration. In *Proceedings of UIST'98*.

CHAPTER 5

Trainable Information Agents for the Web

MATHIAS BAUER

German Research Center for
Artificial Intelligence (DFKI GmbH)

DIETMAR DENGLER

German Research Center for
Artificial Intelligence (DFKI GmbH)

GABRIELE PAUL

German Research Center for
Artificial Intelligence (DFKI GmbH)

Abstract

Software agents are intended to perform certain tasks on behalf of their users. In many cases, however, the agent's competence is not sufficient to produce the desired outcome. This chapter presents an approach to cooperative problem solving in which an information agent and its user try to support each other in achieving a particular goal. As a side effect the user can extend the agent's capabilities in a programming-by-example dialogue, thus enabling it to perform similar tasks autonomously in the future.

5.1   Introduction

Software agents are intended to perform certain tasks autonomously on behalf of their users. Examples include interface agents (Kozierok and Maes 1993), Web-browsing assistants (Lieberman 1995), and personal news agents (Billsus and Pazzani 1999), to name but a few. In many cases, however, the agent's competence might not be sufficient to produce the desired outcome. Instead of simply giving up and leaving the whole task to the user, a much better alternative is to identify precisely what the cause of the current problem is, communicate it to another agent who can be expected to be able (and willing) to help, and use the results to carry on with achieving the original goal.

An ideal candidate for the role of such a supporting agent is a system user who can certainly be expected to have some interest in obtaining a useful response, even at the cost of having to intervene from time to time. Consequently, it seems rational to ask her for help whenever the system gets into trouble. Programming by example (PBE) provides a feasible framework for the particular kind of dialogue required in such situations in which both user and agent use their individual capabilities not only to complement each other to overcome the current problem but also to extend the agent's skills, thus enabling him to deal successfully with a whole class of problems and avoid similar difficulties—and thus additional training effort—in the future.[1]

Imagine a concrete application scenario in which a Web-based travel agent uses dynamic information located at various Web sites to configure a trip satisfying the user's preferences and constraints. Typical information

---

1. Throughout the rest of this article, we will refer to the user in the female form and the agent in the male form.

sources to be used in such a case include the Web sites of airlines, hotels, possibly weather servers, and so on. Unfortunately, many of these Web sites tend to change their look and structure quite frequently, thus exasperating agents who are not flexible enough to deal with this unexpected situation or at least recognize the fact that a problem exists at all.

Wouldn't it be good if this agent could tell his user about his problem and ask her to tell him what to do now and in similar situations occurring in the future? In the remaining sections, we will elaborate on this scenario and in particular describe the way the agent can ask for help without asking too much from the user—after all, the system is intended to provide some service to the user, not the other way round. So the role exchange between user and system (as service provider and consumer) should be as painless as possible to her. To this end, the agent should not remain passive and have the trainer do all the work but instead actively participate in the training dialogue and guide the teacher to give him just the right lessons to solve his problem. So, besides a new *application* for PBE techniques—the generation of scripts for the extraction of information from Web sites—we also advocate their use for a particular type of collaborative problem solving.

5.2 An Application Scenario

To illustrate both the kind of situation in which the aforementioned training dialogue takes place and the collaborative nature of such a session, consider the following instantiation of the trainable information assistants (TrIAs) framework as depicted in Figure 5.1. Assume a user is preparing for a trip. Using her Web browser, she enters the relevant data, such as cities to be visited, budget limitations, and time constraints, leaving the rest to a Web-based travel agent who is expected to fill in all the missing details and suggest a journey satisfying the user's preferences. For most of this planning process, the agent has to make use of information that is not locally available but must be fetched from the Web at planning time. Examples include departure times from train or flight schedules, prices for hotel rooms, and so on.

Using the terminology defined by a domain ontology, the trip-planning agent formulates corresponding information requests to be answered by an *information broker* (called InfoBroker in the TrIAs context). The latter has at his disposal a database of Web site descriptions consisting of

- the respective Web address (the URL);

- one or more query schemes;

FIGURE **5.1**

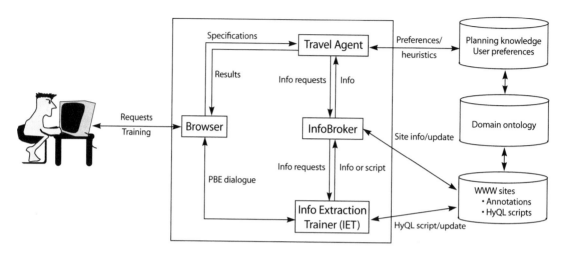

A typical instantiation of the TrIAs scenario.

- the principal information categories to be found at that site, expressed in terms of ontological concepts;

- for each information category, a procedure (a HyQL script; see Section 5.3) implementing its identification and extraction.

The query schemes describe which information has to be provided to query a Web site and what can be extracted from the answer document. For example, a query to a flight server requires as minimum input the specification of departure and destination cities, and the preferred date for the flight. The returned information includes departure time, price, carrier, and so forth.

The InfoBroker combines these query schemes using a classical artificial intelligence (AI) planning approach and thus allows intermediate results from a variety of Web sites to be combined so as to best answer the original information request. (For a detailed description of this approach to query planning and information integration, see Bauer and Dengler 1999a.) If everything works out just fine (i.e., if all answers to the travel agent's questions can be found on the Web), the user is presented the final result in her browser.

The interesting case occurs whenever a relevant piece of information cannot be found at a particular Web site although it should have been there.

The typical reason for such a failure is the modification of the site's layout or structure. This often makes useless the information extraction procedure that was stored in the database characterization for this particular site.

The traditional approach of dealing with this kind of problem has at least two drawbacks:

- The user will be frustrated because the agent will not produce the desired outcome but instead an error message, at best (unless alternative sites that have *not* changed recently can provide the same information).

- The expert in charge of maintaining the InfoBroker's database has to program yet another procedure for dealing with the new look of this Web site.

To kill two birds with one stone, why not have the user assume a small part of the system maintenance (by updating the agent's knowledge base in an appropriate way) in exchange for a good answer (a suggestion for a trip), knowing—or at least hoping—that other users are doing the same, thus improving the overall system performance?

To be concrete, the problematic HTML document is handed over to the *information extraction trainer* (IET) along with the current information request (the agent's question whose answer was expected to be in this document but could not be found). After some preprocessing that remains hidden to the user, the document is opened in the user's browser. Some extra frames are used to guide the training dialogue in which the user initially simply marks the relevant portion to be extracted and possibly gives the system some hints on how to facilitate the identification of this particular piece of information. In the end, a new information extraction procedure is synthesized and inserted into the database for future use. To avoid frequent training sessions, the Web query language HyQL (Bauer and Dengler 1999b) is used as the target language. The next section will briefly describe HyQL and its use for information extraction before Section 5.4 gives a more detailed account of the actual training dialogue.

5.3 The HyQL Query Language

Our approach of a Web query language called HyQL is an SQL-like language that supports flexible selection of document parts as well as navigation through the Web. HyQL combines but also extends features found in related language designs with the aim to handle navigation as well as document processing on the level of both structure and content. The main purpose of HyQL is the operationalization of basic information-gathering processes in the sense of document and information selection using guided search and filtering based on content and structure. Elaborating XML's flexible linking and referencing concept, we integrated features to be able to specify robust queries.

HyQL considers the Web as a computable dynamic graph structure where the nodes are static or dynamically generated documents and the edges are the links between them. Navigation and search in the graph structure are specified by constraints on this structure and the contents of the nodes. Searching in the graph is supported by the specification of regular path expressions that, for example, allow specifying that only links on the originating Web site are followed until a depth of 3 is reached.

A sample task of navigation is filling a form on a Web page, submitting it, and reaching the result page. This process involves constraints between two document nodes named by their URLs, U_1 and U_2, respectively. The document of U_1 contains the HTML form that partially specifies U_2 (by the attribute-value pairs and action contained in the form). The pattern of U_2 is completed by an external interaction (by a user filling the form in her Web browser window or by a script setting the respective attributes). Now, establishing the edge between U_1 and U_2—that is, accessing the document of U_2—corresponds to submitting the form successfully in the browser.

The documents themselves are represented as parse tree structures in a canonical form, which means that some obvious faults in documents are repaired, optional start or end tags are added, and additional annotations such as *word* or *number* are integrated.

The expressiveness of HyQL allows document portions to be addressed in a variety of ways. The position of specific elements E in a document tree can be characterized by specifying constraints on the paths from the root to the relevant subtrees, constraints on properties of E, specifying a context of E and E's relative position to it, and so forth. Collections play a key role in the specification of a position. A *collection* is an ordered set of related elements that results from a complete search over a subtree considering specific constraints on the search method used and the nodes to be considered according to their type and attributes. For example, the collection of all tables reached by traversing a document tree in a depth-first, left-to-right manner can be specified. All collections can be accessed as a complete list or indexed forward or backward. In addition to the single element and all collections, selections of intervals are also possible by specifying two single border elements (which may belong to unrelated collections) and implicitly all elements between them.

In the following, a sample HyQL script is presented that could be used, for example, as the program code of an appropriate CGI-Web access (the line numbers are *not* part of the script). It selects the pure table with the current weather forecast for the city of Berlin from the Yahoo! weather site.

```
1.  select info T := root,descendant(1,table)
2.  from document d1 such that
3.  document d in http://weather.yahoo.com/Germany.html
4.  document d ? document d1
5.  d1.url = select root,descendant(1) href
6.  from {select info A := root,descendant(1,a)
7.  from document d
8.  where A match "Berlin"}
9.  where root,child(1,tr)(1,td)descendant(1,b) applies to T
10. matches "Today*"
```

Lines 1, 2, 9, and 10 specify an operation in the SQL style of selecting some part from a specific resource where some qualification conditions must be satisfied. These parts of the script specify that the first table from the collection of all tables (line 1) to be reached by a depth-first, left-to-right search (the keyword descendant) should be selected from the content of document d1 (line 2) that contains a bold-typed part in the first cell of its first row[2] whose content has the string today as a prefix (lines 9 and 10). Lines 3 to 8 contain constraints of how to access the content of document d1. Line 4 specifies that document d1 can be accessed by following a local link (remaining on the same Web site) originating in document d, whose URL is fixed in line 3 (i.e., the host part of the URL of d1 has been fixed). The URL of d1 (line 5) is further constrained by the fact that its document part is given by the href attribute of an anchor in document d whose representation matches with the word Berlin. In fact, document d contains links to a lot of German cities in order to access individual local weather forecasts.

Usually, a HyQL script is specified by a set of queries where let queries providing intermediate results precede the output-producing select queries. This supports the refinement process of information extraction on the syntactic level of the script by avoiding, for example, deeply nested select queries and allows a component-based configuration of scripts.

---

2. Consider the correspondences: cell - td, row - tr, bold-typed - b.

5.3.1 The Construction of Wrappers

The TrIAs context requires the wrappers used for information extraction to be as robust as possible in the sense that they tolerate minor changes of the structure and layout of the documents they work on. As a consequence, it is necessary for the script not simply to implement a simple search, following strict paths in the documents' tree structures, but to exploit the document structure on a more abstract level.

The categories considered to be relevant with regard to the items to be selected are context, landmark, and characterization. A *context* is a part of a document covering and surrounding the selection that can be easily characterized and located (e.g., the only table contained in a document that has at least five columns and more than three rows). A *landmark* is a prominent feature of the document that is in close relation to the selection and works as a navigational hint (e.g., a particular image just before the text to be selected). A *characterization* of a selection deals with the specific format and style of the selected items. HyQL scripts can be constructed in such a way as to mirror the use of the structural criteria just mentioned. The following skeleton of a script explains the idea.

```
{ let info CONTEXT := . . .
from document d such that . . . }
{ let info LANDMARK := . . .
from CONTEXT
where . . . applicable to LANDMARK }
{ select here,following(1,font,{size = "+1"})
from LANDMARK in context CONTEXT }
```

The first part of the script assigns the variable CONTEXT to some specific part of the document named d (i.e., the result of some selection operation is now internally available for further processing). The second part of the script tries to find a specific landmark in the document portion assigned to CONTEXT. If it can be located, then it is assigned to the variable LANDMARK and again is internally available. Now, the last part of the script specifies that we start a search from the LANDMARK location in the document to find a font tag with a specific size attribute, but the search is limited to the area covered by CONTEXT. If this font is found, then it is provided as an output of the script. More complex scripts can be built, for example, by combining more than one of the script blocks of the kind sketched earlier.

Figure 5.2 explains the idea of the script illustrated here from the document tree point of view. HyQL parses each relevant HTML document and

FIGURE **5.2**

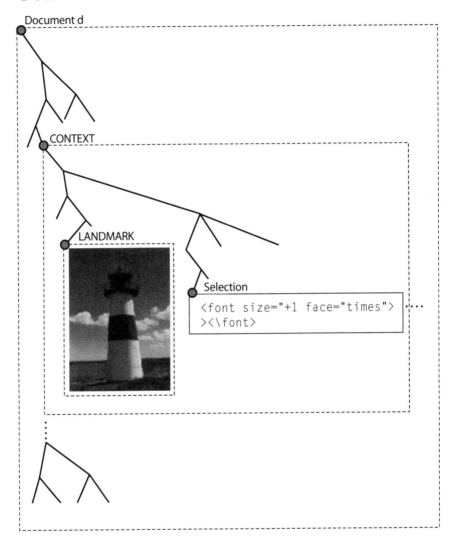

Extraction refinement process of a HyQL script.

transforms it into a tree representation where the nodes correspond to HTML tags and the outgoing edges represent the content and children tags covered by these tags. Then, the context part of the respective HyQL script is given by the subtree of the document tree labeled by CONTEXT. This subtree contains at a specific location a landmark (e.g., a salient feature such as a specific image)—that is, a subtree of a specific kind labeled as LANDMARK. The document portion that should be selected as the relevant information can be located considering a particular relation with regard to the landmark position (e.g., the first specific font tag that follows the specific image object[3]).

5.4 The Training Dialogue

Throughout the rest of this section the terms *user* and *trainer* will be used synonymously (and referred to in the female form). *Learning agent* (or simply *agent,* addressed in the male form) refers to the InfoBroker who is to be trained on how to extract a particular piece of information from an online document. The IET (see Figure 5.1) provides the interface in which both partners can collaborate to accomplish this common goal.

As mentioned in Section 5.2, the training dialogue is invoked whenever the InfoBroker does not succeed in extracting some piece of information (e.g., the price for a hotel room) from an online document delivered by some Web server. In this case, the IET

1. repairs the HTML code of the document under consideration (if necessary),

2. enhances the so obtained document with additional tags (HTML formatting instructions) and JavaScript code, and

3. loads it into a new browser window containing additional buttons for PBE functionality (see Figure 5.4 later) and explains to the user the current problem.

These points have to be clarified. First, regarding point 1, most documents found in the Web are not made of absolutely correct HTML code. Instead, most authors rely on the various browsers' capabilities to somehow produce a satisfying rendering resembling the author's intended design. As HyQL uses the parse tree of these documents as its main data structure, it is recommendable to bring them into a canonical form before starting to produce a wrapper.

---

3. "Follows" in the sense of traversing the subtree CONTEXT in a depth-first, left-to-right manner starting at the node LANDMARK.

Regarding point 2, the enhanced document structure is used in two ways. First, the JavaScript code serves the purpose to add some interactive functionality to the document such as highlighting some portion of the document by moving the mouse over it. Additional tags give the whole document a more fine-grained structure, allowing even single words or special characters to be recognized and providing a unique identifier for each document part. As a result, it is easy to find out exactly which document portion was selected (highlighted) by the user. Note that these first steps remain invisible to the user; that is, the visual appearance of the document in her browser will remain unaffected.

Finally, regarding part 3, the training dialogue is initiated as a reaction to the InfoBroker's futile attempt to extract information from a particular document in order to satisfy an information request forwarded by the travel agent. The agent uses all the information found so far to explain the current task to the user. In the example described in Section 5.4.4 the agent tries to find the price for a twin room in some Berlin hotel. Figure 5.3 shows how the user is presented this problem by referring to the already known values for hotel name, city, and so forth.

The actual training dialogue (Figure 5.4) itself starts with the user accepting the task presented by the agent and selecting that part of the document containing the desired information—in this case, the price of "475.00". Then the following cycle starts:

1. The agent synthesizes a wrapper using only the information he obtained so far and computes a numerical measure of goodness for it.

2. He checks what could possibly be done to improve this wrapper and suggests the corresponding actions to the user (examples include the definition of a landmark or a context; see Section 5.3.1 for details on the general structure of wrappers); if no improvement can be expected, the agent suggests to terminate the training dialogue.

3. The user picks one of the actions suggested by the agent and executes it with the agent's aid.

4. The process returns to step 1.

These steps will be explained in some detail in the following sections.

5.3

Looking for HOTEL information	
city:	Berlin
hotel name:	Inter-Continental
check-in date:	07/11/00
type of room:	Twin
price:	

Explaining the current task.

5.4.1 Wrapper Generation and Assessment

Given some selected portion of a document, the agent computes the assessments of possible wrappers, disregarding cases under a certain threshold. To this end, he uses a hierarchy of wrapper classes for the characterization of the selection. Each class is a kind of template containing wrapper building blocks (implemented as HyQL snippets) with parameters yet to be specified and is associated a numerical valuation reflecting its estimated utility. This measure mainly refers to the expected robustness of a wrapper containing a HyQL construct of some sort.[4] For example, those exploiting the document structure can be expected to be more robust than those simply counting the distance of some selection from the beginning of the document.

Apart from this intrinsic valuation of the various wrapper classes, a wrapper assessment must also take into account the cost for localizing the current selection, given navigational aids such as contexts, landmarks, and a characterization of the target selection on the basis of syntactic features such as style and font.[5] Here the basic idea is that the more complicated this navigation is, the more likely it is to fail due to document modifications. For example, always finding the *first* occurrence of some text written in red

---

4. Whenever a wrapper fails to produce the desired information and a training dialogue becomes necessary, it is analyzed and the assessment of the components responsible for this failure is decreased.

5. Referring to Figure 5.2, this corresponds to moving from one localization point (e.g., the start of a context) to the next one—in this case, the landmark—until the selection is reached.

FIGURE **5.4**

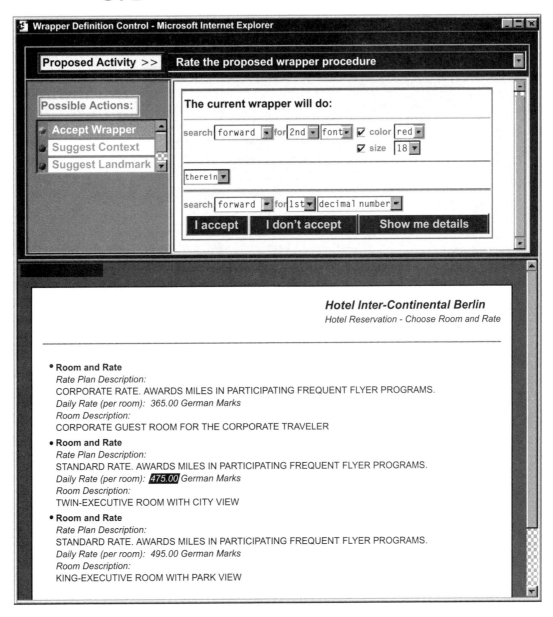

A sample training dialogue.

within some section of a document can be expected to be more robust than the search for the twenty-third occurrence (due to the fact that the chance for something unforeseen happening in between is much higher).

To summarize, at each step the agent must consider all reasonable combinations of landmark, context, and selection characterization. Their respective assessments are computed taking into account

- the valuation of the selection characterization and its localization cost with respect to the other defined parts (i.e., the estimated robustness of the wrapper and the actual localization cost);

- the valuation of context and/or landmark and the resulting localizations;

- the user's acceptance, depending on the user's expertise. Components explicitly suggested by the user obtain a higher value than those proposed by the agent and simply accepted by the user (discussed later).

5.4.2 Suggesting an Action

The agent has at its disposal a *task library* containing "recipes" of how to construct a wrapper of a certain class. The actions they are made of include

- characterizing the selection,

- defining a landmark,

- defining a context, and

- accepting the current wrapper.

More details about these actions will be given in Section 5.4.3.

To suggest an appropriate action to be carried out next, the agent

- evaluates the document structure to identify those wrapper classes that are, at least in principle, applicable to the current document;

- checks what remains to be done to complete the corresponding task;

- computes the *expected utility* of each feasible action; and

- presents them to the user in a ranked order reflecting their respective estimated usefulness, including a brief help text describing the meaning of these actions. Note that the user is free to choose *any* feasible action, not only the one considered best by the agent.

How can the expected utility of an action be estimated? To make the whole training process as painless as possible to the user, only those actions should be suggested that actually advance the dialogue by providing valuable information to the agent. The numerical wrapper assessment explained in the previous section forms a good basis for estimating the effect of an action on the expected wrapper quality. Using the formula

$$EU(a, u, n) = [ass(w_a) - ass(w_{curr})] \cdot P_u(a) - annoy\,(u, n), \qquad (1)$$

the expected utility for action a and user u can be computed. Note that n is the number of actions already carried out during the current training dialogue; $ass(w_a)$ and $ass(w_{curr})$ are the assessments of the best wrapper possible *after* and *before* executing action a, respectively. $P_u(a)$ is the probability of user u successfully carrying out action a, and *annoy* is a function that, depending on the user's characteristics, grows monotonically as the length of the training dialogue increases. Formula (1) thus represents the expected increase in wrapper quality decreased by a penalty for annoying the user with yet another action.

In case none of the available actions is assigned a positive utility value—that is, if no action is expected to provide a sufficient improvement to justify continuing the training process—the agent suggests to finish the dialogue.

This is the case in the situation depicted in Figure 5.4. As the upper left window titled Possible Actions indicates, Accept Wrapper (the final action of each dialogue) is preferred over Suggest Context and Suggest Landmark. The details of how the user's preferred action is actually being executed are explained in the following section.

5.4.3 Executing an Action

Once the user has selected an action to be executed from the ranked list of alternatives *other than* terminating the dialogue, the agent tries to give optimal support to facilitate the user's task. (This special case will be described later.) To this end, he applies a number of strong heuristics to identify and suggest candidates for the wrapper component the user is just trying to define.

To find a candidate for a landmark such as a heading, the agent looks for boldface text (like **Room and Rate** in the example of Figure 5.4), text followed by a colon, or an image. Tables and regions enclosed between two objects (e.g., horizontal rules) are considered to be good candidates for contexts. Any syntactic feature that distinguishes the selected text from its surroundings (e.g., a special color or font) could make a good characterization.

With each possible component found, the agent generates a wrapper, computes its quality, and from these results derives a ranked list of suggestions for contexts, landmarks, and so forth. By clicking through this list of suggestions (and thus highlighting the corresponding parts of the document), the user can explore the set of alternatives provided by the agent and simply accept one of these suggestions or define a new one on her own. In the case of landmarks and contexts, the latter can be easily accomplished by just marking the corresponding region with the mouse. The agent then simply checks for structural correctness and, for example, rejects contexts that do not contain the target selection. When it comes to characterizing a selected area, the agent lists all applicable syntactic features (e.g., font, color, size, etc., but also possible "types" such as decimal number or ZIP code that can be recognized automatically) from which she can select the ones she considers relevant. So in any case, the user is forced to make only structurally correct decisions. This interplay between the complementary capabilities of agent and user will be discussed in Section 5.6.

As already mentioned, terminating the training dialogue is a special case. Whenever the user decides to accept the agent's currently best wrapper, she is presented with a simple representation of this wrapper in terms of its components and the way they interact with each other (see Figure 5.4). The user can easily modify this wrapper by switching components on and off and changing the way they are combined. Every time, the effect of such a modification is immediately displayed in the lower window containing the current HTML document. This provides a way for the user to experiment with the agent's construction and find out whether it actually does what she intended.

5.4.4 A Sample Training Dialogue

Take as an example scenario for PBE the document shown in Figure 5.4. We assume the user is planning a trip to Berlin with a stay at Hotel Inter-Continental. With the wrappers at hand, the trip planner has not been able to extract the room rates from the hotel page, so the agent initiates a dialogue with the user.

The PBE dialogue is presented in the browser together with the relevant document in the lower frame. The upper frame is reserved for the communication with the user. The Proposed Activity field verbalizes the next step the user should take for a successful wrapper construction. An interaction history with undo mechanism is available through a pull-down menu in the top line. The list of ranked possible actions is given on the left side of the upper frame. A green light indicates that the corresponding action is explicitly suggested by the agent, whereas actions with a red light can be executed "at the user's own risk" as they will not lead to the best possible wrapper according to the agent's computations.

The best choice in the agent's view is already preselected. Most actions require an additional communication with the user. This is done in the area to the right where the user is presented the respective submenus and relevant information for her decision making (e.g., wrapper components proposed by the agent). A red box around an area characterizes a currently relevant interface part for a better orientation of the user.

In an initial step, the user is presented with the task at hand (see Figure 5.3), which in this case is the identification of the price for a twin room. The first—and only—action applicable is the selection of the desired information. The user marks the price of "475.00" displayed in a red font, as are all other prices on the Web page.

Having done so, the proposed actions comprise as a first choice to further characterize the selection, which the user accepts. The agent lists the applicable syntactic features (red color, size 18, and italic font, from which the user selects the first two) and types (in this case, only "decimal number," which is also accepted by the user).

Applying his aforementioned heuristics, the agent tries to identify reasonable contexts and landmarks he could suggest to the user to improve the current wrapper. However, due to the limited capabilities of these heuristics, he fails to find any document features that could be used as additional aids and make the wrapper more robust. Consequently, he suggests that the user accept the current wrapper, thus terminating the training dialogue.

After accepting this suggestion, the user is presented with the simple representation of the current wrapper displayed in Figure 5.4 and asked to check whether this is what she wanted. As already mentioned, the user can test what effect minor modifications of the various wrapper components and their combination will have on the search result. The current wrapper exclusively makes use of the syntactic features of the selected text area (looking for the first decimal number in the second occurrence of a text of size 18 in red) and thus ignores the user's reason for selecting just *this* occurrence of a room price in this document instead of the first or third one—namely, the fact that only this price applies to a twin room.

5.5

```
{ let info X1 := root, descendant(1,font,{color="red"
  size="18"})
  from document d in ...
  where text root,ancestor(1,li)
                child(-1,br)next(all,span
        applies to X1 matches "TWIN EXECUTIVE ROOM*" }
{ select info X2 := root,descendant(1,span)
  from X1
  where X2 recognized as 'decimal_number' }
```

The final version of the wrapper.

She decides not to accept this wrapper and adds a landmark to it to connect more strongly the wrapper's functionality to the *semantics* of the document. Using his purely syntax-based heuristics, the agent suggests a number of landmark candidates, none of which is suited to robustly identifying the price of a twin room. In the given example, the agent suggests using one of the occurrences of **Room and Rate** or the second occurrence of *Daily Rate (per room):*. The user, recognizing the semantic relationship between the words TWIN-EXECUTIVE ROOM in the room description and the price for a *twin* room suggests using these three words as a navigational aid. After integrating this landmark into the wrapper (and giving this component an especially high valuation as it was suggested by the user herself), the agent again checks whether any further improvements are possible. As this is not the case, the user is again advised to accept the current wrapper and terminate the training dialogue, which she does.

Figure 5.5 depicts the final wrapper generated by the IET and used to satisfy the travel agent's information request.

5.5 Lessons Learned

Although we have not yet performed a rigorous evaluation of the dialogue strategies sketched here, a few general lessons can already be derived from the first prototype of the PBE environment (Bauer and Dengler 1999a). This first version did not provide ranked suggestions for future user actions but came with a simple graphical interface that left all decisions exclusively to the user. In particular, the following two problems repeatedly occurred in our own interaction with the system:

What to do next? To make this decision, the user has to have some idea of what benefit the learning agent will have from some action taken by the user (i.e., which action would provide the most valuable information for the agent).

Can I stop? Related to the first point is the question of whether or not the user should continue the training process at all. After all, it makes no sense to provide more and more information to the learning agent if he has already acquired enough knowledge about the task at hand to generate a good solution. To make this decision, the user again has to reason about the potential impact of further actions on the quality of the learning result.

To overcome these difficulties, we analyzed the training situation at the respective knowledge levels of the two partners involved. The results of this analysis led to the utility-based approach to dialogue guidance described earlier, and they will be presented in some detail in the next section.

5.6 The Communication Problem

Effective communication between user (trainer) and agent (student) is hard to achieve. This is particularly true in scenarios such as the one sketched in Section 5.2 in which an agent is to be trained to interact with an already existing application that was not designed to be "programmed" this way. One of the most fundamental obstacles is the lack of shared knowledge or insight into the various aspects of the training task at hand. As depicted in Figure 5.6, at least four different types of information play a key role during a training dialogue:

- *Structural* knowledge refers to the internal properties of the programming domain (in this case, the HTML structure of a document to be processed).

- *Procedural* knowledge refers to the understanding of (at least) the basic concepts of the target programming language (in this case, HyQL) and the way the programs to be developed are intended to work (here, the principal functioning of wrappers).

- The *visual/semantic* category is composed of the optical perception of the application system to be dealt with, the representation of domain

FIGURE **5.6**

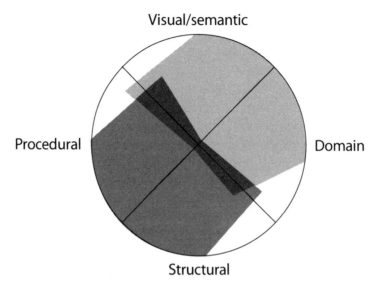

Knowledge shared by user and agent.

objects, and its interpretation allowing, for example, semantic relationships to be derived. Examples include the rendering of an HTML document in a browser and the identification of some particularly formatted portion of text as a heading describing the subsequent paragraph.

- Finally, *domain* knowledge includes the basic understanding of concepts from the application domain (e.g., about hotels, room categories, etc.) and the wording typically used to describe them.

These various categories are not mutually independent. Rather, a lack of structural knowledge prevents a sufficiently deep insight into the procedural aspects of the task at hand; little or no domain knowledge exacerbates the interpretation of visual encoding of information beyond purely syntactical aspects. Unfortunately, only a relatively small part of this information is shared by the user and agent and can thus be used for communication purposes.

As depicted in Figure 5.6, the learning agent, for example, possesses deep insight into the (programming) domain *structure*. In the given example, this refers to the system's ability to evaluate and exploit the underlying document structure induced by the HTML code.

While the typical user can be expected to have some basic understanding of HTML at best, this overlap usually proved to be insufficient to explain the system behavior—its suggestions regarding next actions or wrapper components—referring to such structural document properties.[6]

The user's most prominent capability is in interpreting and understanding the *visual appearance* of a document in her Web browser. Doing so, she can easily identify "important," never-changing aspects of a document and *semantic* relationships among objects (e.g., a graphic and its title) by exploiting her background domain knowledge. The system, on the other hand, has to rely on a number of more or less feasible heuristics (e.g., "the first line of a table column typically contains a header describing its contents") to at least make a guess of which objects are related and might thus make a good navigational aid.

The coverage of *procedural* aspects of the training task (i.e., details of the target language and the general functioning of wrappers) largely depends on the user's experience in such training activities, on the one hand, and on the system's learning bias, on the other hand.

Even without taking into account misconceptions on either side,[7] this discussion indicates that an effective communication providing perfect mutual understanding of both partners is almost impossible.

What are the consequences for the training dialogue in the TrIAs scenario? Obviously there exist two almost disjoint, complementary *competence areas*. The learning agent suggests the next actions to be taken or wrapper components (e.g., a landmark) to be used mainly based on its understanding of the underlying HTML structure. The user—in her role as a trainer—evaluates these suggestions based on her domain knowledge and the visual impression of the document's rendering in the browser. Depending on the user's estimated expertise, either the agent autonomously decides on how to continue the training dialogue—that is, the user is only presented the seemingly best action at each point in time—or the user is free to accept or ignore the agent's suggestions, taking over control by herself.

---

6. The fact that the same visual rendering can be achieved using a number of different HTML encodings (just think of the many creative ways to use tables) aggravates this problem, because it is almost impossible to guess correctly the actually used HTML code just by looking at its rendering.

7. Some of the heuristics used by the system might be perfectly wrong, as might be a user's guess of the document structure derived from its visual appearance.

Adding image-processing capabilities to the learning agent, as is done in Chapter 19 of this book, enables it to (at least partially) understand the structure and functionality hidden in the user interface. In terms of the previously mentioned categories, this means that the agent's coverage of the "visual" information portion is significantly extended. Equipped with this enhanced insight into the visual appearance of an application, the agent can try immediately to interpret and generalize the user's interaction with the various interface elements, thus enabling it to program applications without an API.

Applications specifically *designed* to be programmed by example try to bridge the gap between user and system by providing a visual access to both the programming domain structure and the procedural aspects of the program to be developed. A typical example of this class is Stagecast (see Chapter 1), a system intended to enable its user to program a kind of video game. The world inhabited by various kinds of creatures has the structure of a (visually perceivable) grid, and program steps consist of simple state transition rules represented by the respective states before and after rule application.

Even here, however, not all interaction can be solely grounded on visual perception. Instead, the user must be willing to delve into some of the more advanced features of the system to describe what is called "hidden states" in McDaniel (see Chapter 8). This notion refers to additional aspects of the world that cannot be inferred from just one example but have to be explicitly stated by the user or inferred by the system. In the Stagecast example, such additional information includes abstractions such as "*any* kind of object should be in this place in order to make the rule applicable" or "variables" that represent the internal state of the characters.

This perspective is somewhat similar to the one taken in the Gamut project (see Chapter 8) in which the user is considered to be actually programming. That is, the user is in charge of conveying all required information to the system, which in turn has to provide appropriate communication channels to facilitate this task for the user.

Again, this approach differs from the TrIAs perspective, in which the user initially did not intend to *program* a system but to *use* it. Consequently, she cannot be expected to be infinitely patient and willing to invest her time and effort to teach the system something she expected it to already know. In other words, it's not (only) about making *learning* as easy as possible for the agent (compare VanLehn 1987). Thus, the system's contribution must clearly exceed the simple check for structural properties of a document. In TrIAs this additional accomplishment is achieved by the library of numerically assessed wrapper components and the strong heuristics enabling the system to hypothesize semantic relationships among (graphi-cal) objects.

5.7 Another Application Scenario

One peculiarity of the TrIAs scenario was the exchange of the roles as ser-vice provider and consumer between user and system. This made it neces-sary to consider carefully the user's "felicity" (in contrast to concentrating exclusively on the learner's state as described in VanLehn 1987).

However, not only applications in which a (possibly unwilling) user happens to be involved in a training session benefit from the careful de-sign of their trainable components. In fact, the same PBE approach as described earlier was used to implement the InfoBeans system (Bauer, Dengler, and Paul 2000) in which even naive users could configure their own Web-based information services, satisfying their individual informa-tion needs.

Figure 5.7 depicts an *InfoBox*, a personal information system composed from a number of simple information services. Each of these so-called *InfoBeans* represents an information agent that deals with one particular information source only. Using HyQL wrappers, these agents can query Web servers, extract interesting pieces of information from the documents deliv-ered, and communicate these through input and output channels to the other InfoBeans, thus providing the basis for effective information integra-tion. Whenever the user wants to create a new InfoBean or modify or extend an existing one, a training dialogue similar to the one described earlier is initiated.

The sample InfoBox depicted in Figure 5.7 compares the prices of two online bookstores. To this end the initial input, author and title of a book, are forwarded to the InfoBean dealing with Amazon.com, from which the book price in U.S. dollars is extracted and forwarded to an online currency converter to obtain the value in German marks. Additionally, the corre-sponding ISBN number is extracted and delivered to the InfoBean in the lower left corner that addresses Libri.de and tries to find the same book. This way a comparison shopping system, although admittedly simplistic, can be implemented.

Because the InfoBeans application is in the tradition of PBE systems (e.g., Lieberman, Nardi, and Wright 1999) in which the user trains the sys-tem to recognize certain types of situations to be dealt with autonomously, we removed the "annoyance" factor when assessing the expected utility of

FIGURE **5.7**

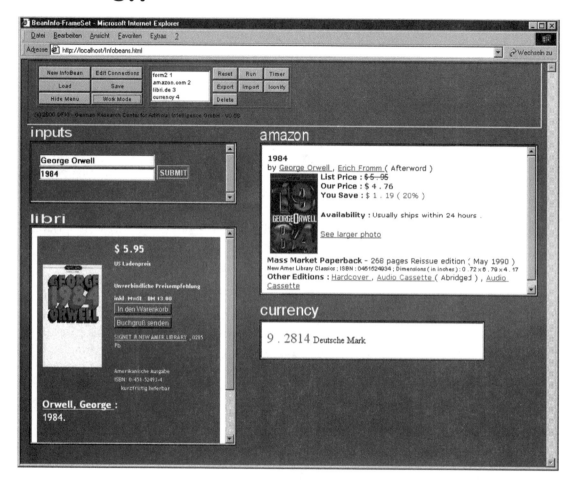

A sample InfoBox.

some system suggestion. Experiments will show which of these versions will have the better user acceptance.

5.8   Related Work (Non-PBE)

Instantiations of TrIAs are in the tradition of information integration systems such as the Information Manifold (IM) and Ariadne (see Levy,

Rajaraman, and Ordille 1996 and Knoblock et al. 1998, respectively). While these concentrate on efficient generation and execution of query plans and the integration of information from previously unrelated sources, TrIAs add the aspect of cooperative problem solving by getting the human user involved in both training the system and gathering information.

Other differences can be found—for example, in the basic assumptions regarding the information sources available. IM, for example, makes use of detailed source descriptions that explicitly represent constraints regarding the information contained at a particular site (e.g., information about cars *with price > $20000*) to optimize the query process. TrIAs, on the other hand, rely on user interaction to correct obviously wrong source descriptions or add missing details whenever the need arises. This, in turn, is in contrast to automatic approaches to capture the contents of an information source in terms of users' categories such as ILA (Perkowitz and Etzioni 1995).

Current wrapper generation approaches such as those in Hsu (1998) and Muslea, Minton, and Knoblock (1998) use "landmark grammars" working on the tokenized document string as a means to specify wrappers. Since we use a canonical parse tree structure extending the sequential token representation, we are able to specify more robust wrappers integrating more abstract landmark patterns. The *wrapper induction* methods in Kushmerick, Weld, and Doorenbos (1997), Hsu (1998), and Muslea, Minton, and Knoblock (1998) mainly aim at automatically constructing content extraction procedures for Web sources. They usually require more than a few examples to work, and a user-interactive approach with online integration of new information sources is not adequately supported.

With an increasing interest in building software agents that use information available on the Web as one of their main knowledge sources, the problem of learning how to handle these sources at least semiautomatically arises. The wrapper induction method (Kushmerick, Weld, and Doorenbos 1997) aims at automatically constructing content extraction procedures for Web sources. The system inductively learns a wrapper generalizing from example query responses. Opposed to our approach, the information sources considered (and also the wrapper class intended) are limited to have a very specific structure. Since their approach also requires more than a few examples to work, a user-interactive approach with online integration of new information sources like our TrIAs architecture is not adequately supported.

In ILA (Perkowitz and Etzioni 1995), the *category translation* problem is concerned—that is, how to translate information from Web sources into internal concepts of the information broker. We extend ILA's approach of using a fixed ontology in that we additionally allow the integration of a user-specific ontology.

The HyQL language incorporates some ideas from other approaches. Both WebSQL (Arocena, Mendelzon, and Mihaila 1997) and W3QL (Konopnicki and Shmueli 1995) provide sophisticated constructs for navigation on the Web, but they lack an integrated model of parsing documents and selecting specific parts of them. SgmlQL (1997) is a nice SQL-style programming language for manipulating SGML (HTML) documents but lacks any navigation constructs. XML (Extensible Markup Language 1997) allows with its linking concept based on XML parse trees a precise specification of resource locations, especially within documents.

5.9 Conclusion

We have tried to make a case for the use of PBE techniques not only in an initial, offline training phase but also during the execution of the procedures so acquired. As was mentioned, this particular setting requires the user to be taken into account much more carefully. After all, she has to "repair" the faulty behavior of a system or agent from which she expected some useful service.

Early informal tests with nonexpert users indicate that the training mechanism provided enables (many) end users to deal successfully with delicate problems of identifying and extracting information from Web-based information sources. Besides the two application scenarios sketched earlier—the TrIAs framework that can be instantiated with a number of different applications and the InfoBeans system—many other uses of instructable information agents are conceivable, ranging from intelligent notification services to data warehouses.

Acknowledgements

This work was supported by the German Ministry of Education, Research, Science, and Technology under grant ITW 9703 as part of the PAN project.

References

Arocena, G., A. Mendelzon, and G. Mihaila. 1997. Applications of a Web query language. In *Proceedings of the 6th International WWW Conference* (Santa Clara, Calif.); www.cs.utoronto.ca/~websql/.

Bauer, M., and D. Dengler. 1999a. InfoBeans—Configuration of personalized information services. In *Proceedings of the International Conference on Intelligent User Interfaces (IUI'99)* (Los Angeles), ed. M. Maybury. New York: ACM Press.

———. 1999b. TrIAs: Trainable information assistants for cooperative problem solving. In *Proceedings of the 1999 International Conference on Autonomous Agents (Agents'99)* (Seattle, Wash.), ed. O. Etzioni and J. Müller. New York: ACM Press.

Bauer, M., D. Dengler, and G. Paul. 2000. Instructible agents for Web mining. In *Proceedings of the International Conference on Intelligent User Interfaces (IUI 2k)* (New Orleans), ed. H. Lieberman.

Billsus, D., and M. Pazzani. 1999. A hybrid user model for news story classification. In *User modeling: Proceedings of the Seventh International Conference* (Banff, Canada), ed. J. Kay. Wien, New York: Springer-Verlag.

Hsu, C.-N. 1998. Initial results on wrapping semistructured Web pages with finite-state transducers and contextual rules. In *Workshop on AI and Information Integration;* see also www.isi.edu/ariadne/aiii8-wkshp/proceedings.html9.

Knoblock, C., S. Minton, J. Ambite, N. Ashish, P. Modi, I. Muslea, A. Philpot, and S. Tejada. 1998. Modeling Web sources for information integration. In *Fifteenth National Conference on Artificial Intelligence* (Madison, Wisc.). Menlo Park, Cambridge, London: AAAI Press/The MIT Press.

Konopnicki, D., and O. Shmueli. 1995. W3qs: A query system for the World-Wide Web. In *Proceedings of VLDB Conference;* see also www.cs.technion.ac.il/~konop/w3qs.html.

Kozierok, R., and P. Maes. 1993. A learning interface agent for scheduling meetings. In *Proceedings of the 1993 International Workshop on Intelligent User Interfaces* (Orlando, Fla.), ed. W. Gray, W. Hefley, and D. Murray. New York: ACM Press.

Kushmerick, N., D. Weld, and R. Doorenbos. 1997. Wrapper induction for information extraction. In *Proceedings of the 15th International Joint Conference on Artificial Intelligence* (Nagoya, Japan, August). San Francisco: Morgan Kaufmann.

Levy, A., A. Rajaraman, and K. Ordille. 1996. Querying heterogeneous information sources using source descriptions. In *Proceedings of the 22nd VLDB Conference.* San Francisco: Morgan Kaufmann.

Lieberman, H. 1995. Letizia: An agent that assists Web browsing. In *Proceedings of the 14th International Joint Conference on Artificial Intelligence* (Montreal, August), ed. C. Mellish. San Francisco: Morgan Kaufmann.

Lieberman, H., B. Nardi, and D. Wright. 1999. Training agents to recognize text by example. In *Proceedings of the 1999 International Conference on Autonomous Agents (Agents'99),* (Seattle, Wash.), ed. O. Etzioni and J. Müller. New York: ACM Press.

Mellish, C., ed. *Proceedings of the 14th International Joint Conference on Artificial Intelligence* (Montreal, August 1995). San Francisco: Morgan Kaufmann.

Muslea, I., S. Minton, and C. Knoblock. 1998. Learning wrappers for semistructured, Web-based information sources. In *Workshop on AI and Information Integration* (AAAI); see also www.isi.edu/ariadne/aiii8-wkshp/proceedings.html9.

Perkowitz, M., and O. Etzioni. 1995. Category translation: Learning to understand information on the internet. In *Proceedings of the 14th International Joint Conference on Artificial Intelligence* (Montreal, August), ed. C. Mellish. San Francisco: Morgan Kaufmann.

SgmlQL: SGML Query Language. 1997. See www.lpl.univ-aix.fr/projects/SgmlQL/.

VanLehn, K. 1987. Learning one subprocedure per lesson. *Artificial Intelligence* 31: 1–40.

Extensible markup language (XML): Part 2. Linking. 1997. W3C Working Draft, July 31, www.w3.org/TR/WD-xml-link.

CHAPTER 6

End Users and GIS: A Demonstration Is Worth a Thousand Words

CAROL TRAYNOR

Saint Anselm College

MARIAN G. WILLIAMS

University of Massachusetts, Lowell

Abstract

This chapter presents a programming-by-demonstration (PBD) approach to geographic information systems (GISs). The aim of our approach is to enable nonspecialist users to avail themselves of the software without having to resort to the help of expert users. We begin with a story of one group of nonspecialist users who encountered difficulty with GIS software. Next we summarize findings of a study of why GIS software is hard for nonspecialist users to use. Then we describe in detail the PBD approach for GIS and explain how this component may be integrated into a GIS.

6.1   Introduction

Geographic information systems (GISs) are in wide use by city planners, landscape architects, natural resource managers, and other specialists who have the expertise—or the trained staff—to use them. Many nonspecialists (e.g., community activists lobbying for change in their inner-city neighborhoods) would like to be able to use GIS. However, GIS software is not accessible to them, because, in its current incarnation, it requires a knowledge of geography, cartography, and database systems. Despite an enormous pool of potential nonspecialist users, GIS is not at this time a mainstream, mass-marketed application.

In this chapter, we present a programming-by-demonstration (PBD) approach to GIS that offers promise for enabling nonspecialists to avail themselves of the power of GIS. We begin with a story of a group of nonspecialists who encountered major difficulties when they tried to use a GIS. We summarize the findings of a study about why such users find GIS so very difficult to use. We then describe a PBD approach to GIS that shows promise for making GIS accessible to nonspecialist users, and we explain how this PBD component may be integrated into a GIS.

6.2   A Story of End Users and GIS

Several years ago, we had the opportunity to observe a group of faculty from a local university as they embarked on a project to make a GIS available to residents of a nearby inner-city neighborhood. The goal of the project was to equip residents of the economically depressed neighborhood, many of whom were recent immigrants, so that they could effectively influence governmental decisions impacting their quality of life. With a GIS, the residents should be able to study and present maps showing the distribution of crime across the city, thereby bolstering their arguments for the placement of a new police precinct within the neighborhood. With a GIS, they should be able to arm themselves with maps showing the proximity of toxic waste sites to their children's schools and lobby effectively to have the sites cleaned up.

The faculty members came from diverse disciplines, including community psychology and public health nursing. They were smart, capable people with advanced degrees and good problem-solving skills. They were regular computer users, proficient with applications for word-processing their academic papers, making slides for presentations, and exchanging email. They approached the adoption of GIS with careful planning. To help them select the right GIS software and get them started using it in the neighborhood project, we engaged a GIS expert for them to consult (Kuhn, Richardson, and Williams 1994). After several long sessions with the consultant, they purchased one of the best-known mass-marketed GIS products.

Despite the careful approach and the consultations with the expert, they found it dauntingly difficult to use the GIS. They were, of course, perfectly capable of going out and taking training courses and understanding the material in such courses. But their time, attention, and brainpower needed to be directed at the content of the project, not at how to use a complicated software tool. Needless to say, it was obvious from the start that if the faculty members could not use the GIS, then it would be even further beyond the abilities of non-computer-using neighborhood residents.

What did the faculty members do? They hired computer science graduate students to use the GIS for them. We call these grad students their *surrogate users.* In styling them thus, we mean no disrespect for the faculty members, who retained responsibility for the intellectual content of the project and who specified the nature of the information displays to be created with the GIS. The surrogate users provided a human interface between the faculty members and the software interface. It was the graduate students who produced the displays that the faculty members and neighborhood residents needed.

Engaging surrogate users has been observed in a variety of other circumstances, when technology has been (intentionally or unintentionally) unavailable for direct use by nonspecialist end users. For example, directory assistance operators have long served as surrogate users of technology to search for telephone listings, though some of that technology has now been made available to end users on the Web. Like us, Garson and Biggs (1992) and Egenhofer (1995) have observed the need for surrogate users for GIS software.

What exactly did the grad students do for the faculty members? The first task, after spending a nontrivial amount of time learning how to use the software, was to locate, reformat, and import data files. Once the data sets were installed, they used the GIS to create information displays on maps. They also attempted, unsuccessfully, to use the GIS's built-in scripting language to create an application that the social scientists could use. However, the possible customizations were too minimal to help solve the problems. In simple terms, the grad students were needed for (1) getting data in and (2) getting information out. We focus here on the problem of getting the information out of a GIS and on the characteristics of the current crop of GIS software that make it so very difficult for nonspecialists to use.

6.3   Why Is GIS Software So Hard to Use?

What is it about GIS software that makes it so hard to use, so hard to get the information out?

To answer this question, we looked closely at seven commonly used GIS software packages, including the one the faculty members were using. We chose some simple tasks that GIS users are apt to perform repeatedly—for example, opening a map—and analyzed the knowledge and steps necessary for performing them (Traynor and Williams 1995). This task analysis showed that, in general, the GISs had three serious obstacles to use by nonspecialists:

1. They used *technical terminology* and *technical concepts* from cartography, geography, and database systems (e.g., the user needs to know what an overlay is in the cartographic sense and what a query is in the database sense).

2. They required the user to have a mental model of the *software architecture* to perform a task, since the sequence of steps was based on the way data were stored and represented (e.g., the user needs to know the structure of the database).

In other words, each of the GISs required users to translate a task from their own language into its language, as well as to understand its software architecture. Little wonder, then, that the grad students hired to work on the neighborhood project became immersed in the terminology of GIS and in a way of thinking about their work that the software imposed on them. Even when coached, they had trouble communicating with the users they served, because of the burden of translating between GIS-speak and the real-world terminology of the users.

Another issue common to all of the GISs we examined was the following:

3. They provided *no record of how a display of information on a map was created,* other than, perhaps, a representation in a database query language.

The GIS users we observed created information displays by trial and error, with the result that once they arrived at a useful display, they had no record of how they had achieved it. Also, they had no way to create a similar, but different, display, other than more trial and error. Without a record of how an information display was created (except, perhaps, in a database query language such as SQL that nonspecialists cannot read), a GIS user has no way to *program* the GIS. He or she tends to start over from scratch all the time.

Heuristics for designing this next-generation GIS software follow naturally from the problems we identified with the current generation:

1. Present the human-computer interaction in terms of the user's task.

2. Protect the user from needing technical expertise from cartography, geography, or database systems.

3. Protect the user from having to know about the software architecture.

4. Provide a program representation of the steps for creating an information display.

Some of these heuristics are widely accepted principles of software human factors and familiar rules of thumb for designers of interactive systems. However, they have special applicability to software, such as GIS, that has arisen out of a particular technical community. Interaction that fits the task model and the expertise of a specialist may be incomprehensible to a nonspecialist. Similarly, a program representation, if present, may be represented in a language familiar to the specialist but alien to the nonspecialist.

We observe a pattern to the way technical software gets mainstreamed and becomes successful in the mass market. First, its applicability beyond the original technical domain becomes widely recognized. There follows a phase in which new users become specialists, or engage the help of surrogate users. Then attempts are made to modify the software to make it usable by nonspecialists. Finally, the software is reconceptualized for the nonspecialist end users. Only then does it succeed in the mass market. Spreadsheets, CAD, and Web browsers are examples of software that has traveled this route.

GIS originated in the geographers' community. Its enormous applicability beyond that community is clear, though at the moment, nonspecialists need surrogate users to exercise the software for them. Now the question is whether we are still tweaking the software in the hopes that small changes will make a difference to nonspecialist users, or whether designers are finally starting to think about GIS from the nonspecialist's point of view.

6.4   Are Things Improving for GIS Users?

We recently revisited the GIS packages that we looked at a few years ago and can report that things have improved for GIS specialist users. The software packages now reside on mainstream platforms, such as Windows. The vendors have started to take usability issues seriously. And more research has been done on how people use spatial data. But what about nonspecialist users?

One of the major vendors of GIS software now has a product aimed at first-time GIS users and has published a book to accompany it. The company's Web site suggests that "everyone" can now use GIS: "Within minutes, you'll be able to create attractive and accurate digital maps that you can print, embed in documents, e-mail, or publish on the World Wide Web." Unfortunately, interacting with the software requires learning many of the same technical concepts and terms (e.g., the technical meanings of "theme" and "coverage") that full-fledged GIS software requires. Queries are just thinly disguised SQL.

In research labs, new ways of querying a GIS are being explored. For example, Standing and Roy (1997) have proposed a visual functional query language for creating macros. Aufaure-Portier (1995) has devised a visual gesture language for describing spatial relationships, such as adjacency and inclusiveness. Richards and Egenhofer (1995) have designed a drag-and-drop interface that lets the user stack up icons, as if they were blocks; the resulting stack shows how information should be used on a map. Ahlberg and Shneiderman (1994) have shown the usefulness of letting users create dynamic database queries by manipulating alphasliders to select values for the various parameters. Some of these approaches require technical knowledge (e.g., Standing's query language uses icons representing functions such as Union and Buffer). None of them provides a savable, retrievable, editable program representation written in a language that nonspecialists can read.

6.5 How Can Programming by Demonstration Help?

In the PBD paradigm, the software "watches" while the user "demonstrates" how to do a task. The software makes inferences about what the user is doing and creates a program that will do the same thing. Depending on the sophistication of the software, the resulting program may be hard-wired for the specific task the user demonstrated (in which case it functions like a macro), or it may be generalizable to similar tasks. (See Cypher 1993 for extensive discussion and case studies of PBD.)

The PBD software creates a representation of the program it has inferred. Sometimes, the representation is internal and cannot be viewed by the user. Often, it is accessible to the user but written in a language best understood by a trained programmer (e.g., Lisp). However, to be usable by nonspecialists, the program representation needs to be written in a language that is accessible to nonprogrammers. The program representation language needs to be

- free of technical terminology,
- independent of the software architecture, and
- expressed in terms of the user's task.

For the program representation to be useful, the user must be able to do more than just see it and read it. The user must also be able to:

- *view it while it is being constructed,* to check whether the software is making correct inferences;
- *save and retrieve it* for later use;
- *execute it* on demand; and
- *edit it* for performing similar tasks.

FIGURE **6.1**

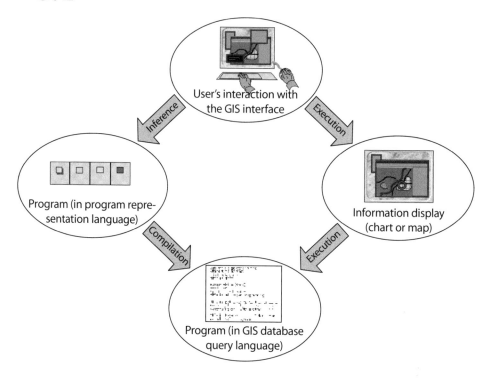

How a user's interactions with the GIS interface are processed.

For a GIS, having a program representation that can be understood by non-specialist users means that a user's interactions with the interface of the GIS are processed in two different ways. First, the instructions are executed and the results shown in an information display, either in a chart or on a map. Second, a program is inferred from the user's actions and encoded in the program representation language. If the user wishes to run the program later on, it needs to be compiled into the GIS's database query language for execution. Figure 6.1 shows the two different ways that the user's interactions with the interface are processed.

If the program has been inferred from the user's actions and the program is run later, the resulting information display should be identical to the one that the user constructed by hand. Of course, if the user has edited the program, then the information display would differ accordingly.

6.6 A Programming-by-Demonstration Approach for GIS: C-SPRL

We are using a PBD approach to making GIS accessible to the nonspecialist user. The specific user population we are designing for can be characterized as people who

- wish to focus on their own domain tasks;

- use a computer as a vehicle to accomplish those tasks;

- have little or no programming knowledge; and

- have no expertise in geography, cartography, database systems, or GIS.

Examples of this kind of user include the concerned mother who wants to ask, "Show me the bars and liquor stores within a mile of my child's school" or the community activist who wants to say, "Show me data on traffic problems in all of the city's neighborhoods"—and who should not need to understand cartography and database systems to formulate their questions.

Figure 6.2 shows the PBD GIS user interface. There are two main parts to the interface: the GIS component (upper part) and the PBD component (lower part).

The architecture of the GIS for nonspecialist users corresponds to Figure 6.1. The user interacts with a graphical user interface (GUI) designed to support the way the nonspecialist user thinks about his or her tasks (e.g., *map* is used in the common, everyday sense, not the cartographic sense). His or her instructions are carried out, and an information display is created on a chart or a map or both. Simultaneously, a program representation is created and displayed.

The PBD component for GIS allows the user to interact in two modes: Record and Edit. In Record mode, the user interacts with the GIS GUI, and the system infers the program representation based on the user's actions. Record mode is the default mode. Edit mode allows the user to edit the program representation directly so that he or she can correct or modify a query or create a new query. The user can switch to Edit mode by choosing Edit from the Mode menu from the GIS GUI. In Edit mode a menubar is displayed in the PBD window. (See Figure 6.8 later for the options available in Edit mode.)

The program representation language uses a comic-strip metaphor. A program consists of a series of panels, just the way a comic strip does. A

FIGURE **6.2**

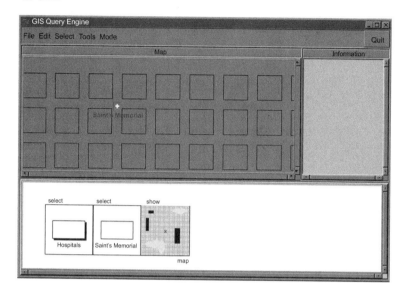

The PBD GIS interface in Record mode. The query depicted is "Show me the location of Saints Memorial Hospital."

panel to the left of another is a *before panel;* one to the right is an *after panel.* An operation on the contents of the before panel results in the contents of the after panel. Thus, a series of panels represents a sequence of transformations, in the temporal order in which they occur. We call the language the Comic-Strip Program Representation Language (C-SPRL, pronounced, "c-spiral"). C-SPRL is an extension of the Pursuit program representation language devised by Modugno (1995). C-SPRL uses the notion of categories of data, in which *category* is used in the normal everyday sense of the word. A category may be composed of one or more subcategories and/or of a number of individual category members. For example, the school system in many U.S. school districts consists of three categories of schools—namely, elementary schools (kindergarten to fifth grade), middle schools (sixth to eighth grade), and high schools (ninth to twelfth grade). In this case the overall category would be "Schools." The category Schools would contain three subcategories: High Schools, Middle Schools, and Elementary Schools. Each of these three subcategories would contain a list of the individual schools in that subcategory. Categories form the basis for queries. Categories, subcategories, and individual members of categories

6.3

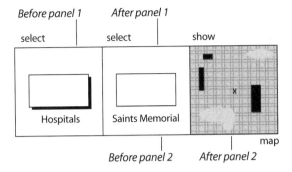

Programs consist of before and after panels. This program depicts the query "Show me the location of Saints Memorial Hospital."

are represented by rectangles. A shadow under a rectangle indicates a category or subcategory. A rectangle without a shadow represents an individual member of a category. Data displays are represented by chart panels (called "info") and by map panels (called "map"). (Figure 6.7 later shows the symbols for both the chart and map panels.) The data display panels are abstractions, not realistic representations of actual screen objects as in, for example, Mondrian (Lieberman 1993).

Figure 6.3 shows a very simple C-SPRL program representation with three panels. The query represented is "Show me the location of Saints Memorial Hospital." When a user interacts with the GUI of the GIS, the software infers a program and builds a representation of it, panel by panel, in a program display window. To construct the simple example of Figure 6.3, the user interacts with the GUI and begins by selecting the category Hospitals from the Select menu on the menubar (Figure 6.4 [a]).

Once this action has been completed, the first panel appears in the PBD program area (Figure 6.4[b]). Notice that the category Hospitals is represented by a shadowed rectangle.

A pop-up window with a list of choices appears in the GIS GUI (Figure 6.5). Since there are no subcategories in this category, a list of individual hospitals and a list of the actions or information that can be requested about the available hospitals are displayed.

The user clicks on Saints Memorial. At this point the user can also indicate that he or she would like to see the location displayed on a map by clicking on the map button on the pop-up window. When the user has

FIGURE **6.4**

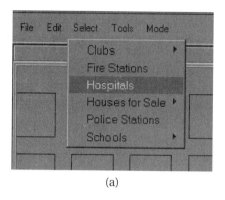
(a)

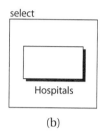
(b)

(a) The categories from the Select menu on the GIS GUI and (b) the panel created in the PBD area as a result of choosing Hospitals (a shadowed rectangle) from the Select menu.

FIGURE **6.5**

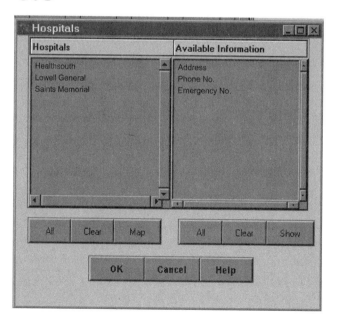

When the user selects Hospitals from the Select menu, a pop-up window with the list of hospitals and actions and/or information that can be requested about the available hospitals appears on the screen.

finished choosing items from the Hospitals pop-up window, he or she clicks on the OK button. The second and third panel of the program representation now appear on the PBD screen. The location of Saints Memorial Hospital also appears on the map in the GIS GUI. Figure 6.2 shows both the GIS and PBD GUI for the results of this query. Notice also in the program representation that Saints Memorial Hospital is represented by a rectangle without a shadow. The third panel is an example of a map panel.

More complex user actions would result in multiple panels being added to the program representation. In building a query, the user uses a top-down approach. At each step in the query-building process, the user refines and narrows the search until reaching the level of granularity that he or she is looking for.

The program representation does a variety of things for the user. First, it provides a visualization of the software's inferences about the user's actions, so the user can correct the software's understanding, if necessary. Each panel depicts a user action, so the user has a step-by-step account of how the query was created. This is also helpful in identifying user errors. Second, the gradual construction of the program representation helps the user to learn C-SPRL by watching what happens as he or she interacts with the GIS's GUI. The representation provides the user with continuous feedback, so if the program representation depicts an "incorrect" action, the user can immediately backtrack and rectify the situation. Third, the program representation is editable. The user can edit the program to modify it or to create a similar, but different, program. The user saves time by being able to run a previously constructed query without having to repeat all the steps. The user can even create an entirely new program from scratch. Fourth, the user can save and retrieve programs for later use. Once again this saves the user time by not having to repeat work/steps already done. Users can easily share results of queries with others. Finally, a program can be executed on demand. Figure 6.6 summarizes the various uses that a user can make of a program representation.

The set of symbols used in C-SPRL program representations is not large in number (Figure 6.7). As a result, users do not have to spend much time familiarizing themselves with the terminology. All program symbols have self-identifying labels that aid user comprehension. C-SPRL also has a set of commands: select, show, and draw. The select command indicates the selection of a category, subcategory, category member(s), or one or more items from the list of available information about a category or category member. The show command indicates the display of information on a map or in text format. The draw command indicates that a user has narrowed the search to the area highlighted on the map. These commands appear above the panels in the program representation.

6.6

- Check whether the software is making correct inferences
- Learn C-SPRL by watching the correspondence between GUI interactions and program constructs
- Save and retrieve a program
- Edit a program to modify it or to create a similar program
- Write a program from scratch

Summary of uses of a C-SPRL program representation.

6.7

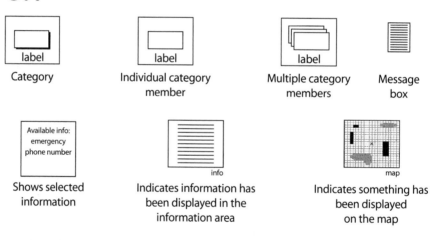

C-SPRL panel icons.

C-SPRL program representations can be edited directly with a special-purpose editor. Figure 6.8 shows the menu options available in the PBD program editor. Panels and program constructs may be added, edited, and deleted. If a before panel is edited or deleted, then all of its after panels are deleted, when their preconditions are no longer met.

C-SPRL includes a branching construct, called *do-one*, and an and-ing construct called *do-all*. Figure 6.9 shows a program that uses the *do-all*. The

FIGURE **6.8**

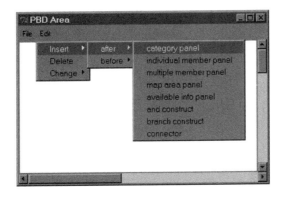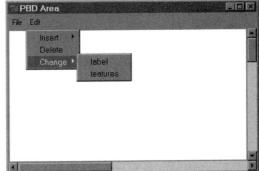

Menu options from the C-SPRL editor.

FIGURE **6.9**

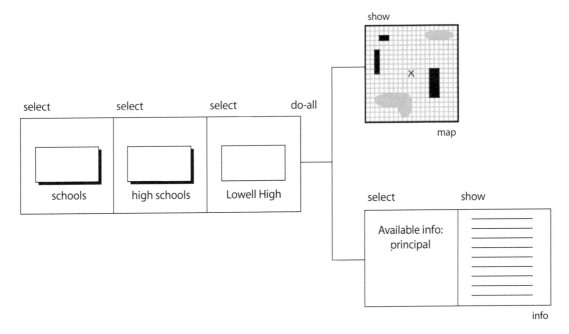

A C-SPRL program with a do-all construct.

schools category is selected, the selection is refined to include just the high schools, and then it is further refined to an individual school, Lowell High School. The panel for Lowell High is the before panel for two after panels, because two simultaneous operations are performed with the Lowell High data: (1) the school's location is shown on a map, and (2) information about the school's principal is displayed in a chart.

User tests of the C-SPRL program representation language indicate that non–GIS specialists are able to read C-SPRL programs (program interpretation), edit programs to create new programs (program modification), and write programs from scratch (program creation). We also gave C-SPRL programs to study participants and asked them to use the GUI to perform the steps that would cause the software to infer the programs (program navigation). The fact that they were able to navigate the GUI successfully indicates that the participants understood the encoding of actions into the C-SPRL representation.

Figure 6.10 gives samples of the different types of queries used in the studies. Two different studies were performed. As a result of the first study, some of the C-SPRL panel icons were modified; hence some of the panel icon symbols in the program navigation may differ slightly from those in Figure 6.7.

The tasks chosen for the user studies were based on a taxonomy of the types of queries that our end users are likely to perform on a GIS. The taxonomy was derived from a requirements definition for a GIS intended for use by one of our target user populations (Traynor 1998). The taxonomy contained six classes of queries:

1. Show me one or more **objects.**

2. Show me one or more **objects** with/without one or more **features.**

3. Show me one or more **objects** with/without one or more **attributes.**

4. Show me one or more **objects** with/without one or more **features** and with/without one or more **attributes.**

5. Show me one or more **objects** within "this" **distance** of one or more **objects.**

6. Show me one or more **attributes** for one or more **objects.**

More details of these studies can be found in Traynor and Williams (1995, 1997).

FIGURE **6.10**

Program Interpretation

Show me the location of all houses for sale with a fireplace.
Show me the practice hours for Pawtucket Soccer Club.
Show me all the liquor stores within a mile of Lowell High and 1.5 miles of my house.

Program Modification

Original Task

Show me all swimming pools.
Show me all parks within a half-mile of Pawtucket Soccer Club and the number of teams in the club.

Modified Task

Show me all parks.
Show me all the swimming pools within a mile of the Wang Middle School and the number of teachers in the school.

Program Creation

Show me the Acre Police Station and the number of policemen assigned to it.
Show me all the fire stations within a mile of Murphy's restaurant and the number of fire engines.

Program Navigation

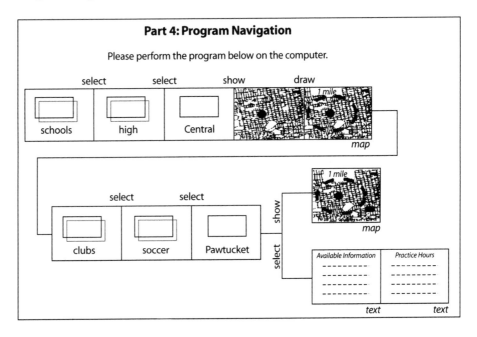

Sample of queries used in the user studies.

6.7 Conclusion

C-SPRL is one possible representation language for a GIS for nonspecialist users. Many others are possible. For example, the block-stacking metaphor of Richards and Egenhofer's (1995) GIS interface would lend itself to a program representation that contains images of stacked blocks. Whatever the representation, it appears possible to create new ways of interacting with GIS software—ways that are not steeped in the traditions of geographers and cartographers. The experts already have GIS software that meets their needs. Attempting to tailor their highly technical software for nonspecialists, either by modifying the interface slightly or by providing a subset of the functionality, has not worked. What is needed is a fresh start, with nonspecialist users viewed as a first-class population of GIS users, rather than an add-on population. Only then will GIS come into its own as a "killer application."

Acknowledgments

We would like to thank the following people for their insightful comments and help in preparing this chapter: the HCI Research Group at the University of Massachusetts Lowell, in particular Dr. J. Nicholas Buehler and Guillermo Zeballos; and Gordon Paynter of the University of Waikato, Hamilton, New Zealand.

References

Ahlberg, C., and B. Shneiderman. 1994. Visual information seeking: Tight coupling of dynamic query filters with starfield displays. In *Proceedings of Human Factors in Computing Systems Conference (CHI '94)*. New York: ACM Press.

Aufaure-Portier, M.-A. 1995. Definition of a visual language for GIS. In *Cognitive Aspects of Human-Computer Interaction for Geographic Information Systems*, ed. T. Nyerges, D. Mark, R. Laurini, and M. J. Egenhofer. Dordrecht, The Netherlands: Kluwer Academic.

Cypher, A. 1993. *Watch What I Do: Programming by Demonstration*. Cambridge, Mass.: MIT Press.

Egenhofer, M. J. 1995. User interfaces. In *Cognitive Aspects of Human-Computer Interaction for Geographic Information Systems,* ed. T. Nyerges, D. Mark, R. Laurini, and M. J. Egenhofer. Dordrecht, The Netherlands: Kluwer Academic.

Garson, G. D., and R. S. Biggs. 1992. *Analytic Mapping and Geographic Databases.* Sage University Paper series on Quantitative Applications in the Social Sciences, series no. 07–087. Newbury Park, Calif.: Sage.

Kuhn, S., C. Richardson, and M. G. Williams. 1994. Meeting of the minds: The challenges of interdisciplinary and inter-occupational communication. In *Proceedings of the Participatory Design Conference (PDC'94),* ed. R. Trigg, S. I. Anderson, and E. A. Dykstra-Erickson. Palo Alto, Calif.: CPSR.

Lieberman, H. 1993. A teachable graphical editor. In *Watch What I Do: Programming by Demonstration.* Cambridge, Mass.: MIT Press.

Modugno, F. 1995. Extending end-user programming in a visual shell with programming by demonstration and graphical languages techniques. Ph.D. diss., Carnegie Mellon University, Pittsburgh, Pa.

Richards, J. R., and M. J. Egenhofer. 1995. A Comparison of two direct-manipulation gis user interfaces for map overlay. In *Geographical Systems* 2, no. 4: 267–290.

Standing, C., and G. G. Roy. 1997. Developing macro queries in geographical information systems. In *Proceedings of the Fourth Conference of the International Society for Decision Support Systems (ISDSS'97).* Lausanne, Switzerland: International Society for Decision Support.

Traynor, C. 1998. Programming by demonstration for geographic information systems. Sc.D. diss., University of Massachusetts, Lowell.

Traynor, C., and M. G. Williams. 1995. Why are geographic information systems hard to use? In *Conference Companion of Human Factors in Computing Systems Conference (CHI'95).* Boston: Addison-Wesley.

———. 1997. A study of end-user programming for geographic information systems. In *Proceedings of Empirical Studies of Programmers: Seventh Workshop.* New York: ACM Press.

CHAPTER 7

Bringing Programming by Demonstration to CAD Users

PATRICK GIRARD

Laboratoire d'Informatique Scientifique et Industrielle
École Nationale Supérieure de Mécanique et d'Aérotechnique

Abstract

This chapter presents a suite of systems we developed that constitute a solution for bringing programming to end users in the field of computer-aided design (CAD), by using programming by demonstration (PBD). This suite includes the LIKE system, which laid the foundations of our method, and the EBP system (Example-Based Programming in Parametrics), which is intended to enable CAD system users to generate every program that describes the geometric shapes of a collection of parts through the interactive graphic design of one example of this collection. From a PBD point of view, they prove that, at least in some application areas where system users have particular skills, complete PBD environments may be developed. From a CAD systems point of view, this approach proves that parametric CAD systems, which are already very successful for sequential (or simple repetitive, pattern-based) parametric design, may be extended to support the parametric design of every conditional or repetitive shape aspect. From a user interface viewpoint, it also proves that very powerful macro-with-example recorders may be developed.

7.1 Introduction

Over the last few years, lots of advances have been achieved to reduce the programming skills and the abstraction level that are required for computer use and programming. Visual programming (Glinert 1990) permits users to select graphically both the functions and the variables that constitute programs. Programming by demonstration, or PBD (Cypher 1993), allows direct interaction with example values that represent the program variables instead of their abstract names, or iconic presentations. Many experimental systems have proved both the usability and the interest of the latter approach. Nevertheless, no PBD system, to our knowledge, has reached the same expressive power as conventional programming in its application area.

The goal of this chapter is to present a suite of systems we developed that constitute a solution for bringing programming to end users in the field of computer-aided design (CAD), by using PBD. This suite includes the LIKE system, which laid the foundations of our method, and the EBP system (Example-Based Programming in Parametrics), which is intended to enable CAD system users to generate every program that describes the geometric shapes of a collection of parts through the interactive graphic design of one example of this collection ("variant programming") (Roller 1990).

7.2 PBD and CAD

In her book *A Small Matter of Programming: Perspectives on End-user Computing,* Nardi (1993) has identified CAD as a natural candidate for end-user programming, because these systems "allow end users to create useful applications with no more than a few hours of instruction." We will see in this section how this can be extended to complete PBD features. First, we describe the application field of PBD in CAD, called *parametrics programming*. Then, we detail two approaches, *variational* and *parametric*, and relate them to PBD terminology. Last, we present the characteristics of the particular PBD approach.

7.2.1 CAD: A Suitable Area for PBD

PBD opens the door to new generations of programming environments. In the fields where some visual appearance may be assigned to variable values, direct manipulation of these values allows implicit program design. SmallStar (Halbert 1984) for iconic desktop programming, Peridot (Myers 1993), Garnet (Myers et al. 1990), Macros by Example (Olsen and Dance 1988) for UIMS programming, KidSim (Cypher and Smith 1995) for simulation, WYSIWYC Spreadsheet (Wilde 1993), Geometer's Sketchpad (Jackiw and Finzer 1993), and ProDeGE+ (Sassin 1994) in drawing systems have proven in different fields the validity of this approach. Despite this success, most systems seem to be at the prototype stage. In the CAD area, PBD, under the name of "parametrics," has actually been shown to be viable in the commercial market.

Designing new products often entails assembling preexisting components intended to be used in different products. These components, named "standard parts," are gathered into families described by a part family model (see Figure 7.1). According to Shah and Mäntylä (1995), "a part family model represents a collection of parts exhibiting some variation in dimensions, tolerances, and overall shape that nevertheless are considered similar from the viewpoint of a certain application." The context of some part family corresponds to some product standard (e.g., the family of ISO 1014 hexagonal screws), to some supplier's parts catalog, or some family of

FIGURE **7.1**

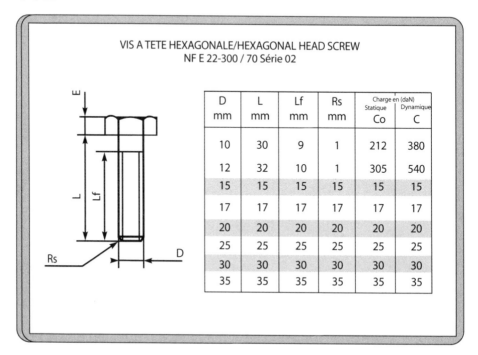

VIS A TETE HEXAGONALE/HEXAGONAL HEAD SCREW
NF E 22-300 / 70 Série 02

D mm	L mm	Lf mm	Rs mm	Charge en (daN) Statique Co	Dynamique C
10	30	9	1	212	380
12	32	10	1	305	540
15	15	15	15	15	15
17	17	17	17	17	17
20	20	20	20	20	20
25	25	25	25	25	25
30	30	30	30	30	30
35	35	35	35	35	35

Example of a part family.

company-specific components, which are described by end users for internal use. Because of the rather large size of these collections, some particular part family is often used to describe the whole collection of corresponding shapes.

In the first generation of CAD systems, part family models were described as parametric programs. In these conventional CAD systems, such programs were textually described, often in Fortran or in the C language. When triggered, they create geometric entities by means of an Application Programming Interface (API). A lot of these systems have been developed at end-user sites where draftsmen were trained on CAD modeling. That end-users went to such trouble to create these programs shows the strong need for better end-user programming facilities in CAD.

The second reason that the PBD approach may be appropriate in the CAD is the kind of dialogue language CAD systems support. CAD models, or

FIGURE **7.2**

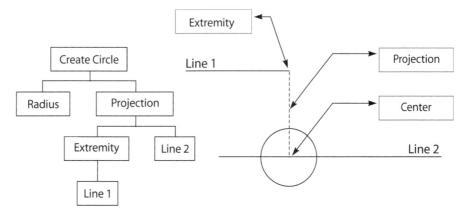

Example of a structured task in CAD.

technical drawings, are very different from pictures or artistic drawings: they must conform to stringent application-dependent rules (for example, in mechanical design, architecture, etc.). When designing such drawings, draftsmen perfectly know the relationships that must exist between the entities of their model, and they want to have the capability of expressing these constraints in their design process. Since the early beginning of CAD, every CAD system provides commands that enable the expression of such constraints. Geometric constraints are specified by means of geometric operators (e.g., *middle_of, starting_point, projection_of . . . onto . . .*). Numerical constraints are specified by *display calculators* that provide both algebraic operators (e.g., +, -, *, /) and geometric functions. These functions (e.g., *distance_of, angle_between, radiu s _ of*) refer to model entities as parameters and return numerical values that, in turn, may be involved in numerical expressions. Therefore, CAD system interfaces enable users to explicitly specify every constraint that should hold between objects, and CAD users are accustomed to specifying such constraints. Just recording these constraints builds the basis of sequential imperative program recording.

Figure 7.2 shows a typical CAD task: assume we want to create a circle whose center is geometrically constructed as a projection of a line extremity on another line (the two lines are assumed to be already drawn). The goal/ subgoal hierarchy, as shown on the left part of the figure, is often broken in CAD systems to allow users to make appropriate constructs. For example, this typical task may be achieved by the following sequence of CAD system primitives (italicized words denote CAD primitives):

- *Create a point* at the end of line 1 (creating point 1).

- *Create a vertical line* through this point (creating line 3).

- *Create a point* at the intersection of this line and line 2 (creating point 2).

- *Create a circle* whose center is point 2 and radius is 10.

This explicit constraint-based definition of geometrical entities is very natural in CAD systems. Rather than direct manipulation, it involves command-operand dialogue style.

7.2.2 Variational and Parametric Solutions

While every modern CAD system supports this kind of constraint-based definition of entities, constraint recording appeared much more recently. Beside the MEDUSA system (Newell, Parden, and Parden 1983), which provided for constraint-recording capabilities in 1983, the generalization of this feature appeared in the late 1980s. At this time, a new generation of systems appeared on the market; they were able to record these constraints, to change the numerical values involved in these constraints, and to compute the new model resulting from these values. These systems, often called *dimension-driven* systems (Roller 1990), have a twofold data structure and a twofold behavior. On the one hand, users may build (or change or compute) the displayed model. On the other hand, users may ask for visualization of the constraints and the numeric values that are involved in the example design. This information, which stands for the program in the PBD terminology, is displayed in some conventional symbolic way—for instance, through dimensioning. Then, users select the values they want to change and enter new values, and the system automatically computes the new model that corresponds to the same constructive process, or to the new solution of the same set of constraints.

In fact, dimension-driven systems proceed from two different approaches: declarative and imperative (Pierra, Potier, and Girard 1994). *Variational systems* hide the declarative program. Users build the example and specify the constraints, either explicitly or implicitly. These constraints are recorded as a set of equations, and some solver derives the solution. Variational geometry is part of geometric problem solving. The user's input may not completely determine the solution. Once constraints are stated, with some approximate geometric description, the solver tries to compute a solution. This approach corresponds to the popular sketchers that are available on most recent CAD systems: users draw some freehand sketch of a 2D model, and the solver computes the exact model after constraints are stated. The user interface is very friendly. Many methods have been used to solve these constraints. The most efficient methods are based on graph reduction (Bouma et al. 1995; Owen 1991).

Despite considerable progress, this approach suffers from three intrinsic weaknesses. First, in general, the set of equations may have an exponential number of solutions, and only system-specific heuristics have been defined so far to guess the "user intent." Very simple examples have been published (Bouma et al. 1995) in which the computed solutions were obviously not those intended by the user. Second, because of the heuristic nature of the solver, different systems may provide different solutions for the same model. Finally, pure variational systems are unable to capture the purely procedural constructs, such as Boolean regularized operations or sweeping. Therefore, every so-called "variational system" is in fact a hybrid system that is variational in 2D and mainly procedural in 3D.

Procedural systems, often called *parametrics,* address a very different problem: "given a class of shapes whose design process is well known and may be supported by the interface of some CAD systems, we want every instance, characterized by its parameter values, to be generated automatically in a deterministic way." *Parametric systems* hide an imperative program. This program is often captured using the example design process: the CAD system "spies" on draughtsmen while they are designing their example. As long as the example model grows, the constructive logic of draughtsmen is captured. Afterward, the CAD system is able to replay the constructive logic, possibly with new input values. The internal representation of programs may be textual, but it is more generally based on data structures (Pierra et al. 1994; Solano and Brunet 1994) such as directed acyclic graphs (Cugini, Folini, and Vicini 1988). The Pro-Engineer system (Parametric Technology Inc.) is the most popular example of this approach.

In the CAD area, the dimension-driven approach is so attractive that presently every competitive CAD system must provide such capabilities. This widespread distribution proves the practical interest of the approach. It also proves that draughtsmen, end users, are able to generate parametrized shapes (i.e., real visual programs) without programming knowledge—that is not to say without any modification of their working process. Effectively, drawing shapes is slightly different from drawing *families* of shapes. Nevertheless, this activity does not stand at the abstract level of a conventional programming activity. Dimension-driven systems, or *parametrics* for short, largely facilitate the design of part family models. For collections or single shapes, just designing one shape provides for generating every family's shape.

7.2.3   Requirements for PBD in CAD

Most choices that have been made for our systems are governed by the domain area (CAD), especially users' habits and needs (particularly their explicit way for describing relations between objects), and by the goals of the PLUS (Parts Library Usage and Supply) project, in which our work took place.

The portability of parts libraries between different CAD systems is a major economic concern for CAD system users, component manufacturers, and CAD systems vendors. This portability would drastically increase the number of available part families on the different CAD systems and therefore would increase the quality and the productivity of the design process for assembly modeling. To allow such a portability, a whole set of concerns, known as the CAD-LIB approach, has been developed (Pierra and Aït Ameur 1994). They constitute the agreed basis of European and International standardization efforts (CEN/TC310-pr ENV 40004 and ISO/TC184/ SC4-ISO 13584 P-LIB).

Besides an object-oriented data model for the exchange of parts library data, the PLUS project had to develop an approach for the exchange of part family geometric models. When the project started (in 1993), the parametric technology did not appear mature enough to be able to commit to the development of a standard exchange format for parametric data models. Therefore, the selected approach has been rather conservative. It consisted in developing a standard API (now available as ISO DIS 13584–31) associated with a Fortran binding. Every CAD system that supports some implementation of this standard API would be able to execute Fortran programs referring to this API. However, this approach was in fact less conservative than it might appear at first glance: the project also included the development of a PBD system that was intended to be able to generate these variant programs through pure graphical interactions.

The design of our EBP system is governed by the following requirements. First, the generation process should be deterministic and fully controlled by the designer: one and only one shape should be generated for every allowed value of the input parameters, and it should be precisely the shape that corresponds to that part. Second, every kind of shape family that might be described using some conventional means of programming should be able to be designed using this system. Finally, the system should be able to generate an external representation of its internal data structures in the format of a Fortran program conforming to the standard API.

Note that if the first requirement is met—namely, to follow a procedural approach without any implicit inference or heuristic mechanism—neither of the two last requirements were fulfilled by either the existing parametric systems or the existing prototypes of PBD systems. While several systems support predefined repetitive pattern structures, none of them, as far as we know, supports a general-purpose program/subprogram structure with graphical parameter-passing mechanisms and recurrence-based iterations where each loop is defined through explicit recurrence relationships within the previous branch.

7.3   Toward a Complete Solution

In this section, we describe the solutions we adopted to build actual PBD systems in the CAD area. First, we briefly describe the system from a standard CAD point of view. Then we focus on the naming problem. Last, we show how we can make the constructed programs sufficiently expressive. The next section focuses on PBD control structure definition.

7.3.1   Classical 2D CAD Systems

As mentioned in the introduction, we developed two CAD PBD systems, named LIKE and EBP. LIKE was built in late 1980s, to study the possibilities of including PBD in CAD. Written on top of the GKS system, it was replaced in 1992 by EBP, which is more complete. In the following, we only describe EBP, because its present features include the results of the LIKE study.

The EBP system (Potier 1995) is a 2D CAD system. It manipulates simple geometric entities (points, unbounded lines, trimmed lines, circles, curves, etc.) and structured entities (composite curves, planar surfaces, and structured sets). Most of the common technical drawing rule constraints are supported. EBP provides a powerful display calculator that enables graphical input of both numerical and graphical expressions. Last, EBP allows model definitions through the use of menus and graphical interactions. The first version of EBP used the X-MOTIF interface and ran on Sun-Solaris (Sun Inc.) and DEC-Alpha (Digital) platforms. A new commercial version has

FIGURE **7.3**

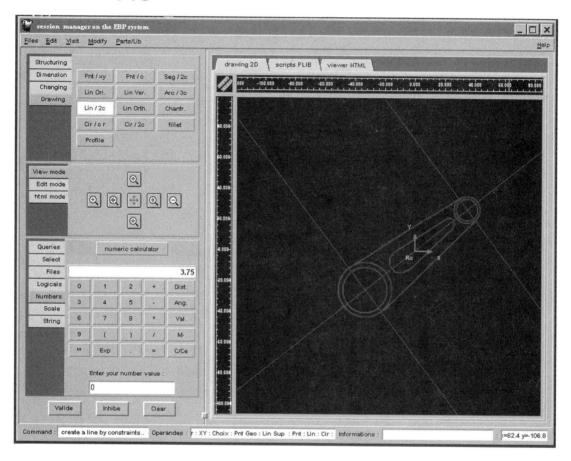

Snapshot from the EBP system.

been developed under TCL/TK, and a complete distribution that runs on PC Windows platforms is available at the URL http://www.lisi.ensma.fr.

Figure 7. 3 shows a snapshot from the "classic" CAD system EBP. On the right, we can see the drawing area, which displays the CAD model. The left part of the window is divided into three command areas. On the top, classic 2D commands are displayed, while in the middle, viewing commands are given. The third area is devoted to low-level entries, such as string or numerical entries. On this snapshot we can see a classical feature of a CAD system: the display calculator, which allows entry of expressions including graphical functions (e.g., *distance between two entities*). EBP includes another calculator, the logical calculator (bottom left). This feature, which shares some commonalities with a mechanism presented in Smith's (1977) Pygmalion system, enables CAD users, trained in using the numerical display calculator, to specify graphically the control predicate of their conditional or repetitive shapes. For instance, a fillet may be defined as dependent on the constraint

val (line_1) > 2 x distance (point_1, point_2),

where *val(line_1)* means the length of line_1, and where *line_1, point_1* and *point_2* are objects that can be graphically selected on the example.

7.3.2 Specificity of Naming in CAD

The major difference between simple scripts that record user interactions and real programs concerns the status of the values involved in interactions. For example, the integer value 3, which is an input in interactive mode, may have, in programs, three different statuses: (1) a constant, (2) a parameter (i.e., a value that must be provided again every time the program is triggered), or (3) an "internal" variable (i.e., a variable whose value results from a previous program statement). Many reasearchers in PBD have addressed this problem, and the first of them, SmallStar (Halbert 1984, 1993), proposed an *a posteriori* explicit differentiation of different types of variables. The specificity of CAD allows us to choose a different solution, but it also highlights the problem of dynamic references to variables. We illustrate our arguments with the LIKE system, in which we first implemented our solutions. EBP has a similar object management.

The Problem of Naming

It is clear that, when it receives the integer value 3, the system cannot decide what the status of this value should be for the program implicitly being constructed. The real challenge for PBD systems is to define conventional dialogue protocols that appear natural enough to users to enable a nearly implicit specification of the status of every object.

CAD systems belong to the general class of interactive applications we can classify as "editors." Their main goal is to create new objects from user inputs. The example of standard parts is more precise: the goal of programs to be constructed is to draw graphical entities (in fact, to create CAD model objects) from numerical parameters. This fact implies, in terms of programming, that a program recorded during the use of such a system would essentially create new objects at any step. Its context (the set of objects it manipulates) would grow after each instruction. To respect this particularity, the LIKE system applies different rules for managing the three classes of objects.

Regardless of their data type (strings, real numbers, or graphical entities), parameters of a program must be explicitly defined by the user, who is supposed to give a name, a question prompt, and a specific example value to each parameter. This constitutes a "parameter context." Furthermore, parameters may be selected for using menus. The way parameters can be defined is not very important: some informal experiments that we conducted show that our class of users (CAD experts) were not afraid to explicitly define the parameters they used. Giving two examples differing by values of parameters (as in Tinker; Lieberman 1993), to let the system "infer" that these values were varying, was not considered to be efficient. They preferred doing it themselves.

Because we chose this explicit solution for parameters, it appeared natural to implicitly consider simple objects, such as numbers or strings, constants when the user enters them. On the other hand, graphical objects, which may be visually selected on the display, are implicitly considered to be internal variables.

During the recording phase, the LIKE system performs two tasks. First, it manages the dynamic context: objects are automatically introduced in the context as soon as they are created by the CAD system. Therefore, the CAD system notifies the PBD manager for each created object. It also provides the database reference of this object. Second, it ensures value/reference substitution. As soon as the user selects them, the PBD manager must identify the objects by comparing them to the values contained in its context. The corresponding variable references are stored in the program. This filtering process also permits the PBD manager to forbid any access to objects that are not considered as visible (i.e., that are neither in the dynamic context nor in the parameter context). Obviously, this automatic naming mechanism is based on numbering (later we will see the consequences of this point).

During the execution phase, symmetrical actions are performed: dynamic context management is performed in the same way, allowing the inverse reference/value substitution needed by the running process in the CAD system. Each time an object is created, its reference is stored in the right variable. Then its value is sent to the CAD system, for each program reference, to the corresponding variable.

In recording mode, each input (command or value) from the user goes through the PBD manager (arrows 1 and 2 in Figure 7.4). The values that correspond to references to model entities are captured in the identification layer (selecting layer) of the user interface, whereas locator positions are

FIGURE **7.4**

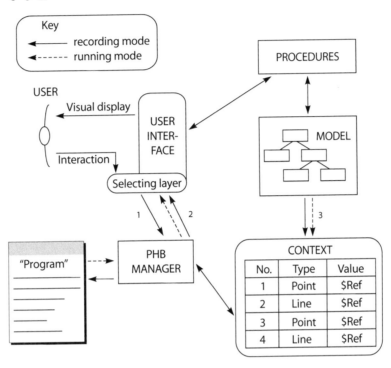

Architecture of the LIKE system.

replaced by entity identifiers. Commands are recorded in the program, together with operators of the display calculator that are considered commands. Each entity identifier is replaced by the corresponding variable, by looking in the dynamic context. The dynamic context manager is notified for every entity creation (arrow 3), and new internal variables are created and assigned to entity identifiers.

The context is dynamically extended during the whole process of the example design. It enables, during the program construction, the substitution of values (system identifiers) by names (numbers) in the recorded program. It permits, while the program is running, the substitution of names (number) by values (system identifier) that are to be sent to the system. The consistency of these rules is obviously based on the assumption that every running of the program will generate the same types of objects in the same order as in the example. In particular, when debugging programs, each change that results in a different number of *object creations* shifts the "naming" of further objects. Consequently, each reference to these shifted variables has to be modified. Moreover, debugging the suppression of actions that generate objects requires the checking and the possible invalidation of further actions that use these particular objects. All this management must be performed by the PBD manager.

Another consequence is more important. The validity of example-based programming is based on one prerequisite: it is assumed that execution will *repeat* the example. Values may change, but actions and control flow have to be the same. This condition, quite natural for purely sequential programs, no longer has meaning in the structured programming context. When conditionals are used, the two branches cannot be assumed to create the same number of objects. For loop structures, the number of iterations may vary in each execution. Hence, the number of variables created may vary. We will see in the following section how this problem may be solved.

Ambiguity Removal and System Determinism

Another characteristic of CAD systems has consequences on inferring user intent. It relates to the ambiguity of geometric constructs. This ambiguity is not specific to variational systems; it is, in fact, intrinsic to geometry, in which every constraint that involves a circle or a distance corresponds, in general, to two different solutions.

For example, building a line that starts on a given point and ends tangential to a circle leads to two possible solutions, as pointed out in Figure 7.5(a). This problem is perfectly solved in interactive geometric design. Most CAD systems use the mouse-click position of each input object to discriminate the possible constructs. They assume that the designer approximately knows the expected solution. For example, in the case of Figure 7.5(b), the position of the mouse click results in the choice of the upper line solution.

If this user-friendly dialogue convention is to be maintained during the design of the example/program in the user interface, it cannot be stored in the parametric program. Different values of the parameters might correspond to different solutions. This problem of constraint-based geometric constructs is also well known in variant programming (Roller 1990), in which programming languages were used for defining part family models.

In such parametrics programs, context-free ambiguity removers are defined. In the target API, ambiguity removal is defined by topological information: geometry entity orientation and in/out for circles. For example, Figure 7.5(c) shows the unique solution of the function *Line_by_Point_and_Circle* from Figure 7.5(b), which is defined by the coherent orientation of graphic entities. EBP ensures the translation from the

FIGURE **7.5**

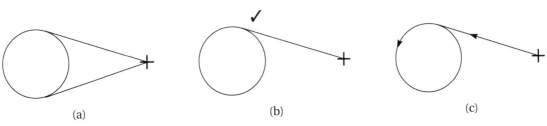

An example of the ambiguity of geometric constructs: (a) the two possible solutions, (b) interactive solving with a click, and (c) a good solution for programs.

context-sensitive information captured at the user interface level (the position of the mouse click) into context-free information recorded in the program.

In EBP, every entity is oriented according to the way it was constructed. Lines are oriented from their origin (first point) to their extremity (last point), circles are oriented according to the given points (when defined by three points) or counterclockwise (when created by center and radius), and so on. During program recording, the system translates the proximity disambiguity mechanism into the orientation mechanism as follows:

- With the proximity mechanism, the system calculates the right construction.

- Then, the system checks for the orientation of the circle.

- If this orientation is consistent with the solution (as in Figure 7.5[c]), the system records the drawing without modification.

- If not, the system records the following sequence: change the orientation of the circle, draw the line, and change the orientation of the circle again.

This mechanism, which remains unknown to users, is completely deterministic.

7.3.3 Expressiveness

In Cypher, Kosbie, and Maulsby (1993), PBD systems are characterized by determining what control structures they support: loops, conditionals, and so on. We considered the problem from the opposite point of view: what mechanisms give programs the most expressiveness?

Following the structured programming paradigm, we decided to include in our systems every classic control structure: (implicit) sequences, iterations, and recursive subroutines. We support both internal construction of these structures by the program mechanisms (essentially the context manager, Girard and Pierra 1990, 1995) and interactive definition by the user.

Support of General Control Structures

Applying the encapsulation principle to the context of subroutines is straightforward: each subroutine has its own dynamic context (internal variables) and parameter context. Subroutines are stored together with the example values for their parameters. This allows running them during program construction, as soon as the user selects parameters, for example, through a menu.

In our current implementation, subroutines have unique output parameters that consist of the set of every graphical entity created by each subroutine. These sets are inserted as unique variables within the dynamic context of the calling program. The content of this variable is a pointer to the dynamic context of the embedded program. When the embedding program is run, the expressions that define the current parameters are again evaluated, and the PBD manager performs parameter matching before triggering the embedded program.

The language is considered as block structured, so each block may access its embedding context. Each control structure is considered as a block and is associated with its own context. Yet, this context is considered as a whole, and is inserted as a unique (pointer) variable in the embedding context. Nevertheless, this context is structured. Each branch corresponds to one context, which is defined during the example phase. In running mode, this context is created again before performing the control structure. The context of an *If Then Else End_If* structure consists of two branch contexts. Both exist in the example definition, but only one is used when the program is run (according to the value of the control predicate).

In a loop structure, the loop context consists of a list of contexts, each one associated with each iteration. Specific associations between objects of each context allow the definition of recurrence relationships and, in so doing, general loops (see the next section).

This block structure of the dynamic context allows the use of a stack mechanism during the example phase or running phase. While executing in either mode, the visible context is the stack of the dynamic contexts in use at the present time. So, implicit references may be searched through the whole stack. In terms of user dialogue, this means that the user is able to refer to the objects of the current branch but also to those of all the including branches.

PBD Control Structure Definition

Purely interactive definition of control structures by PBD is a rather different problem than supporting arbitrary control structures. As for other choices, we have always preferred deterministic solutions and explicit mechanisms triggered by users. Among our systems, EBP is the most complete for control structure definition.

Conditionals and iterations require Boolean expression definition, which is made explicitly through both numerical and logical calculators. The two alternate branches of conditionals may be defined either in a consistent way (running again the instance with alternate parameter values) or in some inconsistent way (drawing the two solutions with the same parameter values).

Several iteration features are provided: set iterations over rubber-band rectangle selections and multiple geometric transformations are straightforward in CAD systems and supported by EBP. As for ambiguity removal, context-dependent information (the two corners of the rubber-band rectangle) are translated into context-free information (the set of entity names that were referenced by this shortcut). But many more general features, such as *Repeat n times, While loops*, and *Repeat . . . until loops* are also provided. They allow recurrence-based definitions in a purely interactive way.

Let us illustrate an interactive REPEAT UNTIL definition. Assume we want to design the drawing shown in Figure 7.6. It is made of circles decreasing by a rate of one-half radius at each loop, to reach a given minimum. In classical CAD systems, the construction process for this drawing is very tedious: while every CAD system provides geometrical transformations that may, for example, duplicate the left part of a figure from the right part, none of them owns the specific geometric transformation that allows building this particular configuration of circles. Each step must be done independently from the previous one, repeating actions such as "creating a circle tangential to a line and a circle, with a radius being half of the one of another circle."

Nevertheless, the definition of a general algorithm to build this drawing is possible. The program to be constructed might be defined as an iteration

FIGURE **7.6**

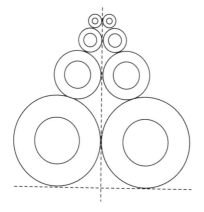

A (rather complex) drawing.

(to obtain one column of circles) and a symmetry (to obtain the other one). We only need to know the value for the maximum and the minimum radius (to stop the construct). Any loop but the first might be defined as follows: first, *build a first circle, tangential to the corresponding circle in the previous loop, tangential to the central vertical axis, and with a radius half that of corresponding circle in the previous loop; then create a second circle whose center is the same as the first circle, and whose radius is half the previous circle.* As shown in Figure 7.6, the first loop has a slightly different specification because the constraints that define the first circle refer to entities of the embedded context (the horizontal line). But, in fact, the only difference is in the nature of the manipulated objects.

If we analyze this problem, three points are to be emphasized: (1) in one loop, objects are defined from objects created during the previous loop and during the current loop; (2) actions performed during the first loop are the same as actions performed during the next ones—the only difference concerns the reference to the objects belonging to the previous loop, which must be found in the embedding context (in the example, the first circle is tangential to both existing lines); and (3) recurrence relationships may be fully defined during the second execution of the first loop actions, just by asking the user for the actual object that shall be used for every referenced object in the first loop. It may be the same object (the vertical line in our example) or any object that has been created during the first loop (in our example, the horizontal line must be replaced by the first circle of the first loop).

These three remarks are the basis of the user interface and the dialogue conventions of the EBP system. The definition process is the following. Two commands are provided: REPEAT and UNTIL. The first one initiates the loop description and allows the user to record the actions of each loop. The second one stops the loop definition and starts the definition of the condition. Because of the PBD process, another step is necessary, which consists of defining the recurrence relationships between one loop and the following loop. After some experience with users, it seemed to enhance usability if we defined the recurrence relation prior to the definition of the condition.

Figure 7.7 illustrates the different steps of this definition. Before the loop, the user has to define the two required parameters (Radius and Minimum, which are displayed as menu options by the system, rectangles in the figure) to create the two lines and then select the REPEAT command (Figure 7.7[a]).

At this point, the first loop can be demonstrated, with full access to the embedding context. So the user selects the Create Circle command (the rounded rectangle "circle"), points out the two lines, and clicks on the menu item that denotes the radius. The first circle is created (Figure 7.7[b]). Then, he or she constructs the second circle: the same command is needed, and the user must point out the first circle (in so doing, they are assumed to have the same center). To give the correct radius, the user must define a formula with the calculator. So, he or she activates the calculator command ("calculus"), specifies the radius of the circle by clicking on the Radius command ("radius") and pointing out the circle, and clicks on the different buttons "/", "2," and "=." The system can build the second circle (Figure 7.7[c]).

The first loop is now complete. To complete the definition of the iteration, the user selects the UNTIL command. The system automatically switches to execution mode, to perform the second loop and to help the user define the recurrence relation. Every command performed during the first loop is run, and the system echoes the embedding context objects. To define the relation, it asks the user to either pick the same (which defines a constant reference during the whole iteration) or pick another object that has been created during the previous loop (which defines a recurrence relation, reevaluated for any loop). Every other entity selection is refused by the system. The same mechanism is provided for any expression, allowing the definition of new expressions (in our example, the expression for the radius of the first circle). Figure 7.7(d) illustrates this interactive phase.

Once each object reference has been confirmed or changed by some reference to entities from the first or the current loop, the system asks the user for the definition of the control expression. This solution implicitly defines

FIGURE **7.7**

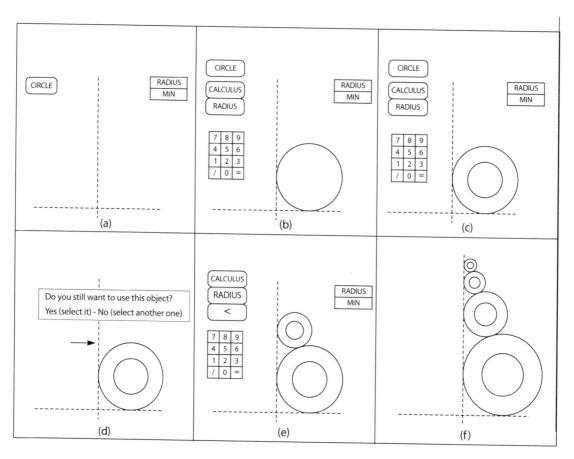

Interactive definition of a loop.

a recurrence-based relation that is consistent for the whole iteration. Using the display calculators (Figure 7.7[e]), the user can access every object from the iteration and the embedding context. In our case, he or she must activate the logical calculator ("calculus" command), and demonstrate the expression: the radius ("radius" command) of the last circle (the user points out the circle) is lower ("<" command) than the minimum (click on the menu item that denotes the minimum, "Min"). Clicking on the "=" box fires the calculus and implicitly asks EBP to handle the execution of the loop (the iteration definition is complete).

After that, the system runs the remaining loops until the controlling expression fires. Each recurrence relation is evaluated from any loop. The result is given in Figure 7.7(f). Finally, the user must define a symmetry of every created circle (a native operation in CAD systems), which involves the whole context of the iteration (any circle).

7.4 True Explicit PBD Solutions

EBP provides for true explicit PBD solutions. In this section, we detail the features of PBD. In the first subsection, we explain the specific commands that have been added to the CAD system to make PBD work, focusing on recording and running programs. In the second subsection, we detail the features that make EBP an actual programming environment.

7.4.1 Fully Integrated PBD Systems

Compared to CAD systems, the EBP system is able to describe every collection of shapes that might be described by conventional programs, even if they contain repetitive or conditional shape aspects. Compared with the existing PBD systems, (1) users may specify on the example every kind of conditional or recurrence-based loop structure without any textual manipulation, (2) the system does not use any inference mechanism but explicit dialogue conventions that are fully integrated within the usual dialogue of the CAD system, and (3) the system generates platform-neutral versions of programs that may be run, later on, on every other CAD system that supports a standard API.

Visual programming by demonstration is achieved by "command recording" mode. This means that, unlike some parametric systems in which "programs" are directly related to example values (e.g., the function *line_2_points* directly refers to the example point), in EBP, programs (which are called *instances*) are separated from examples. Relationships between example values and program variables are given through the dynamic context of the program. This mechanism, usual in programming languages, ensures an indirect reference from the program variables to their current values (in the example). It provides more independence between the PBD manager that deals with variables and the CAD system in which example values are CAD database pointers. When the program is rerun (e.g., during modification), the EBP variables are not changed, but their addresses, stored in the dynamic context, are updated.

After recording mode activation *(Record Instance)*, the EBP system "spies" on the user and builds an instance. Switching to execution mode allows the system to run this instance *(Apply Instance)*.

The only additional commands from traditional CAD systems are designed to RECORD / NAME / LOAD / APPLY instances and to DEFINE / READ / WRITE / ENTER parameters. Adding control structures requires other specific commands (IF / THEN / ELSE, REPEAT / UNTIL), as stated in the previous section.

A typical session of EBP would be as follows: after piece analysis (What are the parameters? Where are the dependencies?), the user begins PBD recording. He or she defines the parameters and then draws an example, using the parameters instead of "direct values." The DEFINE command opens a window, where a name is given (it is displayed every time the program is run). The ENTER command enables entering the values of the parameters for the example. These values are entered through the CAD system interface, and their types define the parameter's types. The WRITE/READ command enables recording/getting values on/from a file that will be linked to the program instance. This is used for recording the allowed sets of parameter values for part families. As soon as parameters are defined, they are displayed in a menu where the user can select them when, for example, defining expressions using the display calculators.

When the example is complete, the user can save the resulting instance, change some parameters, and try a new run. Recording values for parameters in files is very easy; this allows rapid testing. Recorded instances are included in a pop-up menu and are usable with minimal effort.

The LOAD command selects an instance, and the APPLY command runs it. Note that these commands may be selected both outside and inside the recording mode. In the first case, a model will be created in the CAD system database. EBP appears as a macro-by-example facility. In the second case, the APPLY command is recorded as a *call routine* in the embedding instance, and EBP ensures parameter passing. In both cases, after the APPLY command has been selected, EBP displays each parameter name and waits for a value. This value is defined using the whole CAD system user interface. This means that, when applying the instance in recording mode, the parameter value definition consists of every expression that involves entities or parameter values of the embedding instance. These expressions are stored in the embedding instance, and the expression value stands for the actual parameter value in the embedded instance.

7.4.2 An Actual Programming Environment, but for Users...

EBP is a complete programming environment that provides for every usual debugging facility, in a programming-by-example style. Every interaction with programs is done through interaction with examples. Generated programs are shown in a specific window that is only displayed upon user request. A special menu, the *Visit menu*, allows rerunning the instance.

Intelligent UNDO/REDO and Program Modification

During both program recording and debugging, any modification may be done to the program. Successive UNDOs enable returning to previous steps. Then, some additional steps may be done, and some steps may be modified or deleted. EBP manages the program's dynamic context to ensure that addition/deletion does not change references to variables. When REDOing some command that references some deleted entity, EBP asks the user for a new entity to replace the deleted one.

   Note that UNDOing is quite surprising at first use: the system does not record every user interaction, such as pulling down a menu to choose a user command or pointing at a graphical object. Instead, it records CAD actions as a whole, such as "creating a circle . . . ." So, UNDOing and REDOing are done in terms of CAD actions.

   UNDOing and REDOing control structures are even more difficult. Because of control expressions, the definition of these structures is rather different from their simple execution. So, *Undo*ing such a structure "undoes" the structure as one step, and REDOing "redoes" it as a whole, too. Stepping into a control structure is a debugging facility, as stated in the next section.

Debugging on Examples

To have a complete programming environment, debugging facilities must be provided to the user. As in every debugging environment, the EBP manager enables programs to be run step by step or until their end or to be reinitialized. But specific needs result from PBD.

   The first one relates to dynamic context management. At any point of a rerun, inserting or deleting actions is possible. In the first case, it may result in adding new variables in the context of the program. This is handled by the context manager, which adjusts every implicit variable reference. In the second case, consequences may be more dangerous: while debugging a whole program, deleting actions often result in not creating objects that may be used later in the program. After analyzing user behavior, we decided to provide two mechanisms to help good debugging: the user can *replace* or *delete* an action. When the user replaces an action, he or she is assumed to give a new action whose resulting object has the same semantics as the first one. This is the case when an incorrect parameter was first used. For example, in our example of Figure 7.7., the second circle has a radius that is either half the radius parameter or half the first circle's radius (the same value, in fact). But, in the logic of the required algorithm, only the second interpretation is right; the first would result in a surprising effect.

When the user deletes an action (assuming this action really builds an object), the system looks in the program and searches for every object whose construction depends on the result of the deleted action. Then, it can help the user modify the program by deleting invalidated actions or replacing the nonexistent object by a new one. In the same way, control structures can be inspected and modified, as can actions for control or recurrence relation definition.

Another specific feature of EBP must be explained. It may be called "debugging on examples." Because the textual representation of programs is never supposed to be displayed, debugging "virtual" programs might appear difficult. Fortunately, the example always provides an input/output interface with the program: It is possible to run the program *until one entity is drawn*. The user graphically selects this entity, and the program is run until it is drawn. The user may then make any modification on the example/program, before rerunning the remainder of the program. This point is very important, because it shows that the concrete representation of programs is not needed to achieve a complete programming environment.

Program Generation and New Features

EBP was designed to produce standard parts-portable program libraries (ISO13584-compliant Fortran programs reference the ISO 13584–31 API). Figure 7.8 illustrates this code generation.

Within the PLUS project, EBP is already used to generate the library of a bearing and linear system supplier. Some other exchange formats have been generated, including AutoLISP, Java classes, and a STEP-compliant parametric exchange format that was recently proposed (Pierra et al. 1996). Future work includes the development of an industrial product for an ISO 13584-compliant file generator and 3D extensions.

Another point under study in our laboratory is to progress from structured PBD to object-oriented PBD. Nontrivial problems, such as new PBD classes' definitions, and "PBD in the large" have to be addressed. Recent

Figure **7.8**

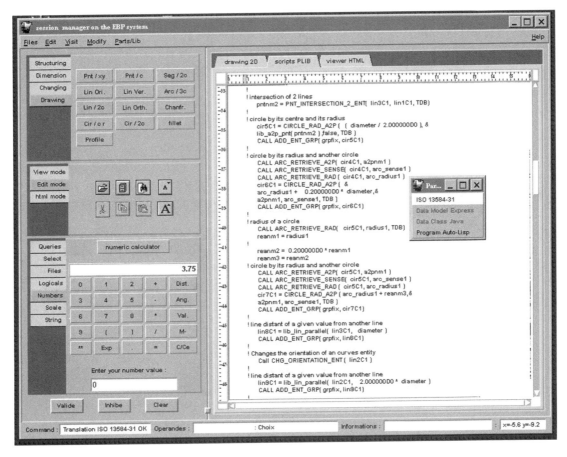

Illustration of program generation.

advances have been made for the first issue (Texier and Guittet 1999), and need to be extended.

7.5 Conclusion

In this chapter, we have presented a series of PBD environments for CAD systems. These systems

- do not use any inference mechanism to ensure full user control over the (implicit) program,

- support every control structure of imperative programming without any direct interaction with the program,

- are able to generate conventional programs that may be used on different CAD systems, and

- constitute a full PBD environment.

From the PBD point of view, the EBP system proves that, at least in some application areas in which system users have expert domain skills, complete PBD environments may be developed. "Complete PBD environment" means both computational completeness of the generated programs and real debugging with example facilities.

From the CAD system's point of view, this approach proves that parametric CAD systems, which are already very successful for sequential (or simple repetitive, pattern-based) parametric design, may be extended to support the parametric design of every conditional or repetitive aspect of shape.

From a user interface viewpoint, most interactive systems are limited to sequential execution. The EBP system suggests extending the dialogue command language toward recurrence-based repetitive command constructs. It also proves that very powerful macro-with-example recorders may be developed.

References

Bouma, W., I. Fudos, C. Hoffmann, J. Cai, and R. Paige. 1995. Geometric constraint solver. *Computer Aided Design* 27, no. 6: 487–501.

Cugini, U., F. Folini, and I. Vicini. 1988. A procedural system for definition and storage of technical drawings in parametric form. In *Eurographics '88*. Eurographics.

Cypher, A., ed. 1993. *Watch what I do: Programming by demonstration*. Cambridge, Mass.: MIT Press.

Cypher, A., D. S. Kosbie, and D. Maulsby. 1993. Characterizing PBD systems. In *Watch what I do: Programming by demonstration*, ed. A. Cypher. Cambridge, Mass.: MIT Press.

Cypher, A., and Smith, D. C. 1995. KidSim: End user programming of simulations. In *Human factors in computing systems (CHI'95)*, Denver, May 7–10). New York: ACM/SIGCHI.

Girard, P., and Pierra, G. 1990. End user programming environments: Interactive programming-on-example in CAD parametric design. In *EUROGRAPHICS'90*, (Montreux, Sept 3–7). Cambridge: Eurographics.

———. 1995. Structures de contrôle générales en programmation par démonstration. In *Journées Francophones sur l'Ingénierie de l'Interaction Homme-Machine (IHM'95)*, Toulouse, October 11–13, ed. P. Palanque. Cépaduès.

Glinert, E., ed. 1990. *Visual programming environments*. IEEE Computer. Los Alamitos, California.

Halbert, D. 1984. Programming by example. Ph.D. diss. University of California, Berkeley.

———. 1993. SmallStar: Programming by demonstration in the desktop metaphor. In *Watch what I do: Programming by demonstration*, ed. A. Cypher. Cambridge, Mass.: MIT Press.

Jackiw, R. N., and W. F. Finzer. 1993. The Geometer's Sketchpad: Programming by geometry. In *Watch what I do: Programming by demonstration*, ed. A. Cypher. Cambridge, Mass.: MIT Press.

Lieberman, H. 1993. Tinker: A programming by demonstration system for beginning programmers. In *Watch what I do: Programming by demonstration*, ed. A. Cypher. Cambridge, Mass.: MIT Press.

Myers, B. A. 1993. Peridot: Creating user interfaces by demonstration. In *Watch what I do: Programming by demonstration*, ed. A. Cypher. Cambridge, Mass.: MIT Press.

Myers, B. A., D. Giuse, R. Dannenberg, B. Vander Zanden, D. Kosbie, E. Pervin, A. Mickish, and P. Marchal. 1990. GARNET: Comprehensive support for graphical, highly interactive user interfaces. *IEEE Computer* 23, no. 11: 71–85.

Nardi, B. A. 1993. *A small matter of programming: Perspectives on end-user computing*. Cambridge, Mass.: MIT Press.

Newell R., G. Parden, and P. Parden. 1983. Parametric design in MEDUSA System. Paper presented at CAPE'83, Amsterdam, April 25–28.

Olsen, D. R., and J. R. Dance. 1988. Macros by example in a graphical UIMS. *IEEE Computer Graphics and Applications* 12, no. 1: 68–78.

Owen, J. 1991. Algebraic solution for geometry from dimensional constraints. In *ACM symposium on foundations of solid modeling*, (Austin, Tex., May 8–10). New York: ACM/SIGGRAPH.

Pierra G., and Y. Aït Ameur. 1994. Logical model for parts libraries. ISO-CD 13584-20.

Pierra, G., Y. Aït Ameur, F. Besnard, P. Girard, and J.-C. Potier. 1996. A general framework for parametric product model within STEP and parts library. In *European PDT Days* (London, April 18–19). London: PDTAG-AM.

Pierra, G., J.-C. Potier, and P. Girard. 1994. Design and exchange of parametric models for parts library. In *27th International Symposium on Advanced Transportation Applications, ISATA'94* (Aachen, Germany, October 31–November 4).

Potier J.-C., 1995. Conception sur exemple, mise au point et génération de programmes portables de géométrie paramétrée dans le système EBP. (Ph.D. diss.): LISI/ENSMA, Université de Poitiers.

Roller, D. 1990. Dimension-driven geometry in CAD: A survey. In *Theory and practice of geometric modeling*. Berlin: Springer.

Sassin, M., 1994. Creating user-intended programs with programming by demonstration. In *IEEE symposium on visual languages,* (St. Louis, Mo., October 4–7), ed. A. L. Ambler and T. D. Kimura. IEEE.

Shah, J. J., and M. Mäntylä. 1995. Parametric and feature-based CAD/CAM: Concepts, techniques and applications. New York: Wiley.

Smith, D. C. 1977. *A computer program to model and stimulate creative thought.* Basel: Birkhauser.

Solano, L., and P. Brunet. 1994. Constructive constraint-based model for parametric CAD systems. *Computer Aided Design* 26, no. 8: 614–621.

Texier, G., and L. Guitter. 1999. User defined objects are first class citizens. In *Third Conference on Computer-Aided Design of User Interfaces (CADUI/99),* (Louvain-la-Neuve, Belgium, October 21–23), ed. J. Vanderdonkt and A. Puerta. The Hague: Kluwer Academic.

Wilde, N. 1993. WYSIWYC (What You See Is What You Compute) spreadsheet. In *IEEE Symposium on Visual Languages, August 24–27, 1993.* Bergen, Norway: IEEE.

CHAPTER 8

Demonstrating the Hidden Features that Make an Application Work

RICHARD MCDANIEL

Siemens Technology-To-Business Center

Abstract

With programming by demonstration (PBD), a user shows examples of a behavior that the computer is meant to perform instead of writing out textual instructions. Many PBD systems use machine-learning techniques to convert the user's examples into executable programs automatically. However, in order to use PBD as a general-purpose programming tool, the user must be able to demonstrate more than just the surface level interactions of a behavior. By combining PBD with interaction techniques for specifying data that is normally hidden, and by selecting important data at key moments, the user is able to give hints to the computer that clarify the vagaries of using examples alone. This enables PBD to be used in more situations where previously only textual languages could be used.

8.1 Introduction

Many programming-by-demonstration (PBD) systems have used machine-learning techniques to understand a user's intention. With machine learning, a PBD system can infer a program automatically without requiring the user to learn a complicated programming language. Unfortunately, machine learning can also be temperamental, unreliable, and, to the untrained user, mysterious. Since machine learning can fail, the system must keep the user in control and informed. Even simple programs can be too difficult to infer by examples alone. The user must be allowed to provide information beyond examples that gives the system information about the program's internal workings. The key is to gather this extra information without placing too many burdens on the user.

In the Gamut project (McDaniel and Myers 1999), I have experimented with techniques for seamlessly gathering the important information needed to infer complex behaviors. These include new interaction techniques that are used to demonstrate the desired behavior as well as new programming elements that the user includes to provide extra information. Many of these techniques were originally developed for other systems, including some that were not PBD systems. By combining these techniques into a single system, along with appropriate machine learning that uses these techniques, we can make PBD as practical as programming using a typical language like C++, while at the same time still much easier to learn for nonprogrammers.

8.2 The Perils of Plain Demonstration

The machine learning in PBD can be seen as a form of *inductive* learning in which the computer infers more general properties from a set of specific examples. The examples thus become the user's primary means for communicating with the system. This method works well in principle because the user knows the task he or she wants the computer to perform. The user can provide examples by simply performing the behavior manually while the system watches. However, the computer cannot read the user's mind. When the user demonstrates, there are always variables inside his or her head. Sometimes the desired behavior depends on these variables, but the user is often not aware that the variables exist and may assume that their state is obvious.

Trying to coax the user to reveal hidden state is quite difficult; as a result, most PBD systems try to work without it. For instance, PBD systems use two typical interfaces to gather examples that I will call the "passive watcher" and using "explicit examples." The main difference between the techniques is who (or what) is responsible for determining when programming is desired. Using explicit examples, the user is responsible, whereas with the passive watcher, the computer is responsible.

The most commonly attempted interface is the passive watcher. The idea is that the computer acts like a helpful assistant who is constantly watching you as you work. Sometimes the system will recognize what you are doing, and if it can offer assistance, it will do so. A good example of this is in Microsoft Word's auto-correct, auto-indent, dictionary, and other features that all occur automatically because the system is passively recognizing patterns in the user's document as it is typed.

A passive watcher cannot normally request hidden state information from the user. The object that the user is creating is usually not a program, so the state cannot be represented as part of the product. For example, in a word processor, the product being created is a text document, not a program. Any behavior that a PBD system generates would not appear in the document itself, so the user has no obvious way to manipulate or refine the inferred behavior without switching to an alternate mode or editor. As a result, the passive watcher style of PBD operates by inferring as little hidden state as possible. This limits it to expressing behaviors with at most one state variable, making general-purpose programming practically impossible. The main advantage of the passive watcher is that its service is not critical in performing the user's task. If it cannot infer a behavior for a particular situation, the user just performs the task manually as though the PBD system did not exist.

In the second PBD approach that uses explicit examples, the user is usually creating an application and has drawn the application's interface components using a graphical editor. The user shows the PBD system before and after samples of the desired behavior using the interface's components. The system then converts these examples into code by noticing which components have changed and inferring the constraints between those changes. Of course, this technique is not restricted to building graphical interfaces. It can be applied to any domain whose essential features can be treated like objects. For instance, consider a greenhouse application in which graphical objects are used to represent water hoses, sprinklers, motors connected to windows, and temperature gauges. Demonstrating behaviors with the graphical objects could be used to create programs for watering the user's geraniums.

Unlike the passive watcher interface, the products the user creates using explicit examples are behaviors within an application. As a result, the user expects the system to create behaviors on demand. The system cannot passively choose to fail when it cannot recognize what the user is trying to accomplish. As a result, inferring behaviors from explicit examples is especially demanding.

If the goal is to make a general-purpose programming system using PBD, one must certainly use an explicit example approach. Unfortunately, many implementations of the explicit example approach still fail to handle hidden state. Without the ability to represent complex state, a system cannot infer behaviors any more complicated than those inferred by a passive watcher and will typically fail.

8.3 Who Is Actually Programming?

A common misconception about PBD is that the computer system performs all the programming work. In truth, the user is performing all the difficult conceptual work. The computer simply provides a more convenient method for recording the user's thoughts. In some senses, a PBD environment is like an advanced programming editor. However, unlike most editors, the user is not expected to write code textually. Instead, code is constructed by demonstrating the key behaviors of the application. This is still programming. The user must still carefully consider how the application works and must plan to demonstrate each behavior so that the computer can record it correctly.

Recognizing that the user is still a programmer eliminates the need for the system to magically interpret the user's every whim. Stated simply, if the user does not know how a behavior works, the system is not going to know, either. The goal of a PBD system should not be to try to do everything for the user but, instead, to facilitate the programming to make it easier to perform.

Since the user is in charge, the system must provide sufficient mechanisms for the user to communicate how a behavior functions. This means that the user must be able to represent the abstractions on which a behavior depends. Properly representing an abstraction is a generally difficult problem. More important, different users will represent the same abstraction differently. Thus, the system must be flexible to allow the user to specify an abstraction in the way that is the most comfortable for that individual.

8.4 Giving the System Hints

To demonstrate a complex behavior using explicit examples, the user must also be able to represent the abstractions that make the behavior work. The visible components of an application's interface do not always show all the aspects of the application's abstractions. For instance, in a chess game, there is nothing about the appearance of a bishop that suggests that it can only move diagonally. The techniques used to communicate information that is not apparent in the application's visible interface to address this problem are typically called *hints*. Hints provide extra channels for the user to represent things that the system would find too difficult to infer on its own.

8.4.1 Creating Special Objects

Many ways to give a system hints are possible including creating special objects and programming widgets, as well as using selection techniques for pointing out objects at key times. Most of these techniques come from

FIGURE **8.1**

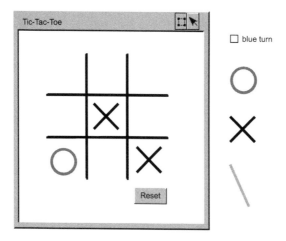

A window frame surrounding a visible game area, with other objects stored along the margins to represent invisible state.

systems that do not use PBD and do not infer code. In many ways, these techniques can be applied to any programming system since the need to represent state is universally applicable.

A common strategy is to give the user a secondary area to draw objects that do not appear in the application's interface. This area acts like the margins in a book where the user can write down notes without writing over the main body of text. In the main application window of my own system, Gamut, which is a PBD programming language for building video games, a window frame encloses the graphics that will become the application's visible area (see Figure 8.1). The rest of the area is all margin space for the user's off-screen objects. Gamut's margins are essentially the same technique as the "offstage area" in Gould and Finzer's (1984) Rehearsal World, which was an application builder that used a stage-acting metaphor. The offstage area was a separate window where the user could place unseen objects.

Objects for representing state can also be intermingled with visible objects on the screen. Several systems use techniques for drawing lines to represent geometric constraints. In Fischer, Busse, and Wolber's (1992) DEMO II, which was a PBD system for inferring small graphical behaviors, these were called "guidewires." In other systems, such as Jackiw and Finzer's

FIGURE **8.2**

*Using an arrow line to indicate an object's
speed and direction.*

(1992) Geometer's Sketchpad, which was a tool for experimenting with geometric constraints, these objects were not even given special names. Figure
8.2 shows a scene in Gamut where an arrow is used to show an object's direction of motion in a video game. The user created the arrow to show the
spaceship's speed and direction, which is not apparent from the ship's image. During demonstration, the user moves the ship and arrow combination to the arrow's end point and highlights the arrow's original position to
tell Gamut that it is important.

Besides representing state, objects can also be used to represent common behaviors. Widgets are objects such as buttons and sliders that have
not only graphical properties but also intrinsic behavior. For example, buttons can be pushed, and sliders can be adjusted to different values. These
behaviors can be incorporated into an application without having to demonstrate the intrinsic behavior of the widget. Widgets can also be used to
specify more complex behaviors. When the behavior of a widget becomes
similar to operations that one performs in a programming language, it becomes a "programming widget." Timers are a common kind of programming widget. For example, the timer in Figure 8.3 causes the ball to move
down the pyramid. The game randomly selects between two colors each
time the timer ticks and moves the ball along the arrow with the matching
color.

Though programming widgets can be powerful, the PBD system designer must be careful not to rely on them too heavily. For instance, in Rehearsal World, widgets were used to represent if-then conditions and for-
loops. The user would draw these widgets in a window and then fill in their
parameters with short segments of code. Widgets, when used in excess, become a programming language on their own. One of the goals of using PBD
is to lessen the need for the user to program the structure of the application's code. If widgets are used too heavily, they can cause the same problems as writing code textually.

FIGURE **8.3**

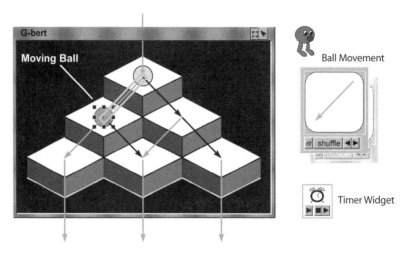

A timer widget used to cause a ball to bounce downward randomly in a game.

8.4.2 Selecting the Right Behaviors

As important as representing state is, it is equally important that the PBD system applies that state in the right way. Like many artificial intelligence (AI) problems, inferring code in PBD can be seen as a searching task. The system must find the appropriate expressions and constraints for representing the behavior the user is demonstrating. Many different behaviors can always be produced from a given set of examples.

Two basic methods are used for bounding the number of choices the system can make when creating a behavior. In the first, the system writes out a list of possibilities and the user picks the most appropriate one. This is the technique that Kurlander and Feiner's (1988) Chimera uses, for example. Chimera was a tool for performing operations such as search and replace on complicated graphical drawings. When the different behavioral choices can be articulated in a few terse phrases, this technique works fairly well. However, for more complicated decisions, such as when the choice concerns an expression that is nested several layers deep within the code, the user cannot always pick the right choice reliably. In these cases, the system can reduce its search space by having the user select the objects that the behavior uses. This technique is sometimes called *giving the system a focus hint.*

Examples of focus hints are shown in Figure 8.2 and 8.3. In both cases, a user is demonstrating to Gamut that a character in a game is following a path. To tell the system that the path is important, the user highlights it. This allows the system to focus on the path object and only generate constraints between the path and the moving object. Maulsby's (1994) Cima, which could recognize textual patterns using examples, also allowed the user to give focus hints. In addition, Cima allowed the user to provide negative focus hints, where marking an object indicated to the system that the object should not be used in the current behavior.

8.5 The Programming Environment Matters

With the ability to specify and point out all the state variables in an application, a PBD language can theoretically be as powerful as any textual language. In fact, Gamut has been shown to be Turing-complete (i.e., it can be used to create any Turing machine, making it computationally equivalent to any another programming language). However, anyone who has ever tried to program a Turing machine knows that theoretical equivalence makes no guarantee that a language is practical. The environment and feel that a PBD system provides are major factors in whether a user would want to use it.

Having a PBD language that is computationally equivalent to textual languages is only one step. People always ask, "Can your system do X?" Where X is some behavior that they think a PBD system could never possibly infer. The answer is invariably no. The fact is that a complete language definition is not sufficient to actually build applications. If one were to take an ordinary programming language like C and ask, "Can I use C to print 'hello world' to the screen?" the answer would also be no if it were not for the presence of the stdio.h library that provides the printf procedure. The power of a language is not entirely in its definition but also in the libraries that allow the language to make interfaces with the world. PBD languages are still immature in that none have any library capabilities. No language can provide comprehensive support for every possible application. At some point, the language has to be extended using a library interface.

Another important aspect of the environment is the manner in which the user fixes bugs. It is essentially impossible in any programming language to produce bug-free code, and this is still true in PBD languages. While it is generally not possible for the system to know whether the user's application has a bug, the system can facilitate how easily the user can find problems and fix them once they are discovered.

The first requirement is that it should be possible to test any change the user makes immediately. If the user is forced to make several changes before the application can be tested and the application still does not work, it is very hard to discern the effects of the changes. It should be possible for the user to correct a problem as soon as it is discovered and see immediately whether the problem has been fixed. In Gamut, the system's inferences are represented as interpretable code. When the user adds a new example, the code is immediately modified to reflect the change, and it can be run as soon as desired.

The second requirement is that the user needs feedback to understand what the system is creating. For example, the system can use visualization techniques to show the user pictorial representations of the code, as in Chimera. One might also draw a dependency network to show which objects have behaviors and which objects those behaviors will affect.

The most explicit kind of feedback the system can provide for a behavior is to show its code. In fact, in some systems, the user might only demonstrate one example, after which the user is required to edit the code in order to fix all the errors the inference system made. This is essentially how a macro recorder works. The user records a single example using the macro recorder and then edits the code the recorder produces to add parameters, loops, and conditional expressions. Though this method works in principle, nonprogrammers generally find it difficult to write code even in small doses. So, although it is probably a good idea to make the inferred code available, forcing the user to write code is generally not good for a PBD system.

8.6 Conclusion

Programming by demonstration can be a powerful method for building applications, but it is still the user's responsibility to know how the behaviors in the application work. By using the proper objects and techniques, a user can create practically any behavior, but the user must still learn how to use those objects and techniques. The user must still convert the abstract concepts that the behaviors use into representations that the computer can understand. While PBD can help make this process easier, it cannot eliminate the creative process the user must perform to turn an idea into code.

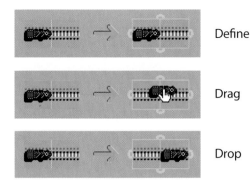

FIGURE 1.1 *Defining a rule by demonstration.*

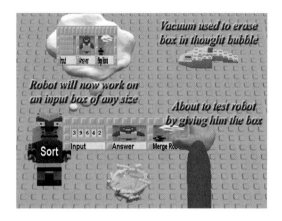

FIGURE 2.7c *Testing the newly trained and generalized robot.*

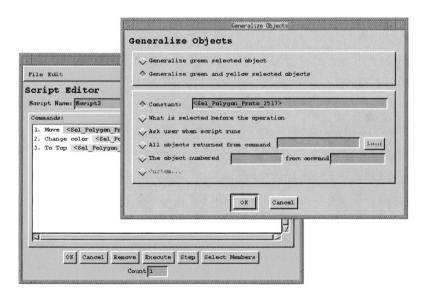

FIGURE 3.1a *The dialogue box for generalizing objects in Topaz, with the script window in the background.*

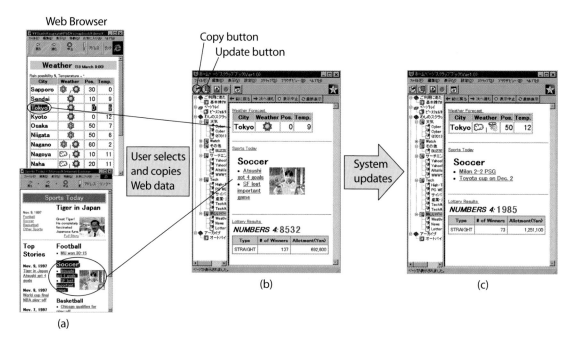

FIGURE 4.1 *Overview of Scrapbook: (a) user selection in Web browsers; (b) Scrapbook page created by the user; and (c) page updated by the system.*

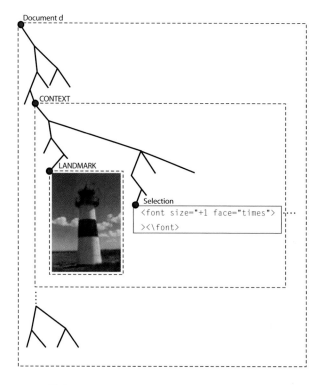

FIGURE 5.2 *Extraction refinement process of a HyQL script.*

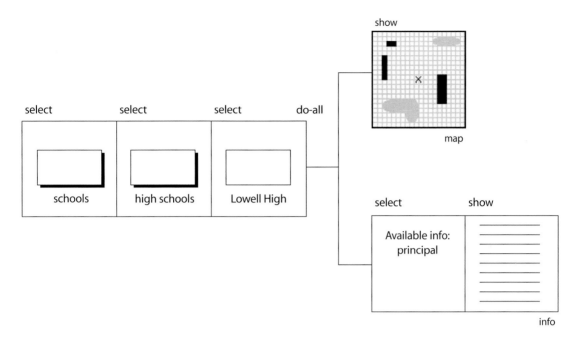

FIGURE **6.9** *A C-SPRL program with a do-all construct.*

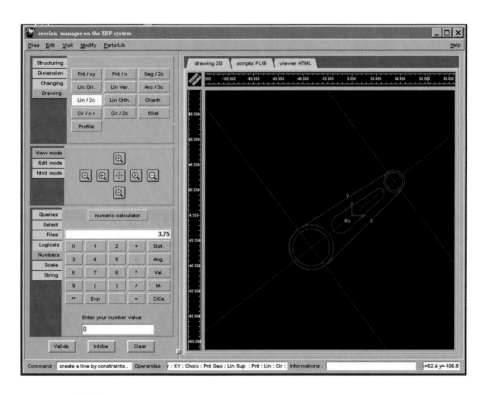

FIGURE **7.3** *Snapshot from the EBP system.*

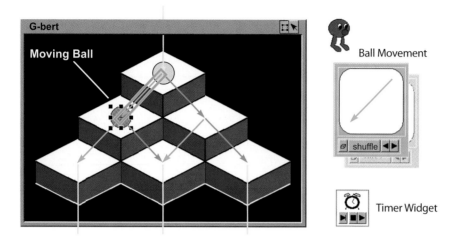

Ball Movement

Timer Widget

FIGURE **8.3** *A timer widget used to cause a ball to bounce downward randomly in a game.*

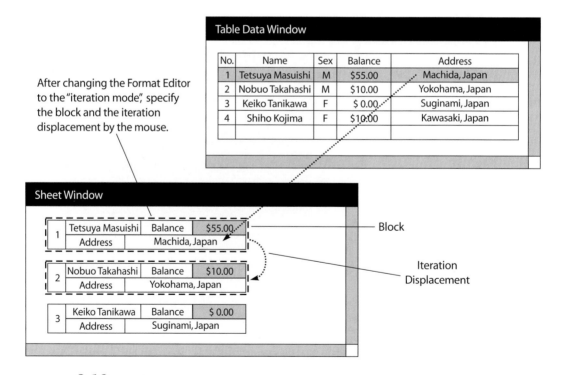

After changing the Format Editor to the "iteration mode", specify the block and the iteration displacement by the mouse.

FIGURE **9.10** *Specifying iteration.*

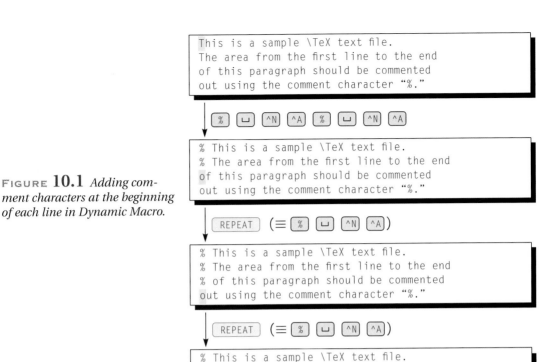

FIGURE **10.1** *Adding comment characters at the beginning of each line in Dynamic Macro.*

FIGURE **11.4**
The macro predicting deletion of the entire HTML comment.

FIGURE **11.5**
Pressing the Step button once more to start deleting the net HTML comment with 100 percent probability.

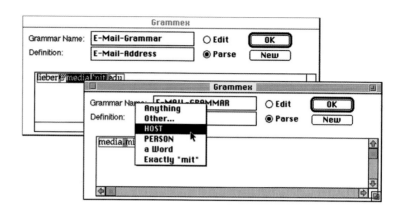

FIGURE 12.9 *Recursively defining a Host.*

FIGURE 13.11 *User interface for specification and display of regular expressions. The word "wobble" on the second row from the top is annotated in red, and the box around the letter "o" in the center of the screen is red.*

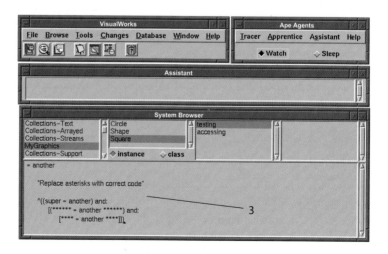

FIGURE 14.8b *The user has written several similar methods named "=" for various classes of MyGraphics. He has just mouse-clicked the suggestion, and the template has been inserted (3).*

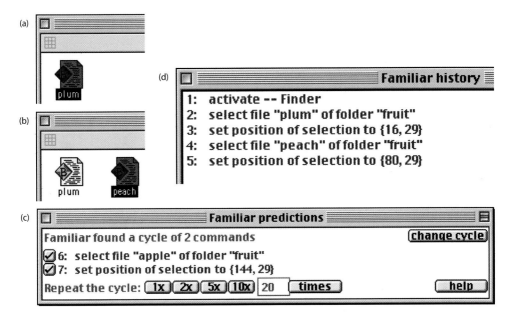

FIGURE 15.2 *Using Familiar to arrange files: (a) a demonstration is recorded; (b) the history window; (c) a second demonstration is recorded; (d) a prediction is made.*

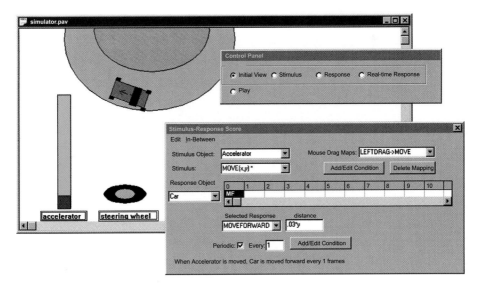

FIGURE 16.4 *A driving simulator built in Pavlov. The arrow on the car is a guide object denoting the direction of the car.*

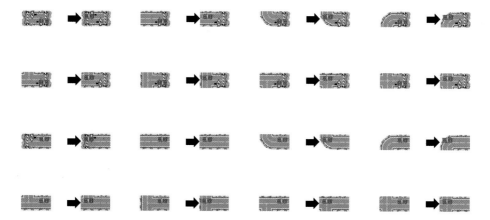

FIGURE **18.9** *Only the first few out of a set of 256 rules created by AgentSheets' "Semantic rewrite rule" system to define the "Cars follow Streets like Trains follow Tracks" behavior.*

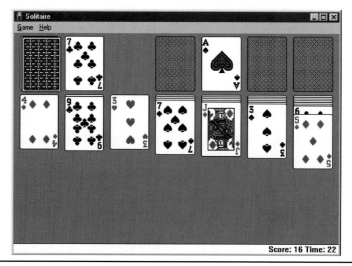

FIGURE **19.3** *VisSolitaire source data and visual processing results.*

To represent the state, the user must be able to create objects that are not visible in the application interface. These objects might be placed in the margins of a window or in separate regions entirely. The user should also be allowed to draw special-purpose objects in the visible regions of the application to show the invisible graphical constraints that the application uses.

For a behavior to use hidden state, the user should be able to point out appropriate objects at key moments during demonstration. This can be accomplished by selecting objects or by selecting which code the system creates. Generally, techniques that do not rely on using code are more appropriate for nonprogrammers, but in some circumstances, selecting from a list of choices is fairly easy. Selecting objects, though, can apply to situations where the system cannot present a terse description.

Finally, the programming environment that the system presents is as important as the PBD language itself. The environment plays a key role in making an application easy to debug and to understand. Program visualization and other feedback are important in keeping the user informed. Furthermore, being able to test behaviors immediately allows the user to know quickly whether a change has been effective and allows the user to be confident that a behavior works.

One might ask that if PBD is not the panacea that lets every user program regardless of what they know, why bother in the first place? Why not encourage users to learn to program using standard techniques? The answer is simply that expressing a program using examples is tremendously easier and faster than writing a program textually. Any mental gymnastics that the user must make to represent hidden data in a PBD interface pales in comparison to the representational nightmares that the user might undergo to represent an equivalent structure in a programming language. Seasoned programmers can sometimes forget the years of training and effort required to learn a textual language. On the other hand, I have seen novices learn to construct complex data structures graphically in Gamut in hours. Granted, using PBD is not free from mental commitment. It only seems that way when compared to textual programming languages.

Though it has strong potential, PBD has not had much commercial success, but PBD research has only recently moved out of the laboratory and into real products. PBD seems to be following the path that AI software has blazed. The initial systems showed promise but fell short of expectations and languished in the backlash. But slowly, the concepts worked their way into common systems with new names such as *fuzzy logic* and *search engines*. PBD will also work its way into the mainstream.

References

Fischer, G. L. Busse, D. E., and Wolber, D. A. 1992. Adding rule-based reasoning to a demonstrational interface builder. Paper presented at *ACM Symposium on User Interface Software and Technology, UIST'92,* Monterey, Calif., November. New York, NY: ACM.

Gould, L., and Finzer, W. 1984. *Programming by rehearsal.* Palo Alto, Calif.: Palo Alto Research Center, Xerox Corporation.

Jackiw, R. 1992. *The geometer's sketchpad.* Berkeley, Calif.: Key Curriculum.

Kurlander, D., and Feiner S. 1988. Editable graphical histories. Paper presented at *IEEE Workshop on Visual Languages,* Pittsburgh, Penn., October. New York, NY: Computer Society.

Mauslby, D. 1994. *Instructible Agents.* Ph.D. diss. University of Calgary, Calgary, Alberta.

McDaniel, R. G., and B. A. Myers. 1999. Getting more out of programming-by-demonstration. Paper presented at *ACM CHI'99, Human Factors in Computing Systems,* Pittsburgh, Penn., May. New York, NY: ACM.

CHAPTER 9

A Reporting Tool Using Programming by Example for Format Designation

TETSUYA MASUISHI

Hitachi, Ltd.

NOBUO TAKAHASHI

Hitachi, Ltd.

Abstract

This chapter describes a report tool in which report formats are designated by PBE-like (programming by example) operations. Users specify a sample layout of an example row of relational table data on a sheet and select an iteration pattern of the sample layout. The tool extracts a set of general formatting rules from the sample layout. The rules consist of absolute positions of noniterative data, relative positions of iterative data, the iteration pattern, and the increment of the iteration. The tool interprets the rules and generates new reports of the format for different table data.

9.1   Introduction

Data warehouse technologies have enabled centralized data management for decision support and planning applications. The decision makers print various formats of reports based on the data of the centralized database. Many end users, sometimes decision makers themselves, have to design the report formats, since the formats represent the view of the data and cause considerable effects on the decision. Such reports for decision making in Japan are reconstructed table-style reports that include instance text strings and numerical data, while most of such reports in the states include graphs that already imply analysis of the results.

The reconstruction is needed because relational tables in practical use usually have many columns. (We have assumed the data are stored in a relational database.) The reconstruction is applied so that several columns of data can fit within the width of the paper. It is difficult to grasp reports that exceed both of the width and the height of the paper. Since the number of rows of tables is usually big enough to exceed the height of the paper, we need to reconstruct the relational table to make reports of many pages flow in one direction that we can handle easily. Figure 9.1 shows an example of a Japanese-style reconstructed table report. Japanese reports usually include many ruled lines to separate adjacent data, rather than tabulation spaces, perhaps because Japanese words are not separated by spaces.

Many software packages called *reporting tools* support such reconstruction. Reporting tools usually have a scripting language to make programs. A program generates a report of a fixed format by embedding various data of a relational database.

FIGURE **9.1**

Relational Table Data

No	Name	Sex	Balance	Address
1	Taro Suzuki	M	$ 88.75	890 Kashimada, Saiwai, Kawasaki
2	Hanako Sato	F	0	549-6 Shinano-cho, Totsuka, Yo..
3	…	…	…	…

 Reconstruction

1	Taro Suzuki	Balance	$ 88.75
	Address	890 Kashimada, Saiwai, Kawasaki	
2	Hanako Sato	Balance	0
	Address	549-6 Shinano-cho, Totsuka, Yo..	
3	…	Balance	…
	Address	…	

Typical Japanese reconstructed report.

This chapter describes the user interface of a report tool that designates formats of reports. The user interface is designed in a programming-by-example (PBE) manner (Cypher 1993; Myers 1992). A user creates a sample report for example table data. The tool extracts the implied formatting rules. The tool interprets the rules to generate reports reading relational table data as input. The extraction process is deterministic and does not include any statistical recognition or learning process.

Sugiura and Koseki (1996) show a data entry system from email text into a database. The system generates a macro program that reads email text, extracts data from the text, and inserts the data into a database. A generalization process is employed to generate a general–purpose macro program from a history of sample operations. Our problem is easier because the input is a structured table in a database, not email text in natural language.

Instead, our system employs a simple generalization process for just one example.

Myers (1991) uses just one example for text formatting. The generalization process includes parsing the example text's special words (e.g., *Chapter, Section,* and *Appendix*), numbers, separators, and decorations (e.g., lines and boxes). The parsing process encounters ambiguity. Our problem is well structured enough to make the system deterministic and easy to use.

9.2   System Overview

The reporting tool is used in two phases: the format-making phase and the report-generating phase. The two phases can be done by different users, and some users may do just the latter phase.

- *Making formats:* In this phase, a user makes a format, not a report. Conventional reporting tools do not require table data for making formats, but this tool requires table data to make a sample report. (Users always need table data even for the usual tools used when they "debug" their formats.) The tool extracts a set of formatting rules and stores them in a persistent file called a *format file.*

- *Generating reports:* Other users generate reports by specifying a format file and table data. Table data can be specified by a file name if the data are stored in a file such as in CSV (Comma Separated Value) file format or a set of retrieval statements such as select statements in SQL (Structured Query Language) for a connected relational database.

9.2.1   System Configuration

The tool consists of the Format Editor, which enable users to edit interactively to make format files, and the Report Generator, which allows users to generate reports by specifying a format file and relational table data (Figure 9.2). The Format Editor is an interactive editor for a user to make a sample report using a set of relational table data, extract a set of formatting rules, and save them into a format file. (A format file is a conventional file that includes a set of formatting rules in our proprietary file format.) The editor reads a format file and example table data.

FIGURE **9.2**

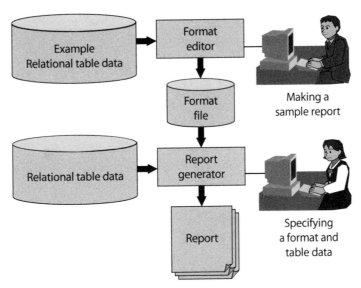

System configuration.

9.3 User Interface of Format Editor

We have employed a PBE-like user interface for the Format Editor. A user makes a sample report to make formatting rules, without needing to specify general formatting rules directly. The set of rules works as a program that generates reports for other sets of relational table data. So, the process of the format editor is a kind of programming by example. Since some of the rules are specified directly by the user for practical use, the process is a simple and practical version of PBE.

9.3.1 Window Configuration

The Format Editor consists of two main windows: the *Sheet* window and the *Table Data* window. The Sheet window shows the sample report as a sheet image. The Table Data window shows the example table data as a relational table image. The user can copy and paste table data (both numerical and string) to the Sheet window.

The editing scheme of the Sheet window is as follows:

1. Put objects on the Sheet window.

2. Specify iterative objects, called a *block*.

3. Specify iteration pattern for the block.

4. Specify increment of the iteration.

The objects on the Sheet window consist of a fixed text string, including column names, functions, ruled lines, and example data. Any text strings can be put on the Sheet window, and usual text string attributes such as fonts can be specified. The user can also copy and paste useful column names from the Table Data window to the Sheet window. Some built-in functions are provided (e.g., date, time, etc.); they work as variables. Ruled lines can be drawn on the Sheet window, and usual line attributes such as width and pattern can be specified.

When starting up the Format Editor, a default example row—the first row—is highlighted on the Table Data window. The user can change the example row by clicking the mouse button. Multiple example rows can be selected for special cases. For example, seven example rows are necessary to make a report showing weekly trends generated from daily table data.

9.3.2 Specifying Iteration

The system makes a report by iterating a print of a specified set of objects with a fixed increment of position. The user specifies which object is iterative or not. A rectangular area that surrounds the iterative objects is called a *block*. The user can specify iterative objects by specifying a block by a rectangular rubber band of the mouse.

The system also provides iteration patterns, some of which are shown in Figure 9.3. The user chooses a pattern from the menu of the provided patterns. The increment of position for the iteration can be specified in two ways: the user can specify the increment directly, or the system can calculate the increment when the user puts in data other than those from the example row(s) (Figure 9.4).

The Sheet window displays the final image of the sample report, which includes iterated images of the iterative objects. The iterated images are produced by the example table data of the corresponding rows, which are calculated by incrementing the row numbers of the specified example row(s) by the number of the example row(s), typically one.

FIGURE **9.3**

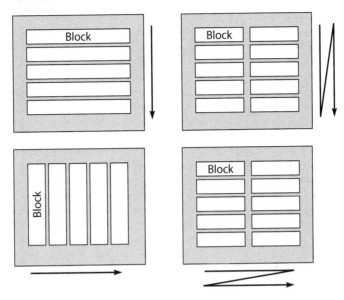

Examples of iteration patterns.

FIGURE **9.4**

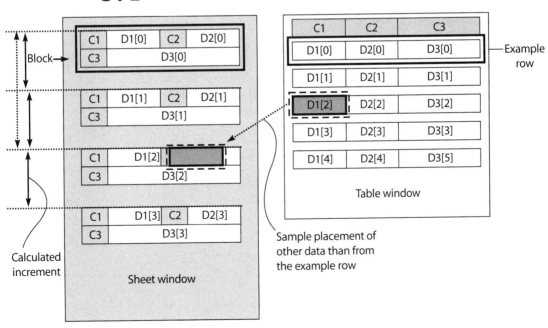

Calculating the increment and the image of the sample report.

FIGURE **9.5**

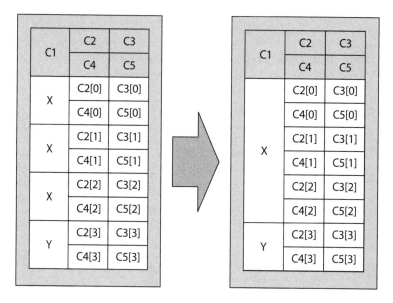

Unification of repeatedly occurring data.

9.3.3 Adjustment

After the image of the sample report is displayed, some adjustments can be made to create sophisticated reports. For example, conditions for page and column breaks can be specified. The typical condition is "When the data of the specified column change, create a new page." Also, when a column has repeatedly occurring data, they may be unified (Figure 9.5).

9.4 Extracting Formatting Rules

The Format Editor stores a set of formatting rules for a sample report. Formatting rules consist of the following information:

• the list of objects on the sheet;

• information about the block, including its absolute position and size;

- the attributes of noniterative objects and their absolute position on the sheet;

- the attributes of iterative objects, including, for example data, (1) column name, (2) relative row displacement in the example table from the base of the example row, and (3) relative position in the sheet from the base position of the block, and, for other objects, (1) their attributes and (2) relative position in the sheet from the base position of the block (delta X and delta Y);

- the specified iteration pattern and the increment; and

- specified adjustments.

9.5 Generating Reports

When a format file and a set of table data are given to the Report Generator, it creates a report according to the algorithm, briefly described as follows:

1. Put the entire noniterative object on the sheet.

2. Iterate the following substep for all rows of the table data: Put all of the iterative objects at the current position, substituting the example data to the given table data at the current row of the iteration.

3. Apply any adjustments.

9.6 Example of the Process

We describe here an example of how the system works, starting with making a format. Figure 9.6 shows the window status of the Format Editor just after the user has specified an example data file. The Table Data window displays the example data as a table. The Sheet window displays an empty sheet on which the user is drawing an example report.

The user draws an example report on the Sheet window by copying and pasting objects from the Table Data window to the Sheet window (Figures

FIGURE **9.6**

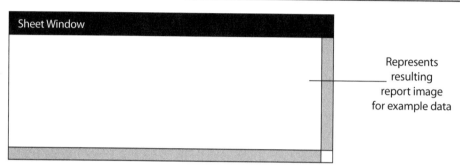

Represents example data

No.	Name	Sex	Balance	Address
1	Tetsuya Masuishi	M	$55.00	Machida, Japan
2	Nobuo Takahashi	M	$10.00	Yokohama, Japan
3	Keiko Tanikawa	F	$ 0.00	Suginami, Japan
4	Shiho Kojima	F	$10.00	Kawasaki, Japan

Represents resulting report image for example data

Format editor.

FIGURE **9.7**

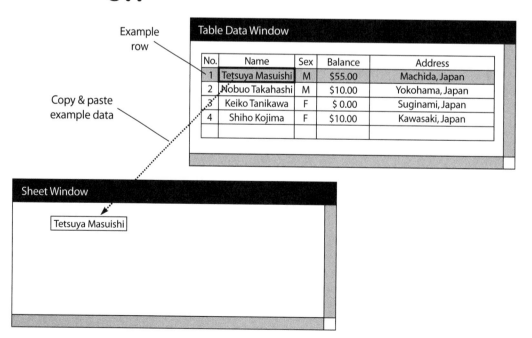

Copy and paste.

FIGURE **9.8**

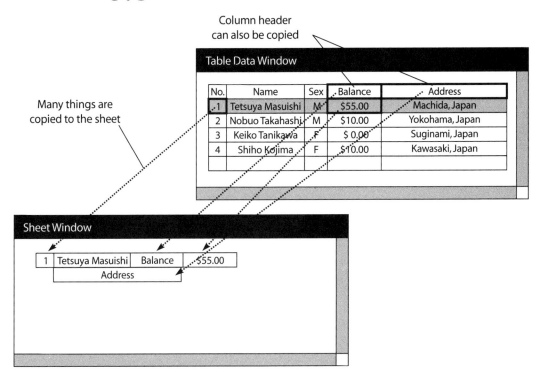

Copy and paste (continued).

9.7 and 9.8). The objects include the table data of the example row and column header. The Sheet window works as a usual drawing program (Figure 9.9). The user can put text strings directly from the keyboard and draw lines using the mouse.

When the user has finished editing the block, the next thing to do is specifying the iteration. The user changes the Format Editor to the iteration mode and specifies the block and the iteration displacement with the mouse (Figure 9.10). He or she can imply the iteration by copying and pasting the other data from the example row (Figure 9.11). This implication does not require that the user change the editor mode.

When the user sees the example report image on the Sheet window, the user saves the format to a file, as one usually does in drawing programs. The

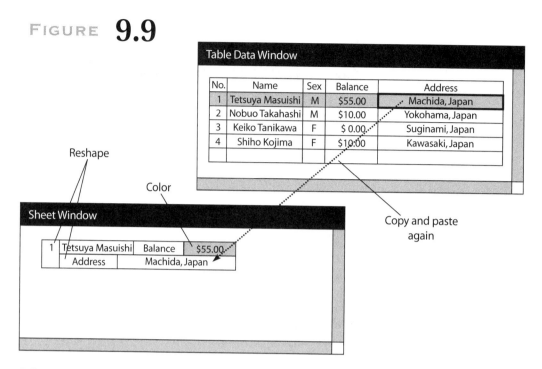

FIGURE **9.9**

Reshape

Color

Copy and paste
again

Edit on the Sheet window.

FIGURE **9.10**

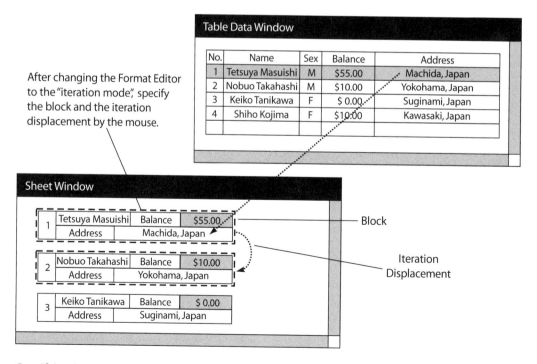

After changing the Format Editor
to the "iteration mode", specify
the block and the iteration
displacement by the mouse.

Block

Iteration
Displacement

Specifying iteration.

FIGURE **9.11**

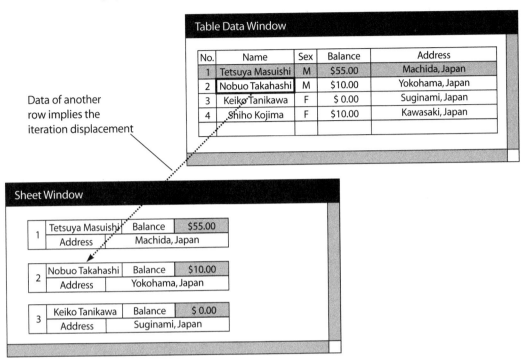

Implication of iteration.

Format Editor extracts the format rules from the example report (Figure 9.12) and saves the rules to the file.

The extracted formatting rule works as a report generation program. Figure 9.13 shows a pseudo-expression of the formatting rules in C-like language. Another user can apply the formatting rules in the file to other data and generate another report (Figure 9.14).

9.7 Evaluation

We have applied the system described here to a real project at a Japanese company. End users and information technology (IT) staff there have developed more than five hundred formats. The applied formats include the following:

FIGURE **9.12**

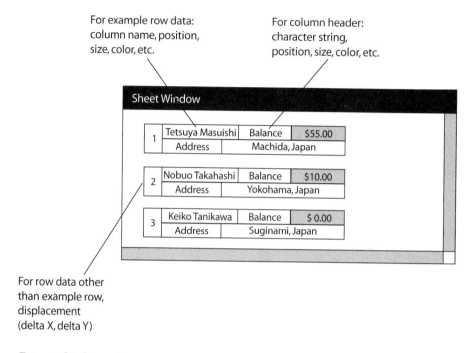

Extracted information.

FIGURE **9.13**

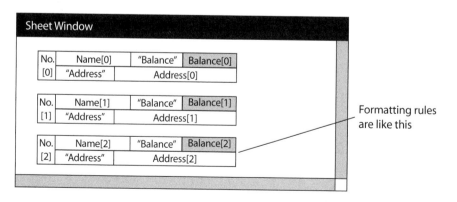

Pseudo-expression of formatting rules.

FIGURE **9.14**

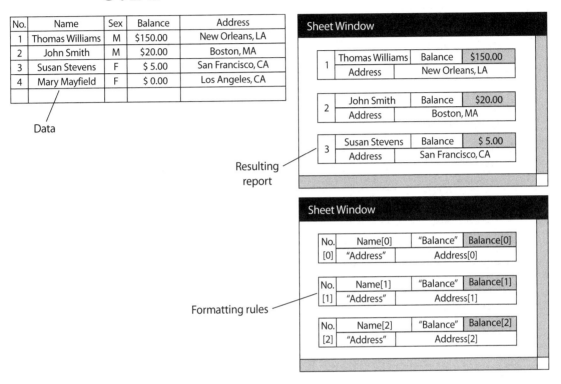

Report generation for other data.

- *Reports for planning and decision making*—sales reports for sales persons and divisions, sales reports for products and areas, and cost reports for products

- *Mission-critical forms*—monthly reports to customers, bills, and in-house order forms

- *Images*—employee files including facial photo images and price lists with product photo images

We have been informed that staff could make all the formats using the Format Editor. They required using some functions for more detailed presentation, such as round corners for crossing ruled lines.

End users could make report formats as well as IT people—there was no difference between the two groups' products. End users, who usually do not make general programs, could also make report formats that generate many reports according to data. This result indicates that the PBE paradigm worked well at this evaluation site.

9.8 Conclusion

We have designed the extraction process to be deterministic for practical use. The system extracts formatting rules deterministically, not statistically. Just one sample report is needed for extracting general formatting rules. To make this possible, some generating information, such as iteration, can be specified directly. This design was possible because the problem of generating reports from relational table data is well structured.

References

Cypher, A., ed. 1993. *Watch what I do: Programming by demonstration.* Cambridge, Mass.: MIT Press.

Myers, B. A. 1991. Text formatting by demonstration. In *Proceedings CHI.*

———. 1992. Demonstrational interfaces: A step beyond direct manipulation. *IEEE Computer* (August): 61–73.

Sugiura, A., and Y. Koseki. 1996. Simplifying macro definition in programming by demonstration. In *Proceedings UIST.*

CHAPTER 10

Composition by Example

TOSHIYUKI MASUI

Sony Computer Science Laboratories, Inc.

Abstract

Programming by example (PBE) literally means making "programs" from examples, but PBE techniques are also useful for automating text composition tasks by creating editing procedures from the history of a user's editing operations. *Composition by example* (CBE) is a practical approach to improve the efficiency of text composition tasks using various simple PBE techniques. Thousands of people are composing texts daily on handheld computers and Emacs using CBE tools that I have distributed for years.

10.1 Introduction

Although text composition is a highly creative task, it can be full of repetitive menial subtasks. For example, people sometimes compose letters by duplicating an old letter whose topic is close to the new one. They repeat the same search-replace operations or type the same phrases (e.g., their names and addresses) again and again in different documents. The popularity of small portable text devices is now presenting users with new classes of repetitive text composition subtasks. On cellular phones, for instance, the user must type small keys many times when composing messages. If a system could automatically perform these repetitive tasks based on examples given implicitly by the user, people could compose texts much more efficiently.

To automate text composition tasks, many text editors support end-user programming features so that repetitive tasks can be programmed by users. For example, on GNU Emacs, users can define and execute arbitrary functions by writing Emacs Lisp codes. Users of Emacs can also define a sequence of keystrokes as a macro command and later invoke the sequence by a single keystroke. With these features, any repetitive task can be defined as a function or a macro.

However, writing a program or defining a macro is not always a convenient way for performing repetitive tasks, even for trained programmers. If a user has to enter a symbol at the beginning of 5 consecutive lines of a text file, he would use a text editor and perform the task manually. If he has to do the same thing for 10,000 lines, he would write a program. But what if he has to do it for 100 lines? Is it worthwhile writing a program?

In this chapter, I show that simple example-based techniques can make various text composition tasks much easier. The first example is the *Dynamic Macro* system (Masui and Nakayama 1994), which enables users of text editors to repeat arbitrary editing operations after executing the same operations more than once. The second example is the *POBox* system (Masui 1999), which enables efficient text input by predicting the next input word from the context, using a dictionary created by the user's text input histories. Using these CBE techniques, users can efficiently create and edit texts without noticing that they are giving examples and making programs from them.

Dynamic Macro and POBox are not paper systems but are actually being used by thousands of people. Dynamic Macro has been very popular in the Emacs user community for several years. I have been using POBox for all my Japanese composition on handheld computers and Emacs. The Japanese version of POBox on Palm Pilot has been available on the Web for more than two years, has been updated many times after receiving suggestions and bug reports from the users, and is currently used by thousands of people. POBox has been adopted as the official text input method of Sony's cellular phones and information appliances, which expect millions of users.

10.2 PBE-Based Text Editing Systems

Many researchers noticed that text-editing tasks involved a lot of menial routine works and tried to improve the efficiency by various PBE techniques. In Nix's (1985) Editing by Example system, users can tell the system to infer the editing procedure by showing the text both before and after modification. The inferred procedure should be of the "gap programming" form, which is a subset of string substitutions using regular expressions. Mo and Witten's (1992) TELS system generalizes users' iterative operations and infers an editing procedure including loops and conditional branches. If the system's guess is wrong, users can incrementally correct it until it does the right thing for them. Since the procedure generated by TELS can include branches and loops, it can perform complex tasks that cannot be done by mere string substitutions. GNU Emacs provides the "dabbrev" function, which expands the substring entered by the user into a full string in the same document beginning with the same substring.

10.3 Dynamic Macro: A PBE-Based Text Editing System

Dynamic Macro is a simple and powerful tool for automatically creating a keyboard macro from repetitive user operations in a text editor. In many text editors, a keyboard macro is used to substitute a long sequence of operations by another single operation. It is usually defined through the following steps: First, the user tells the editor to start recording a keyboard macro; second, she types the sequence of commands that she wants to define as a new macro; and finally, she tells the editor to stop the recording. For example, if a user of GNU Emacs wants to define a macro to insert a "%" at the top of every line, he types "^X (" to start the recording; then he types "^A % ^N" to insert a "%" at the top of the current line and go to the next line; then he types "^X)" to finish the recording. After the recording is finished, he can invoke these operations by typing "^X e". Although keyboard macros are general and powerful tools for repetitive editing tasks, they have several disadvantages. First, users have to remember three commands to record and invoke a keyboard macro. Second, it is not possible to define the command sequence after they are executed: that is, a user should know that a sequence of commands is used many times, well *before* actually executing them. In reality, repetitive tasks are often recognized *after* execution. Third, since the procedure of defining a keyboard macro is not simple, it is not useful for short, small repetitive operations.

Using Dynamic Macro, keyboard macros for repetitive operations are defined and executed automatically. When a user hits a special "REPEAT" key after performing repetitive operations, an editing sequence corresponding to one iteration is detected, defined as a macro, and executed at the same time. Although simple, a wide range of repetitive tasks can be performed just by hitting REPEAT.

Dynamic Macro works as follows: All the recent user operations in a text editor are logged as a string, and when a special repeat command is issued by hitting REPEAT, the system looks for repetitive operations from the end of the string. If such operations are found, they are defined as a macro and executed. If REPEAT is struck again, the macro is executed again. For example, when a user enters the string abcabc and then hits REPEAT, the system detects the repetition of abc, defines it as a macro, and executes the macro, resulting in another abc. When the user hits REPEAT again, one more abc is inserted.

Similarly, when a user inserts a "%" at the top of two lines by doing the same operations twice and hits REPEAT, the operations are defined as a macro and executed. As a result, another "%" is inserted at the top of the third line.

Dynamic Macro does not suffer from the shortcomings of keyboard macros. Users should only remember that striking REPEAT makes the system do the repetitive task once more, instead of remembering three different operations of a keyboard macro. The macro is defined after doing

FIGURE **10.1**

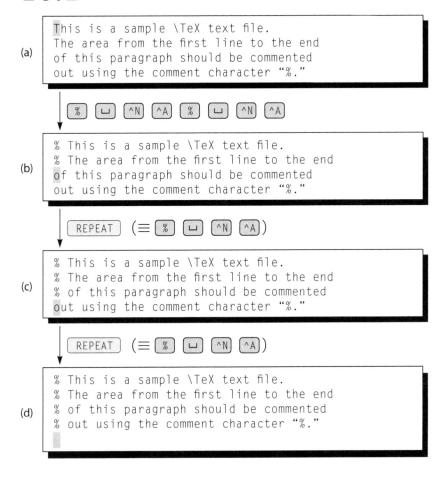

Adding comment characters at the beginning of each line in Dynamic Macro.

ordinary editing tasks, without telling the editor when to start the recording. In spite of its simple-looking appearance, Dynamic Macro is applicable to various editing situations.

Figure 10.1 shows how Dynamic Macro works for simple tasks such as adding comment characters to consecutive lines. Figure 10.1(a) shows the original text. When a user types "% ␣ ^N ^A % ␣ ^N ^A", she gets Figure 10.1(b). If she hits REPEAT here, the system detects the repetition of "% ␣ ^N ^A", defines the sequence as a macro, executes the macro, and gets Figure 10.1(c). Hitting REPEAT again results in Figure 10.1(d).

FIGURE **10.2**

(a)
```
(define (factorial n)
  (if (< = n 1) 1 (* n (factorial (− n 1)))))
(define (halts f)
  ( .... ))
```

```
(search "(define")
(save the string from there to EOL into temporary buffer)
(insert ";*** " above)
(insert the contents of temporary buffer)
(insert ";*** --- ...;***")
search "(define")
```
REPEAT

(b)
```
;*** (factorial n)
;*** ------------------------------------------------
;***<perspicuous description here>
;***
(define (factorial n)
  (if (< = n 1) 1 (* n (factorial (− n 1)))))
;***(halts f)
;*** ------------------------------------------------
;***<perspicuous description here>
;***
(define  halts f)
  ( .... ))
```

Adding comment lines before each function definition.

Figure 10.2 shows a more complicated example. The job here is to add several comment lines above every function definition of Figure 10.2(a). This is done by long steps of operations, but striking REPEAT after doing the first part of the second iteration results in Figure 10.2(b). More hits will add similar comment lines to the following function definitions. In this case, since no sequence of operations is executed twice before REPEAT, the system searches the pattern XYX and defines XY as the macro.

The advantages of Dynamic Macro are as follows. First, it is *simple to use.* Users only have to remember that they can hit REPEAT to make the system do their repetitive chore. They can strike REPEAT at any moment during the repetitive operations, and they do not have to tell the system to start or stop recordings. Second, it is *powerful*. Dynamic Macro works well for a variety of simple to complex repetitive tasks where once only keyboard macros were applicable. Third, it is *easily implemented*. The system just keeps a log of recent user actions for the implementation of Dynamic Macro. Fourth, it *does not interfere with users* in any sense. Logging user actions is an easy task for most systems, and it does not slow down the application. Nothing happens unless users touch REPEAT. Finally, it is *general* in that any system with a keyboard interface can adopt this technique.

10.4 POBox: A PBE-Based Text Input System

Although millions of handheld computers and mobile phones are used today, and email and short messages are exchanged throughout the world, handheld and wearable computing have not really taken off, partly because of the lack of efficient text input methods. POBox is an example-based text input method especially effective for handheld and wearable computers where a full-size keyboard cannot be used and fast text input is difficult.

10.4.1 Various Text Input Techniques

Traditionally, on pen-based handheld computers, handwriting recognition techniques and the soft keyboard (i.e., the virtual keyboard displayed on the tablet of a pen computer) used to be the main techniques for entering text, along with others. However, using any of these techniques takes much longer to enter text than with a standard keyboard.

The situation is worse for East Asian languages such as Chinese and Japanese. Unlike European languages, these have thousands of character faces. Even with a keyboard, it is not easy to enter a character. A variety of techniques for entering text into a computer have been investigated. The most widely used Japanese input technique is Roman-Kanji conversion (RKC), in which a user specifies the pronunciation of a word with an ASCII keyboard, and the system shows the user a word with the specified pronunciation. If the word was not the one that the user intended to use, the user hits a "next-candidate key" until the correct word appears as the candidate.

Figures 10.3 shows an overview of various existing text input systems. Arrow A shows how an English text is composed using a standard keyboard. Roman character codes are directly generated by the keyboard and concatenated to generate a text. Arrow B shows how a Japanese text is

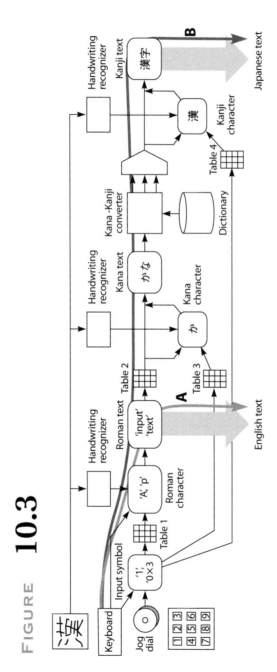

FIGURE **10.3**

Structure of various text input methods.

composed using a standard keyboard. Roman character strings are first converted to Kana texts that represent the pronunciation of Japanese words, and then they are converted to Kanji characters by a Kana-Kanji converter. Since multiple Kanji characters often have the same pronunciation, the user must choose the correct one with the selector.

Text input on handheld computers is very slow for many reasons. First, typing a key or writing a character is much slower than using a standard keyboard. Second, users have to type keys more times than when using standard keyboards, since small input devices often have fewer keys (e.g., cellular phones usually have only 20 keys). These keys can generate only a small number of input symbols, and combinations of the keypress must be converted to Roman characters using a mapping table. In this way, input symbols must be converted more than once until the final text is composed.

Entering Japanese text on a cellular phone is also very slow. The input symbols must first be converted to Kana characters using Table 3 in Figure 10.3, and then a Kana character string is converted to a Kanji character using the Kana-Kanji converter. A proper Kanji must then be selected using the selector.

Several techniques for fast text input on handheld machines have been proposed. One approach is to make the speed of using a software keyboard faster. The QWERTY layout is often used for the software keyboard, but QWERTY is not the best layout for a pen-based software keyboard, since frequently used key combinations are sometimes laid out far apart and users must move the pen for a long distance to enter a text. The Fitaly keyboard[1] is a layout for minimizing the pen movement on software keyboards. Since "e" and "n" often appear next to each other in many English words, they are put in an adjacent position on the Fitaly keyboard. Other layouts have also been proposed to improve the input speed on software keyboards (see Hashimoto and Togashi 1995; MacKenzie and Zhang 1999).

Another approach is to use fast handwriting recognition systems. Unistroke (Goldberg and Richardson 1993) was one of the first approaches in this direction, and similar techniques such as Graffiti have become very popular on recent handheld computers including Palm Pilot. More sophisticated gesture-based techniques such as T-Cube (Venolia and Neiberg 1994), Quikwriting (Perlin 1998), and Cirrin (Mankoff and Abowd 1998) have also been proposed.

Yet another approach is to give up entering characters one by one and to use a word dictionary for composing a text. Textware's InstantText system

---

1. Textware Solutions, 83 Cambridge St., Burlington, Mass., 01803. *www.twsolutions.com/fitaly/fitaly.htm.*

(see footnote 1) allows users to use an abbreviated notation of a sentence to reduce the number of input. For example, users can type `oot` to enter "one of the" or type `chrtcs` to enter "characteristics". These abbreviations are dynamically created, and they do not have to be predefined.

Tegic's T9 system[2] takes a different approach. T9 was originally developed for composing texts using only nine keys on a standard telephone. On T9, instead of typing keys more than once to select an input character, users assign more than one character to the digit keys of a telephone so that they do not have to be concerned about the differences. Figure 10.8(b) on page 205 shows a typical key assignment on a telephone keypad. When a user wants to enter `is`, he pushes the 4 key first, where `G`, `H`, and `I` are printed, and then pushes the 7 key where `P`, `Q`, `R`, and `S` are printed. Using the combination of 4 and 7 corresponds to various two-character combinations, including `hr`, `gs`, and so on, but `is` appears most frequently in English texts, and the system guesses that `is` is the intended word in this case.

On almost all the pen-based computers available in Japan, either RKC or handwriting recognition is supported. Text input is slow and tiring using either of the techniques for the following reasons. Specifying the pronunciation of every input word using a soft keyboard takes a lot of time, and the user must convert the pronunciation to the desired Kanji strings with extra keystrokes. Handwriting recognition has more problems. First, the recognizer has to distinguish between thousands of characters, often making errors. Many of the characters in the character sets have similar shapes, so it is inherently difficult to make recognition reliable. Second, in many cases, users do not remember the shape or the stroke order of Kanji characters, even when they have no problem reading them. Finally, writing many characters with many strokes on a tablet is very tiring. With these difficulties, it is believed to be difficult to enter Japanese text faster than thirty characters per minute on pen-based computers, which is several times slower than using keyboards.

1 0 . 4 . 2 POBox Architecture

Since people usually compose texts that are in some way close to old texts, an example-based approach can be applied to solve this problem. Using POBox, text is not composed by entering characters one by one, but by selecting words or phrases from a menu of candidates created by filtering the dictionary and predicting from context. The word dictionary and phrase dictionary are first created from existing corpus, and updated by examples

2. Tegic Communications, 2001 Western Ave., Suite 250, Seattle, Wash. 98121. *www.t9.com.*

FIGURE   **10.4**

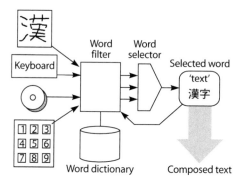

A POBox architecture.

given by the user. With this example-based approach, users can enter text much faster than recognition-based and other existing text input methods. Figure 10.4 shows the architecture of POBox. A text composition task with POBox consists of repetitions of the following two steps.

1. *Filtering step:* First, a user provides prediction keys for a word she wants to enter. Prediction keys can be the spelling, pronunciation, or shape of a character. As soon as she enters prediction keys, the system dynamically uses the keys to look for the word in the dictionary and shows candidate words to the user for selection.

2. *Selection step:* Next, the user selects a word from the candidate list, and the word is placed in the composed text. The selected word and the current context are saved in the dictionary as a new example and used in the future filtering step, so that the word is properly picked up as a candidate in the same context next time.

In most existing text input systems, users must provide all the information for the input text, either by specifying input characters or by showing the complete shape of characters by giving handwritten strokes. In POBox, users do not have to give all of them to the system; they only have to give information to the system that is enough for the prediction. Users also do not have to specify all the characters or stroke elements that constitute a word; they only have to specify part of the input word and select it from the candidate list. This greatly reduces the amount of operations and time for composing a text, especially when selecting input characters is very slow or

difficult. This architecture can be applied to a variety of nonkeyboard devices, including pen tablets, one-hand keyboards, and jog-based phones.

10.4.3 POBox for Pen-Based Computers

Figure 10.5(a) shows the startup display of POBox running on Windows95.
When the user pushes the F key, the display changes to Figure 10.5(b),
showing the frequently used words that start with F in a candidate word list.
Since the word first is a frequently used word and is found in the candidate list, the user can tap the word first so that it is put into the text area.

FIGURE **10.5**

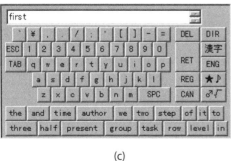

(a)

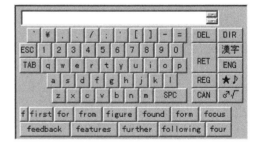

(b)

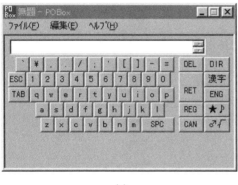

(c)

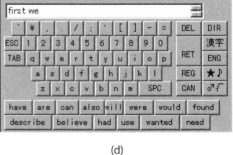

(d)

*POBox running on Windows95: (a) POBox's startup display; (b) frequently used words starting with f;
(c) words that often follow first; and (d) user-chosen word order of first we.*

FIGURE **10.6**

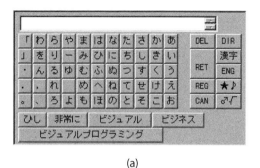
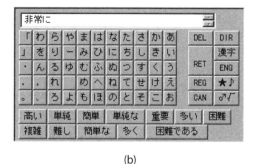

(a)   (b)

Japanese input mode of POBox: (a) a Hiragana character table and (b) a user-selected word from Hiragana display.

After `first` has been selected, the display changes to Figure 10.5(c). In the menu at the bottom, the words that often come after `first` are listed in order of frequency.

The next word, `we`, often comes after `first`, and this word is again in the predicted list of candidate words. The user can directly select `we` by touching it in the menu. After `we` has been selected, the display changes to Figure 10.5(d). In this way, users can repeatedly specify the prediction key and select a candidate word to compose a text.

In the Japanese input mode of POBox, a Hiragana character table is displayed for entering pronunciations, instead of the Roman alphabet in English mode. The pronunciation of the first word 非常に is hi-jou-ni, and the user can select the word by choosing the word ひ (hi) and the word し (shi) from the Hiragana keyboard, just like in the English example (Figure 10.6[a]).

When the user selects the word 非常に, the display changes to Figure 10.6(b), and the next word 簡単 is displayed as a candidate in the candidate word list at the bottom. In this way, the user can enter Japanese text by specifying the pronunciation of the first portion of the word and then selecting the desired word from the menu, just like specifying the spelling for English words.

Figure 10.7(a) shows the display of POBox on a Palm Pilot after the user hits the `ma` key on the software keyboard. The words listed are candidate words beginning with the pronunciation "ma". When the user moves the pen after touching the tablet instead of tapping the software keyboard, the system starts handwriting recognition and interprets the strokes incrementally, showing candidate words that begin with the strokes. Figure

F I G U R E **10.7**

The display of POBox on Palm Pilot (a) after the user hits the ma key and (b) after the user has drawn a line from the center of the keyboard to the lower-left corner.

10.7(b) shows the display after the user has drawn a line from the center of the software keyboard to the lower-left corner. This is the first stroke of the Kanji character "nyuu", and those words that begin with the character are shown as candidates. Unlike existing handwriting recognition systems that recognize characters only after all penstrokes that constitute the character have been written, incremental recognition can greatly reduce the number of penstrokes that users have to draw. In this way, software keyboards and handwriting recognition are seamlessly integrated in POBox for pen-based computers.

1 0 . 4 . 4 Using POBox on a Cellular Phone

POBox can be used for handheld devices that do not have pen tablets. Instead of using a software keyboard or pen operations on a cellular phone, digit keys and a jog dial can be used for the filtering and the selection steps.

Figure 10.8(a) shows the implementation of POBox on a CDMA (code-division multiple access) cellular phone. The phone has about twenty keys on the surface and a jog dial at the left side of the LCD display. Three or four alphabetical characters are assigned to each digit key (Figure 10.8[b]) like standard push-button phones in North America. Hiragana characters

FIGURE **10.8**

 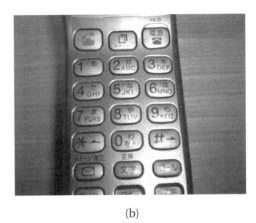

(a)   (b)

(a) The implementation of POBox on a CDMA cellular phone and (b) a display of the digit keys containing alphabetical characters.

are also assigned to those keys to specify the pronunciation when used for Japanese text input.

Figure 10.9(a) shows the initial display of the phone. Frequently used words are listed as candidates at the bottom of the display. When a user pushes one of the digit keys, the character printed on the key is shown at the cursor position, and candidate words starting with the character are shown at the bottom of the display (Figure 10.9[b]). When the user pushes the key again, the next character printed on the keytop is shown, and corresponding candidate words are displayed (Figure 10.9[c]). A user can rotate the jog dial clockwise at any time to select a candidate word. If user is the desired word, the user can rotate the jog dial and display user at the top of the display. As the user changes the selection, more candidate words appear at the bottom of the screen for selection (Figure 10.9[d]).

The user can then push the jog dial to make the selection final. At this moment, the next word is predicted just like in pen-based POBox, and the next candidate words are displayed at the bottom. The user can again rotate the jog dial to select a candidate from the list (Figure 10.9[e]). In Figure 10.9(c), if the user pushes the 7 key, p is selected as the next character for the input word (Figure 10.9[f]). When a user begins rotating the jog dial counterclockwise, she can select input characters by the jog rotation. Input characters are sorted in frequency order; e, a, i, and so forth appear as the candidate input character as the user rotates the jog dial. Figure 10.9(g) shows the display after the user rotated the dial three steps.

FIGURE **10.9**

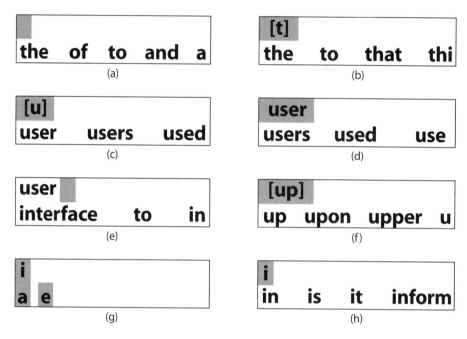

Text input steps on a CDMA phone: (a) initial display; (b) after pushing the 8 key; (c) pushing the 8 key again; (d) rotating the jog dial clockwise; (e) pushing the jog; (f) pushing the 7 key after (c); (g) rotating the jog dial counterclockwise; and (h) pushing the jog.

When the user pushes the jog dial, the search character becomes fixed, and words that begin with the pattern are displayed as candidates (Figure 10.9[h]). The user can then rotate the jog dial clockwise to select the candidate input word (e.g., `information`). Although using a jog dial for character input takes more time than using digit keys, using a jog dial has an advantage; users do not have to touch the digit keys at all, so composing text using only one hand is possible.

10.4.5 POBox Server on the Internet

If POBox can be implemented as a server, various client computers can connect to it and ask the server to do the prediction. In this case, users can use the same system from any terminal, and all the example words and phrases are saved in the server for later prediction. For example, when a user enters a proper noun on a handheld computer, the name can be used for prediction on a desktop computer. If everyone has his or her personal POBox server on the Internet, people would no longer have to enter difficult spelling more than once.

10.5 Conclusion

This chapter introduced two very practical PBE-based tools for text composition. Some people argue that PBE is sometimes not as effective as it is expected to be. However, text composition is one of the areas where PBE-based technique is truly effective. I use Dynamic Macro almost every day and POBox for all the Japanese documents on Emacs and my Palm Pilot, getting rid of all other Japanese text input methods. POBox for Palm Pilot has been on the Web for more than two years, and tens of thousands of people have downloaded it, since it is the fastest Japanese text input method on handheld computers.

I believe that PBE techniques are most effective in the following two cases: when very simple prediction is enough for the task, such as the case of Dynamic Macro and POBox, and when the task is very complicated and even human programmers cannot easily create programs to solve the problem. In this case, stocastic methods for creating programs from examples are effective. Graphic layout tasks and other aesthetic tasks are in this category. In short, PBE is effective for a variety of composition tasks that entail both highly creative aspects and routine work. I hope that more PBE-based techniques are investigated for various composition tasks.

References

Goldberg, D., and C. Richardson. 1993. Touch-typing with a stylus. In *Proceedings of ACM INTERCHI '93 Conference on Human Factors in Computing Systems (CHI'93)*, April 1993. Reading, Mass.: Addison-Wesley.

Hashimoto, M., and M. Togasi. 1995. A virtual oval keyboard and a vector input method for pen-based character input. In *CHI'95 Conference Companion*, May 1995. Reading, Mass.: Addison-Wesley.

MacKenzie, I. S., and S.-Z. Zhang. 1999. The design and evaluation of a high performance soft keyboard. *In Proceedings of the ACM Conference on Human Factors in Computing Systems (CHI'99)*, May 1999. Reading, Mass.: Addison-Wesley.

Mankoff, J., and G. D. Abowd. 1998. A word-level unistroke keyboard for pen input. In *Proceedings of the ACM Symposium on User Interface Software and Technology (UIST'98)*, November 1998. ACM Press: http://mrl.nyu.edu/perlin/demos/quikwriting.html.

Masui, T. 1999. POBox: An efficient text input method for handheld and ubiquitous computers. In *Proceedings of the International Symposium on Handheld and Ubiquitous Computing (HUC'99)*, September 1999.

Masui, T., and K. Nakayama. 1994. Repeat and predict—Two keys to efficient text editing. In *Proceedings of the ACM Conference on Human Factors in Computing Systems (CHI'94)*, April 1994. Reading, Mass.: Addison-Wesley.

Mo, D. H., and I. H. Witten. 1992. Learning text editing tasks from examples: A procedural approach. *Behaviour & Information Technology* 11, no. 1: 32–45.

Nix, R. P. 1985. Editing by example. *ACM Transactions on Programming Languages and Systems* 7, no. 4 (October): 600–621.

Perlin, K. 1998. Quikwriting: Continuous stylus-based text entry. In *Proceedings of the ACM Symposium on User Interface Software and Technology (UIST'98)*, November 1998. ACM Press: http://mrl.nyu.edu/perlin/demos/quikwriting.html.

Venolia, D., and F. Neiberg. 1994. A fast, self-disclosing pen-based alphabet. In *Proceedings of the ACM Conference on Human Factors in Computing Systems (CHI'94)*, April 1994. Reading, Mass.: Addison-Wesley.

CHAPTER 11

Learning Repetitive Text-Editing Procedures with SMARTedit

TESSA LAU

University of Washington

STEVEN A. WOLFMAN

University of Washington

PEDRO DOMINGOS

University of Washington

DANIEL S. WELD

University of Washington

Abstract

The SMARTedit system automates repetitive text-editing tasks by learning programs to perform them using techniques drawn from machine learning. SMARTedit represents a text-editing program as a series of functions that alter the state of the text editor (i.e., the contents of the file or the cursor position). Like macro recording systems, SMARTedit learns the program by observing a user performing her or his task. However, unlike macro recorders, SMARTedit examines the context in which the user's actions are performed and learns programs that work correctly in new contexts. Using a machine learning concept called *version space algebra,* SMARTedit is able to learn useful text-editing procedures after only a small number of demonstrations.

11.1   Introduction

Programming by demonstration (PBD) has the potential to allow users to customize their applications as never before. Rather than writing a program in an abstract programming language to automate a task, users demonstrate how to perform the task in the existing interface, and the system learns a generalized program that can perform it in new contexts.

Our work focuses on the latter class of users: those who don't want to, or don't know how to, construct a program to accomplish some task. In some domains, such as the Stagecast Creator and ToonTalk systems described elsewhere in this book, users' primary goals are to construct programs. In other domains, users are more interested in getting their work done than in programming the system. They are focused on their overall tasks, and constructing programs to automate repetitive subtasks are merely the means to an end.

Ultimately, the process of constructing a program (or recording a macro) boils down to the problem of choosing the correct action for the system to take at each step. A PBD system can make this programming process easier in two ways: by providing a visual representation of the program, thus eliminating the need to understand arcane syntax, and by inferring the user's intent based on demonstrations. For our intended users, the latter approach is more valuable. It places the burden of inference on the system, rather than on the user; the system is responsible for figuring out what the user meant to do and for abstracting enough details to construct a reusable program.

For a PBD inferencing system to be useful, it must be expressive enough to represent the types of programs users want to construct. On the other hand, it must be able to perform its inference based on a very small number of examples—few users would be willing to train the system on hundreds or even tens of examples! These two goals are directly in conflict with each other: as the learning system's expressiveness (and thus the size of its search space) increases, so does the number of examples required to pick out the correct concepts in that space.

The approach we have taken, based on a machine learning concept called *version space algebra* (Lau, Domingos, and Weld 2000), allows us to get the best of both worlds: an expressive program representation language, combined with the ability to make useful inferences after a very small number of demonstrated examples. We do this by carefully crafting our search bias—the kinds of programs we can represent—so as to separate the wheat from the chaff. The version space algebra, which is an extension to Mitchell's (1982) concept of version spaces for machine learning, lets us represent only the programs that users might want to write, without being distracted by nonsensical or useless programs.

We have implemented and tested our framework in the text-editing domain. Examples abound of repetitive procedures for editing text: converting from one file format to another, reformatting address lists, manipulating bibliographic citations, and so on. Our system SMARTedit (Simple MAcro Recognition Tool) uses version space algebra to learn useful programs for editing text based on as little as a single demonstrated example.

Beyond the consideration of a single domain, however, we are also concerned with a system's ability to scale both to more complex domains and to other domains entirely. The variety of systems described elsewhere in this book displays the breadth of application domains that could benefit from PBD. Given such a wide range, an important factor in the design of a PBD system is how domain knowledge is represented in the system. The answer to this question determines how easy it is to add new knowledge to the system and whether it can be easily applied to a different domain.

Previous PBD systems have been built on domain-specific preference biases—knowledge about which actions are more likely than others—to force the system to come to the correct conclusion. Like expert systems, such techniques lead to brittle, poorly understood designs; extending the system to support a new concept requires delving into the depths of the code and understanding all of the ramifications of each change.

In contrast, our version space algebra framework proposes a modular approach to the design of PBD systems: a domain-independent learning algorithm and a structured, high-level domain representation. Adding new features to the system, or applying it to a different domain, requires only changes to the domain representation. We hope that robust solutions such as ours will help PBD spread more quickly to more applications.

1 1 . 2   The SMARTedit User Interface

We illustrate SMARTedit by showing how it automates a simple text-processing task. Suppose the user has some HTML with comments embedded in it and would like to remove the comment tags and all the text inside the comments. An HTML comment is a string delineated by the tokens <!--and -->. The comment may span multiple lines and contain arbitrary characters. To delete all such comments, a Microsoft Word user would have to enter a regular expression of the form \<\!--*--\> into the search-and-replace dialog box. While this syntax may look straightforward to programmers, even we took several tries to figure out the correct syntax to use for that regular expression. In SMARTedit, however, no arcane syntax is required. The user simply demonstrates the desired functionality by deleting the first HTML comment, and the system is able to do the rest. Let's walk through this example to illustrate exactly what SMARTedit can do.

SMARTedit follows the familiar macro recording interface. To begin creating a SMARTedit macro, the user pushes a *Start recording* button. The button then turns red, indicating that her actions are being recorded. She then begins demonstrating what she wants SMARTedit to do. In this task, she first moves the cursor to the beginning of the next HTML comment, right before the <!-- characters, using any combination of cursor-motion keys or mouse clicks (Figure 11.1). She then deletes the entire HTML comment

FIGURE **11.1**

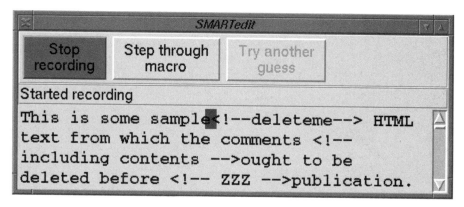

Recording a SMARTedit macro. The blue block is the position of the insertion cursor, the status bar indicates that the user is recording, and the record button has turned red to indicate recording is active.

FIGURE **11.2**

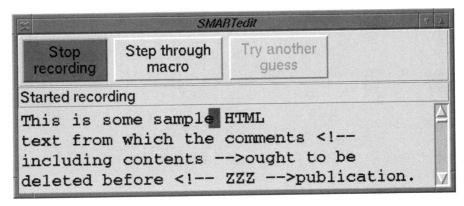

Deleting the HTML comment.

(Figure 11.2). Because the demonstration is now complete, the user presses the *Stop recording* button to indicate that she is finished.

SMARTedit has now learned a macro representing the procedure she has just performed. Looking more closely at the way the user demonstrated this task, she had to hit the *Delete* key fifteen times to delete the extent of the comment. It's unlikely (though possible) that she wanted to delete exactly fifteen characters. What's more likely (and correct) is that she wanted to delete up until the comment closing tag. If she were using a standard macro recorder, she would need to ensure that her exact keypresses would work for future examples as well as the current one. If she were writing a program to delete these HTML comments, she would have had to specify (in some programming language) when to stop deleting, using some abstract representation of the text, rather than the actual text sitting right there.

SMARTedit infers which meaning the user wanted, by using her demonstration as an example of the program she is trying to construct. The next section will show how SMARTedit represents these two possible actions (and others) as different hypotheses in its version space. But first let's see how SMARTedit's knowledge is used to help the user delete the next comment automatically.

SMARTedit learns procedures consisting of a sequence of actions—relatively high-level text-editing commands, such as moving the cursor to a new position; inserting a string; selecting or deleting a region of text; or manipulating the clipboard. The user can invoke SMARTedit's learned macro one action at a time by pressing the *Step through macro* button. SMARTedit will guess what action she's likely to take next. In this case, it correctly

FIGURE **11.3**

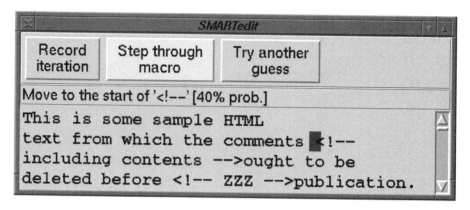

Invoking the macro by pressing the Step through macro button.

predicts that the next action she wants to take is to move the cursor to the beginning of the next HTML comment (Figure 11.3). Given that she's only demonstrated one example, however, SMARTedit could predict this action with only 40 percent probability. (For example, it's possible that she wanted to position the cursor after the word *sample* instead of before the HTML comment; this action and others like it also have nonzero probability.) If the result of this action is not what the user intended, she could use the *Try another guess* button to switch to SMARTedit's next most likely choice of action, and so on, until she finds the desired action. The user is always free to correct SMARTedit and perform the desired action herself.

After the user verifies that SMARTedit has performed the correct action, she steps to the next action by invoking the *Step through macro* button again. This time, it correctly predicts with 27 percent probability that she will delete the extent of the HTML comment (Figure 11.4). The action is visualized by striking through the region that is to be deleted, rather than deleting it without warning (which caused confusion in an earlier implementation).

The user has now finished deleting the second HTML comment in the file. The next time she invokes the *Step* button, SMARTedit will again position the cursor at the beginning of the next HTML comment (Figure 11.5). However, SMARTedit is adaptive, and it has been learning from her choices even while she was asking it to make predictions. It makes this prediction with 100 percent probability based on both the original example as well as the collaborative one.

FIGURE **11.4**

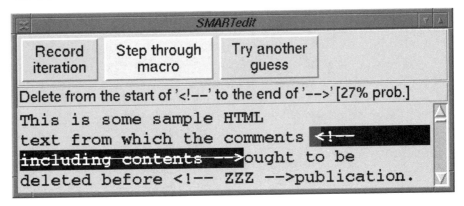

The macro predicting deletion of the entire HTML comment.

FIGURE **11.5**

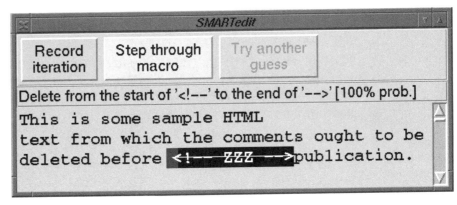

Pressing the Step button twice more to start deleting the next HTML comment with 100 percent probability.

11.3 The Smarts behind SMARTedit

We view text editing as a sequence of changes in the state of a text editor application. The state includes the cursor position (as a row and column pair), the contents of the text-editing buffer, and the contents of the clipboard.

Each text-editing action performed by the user in some state results in a new state. For instance, moving the cursor one row forward results in a new state, which differs from the initial state in that the cursor position is one row greater. Inserting a string by typing a few keys in one state results in a new state where the text-editing buffer includes the inserted string.

SMARTedit learns a macro as a sequence of functions that transform one state to another. For instance, the user's first action in the earlier example was to move the cursor to the beginning of the HTML comment; SMARTedit represented that action as a function that took a text state and output a new state in which the cursor was repositioned to lie in front of the next occurrence of the string <!--.

We have defined several classes of text-editing functions representing the types of text-editing operations people perform in an editor. For example, the class of *Move* functions takes the input state with a particular cursor location into an output state in which only the cursor location is different. Each particular *Move* function moves the cursor for a different reason; possible reasons include moving to a particular row and column, moving to the next row or column, or moving the cursor before or after the next occurrence of a search string. For example, the correct *Move* function in the prior example is the one that moves the cursor before the next occurrence of the string <!—. The class of *Insert* functions models normal typing by mapping from an input state with some text buffer into a new state in which the text buffer includes an inserted string, but nothing else has changed. Each *Insert* function inserts a different string into the text buffer. Other basic functions include deleting text, selecting text, and manipulating the clipboard by cutting, copying, and pasting the selected text.

Given this representation of text-editing actions, we view the learning process as figuring out which functions are consistent with the actions the user performed. In a programming environment, the programmer would have to directly specify exactly which function to perform using programming language constructs. However, SMARTedit reduces user effort by inferring the correct function itself. It performs inference by using demonstrated actions to rule out functions successively until only a few are left.

Figure 11.6 shows the complete space of programs SMARTedit is able to learn. We call this SMARTedit's *version space,* so named because it contains all possible versions of the target function. Mitchell (1982) first introduced version spaces as a method for visualizing and efficiently representing the search for a concept in a space of hypotheses. However, Mitchell's version space contained a single set of hypotheses. In contrast, SMARTedit's version space (as shown in the figure) is organized hierarchically according to the important concepts in the domain, using version space algebra. The algebra defines how smaller, simpler sets can be combined together to construct a

FIGURE **11.6**

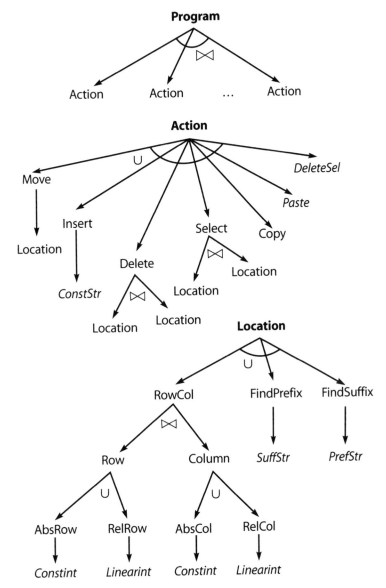

Version space algebra representation in which each node represents a set of functions transforming an input state into an output state. The contents of each node are computed from the contents of its child nodes by either union, cross product (the bowtie symbol), or transformation (unmarked).

single more complex set that retains a hierarchical structure. Functions with a similar purpose (e.g., all movement functions) are grouped together into a single set, rather than being merged with all the other types of text-editing functions.

SMARTedit assumes that the correct function is somewhere in this version space, and SMARTedit's goal is to find it. Each node in the tree represents a set of functions that are consistent with the examples seen thus far; that set is constructed out of the sets beneath it in the tree. For instance, the root of the tree, labeled *Program*, represents the set of all programs consistent with the actions the user has demonstrated. A program is made up of a sequence of *Action* nodes; each *Action* node is a union of all the different classes of text-editing functions. For example, the *Move* node represents the set of all movement functions consistent with the user's cursor repositioning activity.

Before the user records her actions, the version space initially contains the set of all learnable functions. After she has made a recording, some of those functions are thrown out of the version space because they are not consistent with (do not explain) the observed actions. For instance, if the first action a user chooses is to reposition the cursor, all functions for inserting, deleting, or selecting text are inconsistent and can be removed from consideration. The version space for the first *Action* node is updated such that all actions other than *Move* contain the empty set. Moreover, the set of movement functions is constrained to be only those functions that move to locations consistent with the observed movement.

Locations in a text file are central to text-editing programs. The *Location* node in the version space represents this concept as a set of possible locations, specified in a variety of ways. Locations can be specified as row and column position (either relative to the previous position or absolute in the file), after a certain search string, or before a search string. For instance, in the prior example, the user's intent was to move the cursor before the string <!--. In our terminology, she was conducting a suffix search; repositioning the cursor position right before the next occurrence of <!-- is one function in the *Location* version space. Locations are reused by several actions, such as determining the destination of a cursor movement action or specifying the extents of a region to be deleted.

Consider the HTML comment deletion example discussed previously. The program for that task contained two actions: a move and a deletion. Recall that the cursor started at the beginning of the line and was repositioned nineteen characters forward to lie between the word *sample* and the characters <!--. After the user has repositioned the cursor, SMARTedit's version space for the desired location is updated to be consistent with this example. The row and column version spaces are updated according to the observed

difference in row and column positions in this example. For example, a move to the absolute column 19 is consistent, as is a relative move forward nineteen columns (because the cursor started out on the zeroth column).

In addition, various string search functions may apply. In this case, the cursor ended up after the word *sample* and before the string <!--. SMARTedit can't tell whether the word *sample* is the important feature or whether perhaps the string *ample* would suffice or even just the string *le*. (It knows that the prefix *e* alone was not the important feature; otherwise, the user would have positioned the cursor after the *e* in the word *some*.) Any string, including the entire contents of the text file from the beginning to the current cursor position, may be the important feature. In fact, none of these prefix search hypotheses are correct, but SMARTedit hasn't seen enough examples to rule them out yet.

Similarly, a number of suffix search functions are consistent with the example: <, <!, <!-, <!--, and so on up to the entire contents of the text file after the cursor position.

When another example is observed (perhaps as the user is stepping through the macro on the second HTML comment), some of these hypotheses will be thrown out because they are not consistent with this new example. All of the row/column hypotheses are thrown out, because the second comment is not in the same column as the previous one (though in more structured editing tasks, the row/column hypotheses might be more important). All of the prefix search hypotheses are thrown out, because this HTML comment appears after the word *comments,* not after the word *sample.* In addition, the contents of this HTML comment differ from the previous one. Thus, the only hypotheses that remain are those that predict a suffix search of <, <!, <!-, or <!--.

Our version space algebra representation confers two advantages: an efficient representation of the set of consistent functions, and a method for structuring the function space such that related functions (e.g., all *Move* functions) are grouped together. Rather than explicitly enumerating every function hypothesis to determine which hypotheses are consistent with the examples, SMARTedit efficiently searches through this structured version space representation of consistent hypotheses to maintain its knowledge about the actions the user has performed.

11.4 Choosing the Most Likely Action

Using the version space representation, SMARTedit is able to maintain a large and complex space of function hypotheses. Given only a few examples, however, it's rare for the version space to collapse to a single function. If the version space contains several functions, SMARTedit nonetheless picks a single action to perform for the user, as follows.

First, SMARTedit captures the current state of the application. It then treats this state as an input and executes each of the functions in the version space on this input to produce a set of output states. First, SMARTedit captures the current state of the application. It then treats this state as an input and executes each of the functions in the version space on this input to produce a set of output states. If there are indeed more than one of these output states, SMARTedit chooses the most probable one based on the probability of the functions that created them. The probabilities of the functions themselves are provided by the application designer based on domain knowledge.

SMARTedit must also account for the fact that some functions may produce identical output states when applied to the same input state. For example, if the cursor is currently on row 4, moving the cursor to the next row has the same effect as moving the cursor to absolute row 5. In this situation, SMARTedit calculates the probability of each output state as the sum of the probabilities of the functions predicting that output state.

If there is more than one output state predicted by the version space, then SMARTedit must choose between them. It does so by choosing the state that has the highest probability, where an output state's probability is the sum of the probabilities of the functions that produce it.

If the chosen state matches the user's expectations, she can continue executing the next action in the learned macro. If not, she can ask SMARTedit to switch to the next most likely output state, and so on, until she finds the correct one.

In the HTML comment deletion task described earlier, SMARTedit is, in fact, able to learn how to perform the task correctly after only a single demonstration (for a total of three HTML comments correctly deleted). We have also tested SMARTedit's ability in a number of repetitive text-editing scenarios, such as converting from one XML format to another, rearranging the order of columns in a structured text file, reformatting mailing addresses from single-line to multiline, converting C-language comments to C++-style comments, and converting among the Scribe, LaTeX, and HTML formatting languages. In all cases, SMARTedit requires between one and three demonstrations before it is able to perform the task correctly on the remainder of the examples in the scenario.

1 1 .5 Making SMARTedit a More Intelligent Student

SMARTedit's current learning process—learning from observations, guessing a generalized concept, and collaborating with the user to refine those guesses—represents the first step toward "programming by teaching." SMARTedit is an intelligent student poised to learn programs for a teacher. However, it still falls short of fulfilling its role as a student; a truly intelligent student holds a much richer interaction with his teacher. Moreover, SMARTedit is not just a student but also an assistant. An automated assistant shares many traits with a good student but has the added concern of minimizing the user's burden. We see the next major steps for SMARTedit as making it a better student and assistant: taking the initiative to guide the learning process with its own questions, learning from gestures and discussion accompanying the demonstration, carrying knowledge forward from one learning episode to the next, and tempering this process with an awareness of the burden on the user.

To allow SMARTedit to take a more active role in guiding the learning process, we envision a system that takes the initiative, asking questions to clarify its knowledge. Currently, SMARTedit either learns from the user demonstrating an example or from the user's acceptance or rejection of it's guess at the next action. In both cases, the user is in control of the interaction. SMARTedit might instead guide the course of the interaction based on its assessment of the state of its knowledge. As a first step, SMARTedit can inform the user when it needs more examples and when it believes (based on the probability of its hypotheses) that it has discovered the user's procedure. With this feedback, the user can make an informed decision whether to begin examining SMARTedit's guesses or continue demonstrating examples. SMARTedit could take an even more active role by asking for information about the current action (e.g., "Are you searching for a string?"), suggesting that the user demonstrate an example other than the next one in the text or proposing a series of actions for consideration by the user rather than just one (e.g., proposing both the move and deletion from Figures 11.3 and 11.4 in one interaction).

Careful selection of the next question to ask the user will allow SMARTedit to zero in on the user's procedure more quickly. We can make these selections based on their discriminating power in SMARTedit's version space or based on the expected benefit (information gain) of each question given the current probabilities of its hypotheses. The selection of the next question for the user should also take into account the burden that question places on the user. An important, open research question is how we can balance the needs of SMARTedit's learning process against the added burden of its queries to the user. How much and what kind of effort is the user willing to expend answering these queries? How do the different queries inconvenience different users?

We can also enrich the interaction between SMARTedit and its user/ teacher by allowing the teacher to provide information outside the strict bounds of the demonstration. In informal observations, we have found that people find it quite natural to narrate their actions as they perform them. Much of the "teaching" content of the demonstrations may be in these narrations. One could imagine using these narrations in a variety of ways from simple keyword detection (e.g., the word *searching* in the narration might increase the probability of string search hypotheses) to full-fledged natural language understanding. In particular, we speculate that technologies used in information retrieval (e.g., Latent Semantic Indexing, Deerwester et al. 1990) might help connect utterances to the actions the users perform and the text they are modifying. The "hints" we get from the narrations could then be used to change the prior probabilities on each of the different version spaces, so as to prefer some functions over others.

SMARTedit should also carry aspects of its knowledge forward from one interaction to the next. Conceptually, we would like SMARTedit to learn how to deal with different users, texts, and tasks. Context in the form of user habits or document type can dramatically narrow the scope of reasonable hypotheses that SMARTedit need consider. Practically, it can support this kind of adaptation by adjusting the initial probabilities of its various hypotheses based on the identity of the user and type of file the user is editing. For example, if it detects that the user is editing a comma delimited table (e.g., a file with the .csv extension), it can increase the initial probability of string searches containing a comma.

Finally, as an intelligent assistant, SMARTedit should endeavor to reduce the burden it places on the user. Rather than asking the user to start and stop the macro recorder explicitly in between demonstrations, the system should figure out that she has demonstrated the same task twice in a row. Moreover, SMARTedit should be more robust to user errors, such as performing actions in a different order in subsequent examples or pressing the wrong key at the wrong time. A more robust SMARTedit implementation would discount the mistakes, allow the user to correct them, or even automatically correct for errors.

Together, these directions form an ambitious plan for improving SMARTedit: asking questions and proposing examples to direct the learning process, taking advantage of the user's narration of her actions, accumulating knowledge about context (users, texts, and tasks), and balancing the advantages of all of these against their burden on the user. Principled use of these techniques will result in fundamental improvements to SMARTedit—improvements that should carry over to other domains and PBD systems. A more intelligent student will ease the burden on a teacher in any domain.

11.6 Other Directions for SMARTedit

There are many other avenues of research to explore. In the immediate future, we plan to increase SMARTedit's expressiveness by elaborating SMARTedit's state representation (perhaps including features such as sentence, paragraph, and section numbers) and adding to the set of version spaces used to construct programs. Moreover, we plan to construct a larger corpus of repetitive text-editing scenarios with which to evaluate the system's performance. We expect these two avenues to complement each other, suggesting new capabilities to introduce into SMARTedit and highlighting its limitations.

Another dimension to pursue is to evaluate the system's ability to scale, both to larger and more expressive languages, and even to other domains. Will the version space approach suffice when the number of different functions grows to the hundreds or thousands? Is the version space approach appropriate for other domains besides text editing, such as spreadsheets or the desktop? We believe that careful construction of the version space hierarchy will allow our approach to scale; we envision component version spaces becoming part of a generally applicable, reusable library. Furthermore, we believe that the representation of procedures as functions over states is quite general, but undoubtedly we will find limitations in our approach when we consider different domains.

11.7 Comparison with Other Text-Editing PBD Systems

Unlike most previous text-editing PBD systems, SMARTedit uses a formal machine learning technique to describe the generalization that is performed by the system. Witten and Mo (1993) describe the TELS system that records high-level actions similar to the actions used in SMARTedit and implements a set of expert rules for generalizing the arguments to each of the actions. TELS also uses heuristic rules to match actions against each other to detect loops in the user's demonstrated program; it outperforms SMARTedit in this respect. However, TELS's dependence on heuristic rules to describe the possible generalizations makes it difficult to imagine applying the same techniques to a different domain, such as spreadsheet applications.

Nix (1985) describes the Editing by Example (EBE) system that looks not at recorded actions but at the input/output behavior of the complete demonstration. EBE attempts to find a program that could explain the observed difference between the initial and final state of the text editor. In this respect, SMARTedit is a refinement of EBE that uses not only the initial and final states but intermediate states as well. SMARTedit's approach has the drawback that it is sensitive to the order in which the user chooses to perform actions; on the other hand, it is making use of more information than EBE is given, and so SMARTedit is able to learn programs for more complex text transformations than EBE.

Masui and Nakayama (1994) describe the Dynamic Macro system for recording macros in the Emacs text editor. Dynamic Macro performs automatic segmentation of the user's actions, breaking up the stream of actions into repetitive subsequences, without requiring the user to invoke the macro recorder explicitly. Dynamic Macro performs no generalization, and it relies on several heuristics for detecting repetitive patterns of actions.

Maulsby and Witten's (1997) Cima system uses a classification rule learner to describe the arguments to particular actions, such as a rule describing how to select phone numbers in the local area code. SMARTedit is able to learn a program to select all but one of the phone numbers given a single demonstration. The anomalous phone number lacks a preceding area code and is also difficult for Cima to classify correctly. Unlike other PBD systems, Cima allows the user to give "hints" to the agent that focus its attention on certain features, such as the particular area code preceding phone numbers of interest. However, the knowledge gained from these hints is combined with Cima's domain knowledge using a set of hard-coded preference heuristics. As a result, it is never clear exactly which hypotheses Cima is considering or why it prefers one over another. In SMARTedit, these types of hints could be used to bias the probabilities on its different hypotheses.

11.8 Conclusion

We have described the SMARTedit PBD system that automates repetitive text-editing tasks. SMARTedit represents text-editing actions as functions from one text-editing state to another and uses version space algebra to represent efficiently the set of functions that are consistent with the demonstrated examples. The system learns useful text-editing procedures based on a very small number of demonstrations.

SMARTedit's version space algebra representation allows it simultaneously to maintain different beliefs about the user's desired actions. It keeps a record of all functions that could possibly explain the observed series of state changes and throws out only those functions that are inconsistent with the observed data. This representation allows SMARTedit to fail gracefully—if its best guess for the user's next action is not correct, it can fall back to the next best guess, and so on, rather than failing completely.

We believe that the holy grail of an intuitive, intelligent, and flexible PBD system is within reach. The technologies behind SMARTedit are some of the first steps toward this goal.

References

Deerwester, S., S. Dumais, G. Furnas, T. Landauer, and R. Harshman. 1990. Indexing by latent semantic analysis. *Journal of the American Society for Information Science* 41, no. 6: 391–407.

Lau, T., P. Domingos, and D. S. Weld. 2000. Version space algebra and its application to programming by demonstration. In *Proceedings of the Seventeenth International Conference on Machine Learning.* Stanford, Calif.: Morgan Kaufmann.

Masui, T., and K. Nakayama. 1994. Repeat and predict—Two keys to efficient text editing. In *Human factors in computing systems: CHI'94 Conference Proceedings.* Reading, Mass.: Addison-Wesley.

Maulsby, D. and I. H. Witten. 1997. Cima: An interactive concept learning system for end-user applications. *Applied Artificial Intelligence* 11, nos. 7–8: 653–671.

Mitchell, T. 1982. Generalization as search. *Artificial Intelligence* 18: 203–226.

Nix, Robert P. 1985. Editing by example. *ACM Transactions on Programming Languages and Systems* 7, no. 4: 600–621.

Witten, I. H., and D. Mo. 1993. TELS: Learning text editing tasks from examples. In *Watch what I do: programming by demonstration,* ed. A. Cypher. Cambridge, Mass.: MIT Press.

CHAPTER 12

Training Agents to Recognize Text by Example

HENRY LIEBERMAN

Media Laboratory
Massachusetts Institute of Technology

BONNIE A. NARDI

Agilent Labs

DAVID J. WRIGHT

Sun Microsystems

Abstract

An important function of an agent is to be "on the lookout" for bits of information that are interesting to its user, even if these items appear in the midst of a larger body of unstructured information. But how to tell these agents which patterns are meaningful and what to do with the result?

Especially when agents are used to recognize text, they are usually driven by parsers that require input in the form of textual grammar rules. Editing grammars is difficult and error-prone for end users. Grammex (Grammars by Example) is the first direct manipulation interface designed to allow nonexpert users to define grammars interactively. The user presents concrete examples of text that he or she would like the agent to recognize. Rules are constructed by an iterative process, in which Grammex heuristically parses the example and displays a set of hypotheses, and the user critiques the system's suggestions. Actions to take upon recognition are also demonstrated by example.

12.1 Text Recognition Agents

One service that agents can provide for their users is helping them deal with *semistructured information,* information that contains nuggets of semantically meaningful and syntactically recognizable items embedded in a larger body of unstructured information. Since vast amounts of interesting information are already contained in Web pages, application files, and windows, recognition could prove valuable even if that recognition is only partial (Bonura and Miller 1998). The agent can automatically recognize and extract the meaningful information, and take action appropriate to the kind of information found. Existing agents of this kind are generally preprogrammed with a recognition procedure and can only be extended with difficulty by the end user. The aim of this work is to allow users to teach the agent interactively how to recognize new patterns of data and take actions.

Our approach is to let users specify what they want by example, since learning and teaching by example is easier for people than writing in abstract formalisms. The focus in this chapter will be on agents that recognize text in interactive desktop applications, but the general approach is applicable even where the data concerned is graphical or numerical rather than text.

FIGURE **12.1**

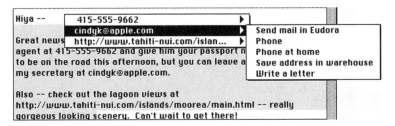

Apple Data Detectors.

The recent advent of the World Wide Web has sparked renewed interest in text-parsing technology. Parsers are also beginning to be deployed as an integral part of the text-editing facilities available across all computer applications. Examples are Apple Data Detectors (Nardi, Miller, and Wright 1998; see Figure 12.1) and the Intel Selection Recognition Agent (Pandit and Kalbag 1997). These facilities allow automatic recognition of simple, commonly occurring text patterns such as email addresses, URLs, or date formats. Whether they occur in electronic mail, spreadsheets, or Web pages, URLs can be automatically piped to Web browsers, telephone numbers to contact managers, or meeting announcements to calendars, without explicit cut-and-paste operations. LiveDoc and DropZones (Miller and Bonura 1998; Bonura and Miller 1998) go further, making recognition by the agent more automatic, highlighting recognized objects in place, permitting drag and drop of recognized objects, and allowing actions to operate on more than one object (see Figure 12.2).

Typically, the set of patterns recognized by the parser is to be programmed by a highly expert user, a grammar writer skilled in computational linguistics. The end user is merely expected to invoke the parser and use its results. However, no set of patterns supplied by experts can be complete. Chemists will want to recognize chemical formulas, stockbrokers will want to recognize ticker symbols, and librarians will want to recognize ISBN numbers, even if these abbreviations have little interest to those outside their own group. Individuals might invent their own idiosyncratic "shorthand" abbreviations for specific situations. We are interested in enabling ordinary end users to define their own text patterns.

We also expect that many text patterns will be programmed by "gardeners," users who have above-average interest and skill in using applications

FIGURE **12.2**

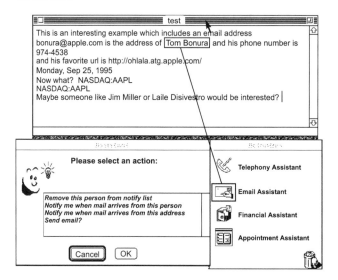

LiveDoc and DropZones.

but are still not full-time computer experts or necessarily even have programming skills. Gardeners often serve as informal consultants for a local group of users (Nardi 1993).

12.2 Writing Conventional Grammars as Text

Grammars are the traditional means of expressing a pattern in a stream of text to be identified by a parser. The usual means of defining grammars is by a text file containing rules specified in a Backus-Naur Form (BNF) syntax. The parser takes the grammar file and a target text and returns a tree of symbols used in the grammar and a correspondence between substrings of the text and each symbol. Grammar files sometimes also serve as input for grammar compilers, which output a recognizer that can subsequently be used to parse text with a single grammar.

First, we'll present a very simple example to establish the methodology. Later, we'll return to questions of complexity and scalability. Let's consider trying to teach the computer to understand the format of an electronic mail address. Examples of electronic mail addresses are `lieber@media.mit.edu`

and

`nardi@apple.com.`

This pattern is expressed in BNF as a set of context-free rules, each of which tells the computer how to recognize a certain grammatical *category*, or *nonterminal*, as a sequence of specific strings, lexical categories such as "Word" or "Number," or other nonterminals.

Below, `E-Mail-Address` is expressed in terms of `Person` and `Host`. We assume `Word` is a primitive token recognized by the parser.

```
<E-Mail-Address> := <Person> @ <Host>
<Person> := <Word>
<Host> := <Word> | <Word> . <Host>
```

Grammars are difficult for end users for many reasons. Users do not want to learn the syntax of BNF itself, and it is very easy to make mistakes. When the grammar does contain mistakes, parsers generally offer little help for determining which rule was responsible or what interaction between rules caused the problem. Grammar categories themselves can seem very abstract to users, and the effect of a set of grammar rules on concrete examples is not always clear.

Despite the difficulty of writing and editing grammars in BNF text form, users may well be comfortable with the idea of a grammar itself. If you asked a typical user, "What does an email address look like?" you'd likely get the answer, "An email address is the person's name followed by an @, followed by a host." To the further question "And what does a host look like?" would come the answer "A host is any number of words, with periods between the words." This indicates that it is the grammar format and syntax itself, and the complexities of applying them in concrete cases, rather than conceptual difficulties surrounding grammars themselves that are the problem.

12.3 Programming Grammars by Example for More Accessibility

Though abstraction is a source of power for grammars, abstraction is also what makes grammars difficult for end users. Because people have limited short-term memory, they find it difficult to keep track of how abstract concepts map to specific instances when systems grow large. People are simply much better about thinking about concrete examples than they are about abstractions such as grammar rules.

Our solution for dealing with the complexity of grammar definition is to define grammars *by example.* The need for a new text pattern will often become apparent to the user when he or she is examining some text that already contains one or several examples of the pattern. Our approach is to let the user use an example that arises naturally in their work as a basis for defining a grammar rule. Abstraction is introduced incrementally, as the user interacts with the system to provide a description of each example.

The idea for the interface is to have the user interact with a display that shows both the text example and the system's interpretation of that example (either simultaneously or at most one mouse click away). At any time, the user can direct the system to make a new interpretation of an example, or to apply the interpretations it has already learned, and display the result. By keeping a close association between the grammar categories and their effects in concrete examples, the user can always see what the effect of the current grammar is and what the effect of incremental modifications will be.

12.4 Grammex: A Demonstrational Interface for Grammar Definition

Grammex is the interface we have developed for defining grammars from examples. It consists of a set of Grammex rule windows, each containing a single text string example to be used as the definition of a single grammar rule. Text may be cut and pasted from any application. The user's task is to create a description of that example in terms of a grammar rule.

Grammex parses the text string according to the current grammar and makes mouse-sensitive the substrings of the example that correspond to grammar symbols in its interpretation. Clicking on one of the mouse-sensitive substrings brings up a list of heuristically computed guesses of possible interpretations of that substring. The user can select sets of adjacent substrings to indicate the scope of the substring to be parsed. At any time, a substring can be designated as a new example, spawning a new Grammex rule window, supporting a top-down grammar definition strategy.

There is also an overview window, containing an editable list of the examples and rules defined so far. The overall structure of the interface was inspired by the Tinker programming-by-example system (Lieberman 1993).

12.5 An Example: Defining a Grammar for Email Addresses

We start defining the pattern for E-Mail-Address by beginning with a new example that we would like to teach the system to handle. We get a new Grammex rule window and type in the name for our grammar, E-Mail-Grammar; the name of the definition, E-Mail-Address; and the example text lieber@media.mit.edu (Figure 12.3).

The Grammex window has two modes: *Edit* and *Parse.* In Edit mode, the bottom view functions as an ordinary text editor; the user can type in it or cut and paste text from other windows as the source of the example.

In Parse mode, Grammex tries to interpret the text in the example view, and the user can interactively edit the interpretation. Grammex makes pieces of the text mouse-sensitive. Initially, *lieber, @, media, ., mit, .,* and *edu* are identified as separate pieces of text, using the parser's lexical analysis. Each displays a box around it. Clicking on a piece of text brings up a pop-up menu with Grammex's interpretations of that piece of text. In Figure 12.4, the user clicks on "mit".

Grammex displays several interpretations of the chosen text, "mit". In the context of an email address, "mit" could be described as being exactly the string "m", followed by "i", then "t", or as an example of any word (string of alphanumeric characters), or as anything, meaning that any string could take the place of "mit". The default interpretation for a string depends first of all on its lexical category. In Figure 12.4, the string "mit" is a sequence of alphabetic characters, so the default interpretation is "a Word." For the punctuation character @, the default interpretation is exactly that string. The user may also select a preexisting grammar to use for the default interpretation. The Other option leads to a dialogue box that allows options

FIGURE **12.3**

"lieber@media.mit.edu" is an example email address.

12.4

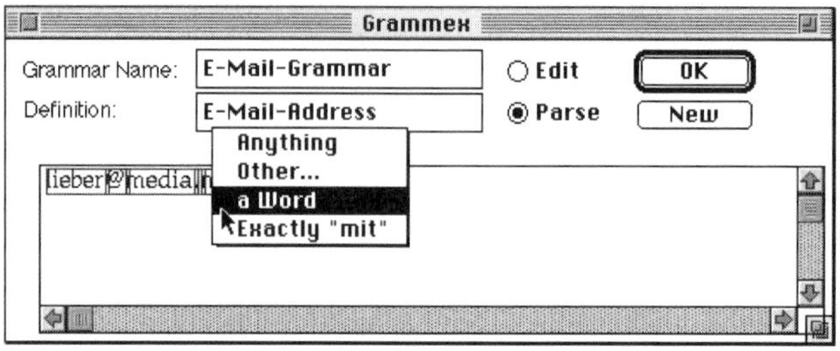

Interpretations of the string "mit."

12.5

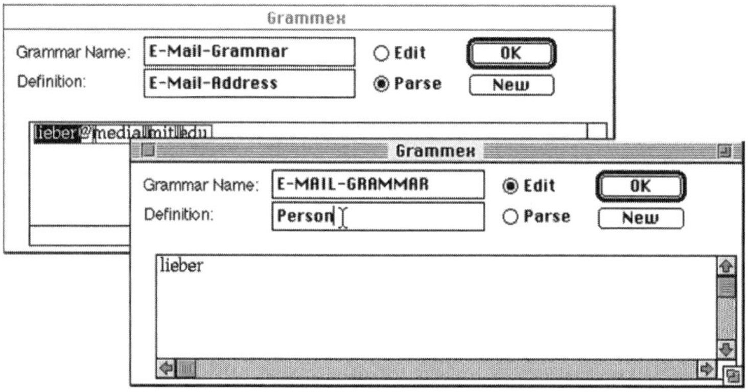

"lieber" as an example of a Person.

specific to the kind of object recognized (e.g., for numbers one can specify a range, for strings a length, etc.).

12.5.1 Top-Down Definition

We start explaining to Grammex the structure of an email address by explaining the meaning of the string "lieber," which represents the Person part of an email address (Figure 12.5). We shift-select the string "lieber," which highlights it, then select the New button, which spawns a new

FIGURE **12.6**

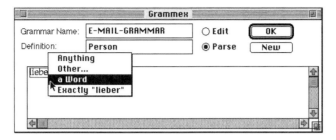

A Person as a Word.

FIGURE **12.7**

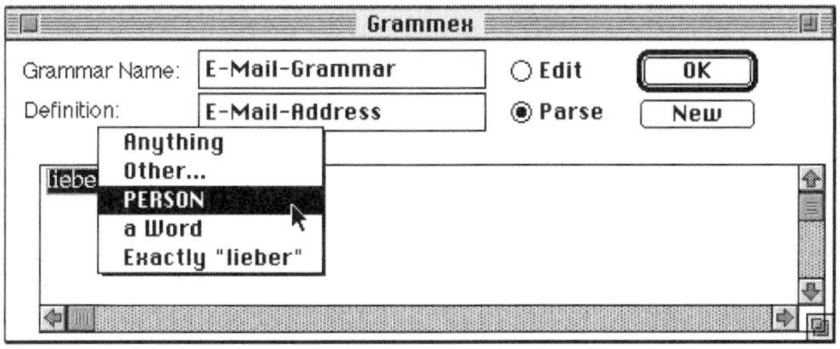

Verifying that "lieber" is recognized.

window containing just the string "lieber" and the name of our grammar, E-Mail-Grammar. We type in the name of the new definition, Person.

For Person, we accept the default interpretation of a Word (Figure 12.6). This tells the system that any word can be interpreted as being a Person. This illustrates a *top-down* style of grammar definition. Underneath the general goal of explaining to the system how to understand the text "lieber@media.mit.edu," we establish the subgoals of explaining "lieber" as a Person and, later, "media.mit.edu" as a Host. Alternatively, we could also adopt a bottom-up style of definition, starting with Person and Host, and only then passing to the full email address.

Now, when we return to defining an email address, "lieber" has an additional possible interpretation, that of a Person (Figure 12.7).

12.6 Rule Definitions from Multiple Examples

The concept of a Host is more complex than that of a Person, because we can have hosts that are simply names, such as the machine named "media", or we can have hosts that consist of a path of domains, separated by periods, such as "media.mit.edu". Thus, the definition for Host requires two examples: one of each important case.

We describe "media" as being an example of a Host being a single word, in the same way we did for "lieber" as a Person. Note in Figure 12.8 that when we choose the word "media," the possible interpretation (plausible, but wrong) of "media" being a Person crops up.

Note that if we wanted to describe a domain as an enumerated type ("edu", "com", "mil", "org", etc.), we could type in each of these as examples and choose the Exactly option for each one, such as "Exactly "edu"."

12.6.1 Definition of Recursive Grammar Rules

The second example for a Host describes the case where there is more than one component to the host name—for example, "media.mit". We select the substring "media.mit" from our original example, "lieber@media.mit.edu", and invoke New.

FIGURE **12.8**

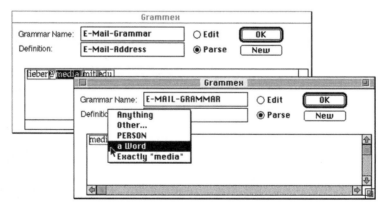

"media" as a Host.

FIGURE **12.9**

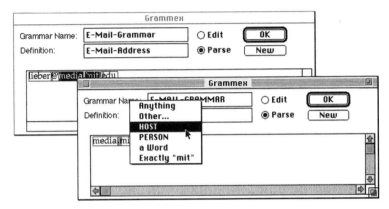

Recursively defining a Host.

The default interpretation of "media.mit" would be as "a Word," followed by a period, followed by another Word. However, while this is a possible interpretation, it does not describe the general case in such a way as could accommodate any number of host components. For that, we need to express the idea that following a period we could then have another sequence of a word, then another period, then a word; that is, we could have another Host. In our example, then, we need to change the interpretation of "mit" to be a Host rather than a word, so that we could have not just "media.mit" but also "media.mit.edu", "media.mit.cambridge.ma.us", and so forth. This is done by simply selecting "mit" and choosing the interpretation Host from the pop-up menu (Figure 12.9).

The result is now that if we ask what the interpretation of "media.mit" is, we get "a Word," then ".", then a Host (Figure 12.10). This is an important and subtle idea, the concept of defining a *recursive* grammar definition through multiple examples. One might question whether this idea might not be difficult for "ordinary end users" to grasp.

While it is unlikely that the concept of defining recursive grammars might occur spontaneously to an untrained user, we believe that Grammex offers users a gentle introduction to the concept of recursion. Initially, a user might have to be shown an example, such as defining the host as in our example. Grounding the definition process in concrete examples gives the user a way to motivate the concept and check his or her understanding at each step. Then, the user should be able to easily acquire the skill for

FIGURE **12.10**

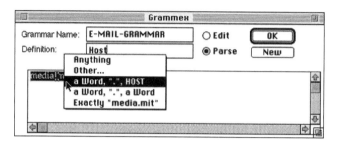

Verifying the interpretation of "media.mit."

defining similarly recursive definitions such as URLs and Unix file paths. Experience with the Logo programming language has shown that even young children can grasp the idea of recursion without difficulty if it is introduced properly.

We also intend to provide a shortcut, the two choices *Optional* and *Repeating*, which will cover the two most common cases where recursive definitions are needed. With this shortcut, one could proceed directly to the example "media.mit" and mark "." and "mit" as Repeating. This will generate two definitions automatically, one for "media" and one for "media.mit", with the same effect as the steps presented earlier.

Finally, note that no great harm is done even if the user simply accepts the initial interpretation of "media.mit" as a Word, ".", then a Word. That definition will only be good for two-component Host names. Then "media.mit.edu" could be presented as a separate example for three-component names. Two-, three- and four-component names probably constitute 95 percent of host names, which might be good enough for most users that the general case might not be worth bothering about.

Returning to our original example, we can now express the description of "lieber@media.mit.edu", verifying that it has been successfully recognized by Grammex as a Person@Host email address (Figure 12.11).

12.6.2 Managing Sets of Rule Definitions

Grammex's Grammar Window holds a list of definitions for the current grammar. Each definition defines a grammar category and has an example of the category. Figure 12.12 presents a grammar window for the email grammar.

FIGURE **12.11**

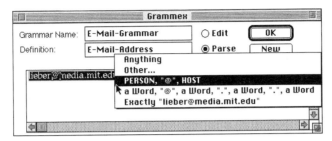

Verifying "lieber@media.mit.edu."

FIGURE **12.12**

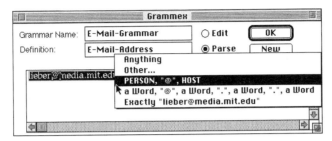

Email grammar, Examples view.

In the Categories view, each definition is represented by its sequence of categories, rather than by its example (Figure 12.13). Seeing both views shows the relationship between the example and its description. In either view, double-clicking on an entry results in editing that entry.

12.6.3 Complexity and Scalability

Although the email address example presented is very simple, the methodology itself is very general and can define grammars of arbitrary complexity. The grammar formalism used by Grammex is equivalent to context-free grammars, which are quite general and can be used to describe a wide

FIGURE **12.13**

Email grammar, Categories view.

variety of text patterns. However, released versions of Apple Data Detectors and Intel's Selection Recognition Agent currently use regular expression recognizers that do not have the full generality of context-free grammars, and some patterns require context-sensitive grammars. Defining grammars is sometimes tricky, and finding exactly the right way to describe examples to cover minor variations in formats sometimes requires some subtlety. Grammex's incremental and iterative approach means that complex grammars can be built up little by little. When an example is found that doesn't yield the desired result, that example can always be fed as input to define or modify a rule.

12.6.4 Defining Actions by Example

To make the paradigm of training agents by example complete, we would also like to define by example the actions to be taken upon recognition of a certain pattern. Previous recognition agents such as Data Detectors and Selection Recognition Agent only allow choosing from a fixed set of actions, provided in advance by someone with expertise in programming. In the case of Data Detectors, actions are programmed in the scripting language AppleScript. LiveDoc's DropZones provides for more sophisticated computation in action selection, but actions still must be programmed in advance. We would like to define the actions just at the time when the user demonstrates examples of the text to be recognized.

Our approach is to use ScriptAgent (Lieberman 1998), a programming-by-example system for the scripting language AppleScript. When the user demonstrates an example to be recognized, the system goes into a "recording" mode in which the user can demonstrate actions using other applications. For example, after we show how to recognize the email address *lieber@media.mit.edu*, the system pushes the recognized text onto the system's clipboard, and we can then demonstrate what to do with it. For example, we can enter the email program, select the *send message* operation, and paste *lieber@media.mit.edu* into the *To:* field of the message window. The system generates an AppleScript program to represent the action, generalized so it can work on any example, not just the one presented.

The clipboard interface, while convenient for actions that simply use the entire recognized text, does not allow direct access to the recognized subcomponents (e.g., user name and host name). We are experimenting with ways of allowing this, but the problem is to find one that integrates well with current Macintosh interface conventions.

The biggest problem with recording actions by example is that it depends on the aspect of applications being "recordable" (reporting user actions to the agent), and to date, very few Macintosh applications are fully recordable.

An end run around the recordability problem is to use the technique of *examinability* (Lieberman 1998), in which the agent polls the state of the applications and uses similarity-based learning to infer user actions. In Lieberman (1998), we discuss an application that achieves recordability of several specific applications (a calendar program and a spreadsheet program) by polling the states of each application (current calendar displayed and current spreadsheet displayed, respectively) and comparing states to induce the operations performed.

12.7 Future Work: Using Grammar Induction to Speed Up the Definition Process

Automatic induction of grammar rules from examples has been a well-studied topic in machine learning (see Langley 1987 for a survey and techniques). Natural language researchers study the topic to try to come to an understanding of how children learn the grammar of English by only hearing examples of adult speech and only occasionally hearing negative examples or receiving explicit instruction in grammar. What is amazing is both the difficulty of the problem and the success rate achieved!

Grammar induction is also studied in finite-state automata, data compression, and data mining applications. Typically, though, the algorithms assume that the examples are processed in a "batch" mode, rather than considering how a user might want to interact with the grammar definition process on the fly.

We have initially been quite conservative in our use of inference techniques, but using Grammex as a "front end" for some of these induction techniques holds promise for speeding up the grammar definition process. Essentially, a grammar induction algorithm could be used to generate and narrow down more intelligently the choices presented in Grammex's pop-up menus. The user need present fewer examples, and the system could even generate examples for the user's approval. Cima, discussed in the next section, represents a step in this direction.

12.8 Related Work

To our knowledge, Grammex is the first direct-manipulation interface to address the question of interactive definition and editing of grammars for end users. The closest work to this is David Maulsby's Cima (Maulsby 1994; Maulsby and Witten 1995), whose goal was also to generate grammatical patterns from presentation of concrete textual examples. Maulsby's work concentrated on developing a more sophisticated inference procedure for determining which features of the text are relevant. However, the proposed user interface for Cima consisted of simply presenting a sequence of examples, and it did not allow the interactive generalizing and specializing of parts of the rules and substrings, as does Grammex. Cima's inference techniques could also profitably be applied within Grammex's user interface framework. Tourmaline (Myers 1993) induced stylistic patterns of text formatting (e.g., fonts, sizes) rather than grammar rules, from examples.

Grammex's approach is strongly related to a similar approach for generating procedures in a programming language, called *programming by example* or *programming by demonstration* (Cypher 1993). In programming by example, the user demonstrates a sequence of operations in an interactive interface, and the system records these steps and the objects they were performed on. Machine learning techniques are used to generalize the program so that it works on examples analogous to the ones originally presented.

In our approach, the examples are sample text strings, and the programs are grammar rules. Many programming-by-example systems use some form of heuristic inference to infer generalized descriptions of the operations used to compute the examples. Unlike programming systems, though, grammar rules themselves can be thought of as generalized descriptions of the examples. We solve the inference problem by heuristically "running the grammar backward" to suggest possible generalizations of a given example. The user chooses from a set of plausible generalizations or proposes his or her own generalizations.

12.9   Conclusion

This chapter has presented Grammex, a demonstrational interface for defining rules for simple context-free grammars from concrete examples. A new rule is defined by directing the system to guess an interpretation of an example string, based on the current grammar, and then modifying this guess using operations that generalize or specialize parts of the rule. By keeping a close association between the grammar rules and their consequences in specific examples of interest to the user, we can give the user the power of grammar and parsing formalisms, without the abstraction and syntactic complications that prevent them from being easy to use.

Acknowledgements

Bonnie Nardi was at Apple Computer at the time of this project, and Henry Lieberman was a consultant to Apple. Jim Miller deserves thanks for providing support for the work on this project. Tom Bonura provided valuable insights and contributed code for the editor. Bob Strong contributed the code for the parser. Lieberman's research was sponsored in part by Apple Computer, British Telecom, IBM, Exol spA, the European Community, the National Science Foundation, the Digital Life Consortium, the News in the Future Consortium, and other sponsors of the MIT Media Laboratory.

References

Bonura, T., and J. Miller. 1998. Drop Zones: An extension to LiveDoc. *SigCHI Bulletin* 30, no. 2 (April): 59–64.

Cowie, J. and W. Lehnert. 1996. Information extraction. *Communications of the ACM* 39, no. 1 (January).

Cypher, A., ed. 1993. *Watch what I do: Programming by demonstration.* Cambridge, Mass.: MIT Press.

Langley, P. 1987. *Machine learning and grammar induction. Machine Learning Journal* 2: 5–8.

Lieberman, H. 1993. Tinker: A programming by demonstration system for beginning programmers. In *Watch what I do: Programming by demonstration,* ed. A. Cypher. Cambridge, Mass.: MIT Press.

———. 1998. Integrating user interface agents with conventional applications. In *ACM Conference on Intelligent User Interfaces* (San Francisco, January).

Maulsby, D. 1994. Instructible agents. Ph.D. diss. University of Calgary, Alberta, Canada.

Maulsby, D., and I. H. Witten. 1995. Learning to describe data in actions. In *Proceedings of the Programming by Demonstration Workshop, Twelfth International Conference on Machine Learning* (Tahoe City, Calif., July).

Miller, J., and T. Bonura. 1998. From documents to objects: An overview of LiveDoc. *SigCHI Bulletin* 30, no. 2 (April): 53–59.

Myers, B. Tourmaline: Text formatting by demonstration. In *Watch what I do: Programming by demonstration,* ed. A. Cypher. Cambridge, Mass.: MIT Press.

Nardi, B. 1993. *A small matter of programming perspectives on end user computing.* Cambridge, Mass.: MIT Press.

Nardi, B., J. Miller, and D. Wright. 1998. Collaborative, programmable intelligent agents. *Communications of the ACM* (March).

Pandit, M., and S. Kalbag. 1997. The selection recognition agent: Instant access to relevant information and operations. In *Proceedings of Intelligent User Interfaces '97.* New York: ACM Press.

CHAPTER 13

SWYN: A Visual Representation for Regular Expressions

ALAN F. BLACKWELL

Computer Laboratory
University of Cambridge

Abstract

People find it difficult to create and maintain abstractions. We often deal with abstract tasks by using notations that make the structure of the abstraction visible. Programming-by-example (PBE) systems sometimes make it more difficult to create abstractions. The user has to second-guess the results of the inference algorithm and sometimes cannot see any visual representation of the inferred result, let alone manipulate it easily. SWYN (See What You Need) addresses these issues in the context of constructing regular expressions from examples. It provides a visual representation that has been evaluated in empirical user testing and an induction interface that always allows the user to see and modify the effects of the supplied examples. The results demonstrate the potential advantages of more strictly applying cognitive dimensions analysis and direct manipulation principles when designing systems for PBE.

13.1 Introduction

Most programming tasks involve the creation of abstractions that can be broadly grouped into two categories: abstractions over context and abstractions over time. An *abstraction over context* defines some category of situations—objects or data—and allows the programmer to define operations on all members of that category. An *abstraction over time* defines events that will happen in the future as a result of the present actions of the programmer. Both of these are potentially labor-saving devices. A good abstraction can be used as a kind of mental shorthand for interacting with the world.

However, creating abstractions is difficult and risky (Green and Blackwell 1996; Blackwell and Green 1999). This is why PBE seems like such a good idea. It is computationally feasible to derive an abstraction from induction over a set of examples. If the abstraction is over context, the examples might include selections of words within a document or files within a directory structure. If the abstraction is over time, the examples can be demonstrations of the actions that the program ought to carry out in the future.

13.1.1 Factors in the Usability of PBE Systems

The consequences for the user that result from this approach to programming can be discussed in terms of Green's framework for usability design of programming languages: the Cognitive Dimensions of Notations (Green 1989; Green and Petre 1996; Green and Blackwell 1998). This chapter will not include an extended presentation of the framework, since many published descriptions are available, but the resulting analysis would include observations of the following kind: PBE offers superb *closeness of mapping* between the programming environment and the task domain, because in PBE the task domain *is* the programming environment. However, PBE imposes severe *premature commitment*—the PBE programmer must specify actions in exactly the same order that the program is to execute them, unlike conventional programming languages. A full cognitive dimensions analysis of PBE systems would be enlightening: they are likely to be *error-prone*, for example, and it is often difficult to apply *secondary notation* such as comments to explain why a particular abstraction was created.

As with all programming languages, most designs for PBE systems have both advantages and disadvantages. No programming language can be the "best" language, because while some tasks are made easier by one language feature, the same feature can make other tasks more difficult (Green, Petre, and Bellamy 1991). In the case of PBE systems, a critical feature of this type is the question of whether a representation of the inferred program should be made visible to the user. This is the cognitive dimension of *visibility*. Some ordinary programming environments make it difficult to see the whole program at once, but in PBE systems the program is completely invisible, on the grounds that the programming process should be completely transparent to the user. These systems create abstractions by induction from examples, but the programmer is unable to see those abstractions. The disadvantage of this approach is that it results in concomitant degradation in other dimensions. An invisible abstraction exhibits high *viscosity* (resistance to change) because it is difficult to change something that you cannot see, and any relationships between different abstractions are certain to create *hidden dependencies* if the abstractions themselves are invisible.

The user's experience of PBE without access to a visible representation of the inferred program might be compared to repairing a loose part inside a closed clock by shaking the clock—you know that everything you do has some effect, but you don't know what that effect has been until you see and hear it working. If the clock is very simple on the inside and you understand how it works, it might be possible to succeed. Unfortunately, the most powerful PBE systems employ sophisticated inference algorithms such that it can be quite difficult to anticipate the effect of adding one more instructional trace. The task of constructing a training set for these algorithms can be difficult for a computer scientist; for an end user, the clock-shaking analogy may be an apt description of the experience of PBE without a program representation. Other chapters in this book, including 3 and 16, have referred to the problem of "feedback" in PBE, but analysis in terms of cognitive dimensions makes it clear that the problem is far more extensive than simply a question of feedback.

13.1.2 A Test Case for Visibility in PBE

This chapter describes an investigation of a very simple experimental case that has been chosen to test the preceding argument. The programming domain is that of the earliest types of PBE system—simple text processing, in which text strings are identified by example, in order to be transformed in a systematic way. The simplest example of such a transformation is a search-and-replace operation. Even search and replace can be regarded as programming, because it is an abstraction-creating activity. The search expression is a transient abstraction over occurrences of some string in a document, although this "program" is usually discarded immediately after it has been executed.

However, straightforward search and replace is not a very interesting task in programming terms. A more interesting case is where the search expression includes wild cards, especially the extended types of wild card matching that are provided by regular expressions. Regular expressions have interesting computational properties, are widely used in powerful programmers' editors, and are of interest in a machine-learning context because the acquisition of regular expressions from examples is a nontrivial induction problem. Furthermore, regular expressions can be used as the core of a powerful language for specifying text-processing scripts, as in sed, awk, or the Perl language (Wall, Christiansen, and Schwartz 1996).

Regular expressions are also interesting from the perspective of usability. In a system in which regular expressions can be inferred from examples, it is still not clear that users will benefit from being shown the resulting expression. This is not because it is a bad thing for users to see the result of PBE inference but because regular expressions themselves are confusing and difficult to read. They appear to be one of the features of Perl that is most difficult for users; popular Perl texts such as Christiansen and Torkington (1998) or Herrman (1997) preface their chapters on regular expressions with grim warnings about the difficulties that are in store for the reader. A brief analysis in terms of Cognitive Dimensions of Notations suggests that the problems with regular expressions may be a result of the notational conventions.

Green (personal communication, 15 June, 1999) points out that the conventional regular expression notation is difficult to parse for a number of reasons:

- some of the symbols are ill chosen (notably / and \);

- the indication of scope by paired elements such as () {} [] is likely to cause perceptual problems;

- the targets to be matched and the control characters describing the match requirements are drawn from the same alphabet; and

- the notation is extremely terse; discriminability is reduced and redundancy is very low, so that in general a small random change produces a new well-formed expression rather than a syntax error.

Furthermore, there is no clear mental model for the behavior of the expression evaluator. If the notation indicated some execution mechanism (Blackwell 1996) or allowed users to imagine executing it themselves (Watt 1998), it could be more easily related to program behavior. These considerations give two potential avenues for improvement of regular expressions; both are tested in the experiment described here.

13.1.3 Summary of Objectives

The system described in this chapter is named See What You Need (SWYN). It is able to infer regular expressions from text examples in a context that improves visibility in several important ways:

- The user is always able to see the set of examples that the inference algorithm is using.

- The user is able to see the regular expression that has been inferred from the examples.

- The regular expression is displayed in a form that makes it easier to understand.

- The user is able to see the effect of the inferred expression in the context of the displayed data.

After the next section, which reviews other similar research, the body of the chapter describes three important components of SWYN. The first is the method by which the user selects examples and reviews the current effect of the inferred expression. The second is the induction algorithm that is used to infer and update a regular expression based on those examples. The third is a visualization technique that allows users to review and directly modify the inferred expression.

13.2 Other PBE Systems for Inferring Regular Expressions

As described earlier, the inference of text transformations such as search-and-replace expressions was one of the earliest applications of programming by example. Nix's (1985) Editing by Example prototype allowed users to define input and output sample texts, from which a general transformation was inferred. The user gave a command to execute the current hypothesis, which resulted in a global search and replace according to the inferred hypothesis. The system provided an undo facility to reverse the command if the hypothesis was incorrect.

Mo and Witten's TELS system (Mo and Witten 1992; Witten and Mo 1993) could acquire complete procedural sequences from examples, including series of cursor movements, insertions, and deletions, in addition to the search-and-replace functionality of Nix's system. If inserted text varied between examples, the inferred program would stop and invite the user to insert the required text, rather than try to infer the text that was required.

Masui and Nakayama proposed the addition of a "repeat" key to a text editor, which would execute dynamically created macros (Masui and Nakayama 1994). Their system continually monitored the user's actions, inferring general sequences. At any time, the user could press the "repeat" key, and the system would respond by repeating the longest possible sequence of actions that had been inferred from the immediately preceding input.

The acquired description of the input text in these systems is in the form of regular expressions (Nix uses the term "gap expression" to describe a regular expression with additional specification of transformed output text). It would be possible to display the inferences to the user in various forms, such as those introduced later in this chapter. However, previous systems that infer text-editing programs from examples have extremely poor *visibility* when considered as programming languages: they effectively hide the completed program from the user. They require that the user work only by manipulating the data, with the option of rejecting incorrect hypotheses after observing the results of executing an undesired inferred program. Several previous PBE systems have recognized this problem and have provided visual representations of the inferred program. Early systems include PURSUIT (Modugno and Myers 1993) and Chimera (Kurlander and Feiner 1993), while SMARTedit, described elsewhere in this book (see Chapter 11), provides a highly expressive program representation language.

Only one example-based text-processing system has addressed the question of how textual inferences should be presented to a user without programming skills. In the Grammex (Grammars by Example) system, also described in this book (see Chapter 12), the user assigns meaningful names to the subexpressions that have been inferred by the system. The result is similar to the process followed when defining BNF grammars for language compilers. No attempt has yet been made to evaluate the usability of the Grammex system, but some of the usability implications can be anticipated on the basis of cognitive dimensions. A system in which the user must identify and name the abstractions being created is *abstraction-hungry*, and this property tends to constitute an initial obstacle for inexperienced users. However, the ability to create names is a simple but effective example of *secondary notation*—allowing users to add their own information to the representation. An even more valuable form of secondary notation would be the ability to add further annotations that could be used to describe intended usage, design rationale, or other notes to future users.

13.3 A User Interface for Creating Regular Expressions from Examples

The usability improvements that SWYN aims to provide over previous demonstration-based systems are

- that the user should be able to predict what inference will result from the selection of examples,

- that the inferred program should be visible to the user,

- that the user should be able to anticipate the effects of running the inferred program, and

- that the user should be able to modify the inferred program.

The initial state of the SYWN interface is a simple display of all the text that is a candidate for selection by a regular expression. If integrated into a word processor as an advanced search-and-replace facility, the display could simply be the regular word processor display, and SWYN could be invoked as a search-and-replace mode analogous to the incremental search mode of the EMACS editor.

The user starts to create the regular expression by choosing a string within the displayed text (dragging the mouse over it). The chosen string is highlighted, and every other occurrence of the same string within the text is also highlighted (in a different color), as in Figure 13.1. What the user sees is the set that would be selected when executing the regular expression defined so far. Of course, after choosing only a single example, the regular expression created so far is identical to the example, so all the highlighted strings are the same.

The user can then refine the regular expression by choosing another example, one that is not already selected. The regular expression is modified by induction over the two chosen examples, using the algorithm described in the next section. The highlighted selection set is immediately changed to show the user the effect of this new regular expression, as in Figure 13.2. At this point the selection set will be larger than the initial selection set,

FIGURE **13.1**

Selection set after choosing "wibble" as an example.

FIGURE **13.2**

wibble wobble tries to nobble
wibbre wobble tries to nobble
wibble wubbse tries to nobble
wibble wobble tries to nobble
wibble wobble tries to nobble
wibble wobble tries to nobble
wibble wobble tries to nobble
wibble wobble tries to nobble
wibble wubble tries to nobble
wibbbbbbble tries to trouble
wibbne wobble tries to nobble

Selection set after adding the new example "wibbne".

FIGURE **13.3**

wibble wobble tries to nobble
wibbre wobble tries to nobble
wibble wubbse tries to nobble
wibble wobble tries to nobble
wibble wobble tries to nobble
wibble wobble tries to nobble
wibble wobble tries to nobble
wibble wobble tries to nobble
wibble wubble tries to nobble
wibbbbbbble tries to trouble
wibbne wobble tries to nobble

Selection set after adding the new example "wubble".

because the regular expression is more general—it includes both chosen examples, and possibly other strings sharing their common features, as described in the next section.

The user can continue to expand the definition of the regular expression by choosing further examples of the kinds of string that should be selected. Every choice of a positive example results in a generalization of regular expression and an increase in the size of the displayed selection set, as in Figure 13.3. However the user can also make the regular expression more specialized by choosing a negative example—a string that should not be

FIGURE **13.4**

wibble wobble tries to nobble
wibbre wobble tries to nobble
wibble wubbse tries to nobble
wibble wobble tries to nobble
wibble wobble tries to nobble
wibble wobble tries to nobble
wibble wobble tries to nobble
wibble wobble tries to nobble
wibble wubble tries to nobble
wibbbbbbble tries to trouble
wibbne wobble tries to nobble

Selection set after choosing a negative example, "wobble".

included in the selection set. Negative examples are chosen by highlighting them in a different color—currently red rather than the green of positive examples (although this brings obvious usability problems for color-blind users). When a negative example is chosen, the regular expression is modified by performing induction on a negative example, which will have the effect of making the regular expression more specialized, as described in the next section. The size of the current selection set will therefore be reduced after choosing a negative example, as shown in Figure 13.4.

The ability to choose negative examples is an extremely valuable way to improve the usability of PBE systems. Much research into the acquisition of programs from examples has concentrated on the theoretical problem of inference from positive examples only (e.g., Angluin 1980). Induction algorithms can be made more efficient and accurate when they have access to negative examples, so training sets can be defined more quickly (Dietterich and Michalski 1984). Furthermore, people naturally describe contextual abstractions in terms of negative exemplars. Human definitions of conceptual categories often employ negative exemplars to describe an excluded category (Johnson-Laird 1983). In the context of SWYN, the ability to work from negative examples also provides an important feature of direct manipulation—the effect of actions should be not only immediately visible but easily reversible (Shneiderman 1983). If I choose an example string that causes the selection set to become too general, it is easy and natural to point to a string that should not have been selected and allow the induction algorithm to correct the problem through specialization of the regular expression.

Future versions of SWYN will add a further means of choosing examples. The probabilistic induction algorithm described at the end of the next section is able to identify strings that are borderline cases—the user may or may not want them included. If the system knew which the user wanted, this would allow the induction algorithm to remove ambiguities from the regular expression. Borderline cases would be highlighted in a different color from the rest of the selection set, giving a cue to the user of the best way to refine the regular expression. The user can then decide on the appropriate action for each borderline case, simply choosing them as negative or positive examples in the usual way.

13.4 A Heuristic Algorithm for Regular Expression Inference

The current implementation of the inference algorithm used in SWYN has been designed to operate using heuristics whose effects can be anticipated by the user. The approach taken is an extension of the heuristic method proposed by Mo and Witten (1992). Their heuristic approach improved on that of Nix (1985) by defining typed character classes as components of the inferred strings. They suggest that users would normally have some class of characters in mind when selecting examples and that the function of the inference heuristics should be to identify the class that the user intended.

The heuristic algorithm currently implemented in SWYN incrementally modifies the regular expression in response to new examples chosen by the user. A graph reduction algorithm identifies common elements of the examples and produces minimal regular expressions composed of common character classes. This process is illustrated in Figure 13.5, which shows the effects of choosing the first two strings in the figures of the previous section.

When a new positive example is chosen, it is added to the graph as a complete alternative expression. Alternatives are branches in the regular expression graph, as shown in Figure 13.5(a). This graph is then reduced by merging common elements at the beginning or end of alternative branches. The result of this merging process is shown in Figure 13.5(b). Where the graph reduction produces alternatives that are single characters, these are merged into the smallest general character class, as shown in Figure 13.5(c). The character class can later be refined by choosing negative examples or by directly manipulating the regular expression itself, as described later in the chapter.

FIGURE **13.5**

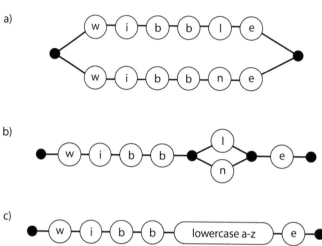

Regular expressions induction by heuristic graph reduction: (a) addition of new exemplar as an alternative, (b) reduction of common elements in alternative branches, and (c) replacement of single-letter alternatives with a character class.

Repeated elements in the regular expression are also inferred using graph reduction heuristics. Figure 13.6 shows the effect of adding an example that can be explained as a repeated character in the regular expression. Where an alternative branch consists solely of repeated elements (either a repeated single character or repeated subexpressions), these are identified as a repeated component of the regular expression, as in Figure 13.6(c). Repeated branches are then merged with any occurrences of the repeat before or after the branch, as in Figure 13.6(d).

13.4.1 Probabilistic Algorithm

The heuristic algorithm described earlier is both deterministic and predictable, but it may not always result in optimal regular expressions. In the context of SWYN, this is completely intentional. It is better that the user should be able to imagine the result of choosing new examples than that the results be optimal. Just as Mo and Witten made some assumption about the classes of characters that would most likely be intended by the user, this heuristic

FIGURE **13.6**

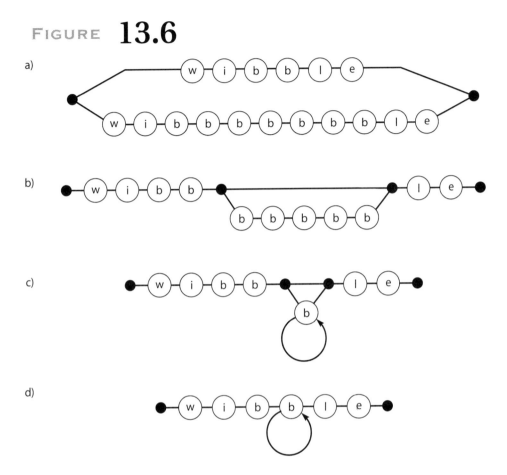

Heuristics for inferring repeated sections of regular expression.

graph reduction approach makes some assumptions about the types of regular expression structure that are most likely intended by the user. This usability feature does result in some loss of generality, but it is always possible for the user to optimize the expression by direct manipulation, as described later in the chapter.

However, an alternative is to use a probabilistic algorithm, in which the examples chosen have more influence on the intended expression. Current work on SWYN is replacing the simple graph heuristics described earlier with a probabilistic model based on stochastic context-free grammars, in which alternative grammars can be assigned probabilities on the basis of the examples that the user has chosen. A great advantage of this new approach is that text not yet chosen by the user can also be assigned probabilities according to different interpretations of the grammar. A string that may be matched by one possible interpretation but not by another can then be classed as ambiguous and brought to the user's attention as a priority for his or her next decision.

13.5   A Visual Notation for Regular Expressions

The previous sections have described the activity of creating a regular expression from examples, as though the user might be able to see and modify not only the examples and resulting selection set but the expression itself. It would certainly be a good thing if that were possible, for reasons described earlier. In fact, the previous section did provide a kind of visual representation of the regular expression for the benefit of you, the reader. The graphs drawn in the discussion of the graph reduction algorithm are very useful in understanding how the algorithm works, and they included some *ad hoc* syntactic elements that provide clues about how one might represent regular expressions visually—a loop with an arrow represented repetition of a character, and a solid black circle represented the beginning and end of alternate subexpressions.

It is difficult to develop usable new visual representations from purely theoretical considerations. The design of visual representations is partly a craft skill and partly a question of cognitive science, in which experimental evidence can be used to assess alternatives. The SWYN project is based on cognitive research into reasoning with diagrammatic representations (Blackwell et al., in press) and has taken the second approach to the design of visual notation.

This section reports an experiment that evaluated four potential representations of regular expressions: conventional regular expressions and three alternatives. Altogether, two of the four alternatives presented the regular expressions in declarative form, while two suggested an explicit order of evaluation. Furthermore, two of the alternative notations used only conventional characters from the ASCII character set, while two used graphical conventions in a way that might be described as a "visual" regular expression. The design of the experiment allowed the effects of these factors to be compared.

13.5.1   Experiment: Evaluation of Alternative Representations

The four notations used in this experiment expressed equivalent information in very different forms. The first of these was that of conventional regular expressions, although a slightly constrained subset was used. One example is that the "+" command was used rather than the "*" command, because the latter often mystifies novices when it matches null strings. Figure 13.7 shows a typical example of a regular expression that was used in the experiment: this example matches a range of English telephone numbers: 01223 613234, 0044 1223 356319, 0044 1223 354319, and so forth. Note that it also matches some strings that are *not* valid English phone numbers, such as 0044 1223 303. This is intentional—it is typical of the problems encountered by novices when using regular expressions, and the experiment specifically tested whether users were able to recognize valid matches even when they were inconsistent with environmental knowledge.

The second alternative notation is still textual, but it defines a strict order of evaluation that can be followed by the user. It also replaces the cryptic control characters of the regular expression with English instructions. An example, logically identical to Figure 13.7, is given in Figure 13.8.

The third alternative notation is declarative, as in conventional regular expressions, but it uses graphical cues in place of control characters. These cues are easily distinguished from the characters in the search expression, both visually and semantically. Some of the cues—spatial enclosure, for example—are so familiar that an explanation seems redundant. Nevertheless, participants in the experiment were provided with a legend defining the meaning of each graphical element. An example of this notation is shown in Figure 13.9(a), and the explanatory legend is in Figure 13.9(b).

The final alternative notation is both graphical and procedural. It might be regarded as a state transition diagram, typical of those used in computer science classes in which regular expressions are taught in terms of finite state automata, or for teaching language grammars. Participants in this experiment, however, treated the notation as an imperative flowchart. An

FIGURE **13.7**

(0|0044)1223 [356][0–9]+

Regular expression defining a set of phone numbers.

FIGURE **13.8**

> Find one of the following:
>   a) either the sequence "0" or
>   b) the sequence "0044"
> followed by the sequence "1223"
> followed by any one of these
> characters: "3" or "5" or "6"
> followed by at least one, possibly more,
> of the following:
>   -any one of these characters: any
>   one from "0" to "9"

Procedural expression defining the same set as that in Figure 13.7.

FIGURE **13.9**

(a)

a	boxes group sequences together
aa / bb	means either the sequence aa, or the sequence bb can go here
?	means any character can go here
k–n / b a	means that one of the characters a, b or k...n (k,l,m,n) can go here
a	means that "a" must occur at least once but possibly more times

(b)

Visual declarative expression defining (a) the same set as that in Figure 13.7, and (b) legend defining notation C.

example of the procedural graphical notation is shown in Figure 13.10(a), and the explanatory legend in Figure 13.10(b).

13.5.2 Method

The participants in the evaluation experiment were thirty-nine post-graduate students from Oxford and Cambridge Universities, studying a wide range of arts and science disciplines. None were previously familiar with regular expressions, but this population clearly has a high level of intelligence and might be expected to learn principles of programming more quickly than average.

Each participant was given an instruction booklet. The first two pages described the experiment and presented the four different notations. This introduction did not refer to programming, which has been found to intimidate participants in previous experiments on programming notations. Instead, it described the expressions as being experimental formats for use in Internet search.

The following twelve pages in the experiment booklet presented twelve different tasks, all chosen to represent typical regular expressions that might be constructed to represent user abstractions. The tasks included identification of post codes, telephone numbers, market prices, food ingredients, car license numbers, examination marks, email addresses, and Web pages. Each page presented a single regular expression in one of the four formats and five candidate text strings that might or might not match the expression. The participant was asked to mark each of the five candidates with a tick or a cross to show whether it would be matched by this regular expression. Participants also used a stopwatch to record the amount of time that they spent working on each page.

The twelve tasks were divided into six pairs. Within each pair the structures of the two expressions were made as similar as possible, then disguised by using examples from different fields (e.g., post codes vs. car registrations). A different notation format was used for each half of the pair. The six pairs of tasks thus allowed direct comparison of all combinations of the four regular expression notations: format A with format B in one pair, A-C in another, A-D, B-C, B-D, and C-D. For each participant in the experiment it was therefore possible to compare their performance on similar tasks using each pair of alternative notations. Performance comparisons were made according to two measures: the completion time for each page and the accuracy of responses for that page.

FIGURE **13.10**

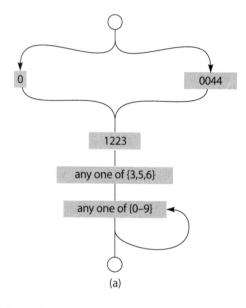

(a)

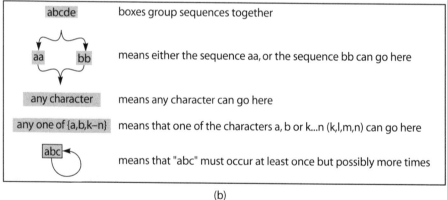

(b)

Visual procedural expression defining (a) the same set as that in Figure 13.7 and (b) legend defining notation D.

The assignment of notational formats to pairs and to individual tasks was varied across all participants, as was the presentation order for the different formats. Each participant carried out three tasks using each of the four notations, but every participant had a different assignment of notations to tasks.

TABLE **13.1**

Overall performance results.

	Time(s)	*N errors*
Conventional regular expression	117.6	60
Procedural text	106.7	48
Declarative graphic	86.1	48
Procedural graphic	86.2	38

13.5.3 Results

The notational format used to carry out the tasks had a highly significant effect on performance, $F(38,1) = 26.8$, $p < .001$. As shown in Table 13.1, all the alternative notations were completed more quickly on average than conventional regular expressions. Furthermore, the two graphical formats resulted in fewer errors.

More detailed analysis shows that the use of a graphical format has a significant effect on completion time: the average completion time for all graphical notations was 86.1 versus 112.1 seconds for the two textual notations, $F(38,1) = 26.0$, $p < .001$. In contrast, the mean difference between the two declarative (101.8 s) and the two procedural (96.4 s) notations was nonsignificant.

An investigation of the individual pairings across all participants confirmed that there were statistically significant improvements in performance, first when using the procedural graphical format rather than the procedural text format and, second, when using the declarative graphic format rather than conventional regular expressions, $t(39) = 2.57$, $p < .02$ and $t(39) = 5.18$, $p < .001$, respectively.

With notational conventions such as these, it is reasonable to ask whether more verbose notations like the procedural text might be appropriate for novices because they are easier at first sight, even though their diffuseness might make them inconvenient after more practice (Green and Petre 1996). In fact, the terse notations of languages such as C or Perl are justified by the complementary argument—that the verbose prompts needed by novices are not appropriate for expert users. A further analysis therefore compared performance on the first task encountered by each participant and on the last six tasks, to test whether any notation provides disproportionate early advantages while being slower with practice. The

TABLE **13.2**

Performance for first and later tasks.

	Mean time on first task(s)	Percentage wrong in first task(s)	Mean time on last six tasks	Percentage wrong in last six tasks
Conventional regular expression	198	64	104	47
Procedural text	207	44	82	37
Declarative graphic	110	25	77	47
Procedural graphic	123	9	71	27

results in Table 13.2 show that procedural text suffers an even greater disadvantage in speed when it is encountered first, and it is still not as accurate as the graphical alternatives. Furthermore, a comparison of performance speed relative to the experimental presentation order found that the most highly correlated improvement in performance over the course of the experiment was for the procedural graphic notation, $r = .41$, $p < .001$. This format was thus the most accurate initially, almost the fastest initially, and still provided the greatest improvement in performance with further practice. The declarative graphical format, on the other hand, appears to have been more error prone toward the end of the experiment.

13.5.4 Discussion

It is clear that graphical notations provide a large improvement in usability over conventional regular expressions for typical comprehension tasks. Clearer text formats that use typographic devices such as indenting and have interpretative information included in the notation may perform slightly better overall. But this slight advantage does not reduce the number of errors, and there is no clear advantage for first-time users.

In fact, the format that is the least error-prone overall also provides the greatest improvements in usability with practice. It has the disadvantage common to many graphical notations: it requires far more screen space than conventional regular expressions. For this reason, the declarative graphical format may be more effective in practical programming applications. It still provides large improvements in usability over the conventional notation, and it is sufficiently compact that it can be used *in situ*, in place of conventional regular expressions. The last part of this chapter describes a prototype text editor using this notation.

13.6 An Integrated Facility for Regular Expression Creation

This section describes an approach toward integrating all of these elements in a text-processing environment such as a word processor. It applies the declarative graphical format that was evaluated in the previously described experiment, and it integrates this into the user's environment so that regular expressions can easily be created from examples. The graphical representation of the regular expression is displayed continuously and is updated in response to each selection of a positive or negative example. The regular expression is overlaid on the text window, so that the direct correspondence between the regular expression and the most recently selected string can be indicated via superimposed graphical links. The simple syntax of the representation means that it can be made partially transparent, so that it is completely integrated into the task context.

13.6.1 Visual Integration with Data

This integration is further enhanced by a simple correspondence between the color of selected example strings in the task domain and coloring of the elements of the visual representation. Required parts of the regular expression are colored green, and parts that must not occur (e.g., excluded character sets) are colored red. This creates a visual link to the green and red colors that are used to highlight positive and negative examples in the text and also to the green outline displayed around all members of the current selection set.

The resulting visual appearance for SWYN is shown in Figure 13.11. The structure of the displayed regular expression is indicated by simple blocks of color, and alternate subexpressions are linked by a containing colored region. Only two special syntactic elements are used: a wild card character to represent potential character sets and a style of decorative border to indicate repetition. Both use existing conventions—the wild card element is represented by a question mark, and the repetition border uses the conventional visual cue of a "stack" of cards.

FIGURE **13.11**

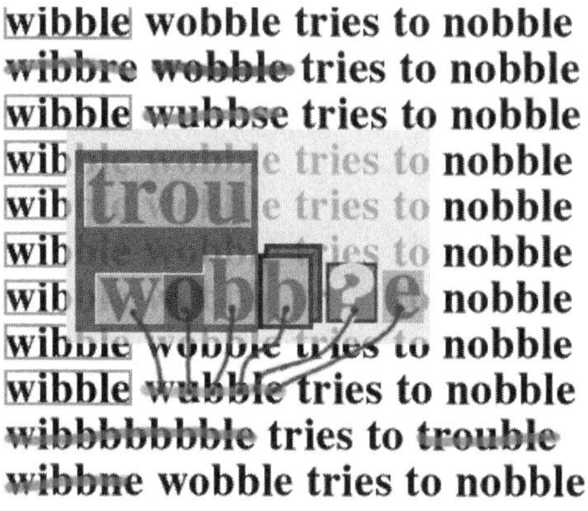

User interface for specification and display of regular expressions. The word "wobble" on the second row from the top is annotated in red, and the box around the letter "o" in the center of the screen is red. (This greyscale reproduction obscures the red and green annotations. See Figure 13.11 in the color insert for full-color image.)

The regular expression is also directly related to the user's most recent action by drawing correspondence lines between the letters of the most recently selected example string and the elements of the visual representation. This allows the user to see immediately what effect each new example has had on the inferred result.

13.6.2 Modification of the Regular Expression

In addition to refining the regular expression by selecting further positive and negative examples, the SWYN visual expression supports two more specialized ways to modify the regular expression. The first of these is by direct manipulation of the visual expression itself. The most important direct manipulation facility supported by the currently implemented algorithms is the ability to select elements of the regular expression and redefine them. As described earlier, the induction algorithm assumes very general character sets when reducing the expression graph. However, the actual characters that were used to infer the graph are recorded as annotations to the graph nodes. If the user wishes to review any character set, he or she can click on that element in the expression in order to see a list of possible interpretations that could be drawn from the original examples. This list could be

F**IGURE** **13.12**

Modifying the expression directly by selecting an intended character class.

presented as a pop-up menu, as shown in Figure 13.12, so the user can select the desired interpretation. Any direct modification of the regular expression will, of course, result in an immediate update of the current selection set within the main text display.

Once the probabilistic inference algorithm described earlier has been incorporated into SWYN, the system will also support active learning by identifying boundary cases and marking them for the user's attention. The user will then be free to refine the current inferred expression by classifying the boundary case, directly modifying the elements of the expression, or simply proceed on the basis of current selections. The result should be both powerful and natural to use, clearly showing the advantages of integrating principles of visual design and direct manipulation into a PBE system. Future work on SWYN will include an empirical investigation of the usability of the novel interaction techniques described here. This will consider both the selection of positive and negative examples to construct a regular expression and the modification of that expression to refine specific boundary conditions or intended character classes.

13.7 Conclusion

The SWYN project aims to help users create powerful abstractions through programming by example. Rather than emphasizing sophisticated inference algorithms, it has applied a relatively simple algorithm for inference of regular expressions from examples but combined it with thorough design for usability. This has taken into account both Green's Cognitive

Dimensions of Notations framework and also the application of direct manipulation principles to the domain of abstraction creation.

The consequences for the system design have been that the results of the inference are made visible to the user—the inferred abstraction and the effects of the abstraction within the task domain. The inference results are displayed using a novel visual formalism that is both motivated by sound theoretical principles and verified in experimental evaluation.

This visualization, the approach to identifying examples in the user interface, and the heuristic algorithms used for inference mean that all user actions have incremental effects whose results are immediately visible. Users can both predict and observe the results of their actions, and either refine their abstractions or correct them accordingly. The result is a tool that, although it has a rather specialized purpose, exemplifies many important future emphases for the development of PBE systems.

Acknowledgements

Kim Marriott first suggested regular expressions as an experimental topic for investigating direct manipulation of visual expressions in programming. Thomas Green, Jonathan Pfautz, and Kerry Rodden have given useful feedback on the form of the regular expression visualizations and also on experiment design. Participants in the experiment were volunteers from the choirs of Darwin College, Cambridge, and Wolfson College, Oxford. This research is funded by the Engineering and Physical Sciences Research Council under EPSRC grant GR/M16924, "New Paradigms for Visual Interaction."

References

Angluin, A. 1980. Inductive inference of formal languages from positive data. *Information and Control* 45: 117–135.

Blackwell, A. F. 1996. Metaphor or analogy: How should we see programming abstractions? In *Proceedings of the 8th Annual Workshop of the Psychology of Programming Interest Group* (January), ed. P. Vanneste, K. Bertels, B. De Decker, and J.-M. Jaques. Ghent, Belgium: Katto Sint Lieven.

Blackwell, A. F., and T. R. G. Green. Investment of attention as an analytic approach to cognitive dimensions. In *Collected papers of the 11th Annual Workshop of the*

Psychology of Programming Interest Group (PPIG-11), ed. T. Green, R. Abdullah, and P. Brna.

Blackwell, A. F., K. N. Whitley, J. Good, and M. Petre. (in press). Cognitive factors in programming with diagrams. *Artificial Intelligence Review* (special issue on thinking with diagrams).

Christiansen, T., and N. Torkington. 1998. *Perl cookbook.* Sebastopol, Calif.: O'Reilly.

Dietterich, T. G., and R. S. Michalski. 1984. A comparative review of selected methods for learning from examples. In *Machine learning: An artificial intelligence approach,* ed. R. S. Michalski, J. G. Carbonell, and T. M. Mitchell. Palo Alto, Calif.: Tioga.

Green, T. R. G. 1989. Cognitive dimensions of notations. In *People and computers V,* ed. A. Sutcliffe and L. Macaulay. Cambridge: Cambridge University Press.

Green, T. R. G., and A. F. Blackwell. 1996. Ironies of abstraction. Presentation at 3rd International Conference on Thinking, British Psychological Society, London, August.

————. 1998. *Design for usability using Cognitive Dimensions.* Invited tutorial at HCI'98, Shefield, U.K., September.

Green, T. R. G., and M. Petre. 1996. Usability analysis of visual programming environments: A "cognitive dimensions" approach. *Journal of Visual Languages and Computing* 7: 131–174.

Green, T. R. G., M. Petre, and R. K. E. Bellamy. 1991. Comprehensibility of visual and textual programs: A test of superlativism against the "match-mismatch" conjecture. In *Empirical studies of programmers: Fourth workshop,* ed. J. Koenemann-Belliveau, T. G. Moher, and S. P. Robertson. Norwood, N.J.: Ablex.

Herrman, E. 1997. *Teach yourself CGI programming with Perl 5 in a week.* Indianapolis: Sams.

Johnson-Laird, P. N. 1983. *Mental models.* Cambridge: Harvard University Press.

Kurlander, D., and S. Feiner. 1993. A history-based macro by example system. In *Watch what I do: Programming by demonstration,* ed. A. Cypher. Cambridge, Mass.: MIT Press.

Lieberman, H., B. A. Nardi, and D. Wright. 1999. Training agents to recognize text by example. In *Proceedings of the Third ACM Conference on Autonomous Agents* (Seattle, May). New York: ACM Press.

Masui, T., and K. Nakayama. 1994. Repeat and predict—Two keys to efficient text editing. In *Proceedings of Human Factors in Computing Systems, CHI'94.* New York: ACM Press.

Mo, D. H. and I. H. Witten. 1992. Learning text editing tasks from examples: A procedural approach. *Behaviour and Information Technology* 11, no. 1: 32–45.

Modugno, F., and B. Myers. 1993. Graphical representation and feedback in a PBD system. In *Watch what I do: Programming by demonstration,* ed. A. Cypher. Cambridge, Mass.: MIT Press.

Nix, R. P. 1985. Editing by example. *ACM Transactions on Programming Languages and Systems* 7, no. 4 (October): 600–621.

Shneiderman, B. 1983. Direct manipulation: A step beyond programming languages. *IEEE Computer* 16, no. 8 (August): 57–69.

Wall, L., T. Christiansen, and R. L. Schwartz. 1996. *Programming Perl,* 2d ed. Sebastopol, Calif.: O'Reilly.

Watt, S. 1998. Syntonicity and the psychology of programming. In *Proceedings of the Tenth Annual Meeting of the Psychology of Programming Interest Group* (Milton Keynes, U.K., January), ed. J. Domingue and P. Mulholland. Milton Keyner, UK: Knowledge Media Institute.

Witten, I. H. and D. Mo. 1993. TELS: Learning text editing tasks from examples. In *Watch what I do: Programming by demonstration,* ed. A. Cypher. Cambridge, Mass.: MIT Press.

CHAPTER 14

Learning Users' Habits to Automate Repetitive Tasks

Jean-David Ruvini

*LIRMM, University of Montpellier-*II

Christophe Dony

*LIRMM, University of Montpellier-*II

Abstract

Adaptive Programming Environment (APE), a software assistant embedded into the VisualWorks Smalltalk interactive programming environment, watches what the user is doing, draws on machine learning to learn the user's habits, and afterward offers to complete repetitive tasks on his or her behalf. The goal of the APE project was threefold: (1) to design an assistant able to automate repetitive tasks with a minimal amount of user intervention, (2) to design an assistant able, as in programming-by-example (also called programming-by-demonstration) systems, to replay and automate complex repetitive tasks, and (3) to design an assistant that disrupts the user's work as little as possible—that is, that makes the right suggestion at the right moment. As a consequence, APE employs a machine-learning algorithm we have specifically designed to learn efficiently and rapidly not only what to suggest to the user but also when to make a suggestion.

14.1   Introduction

Entering repetitive sequences of commands (or repetitive tasks) is a well-known characteristic of human-computer interaction. To deal with this problem, early works have associated macro or script languages with interactive environments—for example, macros in Excel or Lisp scripts in Emacs. They allow the user to write a program that can be invoked later to perform a sequence of commands automatically. The limitation of this approach is that, generally, users do not want to or cannot spend too much effort on programming: Writing a program often takes longer than performing a sequence of commands manually, disrupts the user's work flow, and requires programming knowledge that many users do not have. Recent advances to overcome these limitations came from different correlated fields of research: programming by demonstration (PBD), predictive interfaces, and learning interface agents.

PBD systems (Cypher et al. 1993) let the user demonstrate what the task to be automated should do and then create a program from this demonstration. Macro recorders were the first examples of PBD systems, but they were limited because recorded commands are too specific (rote learning, no parameterization) to be reused. Sophisticated PBD systems, such as Mondrian (Lieberman 1993), create programs containing variables, iterative loops, or conditional branches from observing a user's actions. Although

PBD does not require programming knowledge because the user does not have to write code, demonstrating a program takes time and disrupts the user's work flow.

Predictive interfaces (Darragh and Witten 1991) and learning interface agents (Maes 1994) observe the user while he manipulates the environment. They try to learn from the correlations between situations the user has encountered and the corresponding commands he has performed, and to predict after each new command what the next one will be. They assist him by afterward predicting and suggesting some commands to perform automatically. For instance, CAP (Mitchell et al. 1994), an assistant for managing meeting calendars, suggests default values regarding meeting duration, location, time, and day of the week. OpenSesame! (Caglayan et al. 1997) runs in the background on Macintosh system 7 and offers to open or close files or applications, to empty trash, or to rebuild the desktop on the user's behalf. WebWatcher (Armstrong et al. 1995), an assistant for the World Wide Web, suggests links of interest to the user. Maes's (1994) assistants for handling electronic mail, scheduling meetings, and filtering electronic news advise the user for some application-specific operations such as managing mail, scheduling meetings, or selecting articles in the news. ClipBoard (Motoda 1997), an interface for Unix, tries to predict the next command the user is going to issue. The main advantages of these systems is that they do not require programming knowledge, nor do they disrupt the user's work flow because commands are automatically suggested. However, they do not create programs and thus only suggest single actions and not sequences of actions. Furthermore, the set of actions that most of these systems (expect ClipBoard and WebWatcher) can suggest is small and known in advance.

Eager (Cypher et al. 1993) is one of the most famous attempts to bring together PBD and predictive interfaces. Eager is an assistant for Macintosh Hypercard. When Eager detects two consecutive occurrences of a repetitive task in the sequence of a user's actions, it assumes they are the first two iterations of a loop and proposes to complete the loop. It is a PBD system because it is able to infer loops from observing a user's actions and to replay more than one action at once; it is a predictive interface because it is able to make suggestions without any user intervention. It is able to perform loop iterations until "a condition" is satisfied or following some typical patterns, such as days of the week or linear sequence of integers. Finally, Eager has an important characteristic: it makes a suggestion only after two consecutive occurrences of a repetitive task. As a consequence, it knows exactly when to make a suggestion and which suggestion to make. However, this characteristic is a limitation because in practice such occurrences are frequently not consecutive but interleaved with other actions. Familiar (see Chapter 15) takes on Eager's idea and extends it in many ways but does not address this limitation.

The goal of our work has been to design an assistant operating in a context where the number of possible user actions and possible values for the parameters of these actions are large, where repetitive sequences are not known in advance and not consecutive, and where these sequences are able to predict and replay repetitions composed of several actions, containing loops or conditional branches. None of the previously noted works addresses all these issues simultaneously. In such a context, a key issue is to design an assistant that makes "the right suggestion at the right moment"; an assistant that constantly bothers the user with a lot of wrong suggestions is useless because the user would rapidly ignore it. Wolber and Myers's chapter (Chapter 16) suggests a solution to this problem in the context of a PBD system. It proposes to allow the user to demonstrate "when" to make a suggestion as well as "what" to suggest. APE (Adaptive Programming Environment) takes another approach. It employs machine-learning techniques to learn efficiently and rapidly when to make a suggestion and which sequence of actions to suggest to the user.

As a case study, we present the APE project. APE is a software assistant integrated into the VisualWorks Smalltalk programming environment. Like Eager and Familiar, APE is able to detect loops and to suggest repetitive tasks iteratively.[1]

In the following sections we describe APE, demonstrating what it does and how it can be used. We explain what kind of repetitive tasks it is able to automate and how it automates them. We show what makes learning users' habits difficult, and we describe what and how APE learns. We compare experimental results of alternate approaches. Finally, we summarize lessons learned from this study and give perspectives for future research.

14.2   Overview of APE

APE is made of three software agents—an Observer, an Apprentice, and an Assistant—working simultaneously in the background without any user intervention. Table 14.1 defines our terminology, and Figure 14.1 describes the role of each agent.

---

1. APE is written in VisualWworks Smalltalk 3.0—ObjectShare, Inc., operational and publicly available at www.lirmm.fr/~ruvini/ape.

14.1

Definition of terms used throughout this chapter.

Term	Definition
Action	A high-level intervention of the user on the environment (as opposed to low-level interventions such as mouse movements and keystrokes), window manipulation, menu item selection, button pressing, text entering, etc. An action is parameterized by, among other things, the tool (e.g., *Browser, Debugger, Text Editor*) in which it has been performed.
Trace	A history of the user's actions
Task	A sequence of actions of the trace
Repetitive task	A task occurring several times in the trace
Situation	A sequence of actions of the trace of a given size *n*, *n* being a parameter of the learning algorithms
Current situation	The last *n* actions of the trace
Situation pattern	A regular expression matching one or more situations
Habit	A pair of "set of situation patterns—repetitive task" such that the situation patterns match the situations in which the user performs the repetitive task
When-set	A set of situation patterns that match the situations in which the user has performed repetitive tasks
What-set	A set of habits

14.1

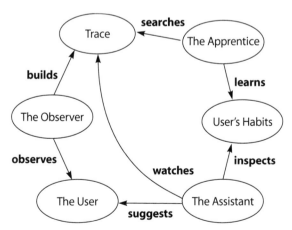

The Observer monitors the user's actions and builds the trace, the Apprentice learns the user's habits, and the Assistant proposes to the user sequences of actions to replay.

1 4 . 2 . 1   **The Observer**

The Observer traps a user's actions, reifies them into dedicated Smalltalk objects (instances of classes shown in Figure 14.2), and stores them in the trace. It then sends messages in the background to the Apprentice and the Assistant to notify them that the user has performed a new action.

For example, when the user selects the "doIt" command of a text editor to evaluate an expression, an instance of the class ActionEditor is created and references to the involved text editor, the evaluated text, and the string "doIt" are stored, respectively, in the toolID, text, and action slots. Figure 14.3 shows an example of a part of a trace where each line is a simplified textual representation of an action (for clarity, we only show the most informative action parameters). Different classes represent the actions held in the different tools of the environment (browser, debugger) because they hold different versions of methods used by the learning algorithm, which does not handle all kinds of actions equally.

In this first implementation, trapping the user's actions has been achieved by directly modifying methods (up to 170) of the user interface

FIGURE **14.2**

```
Object
  Action (type toolName toolID date display)
    ActionApplication (action)
      ActionBrowser (parameter textMode selected)
        ActionDebugger ( )
        ActionFileBrowser ( )
        ActionParcelBrowser ( )
      ActionChangeList (index plug)
      ActionEditor (text index which)
      ActionInspector (parameter on)
      ActionLauncher ( )
      ActionParcelList ( )
      ActionWindow ( )
    ActionError (error object message)
```

Smalltalk hierarchy of action classes.

FIGURE **14.3**

```
ActionEditor(anEditor,'anArray
  stupidMessage','doIt')
ActionError('doesNotUnderstand','stupidMessage')
ActionDebugger(aDebugger,debug)
ActionWindow(aDebugger,'move')
ActionWindow(aDebugger,'resize')
```

A sample of the trace where the user opens, moves, and resizes a debugger to correct an error.

layer in which the user's actions are fired. This result is not very satisfactory and should be improved in the future versions. It is a consequence of the lack of a standard mechanism, such as the "advice/trace" mechanisms of Interlisp (Teitelman 1978) or "wrappers" mechanisms of Flavors (Moon 1986), in the Smalltalk environment we have used (though they have been integrated in other Smalltalk environments; see Böcker and Herczeg 1990).

14.2.2 The Apprentice

The Apprentice activity is twofold: (1) It detects the user's repetitive tasks, and (2) it examines the situations in which repetitive tasks have been performed and uses two machine-learning algorithms to learn situation patterns and build two sets:

- the When-set of situation patterns matching the situations in which the user has performed the detected repetitive tasks, and

- the What-set of the user's habits (i.e., pairs "set of situation patterns—repetitive task," where the set of situation patterns reflects all the situations in which a given repetitive task has been performed).

The Apprentice is able to learn two kinds of situation patterns: situation patterns containing wild cards (i.e., a special character—noted "."—that

FIGURE **14.4**

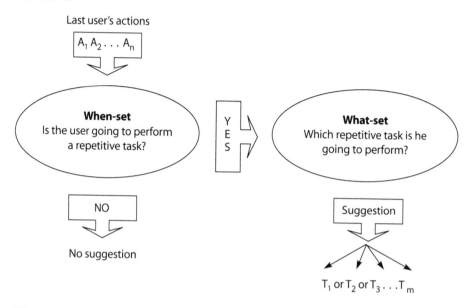

The Assistant inspects the When-set and the What-set to make suggestions.

matches any single action or action parameter) and unordered situation patterns (the order in which some actions are performed does not matter) containing wild cards. The number of wild cards is not limited.

An occurrence of a situation pattern containing a wild card is learned when, for example, the user has examined several methods in a Smalltalk browser, named "=" in the testing protocol, for various classes of the MyGraphics category (see Figure 14.8 on page 285). The detected repetitive task is "select protocol(testing), select method(=)," and the learned situation pattern is "select category(MyGraphics), select class(.)."

14.2.3 The Assistant

Observing the user, the Assistant uses the When-set to determine when to make a suggestion to the user; if it has to, it uses the What-set to determine what to suggest. More precisely, as shown in Figure 14.4, after each user's action, it inspects the What-set to answer the question "Is the user going to perform a repetitive task?" If the last user's actions match none of the situation patterns of the When-set, the answer is "no," and the Assistant makes no suggestion. Otherwise, the answer is "yes," and the Assistant inspects the user's habits (What-set) to answer the question "Which repetitive task is the user going to perform?" It selects all habits[2] with a situation pattern that matches the current situation. Then, it displays in the Assistant window (see Figure 14.5), without interrupting the user's work, the actions composing the repetitive task of the selected habits. The user can ignore this window and these suggestions (nonobtrusive behavior) or mouse-click on one of them. In the latter case, the Assistant successively performs the actions and removes the suggestions from its window.

14.3 Illustrative Examples

This section provides four examples of what APE is able to learn and suggest.

14.3.1 Example 1

Repetitive tasks frequently appear while testing applications. Consider a user testing a multiprocess simulation of the classical "n-queens" problem, implemented by a main-class Board. Figure 14.5 shows two VisualWorks snapshots including both an Assistant window, labeled "Assistant," and the main APE window, labeled "Ape Agents." The Watch button shows that the three agents are active. In the top snapshot, labeled "Situation before firing a habit," the user has selected, in a simple editor (named Workspace), a Smalltalk expression to create a board and to initiate the computation and is about to select the InspectIt item of that editor menu. Because the user is not performing this activity for the first time, a repetitive sequence has been detected and a habit has been learned, a situation pattern that matches the current situation. The Assistant thus fires the habit—that is, displays in its window a text describing the proposed repetitive sequence of actions (opening four inspectors in cascade to show a particular field of a composed object). This repetitive task being exactly what the user intends to do, he mouse-clicks on that text to perform the sequence of actions leading to what is shown in the bottom snapshot labeled "Situation after a habit has

---

2. Browsing through a huge number of suggestions to find the right one puts a workload on the user. The number of suggestions the Assistant can make is a parameter of APE.

FIGURE **14.5**

Situation before firing a habit
The Assistant suggests to open four inspectors.

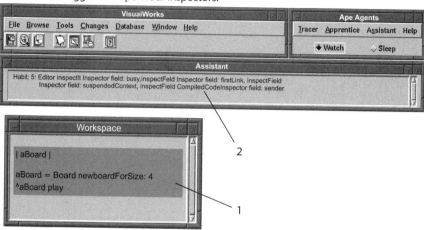

Situation after a habit has been fired
The user mouse-clicked on the proposition.

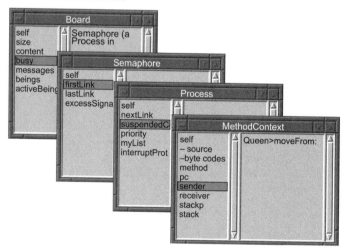

The user has just (1) selected an expression to create and test an instance of class "Board." (2) The Assistant detects a known situation and suggests to execute a registered repetitive sequence of actions, displayed in the Assistant window, that evaluates the expressions and opens four inspectors in cascade, leading to what is shown in the bottom snapshot.

been fired." In this case, the user has performed seven actions in a secure way with a single mouse click.

14.3.2 Example 2

Repetitive tasks also frequently appear while debugging applications. Consider the same user now debugging his "n-queens" application. The user has selected a Smalltalk expression (see Figure 14.6, top snapshot, arrow 1) in the Workspace window, the evaluation of which (arrow 2) has raised an exception leading to the opening of an Exception window (arrow 3). Because this situation matches a situation pattern learned by the Apprentice, the Assistant offers to perform the related repetitive task: "open, move, resize a debugger and select stack index 5." This repetitive task is exactly what the user intends to do, and he mouse-clicks on the proposition (arrow 4), entailing the creation and correct positioning of a debugger window, as shown in the bottom snapshot.

14.3.3 Example 3

This example shows that APE is able to automate sequences of actions iteratively (in a loop), even if the iterations are not consecutive. Suppose a user intends to modify the method "area" of all the classes belonging to a category named MyGraphics. Before working on a method "area," she wants to save it (back it up). She has first selected and saved the area method of the Circle class by performing the following actions: Select the MyGraphics category (Figure 14.7[a], arrow 1), select the Circle class of that category (arrow 2), select the accessing protocol (arrow 3) and the area method of that protocol (arrow 4), and select "file out as . . ." in the browser menu (arrow 5) to save the method. Later, after having completed various tasks such as creating a new Triangle class, the user has selected and saved the area method of the Diamond class (Figure 14.7[b]). At this point, the Apprentice has detected two nonconsecutive occurrences of the repetitive task "select the accessing protocol, select the area method, file out as." The action preceding the first occurrence of this repetitive task is "select the Circle class" and the action preceding the second occurrence is "select the Diamond class." Because classes Circle and Diamond belong to the MyGraphics category, it infers that the user intends to save the area method of all classes of the MyGraphics category. Hence, it assumes that these two occurrences are two iterations of the following loop: "For all classes of the MyGraphics category,

FIGURE **14.6**

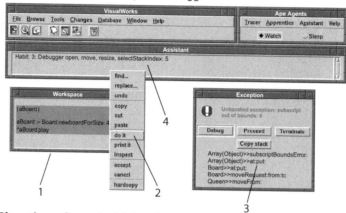

Situation before firing a habit
The Assistant proposes to open a debugger

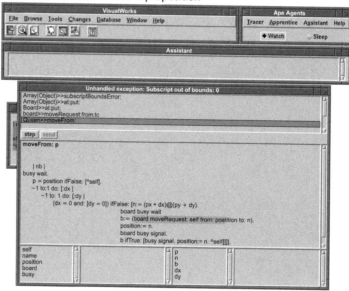

Situation after a habit has been fired
The user mouse-clicked on the proposition

The user has (1) typed and (2) evaluated an expression that (3) raised an exception. (4) The Assistant offers to open, move, and resize a debugger, and to select the fifth item in the debugger stack, as the user typically does (top snapshot). The user has mouse-clicked on the proposition, and the Assistant has performed these actions, resulting in a well-positioned debugger displaying a user's method (bottom snapshot).

FIGURE **14.7**

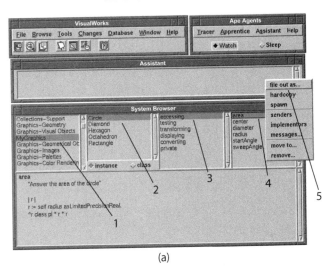

(a)

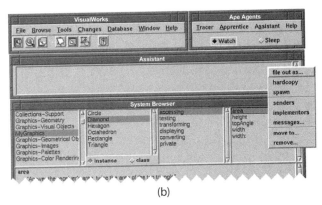

(b)

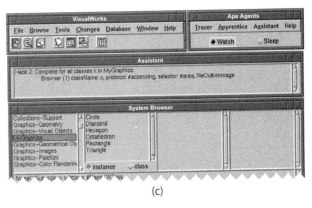

(c)

(a) The user saves ("file out as . . ." command) the method area of the class Circle. (b) After having completed various tasks, the user also saves the area method of class Diamond. (c) The Apprentice has detected a loop in the user's actions and has learned a habit. The Assistant offers to complete the loop (to save all area methods) as soon as it detects that the user is about to save one more area method.

do select the accessing protocol, select the area method, file out as." It learns a habit. As a consequence, as soon as the user selects the MyGraphics category, and whatever actions she has performed before, the Assistant predicts that she is about to save one more method area and offers to complete the loop (Figure 14.7[c]). If the user mouse-clicks on the suggestion in the Assistant window, the Assistant saves all area methods not yet saved (not shown).

14.3.4 Example 4

This last example shows that APE is able to help the user write repetitive pieces of code. Suppose a user has written several similar methods named "=", for various classes of the MyGraphics category in a browser. He has just selected the testing protocol (Figure 14.8, arrow 1) and is about to write a new method "=". The Assistant offers to insert a text template (arrow 2) containing some repetitive code (the asterisks denote nonrepetitive code). The user has mouse-clicked the suggestion, and the template has been inserted (arrow 3).

14.4 Detecting Repetitive Tasks

This section explains what kinds of repetitive tasks the Apprentice is able to detect in the trace and how the Assistant automates them.

14.4.1 Repetitive Sequences of Actions

Detection of repetitive sequences of actions is achieved using a classical text-searching algorithm (Karp, Miller, and Rosenberg 1972). "Open, move, resize a debugger and select stack index 5" (Figure 14.6) is an example of a repetitive sequence of actions. To automate a repetitive sequence of actions, the Assistant simply replays the actions composing it.

14.4.2 Loops

Each time the Apprentice detects a repetitive task, it supposes that the corresponding sequence of actions could be the "body" of a loop and that each occurrence of the sequence could be an iteration of the loop. It then

FIGURE **14.8**

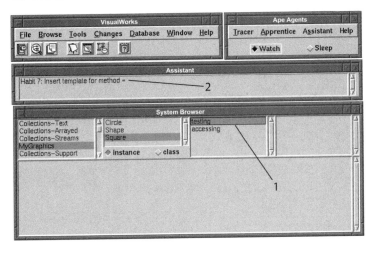

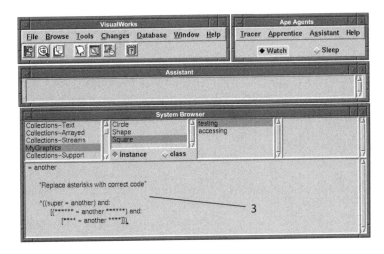

The user has written several similar methods named "=" for various classes of MyGraphics. (1) He has just selected the testing protocol and is about to write a new method "=" for class Square. (2) The Assistant offers to insert a template. (3) The user has mouse-clicked the suggestion, and the template has been inserted.

searches for relations between the actions preceding (or following) each iteration to determine the loop "variable." Example of such relations are classes belonging to the same category, methods belonging to the same class, subclasses of the same class, and so forth. Example 3 in Section 14.3 illustrates this case. The body of the loop is "Select the accessing protocol, select the area method, file out as"; the action preceding the first iteration is "Select the Circle class"; and the action preceding the second iteration is "Select the Diamond class." The relation between these two actions is that classes Circle and Diamond belong to the same category. Thus, the Apprentice then infers that the selected class is the loop variable and builds the following repetitive task: "For all classes x of MyGraphics, select the x class, select the accessing protocol, select the area method, file out as." To complete a loop, the Assistant plays the loop body for all the remaining values of the loop variable.

14.4.3 Writing of Repetitive Pieces of Code

To detect these repetitive tasks, the Apprentice compares the methods created by the user, line by line, using a simple string match comparison function. When it finds a set of methods that have a certain amount of their respective code in common, it assumes it has found a repetitive portion of code and creates a template (Figure 14.8). To replay a writing of a repetitive piece of code, it inserts the template in the code window of the browser (again, see Figure 14.8).

14.4.4 Repetitive Corrections of (Simple) Programming Errors

The Apprentice compares the methods the user has modified and the way he did it. When it finds a set of methods in which the user has replaced a portion C with another portion of code C', it assumes it has found a repetitive correction and records the replacement. To replay a repetitive correction of code, it replays the recorded code replacement.

14.5 Learning a User's Habits

Once it has detected the repetitive tasks, the Apprentice has to learn situation patterns to build the When-set and the What-set. In this section, we explain what makes this learning task difficult and how we overcome this difficulty.

14.5.1 What Makes the Problem Difficult?

We present in this section the requirements that direct the choice of the algorithms that the Apprentice uses to learn the situation patterns of the When-set and the What-set. Let us recall that the When-set is a set of situation patterns that match the situations in which the user has performed repetitive tasks; the What-set is a set of habits (i.e., a set of pair "situation patterns—repetitive task"). Let AL1 denote the algorithm used to build the When-set and AL2 denote the algorithm used to build the What-set.

- *Requirement 1: Low training time.* We distinguish "long-life" and "short-life" repetitive tasks. *Short-life* repetitive tasks are related to specific issues and appear in a small section of the trace, and the corresponding situation patterns have to be learned very rapidly from a few situations. *Long-life* repetitive tasks can reflect the general user's habits and can require a very long trace to be detected. Thus, the Apprentice is, on the one hand, able to learn situation patterns very rapidly on a small section of the trace to capture short-life tasks and, on the other hand, can also consider very long traces corresponding to several work sessions. Let us call *training time* the time required by a machine-learning algorithm to learn situation patterns. AL1 and AL2 must have a low training time.

- *Requirement 2: Low prediction time.* Of course, the Assistant is able to decide when to make a suggestion and which suggestion to make very rapidly. Let us call *prediction time* the time it takes the Assistant to inspect a set of situation patterns and to determine which ones match the current situation. The prediction time depends on the way AL1 and AL2 represent the learned situation patterns. This prediction time must be very low to allow the Assistant to make suggestions (or to decide not to make a suggestion) after each user's actions.

- *Requirement 3: User-intelligible situation patterns.* We want the Apprentice to represent situation patterns in a humanly understandable way. This is not a critical requirement, but it allows the user to inspect or edit the learned habits. Comprehensible and controllable interfaces give the user a sense of power and control.

- *Requirement 4: AL1—Low error rate.* Finally, to be viable our Assistant has to make the "right suggestion at the right moment." This means that it has to determine correctly when to make a suggestion. AL1 is said to "make" an error in two cases: (1) when one of the situation patterns it has learned matches the current situation but the user is not about to perform a repetitive task or (2) when none of its situation patterns matches the current situation but the user is about to perform a repetitive task. In case 1, the Assistant makes suggestions, yet no suggestions should be offered; in case 2, it makes no suggestion when doing so would benefit the user. AL1 must have a low error rate.

- *Requirement 5: AL2—Low error rate and low generalization.* The Assistant also has to determine correctly what to suggest. AL2 is said to "make" an error in two cases: (1) when a situation pattern of a habit matches the current situation but the user is not about to perform the repetitive task of that habit or (2) when a situation pattern of one of the habits matches the current situation but AL1 has made an error[3] and the user is not about to perform a repetitive task. In case 1, the Assistant suggests the wrong repetitive task; in case 2, it makes suggestions but no suggestion is expected. Case 2 may occur if the situation patterns of the habits are too general. A too-general situation pattern will be matched by too many situations and the corresponding task proposed too frequently. AL2 must have a low error rate to make few errors in case 1, but it also has to generalize as little as possible to avoid too-general situation patterns in case 2.

14.5.2   Which Algorithms?

Various kinds of algorithms have been proposed in the field of machine learning. Concept learning, neural networks, and reinforcement learning algorithms do not meet requirement 1; instance-based algorithms do not meet requirement 2; instance-based, statistical, neural networks and reinforcement learning algorithms do not meet requirement 3.

Eligible kinds of algorithms are decision-tree algorithms because they miss none of the requirements 1, 2, or 3. These algorithms, like most of the machine-learning algorithms, have a low error rate and meet requirement 4. Although they have not been designed to generalize as little as possible, they are better suited for requirement 5 than instance-based or statistical algorithms.

---

3. Whatever algorithm is used to build the When-set, it may sometimes make errors: machine-learning algorithms with a null error rate have not been discovered yet and even do not exist for most of the learning tasks.

Decision-tree learning algorithms have notably been used in CAP (Mitchell et al. 1994). The state-of-the-art decision-tree learning algorithm is C4.5 (Quinlan 1993).[4] C4.5 has low computing time (incremental versions of C4.5 exist) and is suited to learn the When-set (AL1). However, our tests (see Section 14.6) have shown that it learns too-general situation patterns and is not suited to learn the What-set (AL2). Hence, APE employs C4.5 to learn the When-set and a new algorithm we have designed to learn the What-set.

14.5.3 A New Algorithm

Our new algorithm, named IDHYS, is a concept-learning algorithm inspired by the candidate elimination algorithm (Mitchell 1978).

Inductive concept learning consists of acquiring the general definition of a concept from training examples of this concept, each labeled as either a member (or positive example) or a nonmember (or negative example) of this concept. Concept learning can be modeled as a problem of searching through a hypothesis space (set of possible definitions) to find the hypothesis that best fits the training examples (Mitchell 1982). Learning users' habits is a concept-learning problem. All the situations preceding a repetitive task T can be seen as positive examples of the concept "situations in which the user is going to perform repetitive task T." The situations preceding any other task can be considered as negative examples of this concept. The searched definition is a set of situation patterns that match the situations in which the repetitive task T has been performed.

IDHYS searches the hypothesis space of the conjunctions of two situation patterns, one for each kind of situation pattern defined in Section 14.2: containing wild cards or unordered containing wild cards. It learns by building hypotheses that are the most specific generalizations of the positive examples. It processes the positive examples incrementally. It starts with a very specific hypothesis (indeed, the first positive example itself) and progressively generalizes this hypothesis with the subsequent positive examples. IDHYS does not build hypotheses for the negative examples, which are only used to bound the generalization process. This incremental bottom-up approach makes IDHYS not sensitive to actions with large sets of possible values for their parameters. As a consequence, it has a low computing time. Our test (see the next section) shows it also has a low error rate and does not overgeneralize to build the situation patterns.

---

4. A commercial version of C4.5, called C5.0, is now available.

Description of an earlier version of IDHYS can be found in Ruvini and Fagot (1998) and of a more complete one in Ruvini (2000).

14.6 Use and Experimental Results

APE, as described in the prior section, is implemented and experimentally used by ourselves and by a pool of fifty students enrolled in a Smalltalk course at the master's level. This section first analyzes user feedback and then describes and analyzes the technical experimental results.

Concerning user feedback, let us recall that our users are Smalltalk beginners; we do not yet have feedback from experienced programmers. About 70 percent of our students have considered the Assistant window for approximately ten minutes and then have forgotten it. Fortunately, results from the remaining 30 percent have been very interesting. The main reasons invoked by those who have not used the suggestions are

- the burden of looking at the Assistant window since nothing, except a modification inside this window, indicates when a suggestion is made; and

- the difficulty of reading suggestions presented as a sequence of actions.

This feedback indicates that a great deal of work in that direction remains— namely, how to gently alert people and provide a better visualization of what the Assistant suggests? In addition, the interesting point is that those who have made the effort to use the tool have rapidly learned how to use it efficiently and have taken advantage of its capabilities. After a while, those users have learned (1) which suggestions are regularly made and which ones interest them and (2) when the suggestions are made. In other words, they have learned to take a look at the Assistant window when they are about to perform a repetitive task and when they do know that the suggestion will be made. The students have been able to anticipate APE's suggestions because APE has a low excess rate and makes few wrong suggestions.

Concerning technical results, APE correctly works and makes the suggestions we expected it to. It also makes many suggestions we did not think of. We report here experiments conducted on ten traces of 2,000 actions, collected during students' usage of the software.

How well does APE assist its users in practice? One way to answer this question is to train APE on a part of a trace (called the *train trace*) and then to test it on another part (called the *test trace*) to see how often one of its suggestions coincides with user's actions.[5] Figure 14.9 plots these data. The horizontal axis gives the size of the train traces and the test traces used. APE employs C4.5 to learn the When-set and IDHYS to learn the What-set (denoted by "C4.5-IDHYS").

However, as a comparison, we also report results when the Apprentice employs C4.5 to build both the When-set and the What-set (denoted by "C4.5-C4.5"), and when it learns the What-set only (and not the When-set) with C4.5 and IDHYS, respectively (denoted by "C4.5" and "IDHYS"). The percentage of correct suggestions (a) is the percentage of repetitive tasks correctly suggested by the Assistant. The percentage of excessive suggestions (b) is the percentage of actions of the test trace not preceding a repetitive task for which the Assistant has made a suggestion. These percentages have been evaluated for a situation length varying from 1 to 10, and Figure 14.9 presents average results. This figure shows that

- the use of the When-set decreases the amount of excessive suggestions without decreasing the amount of correct suggestions,

- employing IDHYS to learn the What-set leads the Assistant to make less excessive suggestions and to suggest correctly more repetitive tasks, and

- the percentage of excessive suggestions increases with the trace size (see "C4.5-IDHYS").

Both the percentage of correct suggestions and the percentage of excessive suggestions increase with the situation length (not shown here). This shows that there is a trade-off between designing an assistant that makes few but correct suggestions (and perhaps misses some repetitive tasks) and finding one that constantly bothers the user with suggestions. Practically, we have chosen a learning frequency of 100 actions and a situation length of 3 actions. In this case, APE correctly suggests 63 percent of the repetitive tasks and makes an excessive suggestion for only 18 percent of users' actions. The average size of the repetitive tasks suggested by the Assistant during this experiment was seven actions (minimum, three; maximum, ten).

Another important question is how long it takes APE to learn users' habits. In practice, it takes APE fifteen seconds (measured on a PC with a 133-Mhz processor) to learn users' habits (i.e., both the When-set and the What-set) from a trace containing 100 actions. A 100-action trace corresponds to about six minutes of user work. In other words, for every six minutes of user work, APE spends fifteen seconds to learn new habits. This result is quite

---

5. This is similar to the machine-learning cross-validation process.

FIGURE **14.9**

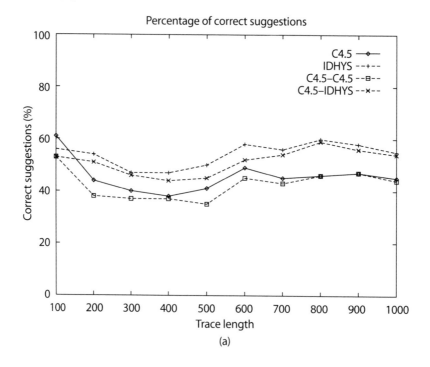

(a)

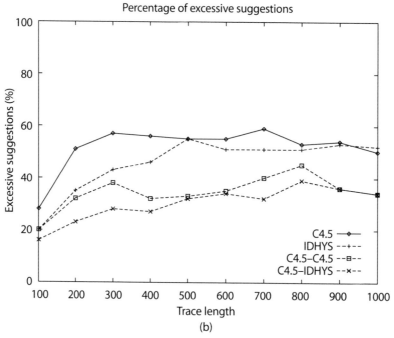

(b)

(a) The percentage of repetitive tasks that APE has correctly suggested and (b) the percentage of actions of the user, not preceding a repetitive task, for which APE has made a suggestion.

satisfactory. Note also that the Assistant makes suggestions (i.e., inspects the When-set and the What-set) in a matter of milliseconds.

14.7 Conclusion

APE is one more step toward assistants that bring together programming by demonstration and predictive interfaces. It works and operates in a context in which the number of possible actions and possible values for the parameters of these actions are large and repetitive sequences are not known in advance and not consecutive. It is able to replay repetitions composed of several actions and containing loops. The lessons learned from this work are as follows:

- Minimizing the number of incorrect suggestions is an important issue. The system has to suggest the "replaying" of the right repetitive task at the right moment.

- Learning when to make a suggestion as well as what to suggest decreases the number of incorrect suggestions.

- The system must not learn habits that are too general. We have shown that our new machine-learning algorithm designed to learn habits reduces the amount of incorrect suggestions without degrading the quality of these suggestions.

- It is possible to learn a user's habits to anticipate repetitive tasks. Experimental tests have shown that APE is usable and efficient: it learns a user's habits in a matter of seconds and anticipates 63 percent of the repetitive tasks. It makes irrelevant suggestions for only 18 percent of the user's actions.

Concerning future work, it is clear that one of the main remaining issues is to present the suggestions made by the Assistant in a more attractive way. Programming-by-demonstration studies have addressed the problem of creating a graphical representation of a program or a sequence of actions, and they offer a direction for future research.

Although the integration of APE into a programming environment is an originality, it is not restrictive. APE could be integrated in other interactive environments such as Microsoft Windows, X window system, or Apple MacOS.

References

Armstrong, R., D. Freitag, T. Joachims, and T. M. Mitchell. 1995. WebWatcher: A learning apprentice for the World Wide Web. Paper presented at the AAAI spring symposium on information gathering.

Böcker, H.-D., and J. Herczeg. 1990. What tracers are made of. *In Proceedings of the OOPSLA/ECOOP '90 conference on object-oriented programming systems, languages and applications* (October). Ottawa, Canada: ACM Press.

Caglayan, A., M. Snorrason, J. Jacoby, J. Mazzu, R. Jones, and K. Kumar. 1997. Learn sesame: a learning agent engine. *Applied Artificial Intelligence* 11: 393–412.

Cypher, A., D. C. Halbert, D. Kurlander, H. Lieberman, D. Maulsby, B. A. Myers, and A. Turransky, eds. *Watch what I do: Programming by demonstration.* Cambridge, Mass.: MIT Press; see also www.acypher.com/wwid/.

Darragh, J. J., and I. H. Witten. 1991. Adaptive predictive text generation and the reactive keyboard. *Interacting with Computers* 3, no. 1:27–50.

Karp, R. M., R. E. Miller, and A. L. Rosenberg. 1972. Rapid identification of repeated patterns in strings, trees and arrays. In *4th Annual ACM Symposium on Theory of Computing* (Denver, May 1–3). Denver, Colo.: ACM Press.

Lieberman, H. 1993. Mondrian: A teachable graphical editor. In *Watch what I do: Programming by demonstration,* ed. A. Cypher, D. C. Halbert, D. Kurlander, H. Lieberman, D. Maulsby, B. A. Myers, and A. Turransky. Cambridge, Mass.: MIT Press.

Maes, P. 1994. Agents that reduce work and information overload. *Communications of the ACM* 37, no. 7 (July, special issue on intelligent agents): 31–40.

Mitchell, T. M. 1978. Version spaces: An approach to concept learning. Technical Report HPP-79–2, Stanford University, Palo Alto, Calif.

———. 1982. Generalization as search. *Artificial Intelligence* 18, no. 2 (March): 203–226.

Mitchell, T. M., R. Caruana, D. Freitag, J. McDermott, and D. Zabowski. 1994. Experience with a learning personal assistant. *Communications of the ACM* 37, no. 7 (July, special issue on intelligent agents): 81–91.

Moon, D. A. 1986. Object-oriented programming with flavors. In *Proceedings of the conference on object-oriented programming systems, languages, and applications (OOPSLA)* (New York, November), ed. N. Meyrowitz. New York: ACM Press.

Motoda, H. 1997. Machine learning techniques to make computers easier to use. In *Proceedings of the 15th International Joint Conference on Artificial Intelligence (IJCAI-97).* (August 23–29). San Francisco: Morgan Kaufmann.

Quinlan, J. R. 1993. *C4.5: Programs for machine learning.* San Mateo, Calif.: Morgan Kaufmann.

Ruvini, J.-D. 2000. Assistance à l'utilisation d'environnements interactifs: Apprentissage des habitudes de l'utilisateur. Ph.D. diss., Université Montpellier II, France.

Ruvini, J.-D., and C. Fagot. 1998. IBHYS: A new approach to learn users habits. In *Proceedings of ICTAI'98*. Los Alamitos, Calif.: IEEE Computer Society Press.

Teitelman, W. 1978. *Interlisp reference manual*. Palo Alto, Calif.: Xerox Palo Alto Research Center.

CHAPTER 15

Domain-Independent Programming by Demonstration in Existing Applications

GORDON W. PAYNTER

Department of Computer Science
University of Waikato

IAN H. WITTEN

Department of Computer Science
University of Waikato

Abstract

This paper describes Familiar, a domain-independent programming-by-demonstration system for automating iterative tasks in existing, unmodified applications on a popular commercial platform. Familiar is domain-independent in an immediate and practical sense: it requires no domain knowledge from the developer and works immediately with new applications as soon as they are installed. Based on the AppleScript language, the system demonstrates that commercial operating systems are mature enough to support practical, domain-independent programming by demonstration—but only just, for the work exposes many deficiencies.

15.1 Introduction

Our aim is to add programming by demonstration (PBD) to commercial platforms in a way that is domain-independent and works with existing applications. Domain independence, if it can be achieved, is of huge benefit because it eliminates the difficult, time-consuming, and error-prone job of encoding domain knowledge in a satisfactory way, and it eliminates the brittleness that is associated with unexpected interactions between different pieces of domain knowledge. The ability to work with existing application programs is highly desirable for any interface agent because it eliminates the restriction that users can only use selected applications and removes the need to reimplement applications.

This chapter describes Familiar, a PBD package that operates on a popular computer platform, the Apple Macintosh. Familiar uses standard software (e.g., the Apple Finder, Microsoft Excel, and lesser-known applications such as JPEGView, Fetch, and GIFConverter) and communicates through AppleScript, a standard protocol. We have succeeded in achieving true domain independence: If you install a completely new recordable application that Familiar has never before encountered, issue the "Begin recording" command, and start interacting with the application, you will reap the benefits of PBD right away. Success will depend on how well the application implements AppleScript, a limitation that we will discuss.

Macro recorders are a rare example of PBD systems that operate on standard computer platforms—both within application packages, such as spreadsheet macro recorders, and on a systemwide basis. Yet they have serious limitations, limitations that have been recognized since the early days of PBD. Cypher (1993a) points out that their main failing is that they are too literal: they replay a sequence of actions at the keystroke and mouse-click level, without taking any account of context or attempting any kind of generalization. Most PBD systems aim higher, recording the user's actions at a more abstract level and making explicit attempts to generalize them. However, they have virtually all been demonstrated only in special, nonstandard, often tailor-made software environments.

Familiar builds on the functionality and interaction style of the Eager PBD system (Cypher 1993b). Familiar extends Eager in three important respects: interface, inference, and domain independence. Eager's "anticipation highlighting" technique presupposes domain knowledge, can only display one action at a time, and provides no explanation of the predictions—users are forced to trust the system (and do so reluctantly). Its inference engine does not tolerate mistakes in demonstrations, cannot explain the predictions it makes, and has a smaller set of generalization techniques available. Although it is domain-independent in principle, Eager requires changes to the operating system and applications and has been demonstrated with only one application (HyperCard). Familiar overcomes these problems by using the AppleScript language to communicate with the user and other applications, gaining generality at the expense of Eager's polished interface.

Other PBD systems have used AppleScript to monitor the user and control applications, but they do not exploit its domain independence and high-level application knowledge. Lieberman (1998) has based two separate PBD systems on AppleScript that are tailored to specific applications. ScriptAgent uses inference techniques from Lieberman (1993) to write scripts for manipulating files in the Finder, and Tatlin seeks similarities between data in a spreadsheet and a calendar by interrogating them with AppleScript. Yvon, Piernot, and Cot (1995) use AppleScript as a macro recorder without generalization.

This chapter begins by describing interaction with the Familiar system, from the user's perspective. Because of space limitations, details of the implementation are beyond our scope (see Paynter 2000 for full information). Commercial scripting architectures that purport to support agents, such as AppleScript, have shortcomings that present significant obstacles to general-purpose systems. One impediment to their development is that the requirements of PBD are poorly defined because (historically) even domain-independent systems have been tightly coupled with prototype applications. We review the requirements of domain-independent PBD and finally discuss how AppleScript meets these requirements and what its shortcomings are.

15.2 What Familiar Does

Familiar's purpose is to help users solve iteration problems in their standard applications and environments. We give three examples of Familiar's use. The first, rearranging a set of files into a horizontal row, demonstrates the ability to iterate over sets and extrapolate sequences. In a variation of this task, the user asks Familiar to explain its predictions and gives feedback about their accuracy. The second is to sort a set of files into two folders. Before it can safely be asked to finish the task, Familiar must learn the sort criteria—and convince the user it has done so. The third is to convert a set of files from one image format to another. It demonstrates the ability to work across multiple domains and infer long cycles from noisy demonstrations.

In each example the user first asks the agent to start observing his or her actions by selecting "Begin recording" from the Familiar menu (Figure 15.1), which is available in every application. They then proceed to demonstrate the task and interact with the agent. When they have finished working with Familiar, they signal that the task is complete by choosing

FIGURE **15.1**

The Familiar menu.

"End task" from the menu. The user can pause a demonstration at any time with the "Stop recording" command and continue it again with "Begin recording."

15.2.1 Arranging Files

To rearrange files into a horizontal row, the user begins by moving a convenient file, "plum," to the top left corner of the folder window (Figure 15.2[a]). These actions are recorded by Familiar and displayed in the Familiar History window (Figure 15.2[b]). The "activate" command (event 1) indicates that the user is working in the Finder. The "select" (event 2) and "set" (event 3) commands describe the positioning of the first file. The user continues the demonstration by moving the file "peach" (Figure 15.2[c]); again, his or her actions are recorded and displayed (Figure 15.2[b], events 4 and 5).

Each time it records a user action, Familiar attempts to generalize the event trace and infer the user's intent. After event 5 it detects a cycle,

FIGURE **15.2**

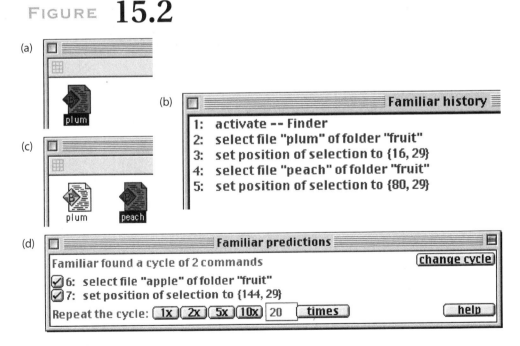

Using Familiar to arrange files: (a) a demonstration is recorded; (b) the history window; (c) a second demonstration is recorded; (d) a prediction is made.

FIGURE **15.3**

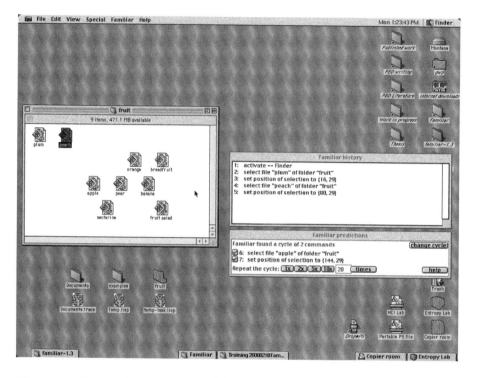

The screen after two demonstrations of the arranging files task.

predicts the next iteration, and presents this prediction to the user in the Familiar Predictions window (Figure 15.2[d]). In this case, Familiar antici-pates that the user's next actions will be to "select file 'apple'" (event 6) and set its position (event 7). The user is satisfied with this prediction—the task involves arranging all the files in a row, irrespective of order, and "apple" has yet to be moved.

Figure 15.3 shows the entire screen as it appears after the user has dem-onstrated the first two examples. The fruit window, in which the user is demonstrating the task, appears on the left. Familiar is a stand-alone appli-cation, so its two windows remain in the background (right-hand side) until the user selects one, bringing it to the foreground. They take up only a small part of the total screen area and can be moved to increase visibility. Note that a flashing tape recorder icon has been added to the top left corner of the screen to show that AppleScript recording is active and that the Familiar menu has been added to the standard Finder menubar.

FIGURE **15.4**

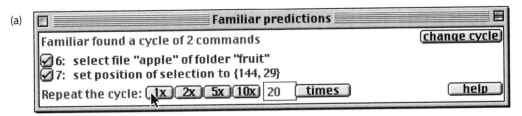

(a)

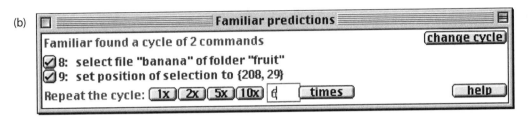

(b)

(c)

Completing an iterative task: (a) a prediction is executed once; (b) the user requests six more iterations; (c) the task is complete.

The Predictions window can be used to perform the task. The "1x," "2x," "5x," and "10x" buttons execute the corresponding number of complete iterations of the cycle (Figure 15.4[a]). The user presses "1x" (one times) to tell Familiar to execute its predictions for events 6 and 7, and it responds by sending the commands to the Finder, which selects and positions the file "apple." The user follows the agent's progress by observing its actions in the Finder and watching the Familiar interface. As each command is executed, it is added to the History window and its color is changed in the Prediction window. When the entire iteration has been executed, Familiar displays its prediction for the next iteration (Figure 15.4[b]).

The user can instruct Familiar to execute a given number of iterations by entering the number from the keyboard. In this example the user, knowing how many files are left to position, replaces the default value of 20 (visible in Figure 15.4[a]) with 6 (Figure 15.4[b]), and presses "times." After each it-eration, Familiar pauses to redraw the Predictions window and decrement the number of cycles to go. When six iterations are finished, the task is com-plete (Figure 15.4[c]).

15.2.2 When Errors Occur

The Predictions window describes Familiar's predictions and accepts feed-back about them. The simplest way to correct a mistake is to demonstrate another example in the standard application interface. Familiar will incor-porate the new demonstration—and the fact that the old predictions were incorrect—into subsequent predictions. If the user clicks on the "tick" but-ton beside any command in the Predictions window, the steps up to this point are executed. For example, if a cycle of six commands is predicted but only the first four are correct, the user can click on the fourth and then demonstrate the remaining two. Familiar will incorporate all six events into its subsequent predictions.

The "help" button gives feedback about Familiar's reasoning. The itera-tive pattern in Figure 15.5(a) is consistent with the two demonstrations of the task (Figure 15.2[a–c]), but the parameter of the "select" command (event 6) has not been extrapolated correctly: Familiar has predicted that the user will select "peach," but the user already moved this file (events 4 and 5) and wants to move a new one.[1] To find out why the agent has made the erroneous prediction, the user clicks on "help." The Macintosh "balloon help" feature is activated (Figure 15.5[a]) and used to explain predictions (Figure 15.5[b–c]). The user is concerned that the "select" parameter is in-correct, and a balloon explains that Familiar has reasoned that the user is positioning the same file in every iteration (Figure 15.5[b]). The prediction can be changed by option-clicking it, whereupon Familiar replaces "peach" with "apple" (Figure 15.5[c]). The new balloon explains that this prediction is generated by assuming that the user is iterating over all the file objects in the folder "fruit." The agent's reasoning—and thus its prediction—is cor-rect, and the task can now be completed.

---

1. Familiar was artificially constrained to cause this prediction; normally, it would predict correctly.

FIGURE **15.5**

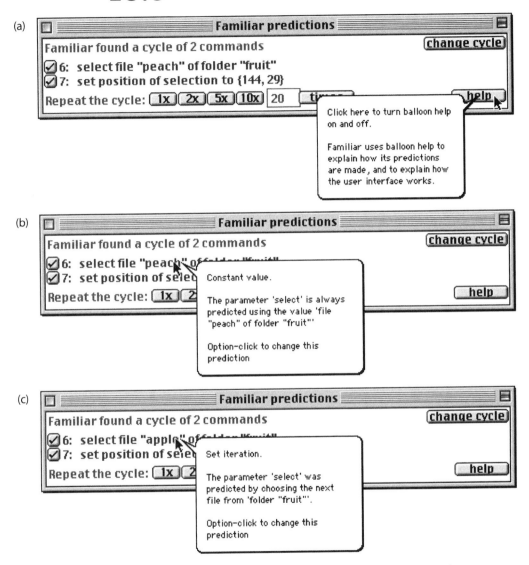

Examining and changing an incorrect prediction: (a) balloon help is activated; and (b-c) two predictions are explained.

15.2.3 Sorting Files

The second task is to sort a set of files into folders for word processor and spreadsheet documents. The user selects "Begin recording" (Figure 15.1) and starts by creating a new folder and renaming it "word processor." These commands are recorded and displayed (Figure 15.6[a], events 1–4) but do not contribute to any iteration—they are once-only initialization steps. The user then moves "ACC01.doc," a word processor document, into the new folder (Figure 15.6[a], events 5–6). To demonstrate the second iteration, the user moves "ACC99.doc" into the word processor folder (Figure 15.6[b], events 7–8). The third file, "Balance sheet," is a spreadsheet, so the user creates a folder called "spreadsheets" (Figure 15.6[c], events 9–11) and moves the file into it (Figure 15.6[c], events 12–13). Three iterations of the task have been demonstrated, but over half of the recorded events are initialization commands that do not contribute to the iterations.

Familiar detects an iterative pattern of seven events in the demonstration and makes a corresponding prediction (Figure 15.6[d]). Unfortunately, it is completely wrong, and the entire cycle it is predicting is incorrect. Each iteration includes creating a new folder and renaming it "spreadsheets"; note that if we permitted Familiar the luxury of domain knowledge, this prediction could be suppressed because it does not make sense to create multiple folders with the same name. The user rejects the pattern with the "change cycle" button. Familiar then suggests a two-step pattern that is correct for the next file (Figure 15.6[e]). The user presses the "1x" button and watches Familiar executing the commands to move file "Balance sheet 1996" to the "spreadsheets" folder.

When Familiar displays its prediction for the next iteration (Figure 15.6[f]), it becomes apparent that there is more teaching to do, for it predicts that the user will select "Corrections," a word processor file, and move it into the "spreadsheets" folder (Figure 15.6[f], event 17). Noticing the error, the user clicks on "help" and moves the mouse over the "move" command's "to" parameter. The help balloon (Figure 15.7[a]) explains that Familiar predicts the constant "spreadsheets" (the value in the last two iterations) and that the user can change this by giving a new example. Familiar gives this advice because it has no other suggestions to make: three examples are insufficient for it to learn this classification task.

The user returns to the Finder and moves "Corrections" into the "word processor" folder. These actions are recorded (Figure 15.7[b]) and used to make a prediction for the next file (Figure 15.7[c]). Unfortunately, the prediction is incomplete: the agent correctly anticipates that the user will select "expenses for 1996" but fails to predict the destination folder, instead

FIGURE 15.6

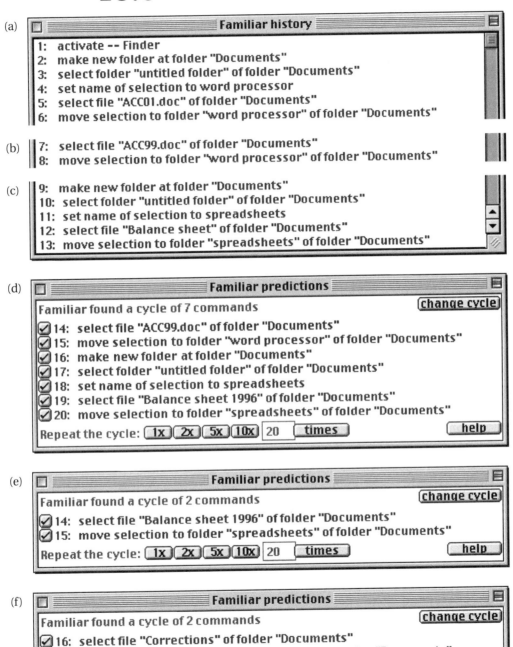

Changing an incorrect cycle: (a-c) three iterations are demonstrated and recorded; (d) the fourth iteration is predicted incorrectly; (e) the fourth iteration is predicted correctly; (f) the fifth iteration is predicted.

FIGURE 15.7

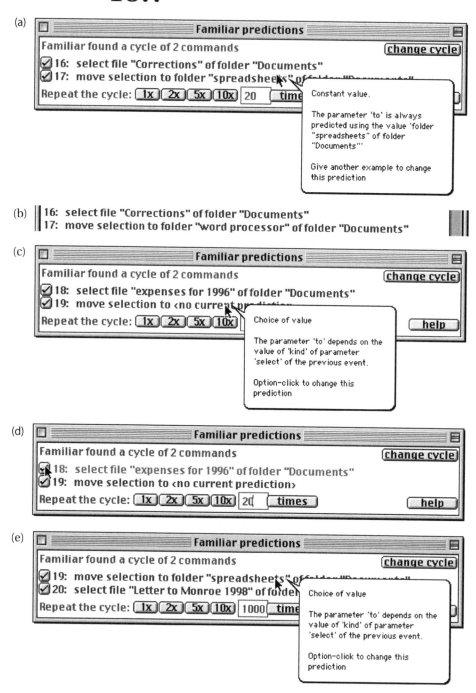

Changing an incorrect parameter: (a) an incorrect prediction is explained; (b) a new demonstration is recorded in the History window; (c) an incomplete, but correct, prediction is explained; (d) the user executes a single command; (e) a correct prediction is explained, and the user requests 1,000 iterations.

giving "no current prediction." The user activates "balloon help" and asks for an explanation. Familiar has found a relationship between the "to" parameter and the "kind" attribute of the previous event and will only make a concrete prediction of event 19 after event 18 has been confirmed. To test the prediction, the user clicks on the "tick" beside event 18. Familiar executes it (Figure 15.7[d]), adds this event to the History window, and displays its prediction of the next two events (Figure 15.7[e]).

Familiar correctly anticipates that the next action will be to move the selected file into the "spreadsheets" folder. Confident that Familiar has grasped the idea, the user types 1000 into the "number of iterations" field and presses "times" (Figure 15.7[e]). After 135 iterations no files are left in the folder. Since Familiar can neither predict nor select the next file, it stops performing the task and awaits new instructions from the user, who chooses "Stop recording" from the Familiar menu and continues with his or her work.

15.2.4 Converting Images

Complex tasks may involve multiple domains, longer demonstrations, and user errors. Figure 15.8 shows History (a-b) and Prediction (c) windows that were generated from a demonstration performed by a subject in a user evaluation. The task (a subtask of a larger task that the subject identified then elected to complete with Familiar) involves two applications and has a noisy event trace.

In this example, Familiar is used to convert a set of graphic files from JPEG format to PICT format. The History window is shown after the first (Figure 15.8[a]) and second (Figure 15.8[b]) iterations have been demonstrated. In each iteration of the task, the user selects a JPEG file in the Finder (events 4, 10), opens it in the GIFConverter image manipulation program (events 5, 11), saves it as a PICT file (events 7, 13), and then deletes the JPEG file (events 9, 16). However, these actions are interspersed with others that are not part of the iterative loop. The first three events of the first iteration initialize the environment. Event 15 is a singular noise event—it was generated when the user shifted a window to get a better view and will never be repeated. In Figure 15.8(c) we see that Familiar has correctly identified a cycle of six significant events and predicted the next full iteration.

FIGURE **15.8**

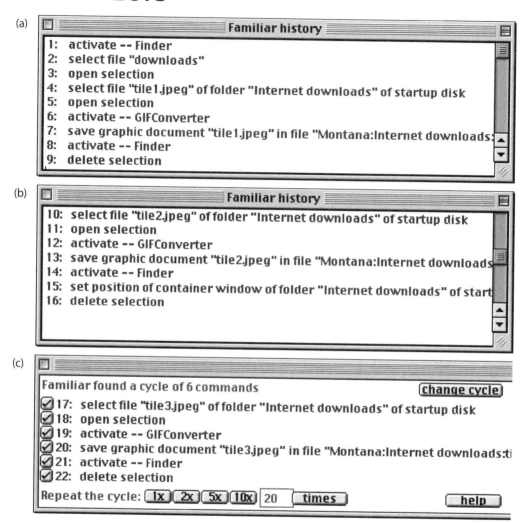

Converting image files: (a-b) two noisy demonstrations are recorded and (c) a correct prediction is made.

15.3 Platform Requirements

Familiar demonstrates that domain-independent PBD can be added to existing applications but is dependent on many services provided by the software architecture. These services are given in Table 15.1, which lists a minimal set of technical and nontechnical platform requirements that must be satisfied before domain-independent PBD is possible in existing applications. Three pertain directly to applications: the ability to monitor user actions, examine application data, and control the application program. Analogous requirements have been identified for intelligent tutoring systems—observation, inspection, and scripting (Ritter and Koedinger 1995; Cheikes et al. 1998). User studies that record user actions (Kay and Thomas 1995; Linton, Charron, and Joy 1999), animated help systems that require complete and exclusive control of the user interface (Bharat and Sukaviriya 1993; Miura and Tanaka 1998), and attachable, application-independent tools (Olsen et al. 1999) make similar demands.

- *Requirement 1: Users and applications.* The principal justification for adding a demonstrational interface to existing applications and environments is that end users know them and are disinclined to alter their habits, so the most basic requirements are nontechnical: a set of applications and a group of existing users. Both are met by any successful commercial computer platform, but not by prototypes and research systems. If there is no established user base, it will be easier and more effective to rewrite an application using an architecture such as Amulet

TABLE **15.1**

Platform requirements of domain-independent PBD systems.

Requirement	Description
R1	Users and applications
R2	Recordability: the ability to monitor the user's actions
R3	Controllability: the ability to control application programs
R4	Examinability: the ability to examine application information
R5	A user interface
R6	Consistency

(Myers and Kosbie 1996) or AIDE (Piernot and Yvon 1993) that is designed to support PBD.

- *Requirement 2: Recordability.* Most kinds of PBD require monitoring and recording the user's actions. Each action is recorded, added to the event trace or command history, and analyzed to infer the user's intent and predict subsequent actions. An ideal recording mechanism will be unobtrusive, so that users can demonstrate tasks under conditions identical to their standard working environment, and detailed enough to support reasoning about the user's intent.

- *Requirement 3: Controllability.* To carry out tasks on the user's behalf, a PBD system must be able to control other applications. This can be accomplished either through application programming interfaces or by emulating the user (Lieberman's [1998] "marionette strings"). The latter is a natural choice because it allows a learned task to be performed in the same way that it was demonstrated by the user.

- *Requirement 4: Examinability.* Information about the application is necessary to infer intent and make predictions. Such information falls into two categories: *class* (or type) *information* and *instance information* (or data). The former describes the capabilities of an application, including the commands and objects it uses, and remains unchanged from one invocation to the next. The latter describes the data the user is working on and the commands he or she has executed recently. It differs each time the program is run and often changes in response to user actions. PBD systems require access to the applications' instance information.

- *Requirement 5: User interface.* Any demonstrational interface must interact with the user. Interaction design is especially challenging for systems that work with existing applications or with multiple applications. Few existing applications are designed to have truly extensible interfaces, and PBD must work around these limitations. Multiple-application systems face a trade-off between consistency and the benefit obtained from domain-specific interaction techniques.

- *Requirement 6: Consistency.* In practice, application independence requires that each application satisfies the technical requirements in the same way, so that a single system can work with every application, represent tasks that span applications, work with unseen applications, and present a single interface to the user.

15.4 AppleScript: A Commercial Platform

AppleScript is an application-independent, high-level scripting language for the Apple Macintosh (Apple Computer 1993–1999). Familiar uses it to record the user's actions and to examine and control target applications. AppleScript is not the only commercial platform that can support PBD (see Paynter 2000 for alternatives), but it is one of the most sophisticated and is consequently an instructive model for future systems. This section describes AppleScript and its effect on the development of Familiar.

The AppleScript language is composed of control structures (loops, conditionals, statement blocks), common data types (numbers, strings, lists), and interprocess communication. Applications extend the language by adding their own commands; every application makes a dictionary of its commands, object classes, and enumerations available to other programs. Familiar uses the dictionary to model the application, making new, unseen applications compatible immediately and without human intervention.

AppleScript is an attractive platform because it satisfies the previously noted requirements and provides an English-like feedback language. Applications that respond to AppleScript commands are called *scriptable*, and they satisfy the controllability and examinability requirements. Some scriptable applications also report what the user does; these are called *recordable* applications and meet the recordability requirement. Familiar can only work with applications that are both scriptable and recordable. The simple syntax of instructions such as "open folder 'fruit'" or "select file 'apple'" allows users to comprehend commands they would be unable to formulate themselves, particularly when the command describes a recently performed action. This relieves Familiar of the need to implement a second program representation (e.g., anticipation highlighting or a visual language) to communicate with the user.

The remainder of this section describes the weaknesses of AppleScript as a platform for PBD. These can be divided into those that are caused by its high-level event architecture, those that are problems with the language itself, and those that result from poor implementations of the AppleScript specifications.

15.4.1 High-Level Event Architectures

The high-level events employed by AppleScript characterize user actions in an abstract form that omits details of how each operation is performed. In contrast, low-level events correspond directly to specific machine input, describing the user's physical actions rather than their effects. Although high-level events are easier to interpret and search for repetition, they do have drawbacks:

- *Data description:* Data description problems arise because application objects are identified by a description, not accessed directly (e.g., by pointers to memory). If an object changes so that it no longer matches its prior description, then it can no longer be accessed by an external system. Furthermore, the description format is chosen by the application developer and may be inappropriate for the purpose of a particular agent. Generating a data description is a well-known problem in the PBD literature (Halbert 1993) and is by no means specific to AppleScript.

- *Mismatch between interaction and a high-level command:* Some user actions do not correspond directly to high-level events. For example, the Finder allows the user to select and copy part of a file name, but this action is not described by an AppleScript command from the Finder dictionary. This deficiency might be addressed by extending the Finder dictionary to cover selection in text fields, but taken to its logical extreme this solution would add every variation on every command to the dictionary, exploding its size and sacrificing the abstraction of high-level events. A further ambiguity is the role of navigation commands that do not affect data—do they represent significant user actions? Kosbie and Myers (1993) suggest that high-level events correspond to actions that the user might wish to undo.

15.4.2 Deficiencies of the Language

AppleScript was designed for human users and has several shortcomings as an agent communication language—shortcomings that should not be confused with poor implementations of the language in recordable applications.

- *Single-user assumption:* Applications treat commands from agents as though they were user actions, which creates contention when agents activate applications, make selections, or use the clipboard at the same time as the user, because such operations involve global variables—the *frontmost* application, the *selection,* the *clipboard.*

- *Examinability:* Familiar regularly accesses data in other applications, but it is hampered by its inability to traverse object hierarchies at run time and find all the properties of specific objects. The "get every" command can be used to examine hierarchies, but it is difficult to tell whether a given application supports it. Inheritance information is optional and often omitted, preventing an agent from finding all the information relevant to an object. These are arguably implementation problems, but they are systemic because AppleScript lacks standards of compliance.

- *Speed:* AppleScript is notoriously slow, although this drawback has been alleviated by recent versions and machines. The consequences are more far-reaching than sluggish response: the user operates in real time, and if the agent does not react quickly, the opportunity for prediction passes. Familiar can and does fall behind the user's demonstration without interfering with interaction, although it may offer predictions too late and retrieve data that are stale.

- *Timing:* High-level events are reported retrospectively, and agents have no access to data the event has overwritten. Various solutions to this problem have been proposed, but most introduce new timing problems. Apple's *Human Interface Guidelines* (Apple Computer 1992) recommend that interaction be structured so that the user first selects an object (noun) and then applies some action (verb), a style that is reflected in "select-set" cycles (e.g., Figure 15.2[d]). An agent, upon recording the "select" command, can immediately examine the relevant object. In practice, however, the two events are reported almost simultaneously, so the agent cannot examine the selection before the subsequent command. Cypher (1993b) describes an unreleased version of AppleScript that lets the agent examine the application before and after each event, but this is incompatible with current software and introduces another potential timing problem: an agent could fall behind the demonstration, forcing the application to suspend interaction with the user while it responds to the agent.

- *Representing spatial relations:* Textual languages are often inadequate for describing graphical data, one of several shortcomings of English-like programming languages (Thimbleby, Cockburn, and Jones 1992). Given application knowledge, it is possible to represent information graphically, but this sacrifices domain independence and consistency.

- *Persistence of objects and references:* AppleScript objects used in commands are not required to exist after the command is executed. If you store a reference, it may be invalid or identify a different object when it is reused. For example, the Scriptable Text Editor identifies documents with index numbers, where the frontmost is document 1, the next document is 2, and so on. The AppleScript command to bring the rearmost of two open documents to the front is "select document 2," but as soon as it is executed the indexes of the two documents are exchanged, and any future references to "document 2" in fact affect the former "document 1."

- *Undo:* AppleScript has inconsistent support for "Undo" and "Redo" commands. Although many applications support these functions, they do so inconsistently and cannot be relied on. As a result, agents are unable to undo their actions.

15.4.3   Deficiencies of AppleScript Implementations

Many problems with AppleScript implementations can be traced to the developer's assumption that recording will be used by humans rather than agents. Others are the inevitable result of ignoring basic design principles (Simone 1995).

- *Syntax:* Syntactic items are often chosen confusingly. The Microsoft Excel (version 5, 98) command to enter the formula =SUM(A1:A50) in cell B1 is

```
Select Range "R1C2"
set FormulaR1C1 of ActiveCell to "=SUM(RC[-1]:R[49]C[-1])"
```

This command exemplifies several problems. First, the user selects a single `Cell`, but the recording describes it initially as a `Range`, then as `ActiveCell`. It is not clear what `FormulaR1C1` means. The formula itself is the aspect of this trace most likely to confound the user: every `Cell` has a `FormulaR1C1` property, used in the trace, and a `Formula` property, which contains the formula as the user sees it. The latter is simpler and more closely reflects the user's actions, but it is not used.

- *Recordings not matching actions:* The single largest problem with AppleScript recording is that the recording does not always reflect the actions the user has performed. This drawback confuses agents that rely on AppleScript recording to monitor the user's actions, and it misleads the user about the syntax of the language and the effect of commands. Two specific problems occur in the applications used with Familiar: recording extraneous commands and failing to record commands. For example, the formatting commands in Microsoft Excel (version 5, 98) misrepresent the user's actions by adding commands, while Netscape Navigator (versions 3–4.6) does not record the user clicking on a hyperlink.

- *Application behavior changing during recording:* Some applications behave differently when recording than they do normally, which impairs the user's ability to demonstrate. For example, Microsoft Word (version 6, 98) disables the mouse when recording is turned on.

- *Incompletely specified objects:* Objects are often described incorrectly in the application dictionary—particularly with regard to object inheritance. In the Finder (versions 7.5–8.1), for example, alias files are subclasses of files, and files are subclasses of items, but no inheritance relationships are specified. Though they may be intuitively obvious to a person, agents have great difficulties with such omissions.

- *Errors (often fatal):* Many AppleScript implementations contain serious bugs. For example, the "set" command is missing from the Fetch (version 3.0.3) dictionary, and the "resize" command recorded in GIFConverter (version 2.4d18) hangs the machine when replayed.

- *Lack of recordable applications:* Finally, there is a shortage of scriptable and recordable applications. Adding these features to an application incurs extra expense, so not all applications are scriptable. Fewer still are recordable—a prerequisite for Familiar.

15.4.4 Learning from AppleScript's Shortcomings

The shortcomings of AppleScript—which, nevertheless, is a usable platform for PBD—provide insight into the design of scripting architectures and scriptable applications. The three most important steps that application developers can take to make their scriptable applications cooperate with PBD systems and other agents are to design well for human users, to implement recording, and to use sensible data descriptions. Simone's (1995) "human scriptability guidelines" explain how to design the scripting implementation well for users. Syntax that is good for a user is good for an agent, because agents aim to understand and emulate the user.

It is important that AppleScript recording is implemented so that the agent can monitor the user. The recorded actions should describe the user's actions as closely as possible: every significant user action should be included, with no "extra" commands. Unfortunately, it is difficult to judge what might be a significant action, and commands that seem obscure may prove important to users. Navigation commands are problematic; it is usually a good idea to merge consecutive navigation commands unless the application is some form of browser or the commands have side effects on data. Recorded commands should both read well and parse easily, so simple terms are essential. Recordings should not include internal information, and the application's behavior must not change when recording is activated.

Many AppleScript implementations suffer from data description problems, preventing an agent from examining their data. Agents have no intuition, so it is important that the dictionary specifies every class completely, without omitting inheritance relationships. Persistent references are essential, because references that become stale or expire are of no use to an agent. Every property of an object should be accessible through the "get" command (including inherited properties). If a requested property does not exist, then it will return a null object, not an error—errors imply a mistake by the user or agent. The "get every" syntax should be universally supported, and every containee object of a class should share a superclass, so that it is possible to retrieve the contents of an object with a single command.

15.5 Conclusion

End users can be loosely defined as nonprogrammers who are skilled computer operators. They form the largest group who stand to benefit from PBD, but they are unlikely to give up the environments and applications they know for new, possibly inferior, research prototypes. Even if a new product were as polished as an existing equivalent, it is unrealistic to expect end users to abandon the applications they are familiar with and learn new ones for the sake of unproven demonstrational tools. Instead, PBD must be added to existing applications if it is ever to be successfully used—or even evaluated—by typical users.

Familiar demonstrates that commercial operating systems are mature enough to support practical, domain-independent PBD—but only just. As more architectures support PBD's platform requirements—users and applications, recordability, controllability, examinability, user interface, and consistency—we anticipate that reliable, intelligent, domain-independent PBD systems such as Familiar will supersede the humble macro recorder.

Programming by demonstration systems are limited by the environment in which they operate, which explains why they are invariably implemented on research platforms. AppleScript is a (barely) adequate platform; it suffers from a number of deficiencies. Most stem from the fact that it was designed for end users, not for agents. We urge future designers of scripting languages to treat agents as first-class citizens.

References

Apple Computer Inc. 1992. *Macintosh human interface guidelines.* Reading, Mass.: Addison-Wesley.

———. 1993–1999. *AppleScript language guide: English Dialect.* Cupertino, Calif.: Apple Computer Inc.

Bharat, K., and P. Sukaviriya. 1993. Animating user interfaces using animation servers. In *Proceedings of UIST '93.* Atlanta, Ga: ACM Press, New York, NY.

Cheikes, B. A., M. Geier, R. Hyland, F. Linton, L. Rodi, and H. Schaefer. 1998. Embedded training for complex information systems. In *Proceedings of Intelligent Tutoring Systems,* Berlin: Springer.

Cypher, A. 1993a. Bringing programming to end users. Introduction to *Watch what I do: Programming by demonstration,* ed. A. Cypher. Cambridge, Mass.: MIT Press.

———. 1993b. Eager: Programming repetitive tasks by demonstration. In *Watch what I do: Programming by demonstration,* ed. A. Cypher. Cambridge, Mass.: MIT Press.

Halbert, D. 1993. SmallStar: Programming by demonstration in the desktop metaphor. In *Watch what I do: Programming by demonstration,* ed. A. Cypher. Cambridge, Mass.: MIT Press.

Kay, J., and R. C. Thomas. 1995. Studying long-term system use. *Communications of the ACM* 38, no. 7: (July): 61–69.

Kosbie, D., and B. Myers. 1993. A system-wide macro facility based on aggregate events: A proposal. In *Watch what I do: Programming by demonstration,* ed. A. Cypher. Cambridge, Mass.: MIT Press.

Lieberman, H. 1993. Mondrian: A teachable graphical editor. In *Watch what I do: Programming by demonstration,* ed. A. Cypher. Cambridge, Mass.: MIT Press.

———. 1998. Integrating user interface agents with conventional applications. In *Proceedings of the International Conference on Intelligent User Interfaces,* (San Francisco, January). New York, NY: ACM Press.

Linton, F., A. Charron, and D. Joy. 1998. OWL: A recommender system for organisation-wide learning. Technical report, The MITRE Corporation.

Miura, M., and J. Tanaka. 1998. A framework for event-driven demonstration based on the Java toolkit. In *Proceedings of the Asia Pacific computer human interaction conference.* Kanagawa, Japan: IEEE Computing Society, Los Alamitos, CA.

Myers, B. A., and D. S. Kosbie. 1996. Reusable hierarchical command objects. In *Proceedings of CHI'96,* Vancouver, Canada: ACM Press, New York, N.Y.

Olsen, D. R., Jr., S. E. Hudson, T. Verratti, J. M. Heiner, and M. Phelps. 1999. Implementing interface attachments based on surface representations. *Proceedings of CHI'99.* Pittsburgh, PA: ACM Press, New York, N.Y.

Paynter, G. W. 2000. Automating iterative tasks with programming by demonstration. Ph.D. diss. University of Waikato, New Zealand.

Piernot, P. P., and M. P. Yvon. 1993. The AIDE project: An application-independent demonstrational environment. In *Watch what I do: Programming by demonstration,* ed. A. Cypher. Cambridge, Mass.: MIT Press.

Ritter, S., and K. R. Koedinger. 1995. Towards lightweight tutoring agents. In *Proceedings of the World Conference on Artificial Intelligence in Education (AI-ED'95),* (Washington, D.C., August). (Cited in Cheikes et al. 1998.)

Simone, C. 1995. Designing a scripting implementation. *Develop* 21 (March): 48–72.

Thimbleby, H., A. Cockburn, and S. Jones. 1992. HyperCard: An object-oriented disappointment. In *Building interactive systems: Architectures and tools,* ed. P. D. Gray and R. Took. Berlin: Springer.

Yvon, M., P. Piernot, and N. Cot. 1995. Programming by demonstration: Detect repetitive tasks in telecom services. In *Proceedings OZCHI '95.* Wollongong, Australia.

CHAPTER 16

Stimulus-Response PBD: Demonstrating "When" as Well as "What"

DAVID W. WOLBER

University of San Francisco

BRAD A. MYERS

Carnegie Mellon University

Abstract

Many programming-by-demonstration (PBD) systems elaborate on the idea of macro recording, and they allow users to extend existing applications. Few, however, allow new interfaces to be created from scratch because they do not provide a means of demonstrating when a recorded macro should be invoked. This chapter discusses stimulus-response systems that allow both the when (stimulus/event) and the what (response macro) to be demonstrated.

16.1 Introduction

When a client hires a programmer, he generally will meet with her to show how he wants the proposed application to behave. Using a graphics editor, scratch paper, or even a dinner napkin, the client sketches the proposed interface and then walks the programmer through its behaviors, first playing the role of the end user and showing what actions he can take, and then playing the role of the system and showing how it will respond to a particular stimulus.

The goal of our research has been to automate this process, to build software tools that do the job of the human programmer in such a scenario. We envision a system that watches a client demonstrate behaviors and automatically creates the desired application.

16.1.1 PBD: An Elaboration of Macro Recording

Our research is based on the programming-by-demonstration (PBD) systems described in Cypher (1993), including Eager (Cypher 1991), SmallStar (Halbert 1984), Chimera (Kurland and Feiner 1991), Mondrian (Leiberman 1993), and Peridot (Myers 1990). These systems elaborate on a concept familiar to many computer users—macro recording. With macro recording, the user tells the system to watch him execute operations so they can be recorded and played back later. The goal is to give a name to a sequence of operations so the user won't have to repeat those operations again and again.

PBD elaborates on the concept of macros by generalizing the sequence of operations demonstrated. For instance, with Lieberman's (1993)

Mondrian system, a user can demonstrate the drawing of three rectangles around a square. Mondrian records the three DrawRectangle operations but generalizes them with parameters so that the recorded macro can be used to draw an arch around any square of any size.

16.1.2 PBD Macro Invocation

Once a macro is created, there must be a way to invoke it. Mondrian creates a new item in the palette of operations—the user just clicks the item to invoke the macro. Other systems just allow the user to execute a previously recorded macro by choosing it from a menu or list.

A standard method of invoking previously recorded macros is sufficient to help a user eliminate repetitive tasks in existing applications. But, as outlined in an earlier article (Kosbie and Myers 1993), sometimes a user would like to create a macro and have it invoked when a particular event occurs. For instance, a user might want to extend her desktop so that the next day's calendar is printed (the macro) when she logs out (the macro invocation event).

Eager (Cypher 1991) and its successors (see Chapters 14 and 15) focus on macro invocation by combining PBD with a predictive interface. They watch a user work and learn to invoke macros after the user has explicitly executed its first few operations (i.e., they finish the job for the user).

But whereas the goal of these systems is to extend existing applications, our goal is to allow users to build complete interfaces starting with a blank canvas. Thus, we must provide mechanisms so that a designer can *explicitly* specify both macros and the events that invoke them.

To facilitate this goal, we have built a number of systems based on a two-phase process called *programming by stimulus-response demonstration* (McDaniel and Myers 1999; Myers, McDaniel, and Kosbie 1993; Wolber and Fisher 1991; Wolber 1997). With this process, the user first demonstrates the stimulus (invocation event), then demonstrates the response (macro procedure) that it invokes. The system then infers a behavior so that, at run time, when the stimulus is executed, it triggers the corresponding response.

The inclusion of macro invocation complicates PBD for both the designer and the underlying system. Macro recording is already difficult for many users, as it is easy to forget whether the Record button is on. Adding another mode button for "Record stimulus" complicates matters even more.

Furthermore, the events that can trigger activity are often more complicated than the activity itself. Actions can be triggered by many different type of events, including low-level actions (e.g., mouse and keyboard actions), high-level operations (e.g., the rotation of an acceleration gauge can speed up a car), or the interface being in a particular context (a bullet intersecting a target).

Thus, it is a challenge to provide a simple "syntax" for demonstrating behaviors. It is also a challenge to provide a powerful enough generalization mechanism to infer the response operations and their parameters. Generalization is complicated because a response operation can be dependent on the stimulus and its parameters. For instance, a car responds (speeds up) an amount proportional to how much the acceleration gauge is modified.

16.1.3   Augmenting the Capabilities of Traditional Interface Builders

Stimulus-response demonstration can augment the capabilities of interface builders such as Visual Basic (Microsoft).[1] These popular tools significantly decrease the time and expertise necessary to define the *layout* of an interface, but the designer must still code its dynamic *behavior*. For instance, a Visual Basic designer can easily change the static location of an object in the interface by dragging it, but specifying that the object should be moved at *run time* in response to some stimulus (e.g., a button click) requires coding.

Our strategy is to provide the designer with a complete set of widget, text, and graphics operations, along with the capability of using them for both drawing the interface and demonstrating its dynamic behavior. With such a capability, the designer is not restricted to wiring together standard widgets such as menus, list boxes, and buttons but can instead draw arbitrary graphics and demonstrate how they respond to stimuli (we call these *application-specific behaviors*). Such capabilities allow nonprogrammers to create animated and graphical applications and not be limited to standard business-type applications.

16.1.4   A Quick Example

Consider how stimulus-response demonstration is used to create a Celsius-Fahrenheit converter in the Pavlov system (Wolber 1997, 1998). The designer first draws two thermometers, as shown in Figure 16.1. Note that the thermometers in Figure 16.1 consist of raw graphics—they are not widgets with predefined behavior. After drawing the thermometers, the designer

---

1. msdn.microsoft.com/vbasic.

FIGURE   **16.1**

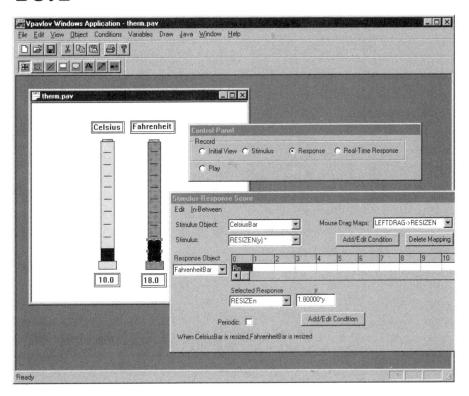

Pavlov development of a Celsius-Fahrenheit converter, with the control panel (upper right) as a video-recorder-like mode palette that allows the designer to draw, record stimuli, record responses, or "play" interfaces. The Stimulus-Response Score (lower right) displays a high-level representation of the behaviors that have already been demonstrated.

uses the same drawing operations to demonstrate the interface's behavior. He first tells the system he is demonstrating a stimulus—he selects "Stimulus" mode in the control panel—then stretches the Celsius indicator ten pixels up. Then, in "Response" mode, he demonstrates how the system should respond to the stimulus: he stretches the Fahrenheit indicator eighteen pixels along the y-axis (he might also modify the text box below the Celsius thermometer if he hasn't already demonstrated this behavior previously).

From the demonstrations, the system infers a generalized behavior. In this case it infers that any time the Celsius bar is moved, the Fahrenheit bar should be moved 9/5 (1.8) as much. When the interface is executed and the end user moves the Celsius bar, the Fahrenheit bar is moved the proportional amount.

16.1.5 Wait a Second!

An example like the Celsius-Fahrenheit converter inspires more questions than it answers. How does the system know to infer the 9/5 proportion? Can the end user move the Celsius indicator outside its enclosing box? How would such a restriction be demonstrated? If the designer doesn't like what the system infers, can she change it? Can animated behaviors and timing be specified? Can more complex stimuli be demonstrated, such as the behaviors of a PacMan character?

Trying to answer such questions is the challenge of our research. This chapter introduces what we have learned over the last decade in building our early systems (DEMO [Wolber and Fisher 1991] and Marquise [Myers et al. 1993]) and their successors (Pavlov [Wolber 1997] and Gamut [McDaniel and Myers 1999], respectively). Our goal is a system that allows the behavior of any interface to be defined without coding. There has been some significant progress: stimulus-response demonstration can be used to create such complex interfaces as diagram editors, driving simulators, shooting arcades, board games, and even PacMan. However, stimulus-response demonstration has not been included in any commercial interface builders, and much research is still needed to reach the ultimate goal.

In this chapter, we'll view stimulus-response as a kind of programming language, in which the language consists of behavior demonstrations instead of code. Thus, we'll provide an overview of alternatives for both the syntax and the semantics of stimulus-response languages. We'll also discuss various alternatives for providing feedback to designers so that they can view and edit a high-level representation of the behaviors that have already been specified.

16.2 The Syntax of Stimulus-Response

The syntax of a stimulus-response system is the mechanism by which a user presents the "example" behaviors to the system. Providing a usable syntax is a challenge because the system is providing the end user with much more power than most software—it is allowing him to create software, not just use it. The key difficulty is that a user must perform the same actions both to use the system and to demonstrate the behavior of the target software being created.

Perhaps the most straightforward syntax is to provide a video-recorder-like mode palette as shown in Figure 16.1 and used in DEMO, Pavlov, and Marquise. The designer uses "Initial View" mode to draw the *initial* interface. The system keeps a record of the initial state of each graphic, so that it can snap back to it after the designer demonstrates stimuli and responses. Pavlov reverts to this initial state whenever "Initial View" or "Play" mode is selected.

In "Stimulus" mode, the designer plays the role of end user and demonstrates an event. This event can be as simple as a button click or key press, or it can be one of the drawing operations (e.g., "Move," "Rotate"). It can also be contextualized; that is, the designer can demonstrate a graphical condition that must be true before a response is triggered.

Often the stimulus is something the end user initiates directly at run time, but not always. For instance, one stimulus might trigger the execution of a series of response operations, and one of those operations in turn might trigger some other response. In such a case, the designer would demonstrate two behaviors, the first with an "end-user" stimulus, the second with a "system" stimulus. The different types of stimuli are discussed in detail later in this section.

After a stimulus is recorded, the system automatically changes the mode to Response mode. In this mode, the designer plays the role of the system by executing the operations that should occur in response to the stimulus. To end the response sequence, the designer changes to any other mode. Play mode allows the interface to be executed. In some systems, the development menus and palettes disappear in Play mode, leaving only the target interface.

16.2.1 Eliminating Modes

Conventional interface builders such as Visual Basic have two modes: "build" and "test." Environments like the one described earlier add at least two more to the mix: "record stimulus" and "record response." We have found that users have significant difficulty keeping track of the current mode when these additional modes are added.

Some systems provide alternative syntax that eliminate one or more of the modes. Chimera (Kurlander and Feiner 1991) effectively eliminates response mode by recording all actions in a history list and requiring the designer, after the fact, to signify which actions in the list should be part of a macro (response). Such a scheme could be applied to a stimulus-response system by requiring the designer also to signify an operation in the history list as the stimulus.

Peridot (Myers 1990) provides an onscreen virtual mouse that eliminates some of the need for a stimulus mode. Instead of choosing stimulus mode and using the physical mouse to demonstrate what the end user might do, the Peridot designer drags the logical mouse to the object and manipulates it.

Gamut (McDaniel and Myers 1999) eliminates stimulus mode by replacing the four-mode palette with two buttons: "Do Something!" and "Stop That!" (see Figure 16.2). When the user performs an action that is supposed to do something and it doesn't, she hits the Do Something! button. The event just prior to pushing the button is assumed to be the stimulus. The system is then in Response mode until the user hits "Done" (the Done button appears when the system is in Response mode). Stop That! is used to give negative examples when the system does something wrong; it also puts the system in response mode, and it tells the system to eliminate the response(s) that were previously recorded. Besides eliminating stimulus mode, the Gamut scheme also eliminates the distinction between build and test mode by having the system always be in test mode (i.e., any previously defined behaviors are always active, even when the designer is editing).

16.2.2   Demonstrating Stimuli

Software systems commonly allow any of the following stimuli to trigger a response in an interface:

- an end user manipulating the mouse or keyboard (physical operations),

- the execution of some drawing editor operation, such as Move or Rotate (logical operations),

- objects in the interface exhibiting some state or context,

- the passage of time, or

- the execution of some application event.

The syntax for demonstrating each of these stimuli are discussed in the following sections.

FIGURE **16.2**

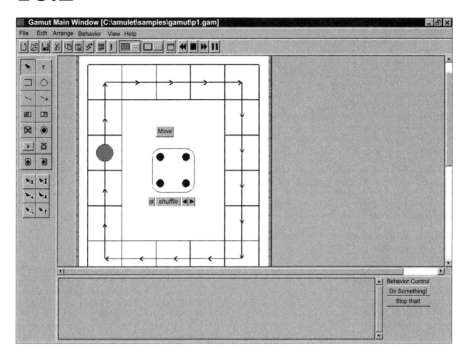

A Gamut screen creating a board game. The graphics, text, and widget operations are accessed in the menus (top and left); the behavior control panel (lower right) provides "Do Something!" and "Stop That!" buttons that both initiate response demonstrations.

Physical and Logical Operations

One key aspect of PBD interface builders, as opposed to PBD macro systems that extend existing applications, is that the base system (e.g., the drawing palette, menu, and other mechanisms) *does not appear at run time.* Thus, unless the designer explicitly demonstrates that end users can perform an operation in the target interface, they won't be able to.

For example, during development, the designer can rotate any object by choosing Rotate in the drawing mode palette. But if the designer wants the end user to be able to rotate that object, she must demonstrate a stimulus-response behavior that maps a mouse drag to a rotate operation.

Some systems require this physical (mouse drag) to logical (Rotate) mapping to be explicitly demonstrated. In DEMO (Wolber and Fisher 1991), when the designer clicks on an object in stimulus mode, she is prompted to choose between the mouse operations up, down, drag, enter, and exit. The designer selects one and then demonstrates the response that should be linked to the chosen stimulus.

Gamut provides special mouse operation icons that can be dragged onto an object to demonstrate the physical operation. (These are visible at the left of Figure 16.2, below the drawing palette). Since there is an icon for each type of operation, no choice dialogue is necessary.

If the physical → logical mapping is explicit, the designer needs two demonstrations for behaviors such as the Celsius-Fahrenheit program in Figure 16.1:

one to specify the physical mapping:

LeftMouseDrag → CelsiusBar.Move

and one for the logical mapping:

CelsiusBar.Move → FahrenheitBar.Move.

Pavlov eliminates the need for two demonstrations in such cases. When the designer moves an object in stimulus mode, the system implicitly infers the drag → Move mapping, and also records that the Move should be mapped to the upcoming response operation(s). The advantage is convenience; the disadvantage of inferring the physical-logical mapping is that sometimes the designer only wants to map a logical stimulus to logical response(s) and doesn't want the physical-logical mapping. For instance, in a shooting arcade game, the designer demonstrates that moving a bullet (and hitting a target) should cause a response of deleting the target. In Pavlov, when the bullet.Move stimulus is demonstrated, the system infers a physical-logical mapping (i.e., that the end user can move the bullet by dragging it). To restrict the end user from doing this, the designer must use the editor to delete the mapping.

Context-Triggered Behaviors

Sometimes the activity in an interface should be executed in response not to an operation but to the interface reaching a particular context or state. For instance, in the shooting arcade game, a target should be deleted only when a bullet intersects the target, as shown in Figure 16.3.

FIGURE **16.3**

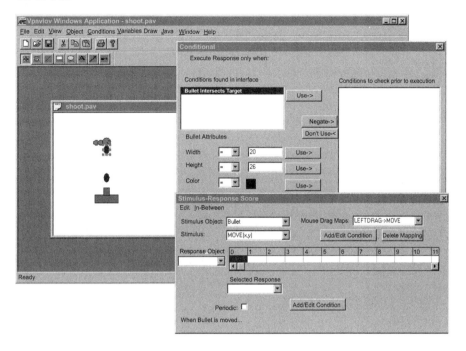

Pavlov development of an arcade game. The condition dialogue (upper right) appears when the system identifies a condition during a stimulus demonstration.

Such context-based stimuli are the focus of graphical rewrite systems such as Creator, which can be considered as a type of stimulus-response system. Demonstrations in these systems consist of selecting a portion of the interface (a set of cells in the grid) that make up a "before state" and then manipulating the objects residing in the selected portion of the grid to show an "after state."

In terms of stimulus-response, the stimulus is the "before picture" instead of an operation. At run time, the system continually tests to see whether the demonstrated "before picture" occurs. When it identifies such a state, it executes the operations required to put the interface in the demonstrated "after state."

Like Creator, Pavlov allows context to be demonstrated, but it does not provide a special "demonstrate 'before-state' stimulus" mode. Instead, it integrates context directly into its stimulus-response model. The rationale is that an interface does not magically enter a particular state but will only do so as a result of some operation. Thus, the designer always demonstrates a triggering stimulus operation, but during or prior to this demonstration, she puts the system in the state that must be true for the stimulus to trigger its response.

Consider again the shooting arcade game in Figure 16.3. In Pavlov, the designer demonstrates a move of a bullet as the stimulus but completes the move (releases the mouse) so that the bullet intersects a target (see Figure 16.3). The system records the move stimulus and identifies conditions, such as "intersect," relating the objects in the interface. Textual descriptions of these conditions are listed so the designer can choose which should be used as part of the stimulus. In this case, the designer selects *Bullet.Intersects(Target)* and then demonstrates the deletion of the target as the response. At run time, every time a bullet moves, the system checks the intersect condition and executes the response only if the condition is true.

Since all conditions are subordinate to a stimulus operation, there is a run-time efficiency gain compared to traditional rewrite schemes. The system need only check a particular condition when the stimulus is executed, instead of after every time stamp. There is a syntactical disadvantage, however. If different stimuli can cause the same result (e.g., there are two objects, and movement of either might lead to a situation where they intersect), then the designer must demonstrate two separate behaviors.

Both Creator's graphical rewrite rule scheme and Pavlov's stimulus-response scheme have limitations in terms of the kinds of context that can be demonstrated. Creator restricts context specification (and object movement) to discrete grid coordinates (e.g., the target game behavior might be described as "trigger the response when the bullet is *one square below the target*"). This grid restriction simplifies the syntax, but it also limits the conditions and behaviors that can be specified.

Though Pavlov's scheme isn't restricted by a grid basis, it is limited by the set of conditions or object relationships (e.g., intersect, encloses, etc.) for which it searches. It also requires the designer to specify AND, OR, and NOT relations in a dialogue when a condition is complex; in a system using graphical rewrite rules, the designer can specify such complex conditions with a single picture.

Gamut, like Pavlov, bases its context identification on object attributes and relationships and not on grid-based relationships. A general goal of Gamut is to eliminate the need for the designer to choose the correct generalization (e.g., condition), as is done in Pavlov. The reasoning is that the representation of context, whether textual or graphical, is inherently complex, so choosing can be difficult. Gamut's philosophy, similar to that of InferenceBear (Frank and Foley 1995), is to allow the designer to perform multiple demonstrations of the same context. The system then uses artificial intelligence (AI) techniques to infer the intended context from the samples. Gamut also asks the designer to provide hints by selecting objects that are relevant to the context. The hints allow more complex conditions to be inferred than are possible in other systems (see Chapter 8).

It should be noted that the idea of demonstrating context is also important in Web information extraction systems. These systems allow designers to build new pages that are composites of information extracted from various other Web pages. Because Web pages change so rapidly, the difficulty lies in centrally describing the information to be extracted so that even if the Web page changes, the description is still valid. Chapters 4 and 5 in this book explore techniques for automatically generating such descriptions from a user's demonstrations.

Time as a Stimulus

Sometimes activity should occur at a certain time, rather than in response to an external event. Gamut allows the designer to drag a special clock widget into the background window and then demonstrate a tick as a stimulus. Pavlov provides a special stimulus called "beginning of execution" that a designer can specify as the current stimulus. He can then select a time frame and demonstrate responses that, at run time, are executed at a particular time.

Structured Text as a Stimulus

Sometimes activity should be triggered when the user types in a piece of structured information. For instance, when a user enters a street address, an interface might automatically open a map with the address as the destination. The work described in Chapter 12 allows a designer to demonstrate example instances of structured types and then automatically build a grammar that can recognize new instances.

System Events as Stimuli

An earlier article (Kosbie and Myers 1993) proposed a generalized event-based invocation scheme for stimulus specification. In this scheme, the system would register events for both low-level user actions (e.g., mouse and keyboard clicks) and the high-level interpretations (e.g., menu item *Delete* selected, or object A moved), and macros created by demonstration could be invoked when these events occur. This would allow such behaviors as creating a macro that copies files to a backup area that is invoked before a delete operation or printing out tomorrow's calendar before logging out.

16.2.3 Demonstrating Responses

A *response* is any action that creates, transforms, or deletes an object in an interface. Though most PBD research systems are based on fairly rudimentary graphics editors, the idea is that a commercial system would provide a full range of graphic and text-editing capabilities, and even access to a database and its operations.

Pavlov combines PBD with some animation mechanisms that allow timing to be specified on behaviors. Using Pavlov's time line, the designer can specify a time stamp, relative to the stimulus, for a demonstrated response. Pavlov also provides a special mode, similar to one in Macromedia's Director (version 7.0) called *Real Time Response* mode. When this mode is chosen, the system records a sequence of time-stamped operations (an animation path) as the designer demonstrates an operation. The designer can also specify animation by stipulating that a response be executed *periodically* at run time.

Pavlov also allows a designer to specify the direction (nose) of an object using a guide object. Consider, for instance, the development of a driving simulator (Figure 16.4). After drawing the car, accelerator slider bar, and steering wheel, the designer specifies the "nose" of the car by manipulating a special guide object representing its direction. She then demonstrates a stimulus of moving the accelerator slider bar, and a response of moving the car, and marks the response as periodic. Because the car has a notion of direction, its movement is restricted—the designer can only demonstrate that it moves forward or backward relative to the direction vector. In Pavlov, the response is recorded not as a Move(x,y) but as a (periodic) MoveForward operation. At run time, the car goes faster or slower as the accelerator is manipulated.

16.2.4 Demonstration Aids: Guide Objects and Ghost Marks

Guide object like the one described above are graphics that the designer uses during development but doesn't want to appear at run time (Fisher, Busse, and Wolber 1992). For instance, the designer might use a directed line to show how a game piece can move around the board. In Gamut, the designer simply sets an object property to specify that it is a guide object. It

FIGURE **16.4**

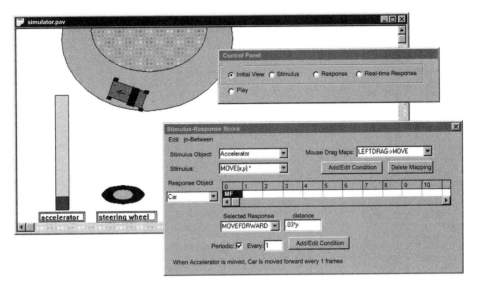

A driving simulator built in Pavlov. The arrow on the car is a guide object denoting the direction of the car.

then appears in pastel colors during development and disappears at run time. In Figure 16.2, the arrow lines in the center of the boxes are guide objects to help show where the pieces can move. When the designer drags a game piece along a line, the system can infer that he is demonstrating a move from one end point of the line to the other (instead of a move by some offset). Thus, behaviors such as moving one (or more) squares in a game can be demonstrated.

Gamut also provides a backstage area in which all objects are guide objects. The objects in this area generally store "computational" information in the form of text boxes or other widgets. For example, a widget might store whose turn it is or the number of lives left. By replacing information traditionally stored in program variables, the need to connect an interface to application code is reduced or eliminated.

Marquise introduced the idea of leaving trails, or ghost marks, of the mouse cursor as it is moved, so the designer can hook responses to points on its path. Gamut extended the idea so that the previous state of an object also appears after it is transformed. Thus, a designer can specify an operation dependent on that previous state (e.g., that Object A is moved to the previous location of Object B after Object B is moved).

16.3 The Semantics of Stimulus-Response

The generalization or inference machine of a stimulus-response system interprets the meaning of the examples a designer provides during the demonstration. It takes the demonstrated stimulus-response examples as input and output behaviors that, if represented as code, would appear something like this:

```
On StimulusObject.Stimulus(<formal parameters>)
{
  if (checkcontext)
    Operation(<ResponseObject>,<other response parameters>)
    . . .
}
```

Some major challenges in interpreting the examples are as follows:

- Which object(s) is the designer signifying with her demonstrations?

- What should the parameters of the response operation(s) be?

- How should context modify the inferred behavior?

There are two main methods of generalization, based on whether the system allows more than one example of a behavior to be demonstrated. Pavlov generalizes from a single example, in the tradition of early PBD systems such as SmallStar (Halbert 1984) and Chimera (Lieberman 1993). In AI terms, such single-example systems are known as *explanation-based learning systems.*

The philosophy behind using single examples is to keep the inference machine simple so the designer can understand it and then provide a second-level editor that allows the designer to modify generalizations easily. Single-example systems use as much domain knowledge as they can so that the single "guess" is as accurate as possible.

In contrast, Gamut generalizes from multiple examples. In AI terms, multiple-example systems are known as *empirical learning systems.* Because more information is provided with multiple examples, these systems can infer more complex behaviors and need not rely as much on domain knowledge. However, it is more difficult for the designer to understand what the system is doing, and the syntax is also complicated because a demonstration can conceivably be performed to edit, refine, or append (add another response) to a particular behavior.

Chapter 3 discusses generalization for PBD systems in general, focusing on the question of how much intelligence should be incorporated. This section explores generalization in the context of stimulus-response systems specifically.

16.3.1 Object Descriptor Problem

Perhaps the most important problem in generalizing from examples is the *object descriptor* problem (Halbert 1984)—determining the object or objects that the designer intends to signify when she demonstrates an action on an example object. In terms of the generated code template shown at the beginning of this section, the problem consists of how to describe the StimulusObject and ResponseObject of the code.

Sometimes no generalization need occur, as there is a one-to-one correspondence between the *demonstrated object* and the *intended run-time object*. For example, in the Celsius-Fahrenheit example, FahrenheitBar is the demonstrated response object, and it is the intended run-time object as well. FahrenheitBar is an example of a *constant object descriptor*.

In some cases, however, the designer intends the demonstration object to be representative of some set of objects or some single object that cannot be described with a constant. When the demonstration object is a dynamically allocated object, the object *can't* be described with a constant. Consider, for instance, the dynamically created bullets in an arcade game. A particular development-time bullet won't appear at run time, because no bullets appear until a "shotgun" stimulus occurs. When an action is demonstrated on a bullet (e.g., movement), a nonconstant descriptor *must* be inferred for it.

There are also cases when a nonconstant descriptor is appropriate even though the demonstration object itself is statically created. For example, consider a board game that has a group of pieces that are statically created. When the designer demonstrates moving a piece, he may be signifying that the piece to move at run time is the one for the player whose turn it is, and he is using the particular piece as a representative of that concept.

Pavlov is a single-example system, so it only infers nonconstant descriptors for demonstrations on dynamic objects, since those *must* be generalized into nonconstants. Pavlov includes a number of heuristics to guide its generalization of dynamic objects. The most simple inference is that the dynamic demonstration object represents all instances, at run time, that have been created by the same stimulus. For example, suppose that the bullets in an arcade game are created by pressing the up-arrow key. If the designer demonstrates a stimulus of clicking a button, and a response of changing a particular bullet's color to blue, Pavlov infers that at run time, clicking the button changes the color of all bullets (created by an up arrow).

Pavlov does identify special cases that use more distinguishing descriptors. For instance, if a transformation is demonstrated in the same response sequence as a creation (e.g., a bullet is created then moved), then the object descriptor will be "the same instance as the one just created." If a response is demonstrated on the same object as the stimulus, the inferred descriptor is "the same instance as the stimulus." And, as mentioned in Section 16.2.2, Pavlov identifies existing conditions that exist when the example is demonstrated, so the designer can add if-then complexity to a descriptor if desired. In practice, Pavlov's special rules and condition identifier cover a wide range of behaviors. But no matter how many heuristics are used, the system will sometimes guess wrong using only a single example. In these cases, second-level editing or coding is necessary.

Because Gamut uses multiple examples, it can infer nonconstant descriptors for static and dynamic objects. After the first example, a constant descriptor is generally inferred, but as more examples are provided, the system analyzes the properties of the example objects to infer more complex descriptors.

Gamut also reduces the number of required examples by asking users to give *hints* about which of the many interface objects are important. With hints, the system can infer object descriptors that depend on objects that are not directly modified by the example action itself. Consider, for example, a two-player board game that has a red piece, a blue piece, and a toggle specifying whose turn it is. To specify the behavior, the designer first sets the toggle to true and demonstrates moving the red piece. He then sets the toggle to false and demonstrates moving the blue piece. At this point the system knows a nonconstant descriptor is needed to describe the piece that should be moved, but it doesn't know where to start. Thus, it asks the designer to select what auxiliary objects, besides the piece, the behavior depends on. When the designer selects the toggle, the system infers an object descriptor such as "the red piece if the toggle is true, the blue piece if the toggle is false."

16.3.2 Response Parameter Descriptors

In addition to the object parameter, PBD systems must infer the other parameters of an operation (see the "<other response parameters>" in the code at the start of Section 16.3). For example, a move operation has both the object to be moved and the position to which it moves. Again, the simplest inference is that the parameter is constant, but even this situation presents ambiguity: Did the designer intend the destination demonstrated or the offset demonstrated (i.e., move to this location, or move by this amount)? Single-example systems must guess in this situation. Multiple-example systems can usually distinguish after two examples.

Inferring constant parameters is hardly the most challenging issue. For instance, the position to which a board game piece should be moved in Figure 16.2 might be described as "take the number on the dice and move that number of spaces clockwise around the board from where the piece used to be." Such a parameter can be inferred by Gamut but not by other systems. The following sections discuss various techniques that can be used for generalizing nonconstant parameters.

16.3.3 Linear Proportions

Pavlov takes advantage of the observation that many interface behaviors have response parameters that are proportional to the corresponding stimulus parameters. The Celsius-Fahrenheit converter is one example: when one gauge is transformed, the other one should be transformed 5/9 (9/5) as much. Another example is a diagram editor in which moving a node should cause the ends of all lines connected to it to be moved by the same amount.

Pavlov uses the heuristic that when a stimulus and response are both transformations (e.g., Moves), each response parameter is inferred to be proportional to the corresponding stimulus parameter. As with object descriptors, Pavlov also watches for special cases. For instance, if the designer demonstrated a Move(20,0) as a stimulus, and a Move(0,40) as a response, it maps the nonzero second parameter of the response to the nonzero first parameter of the stimulus.

InferenceBear (Frank and Foley 1994) infers other linear combinations of parameter values from multiple examples of the desired behavior. This feature eliminates the need for hard-wired special cases but requires the user to choose the examples carefully. Furthermore, InferenceBear can take into account properties of the object that do not participate in the action (Pavlov only analyzes the demonstrated stimulus and response objects). For instance, in the shooting arcade game, Inference Bear can infer after multiple examples that the parameters of the bullet creation depends on the location of the gun, though the gun is not part of the stimulus or response.

16.3.4   Complex Parameters

Gamut adds even more inferencing power by using decision trees and other AI algorithms and by allowing the designer to provide hints to help the system generalize the parameters. For instance, after the first example of a bullet creation was provided, Gamut would ask the designer to point out objects that are important. The designer would select the gun, and Gamut would use this to infer the correct create response parameters (i.e., that the bullet should be created directly above the gun). In this way, hints can allow the system to "guess" the correct behavior more quickly than in systems that don't ask the designer for extra help.

Gamut can also compute the parameters using values from many objects. Examples include setting the color of an object based on the color of a palette or computing the position of the board game piece using the dice as mentioned earlier. As a result, Gamut can be used to create complete applications such as a Turing machine, tic-tac-toe, or a PacMan game.

16.4   Feedback and Editing

When a PBD system infers a program from a designer's demonstration, it doesn't always infer the program that the designer intended. One solution is to allow the designer to demonstrate more examples until, hopefully, the system infers the intended program. But with such a scheme, the designer can never be sure what program the system has inferred and can feel lost not knowing what to do next. Another approach is to ask the designer questions that will hopefully disambiguate the examples. However, our experience with such systems suggest that users have great difficulty answering such questions and generally choose "yes" if given a choice, assuming the computer is right, even when it isn't.

It is clear from our experience that the designer really needs to see some representation of the inferred program and be able to edit it. Here lies the dilemma, called the *PBD representation problem:* Since the goal of PBD is to allow people that aren't programmers to create programs, the system probably shouldn't represent a program as conventional computer code (C++,

FIGURE **16.5**

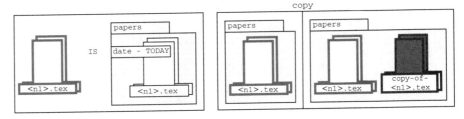

A Pursuit storyboard showing a file manipulation program created by demonstration in Pursuit.

Java, etc.). Even special-purpose scripting languages, such as those generated by DEMO and InferenceBear, are difficult for end users.

16.4.1 Storyboards

One solution is to present a graphical, storyboard representation of the inferred programs (Kurlander and Feiner 1991; Leiberman 1993; Modugno, Corbett, and Myers 1997). Figure 16.5 shows one from Pursuit (Modugno et al. 1997) that represents copying all the files edited today in the papers folder that end in ".tex".

Storyboards allow a designer to see what the system has recorded and what generalizations it has made. These "programs" can also be edited by moving files around, deleting them, or selecting them and redemonstrating the particular operation.

16.4.2 The Stimulus-Response Score

Unlike Pursuit, stimulus-response systems must provide a representation that includes the triggering stimulus. In Pavlov, a dialogue is provided that allows the designer to select an object and a current stimulus (Figure 16.6). When the stimulus is changed, either with the dialogue or by a stimulus demonstration, the corresponding time line (middle of Figure 16.6) shows only the responses corresponding to that stimulus. The designer can edit the parameters of each response (x and y in Figure 16.6) and can click Add/ Edit Condition to view and edit a graphical condition on the stimulus.

FIGURE **16.6**

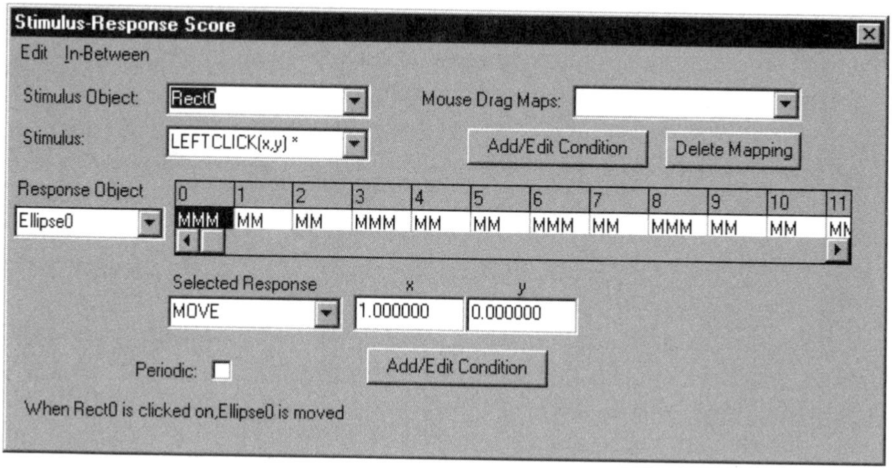

The Pavlov Editor showing an animation path triggered by a button click. In this example, the current stimulus is a LEFTCLICK on Rect0. The displayed response is an animation path (a series of moves) involving Ellipse0.

Because there is a time line for each stimulus, and because operations, not object states, are recorded, the designer can specify interfaces in which objects behave asynchronously. Chapter 17 of this book provides more details.

It should be noted that Pavlov's stimulus-response score not only is used to view and edit behaviors after the fact but is integrated into the demonstration environment. For instance, the designer can choose a current stimulus in the score, instead of demonstrating it, if she knows its name and doesn't need to specify parameters for it graphically. As mentioned earlier, she can also use the time line in the score to specify time stamps prior to demonstrating responses.

16.5 Conclusion

Many people use software, but few can create it. One of the only areas of creation open to most people is to build static Web pages with one type of stimulus: the button click on a link. Stimulus-response systems can open up creativity by allowing people to build applications that come alive, both for the Web and for the desktop.

Our research has introduced some of the alternatives of stimulus-response system design, in terms of syntax, semantics, and feedback. The next step, we believe, is detailed empirical testing between alternatives, either through research or the widespread use that would occur if stimulus-response technology were added to a popular interface builder.

References

Cypher, A. 1991. Eager: Programming repetitive tasks by example. In *Proceedings of CHI'91,* (New Orleans, May).

Cypher, A., D. Halbert, D. Kurlander, H. Lieberman, D. Maulsby, B. Myers, A. Turransky, eds. *Watch what I do: Programming by demonstration.* Cambridge, Mass.: MIT Press.

Halbert, D. 1984. Programming by example. Ph.D. diss., University of California, Berkeley.

Frank, M. R., and J. D. Foley. 1994. A pure reasoning engine for programming by demonstration. In *Proceedings UIST'94: ACM SIGGRAPH symposium on user interface software and technology.* (Marina del Rey, Calif.). New York, NY: ACM Press.

Fisher, G. L, D. E. Busse, and D. Wolber. 1992. Adding rule-based reasoning to a demonstrational interface builder. In *Proceedings of UIST'92.* (Monterey, Calif.). New York, NY: ACM Press.

Kosbie, D. S., and B. A. Myers. 1993. PBD invocation techniques: A review and proposal. In *Watch what I do: Programming by demonstration,* ed. A. Cypher. Cambridge, Mass.: MIT Press.

Kurlander, D., and S. Feiner. 1991. Inferring constraints from multiple snapshots. *ACM Transcations on Graphics* (May).

Lieberman, H. 1993. Mondrian: A teachable graphical editor. In *Watch what I do: Programming by demonstration,* ed. A. Cypher. Cambridge, Mass.: MIT Press.

McDaniel, R., and B. Myers. 1999. Getting more out of programming-by-demonstration. In *Proceedings CHI'99: Human Factors in Computing Systems.* (Pittsburgh, Pa. May 15–20). New York, NY: ACM Press.

Modugno, F., A. T. Corbett, and B. A. Myers. 1997. Graphical representation of programs in a demonstrational visual shell—An empirical evaluation. *ACM Transactions on Computer-Human Interaction* 4, no. 3: 276–308.

Myers, B. A. 1990. Creating user interfaces using programming-by-example, visual programming, and constraints. *ACM Transactions on Programming Languages and Systems* 12, no. 2: 143–177.

Myers, B., R. McDaniel, and D. Kosbie. 1993. Marquise: Creating complete user interfaces by demonstration. In *Proceedings of INTERCHI'93* (Amsterdam, April). New York, NY: ACM Press.

Smith, D. C., and A. Cypher. 1995. KidSim: End-user programming of simulations. In *Proceedings of CHI'95* (May). New York, NY: ACM Press.

Wolber, D. 1997. An interface builder for designing animated interfaces. *Transactions on Computer-Human Interface* (TOCHI) (December).

———. 1998. A multiple timeline editor for designing multi-threaded applications. In *Proceedings of the User Interface and Software Technology (UIST) conference* (San Francisco). New York, NY: ACM Press.

Wolber, D., and G. Fisher. 1991. A demonstrational technique for developing interfaces with dynamically created objects. In *Proceedings of UIST'91* (Hilton Head, S.C., November). New York, NY: ACM Press.

CHAPTER 17

Pavlov: Where PBD Meets Macromedia's Director

DAVID WOLBER

University of San Francisco

Abstract

Pavlov and Macromedia's Director both provide mechanisms for creating animated interfaces. Pavlov's design evolved from programming-by-demonstration (PBD) interface-building research, whereas Director evolved from traditional time-line based animation systems. This chapter presents the basic differences in the way the tools are designed and highlights some advantages of Pavlov's approach.

17.1 Introduction

Pavlov (Wolber 1996, 1997, 1998) combines programming by demonstration (PBD) with animation mechanisms similar to those in Macromedia's Director. Instead of writing scripting code to specify interaction, as is done in Director, the Pavlov designer *demonstrates* the events that trigger activity (and the activity itself). The resulting behaviors then appear in a *stimulus-response score*, as shown in the bottom-right corner of Figure 17.1.

17.2 Example

In the example, the designer first specified a direction (nose) for the car by manipulating the special direction vector on it (the vector does not appear at run time). He then demonstrated a stimulus of dragging the accelerator (the small blue rectangle inside the green one) and a response of moving the car. Because the car has a notion of direction, the designer is only able to move it forward or backward along the direction vector, and the system records the response as a Move Forward instead of a normal move.

The demonstrated behavior is then displayed in the score. When the designer selects a stimulus object and stimulus in the score, the time line displays only the operations that occur in response to that stimulus. As can be seen, the system has inferred that the parameter of the Move Forward operation (distance) be dependent on the vertical movement (y) of the accelerator. The designer can modify this parameter or set the behavior as periodic, which has been done in the example (so movement of the accelerator will speed up the car, not just move it once).

FIGURE **17.1**

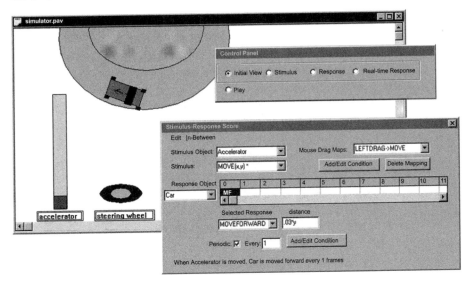

Pavlov development of a driving simulator, with a control panel (top right) to tell the system when to record a stimulus or response and the stimulus-response score (bottom right).

Besides specifying movement as periodic, as in the example, the Pavlov designer can also specify animation paths with in-betweening or with a real-time recording mechanism. With real-time recording, the system records a sequence of time-stamped operations as the designer executes an operation (such as moving an object). A recorded sequence is shown in Figure 17.2.

17.3 Objects that React Asynchronously to Events

Besides eliminating scripting by allowing both triggering events (stimuli) and responses to be demonstrated, Pavlov also allows for the interactive specification of interfaces in which objects react asynchronously to events. Such interfaces can be developed in Director only through coding.

FIGURE **17.2**

Stimulus-Response Score

Edit   In-Between

Stimulus Object: Rect0 ▾   Mouse Drag Maps: ▾

Stimulus: LEFTCLICK(x,y) * ▾   [Add/Edit Condition] [Delete Mapping]

Response Object

Ellipse0 ▾

0	1	2	3	4	5	6	7	8	9	10	11
MMM	MM	MM	MMM	MM	MM	MMM	MM	MMM	MM	MM	MM

Selected Response   x   y

MOVE ▾   1.000000   0.000000

Periodic: ☐   [Add/Edit Condition]

When Rect0 is clicked on,Ellipse0 is moved

A Score showing an animation path as a response to a button click.

FIGURE **17.3**

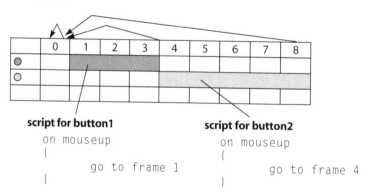

script for button1
```
on mouseup
{
          go to frame 1
}
```

script for button2
```
on mouseup
{
          go to frame 4
}
```

A conceptual illustration of the single time-line view. The colored rectangles represent the animation paths of the respective graphics. The arrows represent frame branch statements that set control to the beginning of a path, or back to the waiting state (cell 0). The "on mouseup" scripting code is typical of how interaction is defined in systems like Director.

For instance, consider an interface in which two objects (Ellipse0 and Ellipse1) follow their respective animation paths in response to clicks on two different buttons (Rect0 and Rect1). In Director, the animation path of each ellipse is stored in separate parts of a single time line, as illustrated in Figure 17.3. When a button click occurs, the system changes the global time frame to the corresponding animation path. Whatever animation paths were already in progress are terminated, as each object has a fixed state in the new time frame. Thus, one object will not continue its animation path when the second object's animation path is triggered. The only way to specify such behavior in Director is to bypass the time line altogether using Lingo puppet code.

Pavlov records operations, not object states. There is no single time-line or global-time frame during execution. When a stimulus occurs, all the time-stamped responses for that stimulus are added to a global execution list, and they are executed when the current time matches their time stamp.

Thus, a Pavlov developer can specify the example without resorting to code. He simply clicks on one button (Rect0) as a stimulus, then demonstrates a real-time response of the first ellipses' (Ellipse0's) animation path. He then performs a similar demonstration for the second button and second ellipse's animation path. By choosing a different button name in the "Stimulus Object" list of the stimulus-response score, the developer can view and edit the two animation paths.

At run-time, when Rect0 is clicked, Ellipse0's animation path is added to the global execution list, and the user sees it moving. If Rect1 is then clicked, Ellipse1's animation path is added to the global execution list, and the user sees it moving along with Ellipse1. The initiation of one object's animation path doesn't affect the activity of other objects.

17.4 Conclusion

Though arguably easier than general programming, script writing is difficult and precludes many from designing interactive animation. PBD along with a stimulus-response based, multiple–time line editor, can eliminate much of the scripting necessary in systems like Director.

References

Wolber, David. 1997. An interface builder for designing animated interfaces. In *Transactions on Computer-Human Interface (TOCHI)* (December).

———. 1996. Pavlov: Programming by stimulus-response demonstration. In *Proceedings of the Conference on Human Computer Interface (CHI'96)*.

———. 1998. A multiple timeline editor for designing multi-threaded applications. In *Proceedings of the User Interface and Software Technology (UIST) Conference* (San Francisco). New York, NY: ACM Press.

CHAPTER 18

Programming by Analogous Examples

ALEXANDER REPENNING

AgentSheets, Inc.
Center of Life Long Learning & Design
University of Colorado, Boulder

CORRINA PERRONE

AgentSheets, Inc.
Center of Life Long Learning & Design
University of Colorado, Boulder

Abstract

Analogies are powerful cognitive mechanisms that people use to construct new knowledge from knowledge already acquired and understood. When analogies are used with programming by example (PBE), the result is a new end-user programming paradigm combining the elegance of PBE to create programs with the power of analogies to reuse programs. The combination of PBE with analogies is called Programming by Analogous Examples (PBAE).

18.1 Introduction

Why do end users need to program? In a world with an ever-increasing flood of information, people become overwhelmed trying to cope with it. With the ubiquity of computer networks, the information challenge is no longer about accessing information but processing it. The direct manipulation paradigm, popularized in the 1980s, begins to break down when it is no longer feasible to directly manipulate the sources of information such as the location of *all* the files on your hard disk or *all* the emails in your in box.

End-user programming (Nardi 1993) is becoming a crucial instrument in the daily information-processing struggle. End-user programming is a form of programming done by the end user to customize information processing. Most computer end users do not have the background, motivation, or time to use traditional programming approaches, nor do they typically have the means to hire professional programmers to create their programs. Simple forms of end-user programming include the use of email filters to clean up email by directing specified emails into separate folders or the use of spreadsheets to explore the total cost of a new house.

Programming by example (PBE) is a powerful end-user programming paradigm enabling computer users without formal training in programming to create sophisticated programs. PBE environments create programs for end users by observing and recording as users manipulate information on a GUI level. For instance, in Microsoft Word PBE is used to build macros.

The focus of this chapter is the problem of PBE *reuse*. A user may find the PBE-generated program useful but may need either to generalize it or to modify it for a related yet different task. Program reuse is a well-known software design problem (Lange 1989). Reuse problems hamper productivity of a wide range of software projects, from those involving individual end-user programmers to large distributed teams of software developers (Roschelle et al. 1999). In the PBE context, reuse poses even more complex issues. While initially PBE shields end users from having to deal with programming issues, reuse will force them to leap cognitively between two levels of representations:

- *The GUI level:* This is the level of representation featuring windows, icons, and menus familiar to users. For instance, in the case of a word processor application such as Microsoft Word, this is the level that represents content directly manipulated by users with operations such as typing in new text, formatting text, using cursor keys to navigate through a document, and so forth.

- *The program level:* This is the level of representation that captures user manipulations into programs so that they can be replayed by the users. In the case of Word, this is the level of Visual Basic. Manipulations by users are recorded as Visual Basic scripts. Users assign scripts to keyboard commands or to user-defined toolbar commands.

The *PBE representation chasm* describes how difficult it is for users to comprehend the mapping between the GUI and the programming levels. In reuse this chasm is especially problematic since users, to adapt representations at the programming level to their needs, will be required to have at least a minimal understanding of the programming level representations. For the end user with no previous exposure to programming in general or to programming in Visual Basic, this transition may be too complex and result in frustration. As a consequence, the user may just give up on the idea of end-user programming and continue to solve the original problem manually again and again for years.

Analogies are powerful cognitive mechanisms that people use to construct new knowledge from knowledge already acquired and understood. When analogies are used with PBE, the result is a new end-user programming paradigm combining the elegance of PBE to *create* programs with the power of analogies to *reuse* programs. The combination of PBE with analogies is called *programming by analogous examples* (PBAE). Analogies are an effective representation level bridging the GUI level with the program level.

In this chapter, we portray the reuse problem with two detailed examples. In the first example, a Microsoft Word macro to do repetitive reformatting is created and the reusability of macros is explored. This example is chosen not because the Word macro-recording mechanism is the most sophisticated PBE system but because Word has a large user base and, consequently, readers may best be able to relate to use/reuse issues in this context. In the second example, a SimCity-like simulation is built using the AgentSheets (Repenning and Sumner 1995) simulation authoring tool. AgentSheets provides an end-user programming approach that is considerably more accessible to most users than Visual Basic. We will show that even if the program level is more accessible, there is still a need for analogies as a PBE reuse mechanism. Throughout these examples PBAE is contrasted with existing reuse mechanisms known from object-oriented programming, such as inheritance.

18.2 The GUI to Program Chasm

As PBE techniques become more widely adopted in both commercial and research systems, users incrementally construct and edit new behavior or commands as needed. As in traditional programming approaches, effective reuse of this new behavior is limited by underlying representations. In fact, these representations run the risk of presenting end-user programmers with the same copy/paste/modify, or inherit, reuse problem that professional programmers have struggled with for years. What makes reuse even more problematic in a PBE situation is that the programs that need to be modified for reuse have been machine generated. Typically these programs contain little information regarding how they could be changed. In this section, we describe a reuse scenario in which an end user is trying to reformat an address list automatically.

Microsoft Word and other applications allow for modular modification through the *macro* mechanism. Users are given an interface to program macros by example through the Record New Macro menu command. Additional support is given by the macro-editing toolbar and menu functions. Once a macro is named and assigned to a toolbar icon or a keyboard command, the macro is created by simply doing the task desired—in our example, repetitive reformatting. The system records keystrokes and compiles the command into Visual Basic, and the command can then be invoked by anyone editing a document.

Often a user would like to modify, and hence reuse, a macro with additional, related actions and have the entire new set of changes assigned to the same keyboard command. There are mechanisms to rename the macro, and thus copy the same behavior, but any modification to an existing macro must be done through the Visual Basic programming language. For

FIGURE **18.1**

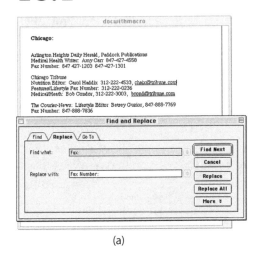

(a)

(b)

Creating a PBE to format all occurrences of "Fax:" into "Fax Number": The GUI level (a) shows a document edited with a find-and-replace dialogue box, and the program level (b) shows a Visual Basic editor.

instance, how would a user have to modify the macro to reformat not just the "Fax:" but also an "Address:" field? To modify this macro through the record function, a user would have to overwrite the old macro, go through the exact actions that were previously recorded, and then record the desired additional behavior.

To be able to reuse existing macros and make them useful in more general situations, users will have to drop from the GUI level (Figure 18.1[a]) to the program level (Figure 18.1[b]). According to the Word documentation:

> Recorded macros are great when you want to perform exactly the same task every time you run the macro. But what if you want to automate a task in which actions vary with the situation, or depend on user input [. . .]? To create powerful automations, you should learn to program in Visual Basic for Applications. (p. 227)

The cognitive chasm between the GUI and program levels is quite large. The GUI level provides only very limited options for reuse. Even though advanced reuse *requires* making the transition into the program level, no intermediate steps are provided to take the user *from* the simple recording mechanism *to* the Visual Basic programming language. At the GUI level, users are limited in reuse to copy macros as black boxes into other documents or to make macros generally available to all documents. At the program level, code may be copied, pasted, and modified with the same difficulty as any other object-oriented program. At this point, the user has jumped from the comfortable environment of direct manipulation at the GUI level directly into the uncomfortable or downright frustrating programming level.

18.3 Programming by Analogous Examples

We use the AgentSheets simulation authoring tool to explain how analogies bridge the chasm between the GUI level and the program level in PBE. AgentSheets is employed to build SimCity-like simulations and export them as interactive Java applets. A large number of simulations have been built by a wide range of users, including elementary school kids and NASA scientists. A detailed description of AgentSheets can be found elsewhere (www.agentsheets.com/userforum-publications.html).

AgentSheets combines PBE with graphical rewrite rules (Cypher and Smith 1995; Lieberman 1987; Repenning 1993, 1995) into an end-user programming paradigm. Graphical rewrite rules (GRRs), which are also used in systems such as Cocoa/KidSim and Creator, are powerful languages to express the concept of change in a visual representation. These rules declaratively describe spatial transformations with a sequence of two or more dimensional *situations* containing *objects* (Figure 18.2[b]). Situations can be interpreted with respect to objects contained and spatial relationships holding between these objects. The differences between situations imply one or more *actions* capable of transforming one situation into another. In AgentSheets, any number of GRRs can be aggregated to create complex behaviors for agents, and these agents and their behaviors combine and interact to simulate anything from heat diffusion to urban planning. We have found that it is highly likely that behavior created in one simulation will be desirable for users building other simulations.

Compared to the previously described GUI/program level chasm in Word, the chasm between the GUI and program levels in AgentSheets is less pronounced. The GRR representation at the program level matches the representation at the GUI level closely. For instance, the user-produced train and train track icons found at the GUI level are also found at the program level. This representational mapping helps users comprehend programs.

FIGURE **18.2**

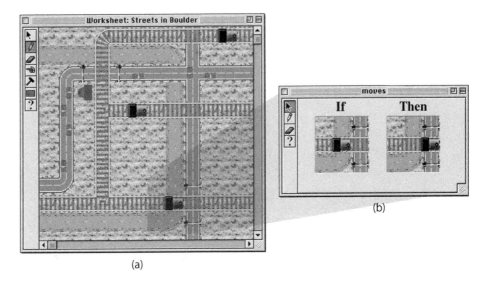

(a)

(b)

Programming a train to follow a train track by example in AgentSheets. (a) When a user moves a train on a train track at the GUI level, (b) AgentSheets records the movement, including context, and represents it at the program level as a graphical rewrite rule.

We argue that despite this closer match between GUI and programming, it is still necessary to have a mechanism to deal with reuse.

18.3.1 Making Cars Move Like Trains: An Analogy

In the application called Sustainopolis (Figure 18.2) used to explore public transportation issues, an end user—in this case, an urban planner—wishes to incorporate cars and streets. Noticing that Trains and Tracks are already successfully programmed, and realizing that cars move on streets similar to the way trains move on tracks, the user wishes to reuse the *move* behavior already written for the Train object and attach it to the Car object.

One approach would be for the user to start from scratch and simply demonstrate all the examples of Car and Street interactions. Unfortunately, the set of rules attached to the Train is quite large. The problem is that even for a relatively simple behavior such as making the Train follow the Track, rules had to be demonstrated to specify all of the meaningful combinations of interactions between Trains and Tracks (see also Figure 18.5, later). Trains are capable of heading in four different directions (north, south, east, and west). A complete specification accounting for fifteen different train track pieces (straight tracks, vertical and horizontal; four orientation of curves, four different T intersections, one crossing, and four orientations of cul de sacs) requires 256 rules. These rules specify behavior in situations such as "If the train drives into a cul-de-sac, which way should the train go if it has a choice of going left or right?" If the Tracks are carefully arranged in the simulation, a good number of rules can be eliminated, but the point remains that it must have taken quite a while and some patience to demonstrate the complete set of rules. Given that in our scenario this behavior already exists, it would be preferable to find a way to avoid having to demonstrate the entire set of rules again to specify the conceptually similar interaction between Cars and Streets.

A different approach is to copy all the Train's rules into the Car and manually edit them by substituting corresponding icons. In most GRR systems, the user would then copy all the rules from Trains and Tracks to Streets and Cars and then simply substitute Cars for Trains and Streets for Tracks. But is time saved? This is basically the same arduous, error-prone process a programmer must go through to reuse a program or a Word user must go through to reuse a macro. Without the understanding of what the user intends, can we facilitate the reuse process? We argue that the mechanism that allows an end user to program allows reuse as well.

Programming by analogous examples supports the reuse of previously recorded example programs. Instead of creating the behavior of cars from scratch either through demonstration or through manual editing, users generate a complete set of rules by specifying an analogy.

It is the *relationship* between Trains and Tracks that the user wishes to reuse by applying it to Cars and Streets (Figure 18.3). In contrast to object-oriented programming, in which inheritance is used to define an ontology of object classes, analogies are used to define an ontology of object relationships represented by verbs such as "move."

The Analogy dialogue box (Figure 18.4) is used to define analogies. The result is that the behavior programmed via a GRR for Trains moving on Tracks is transferred to Cars on Streets. The verb "moves" is differentiated for Trains and Cars, so that Trains do not now move on Streets, nor will Cars move on Tracks, because no relationship is implied between Trains and Streets or Cars and Tracks.

Here, reuse is expressed in terms of existing objects, and no abstractions are required. The result of the analogy is a new set of GRRs attached to Cars that allow Cars to move on Streets. All the rules generated by analogy are

FIGURE **18.3**

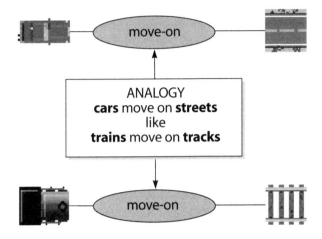

Transferring the relationship between objects.

FIGURE **18.4**

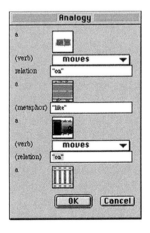

Making an analogy.

like ordinary GRR in that the user can edit them to deal with exceptions to the analogy.

In summary, PBE systems often feature representations that, through the use of analogies, serve as bridge between the GUI level and the program level. Here, a user formulating an analogy created new behavior out of existing behavior. This style of reuse-enhanced programming in which an initial set of programs is created through PBE and then extended through analogies is what we call programming by analogous examples.

18.4 Discussion

So far we have described the user perspective of PBAE. What is the depth at which an analogy mechanism needs to "understand" a program to create an analogous program? On the one hand, mere syntactic symbol substitution will not be sufficient for the transformation of nontrivial programs. On the other hand, a deep understanding of the program semantic is not only an extraordinarily hard and yet unsolved artificial intelligence (AI) problem but would probably also require users to annotate programs extensively with semantic information to enable analogies. We discuss next how PBAE moves beyond simple substitution without becoming an AI complete problem. We also list some of the problems when trying to use inheritance found in object-oriented programming as an improvement over simple substitution.

18.4.1 Beyond Syntactic Rewrite Rules

A first step toward creating more usable and reusable rewrite rules is to move from *syntactic* rewrite rules to *semantic* rewrite rules. To transform programs, it is important for programs to include semantic meta-information. This meta-information can capture—to a limited degree—what the program is doing and how it is doing it. First-generation rewrite rule–based systems such as AgentSheets91 and later Cocoa, Vampire, and Creator operate only on a syntactic level. A rule such as the one shown in Figure 18.5 is rich in meaning to a human being but cannot be interpreted by syntactic rewrite rule systems.

The system does not know what trains and train tracks are, nor does it have any sense of the functional relationship between a train and the train tracks. To a syntactic rewrite rule, systems objects are uninterpretable

FIGURE **18.5**

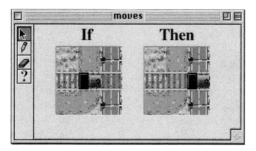

A rule that makes a train follow a train track.

bitmaps, and scenes are patterns containing objects. Without semantics, the system cannot allow users to generalize or reuse behaviors such as the behavior of a train following a train track. The *meaning* of a syntactic re-write rule remains strictly in the programmer's head.

The lack of semantics not only makes reuse difficult but also creates a significant problem for building new behaviors from scratch. Suppose a user would like to create a complete set of rules that makes trains follow train tracks (see Figure 18.6). Through the power of PBE, the rule described earlier is defined in no time. With this one rule, trains can follow any number of horizontal train tracks. However, a track system is not limited to horizontal track pieces—there are also curves, intersections, and so forth. Fortunately, the user does not have to draw all these different track pieces manually but can have AgentSheets generate new bitmaps automatically by transforming the original depiction drawn by the user. The transformation of bitmaps is a syntactic transformation.

Unfortunately, the complete behavior of trains following tracks is made a bit more complex since we now have fifteen different track pieces (Figure 18.8 on page 364). A very large set of rules would have to be defined to specify all the combinations of track pieces that the train is currently on, the track pieces the train can move to, and the four different directions that the train can move onto. What started as a very simple single rule quickly has turned into a tedious PBE exercise. The lack of semantics dramatically reduces the scalability of a PBE approach. In effect, users get trapped by affordances of the programming environment. They are off to a quick start to create a simple behavior only to be "trapped" by the programming approach later when trying to create more complex behaviors.

FIGURE **18.6**

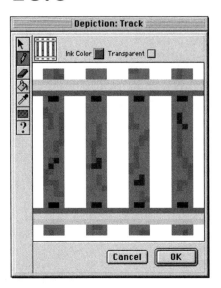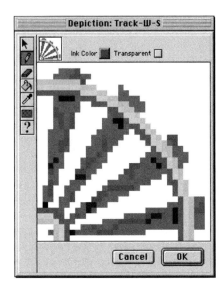

Syntactic transformation: AgentSheets has created a curve by "bending" a track icon designed by the user.

To scale the combination of PBE with GRRs, it is necessary to add at least a limited amount of semantics. Semantics simplifies at least two kinds of programming:

- *Original programming: Building new behavior:* Semantic GRRs simplify programming by allowing end users to annotate the objects that are pro- grammed with semantic information. For instance, AgentSheets94 (Repenning 1994a, 1994b) allows users to annotate objects with connec- tivity information describing whether an object has input and/or output ports in a certain direction. AgentSheets can transform agents syntac- tically (how an agent looks) as well as semantically (what an agent means). The same kind of annotation makes sense for all kinds of agents representing agents in a context of flow. Examples include roads, train tracks, rivers, and wires.

- *Programming through reuse: Analogies:* The same semantics that help a user create original programs simply can also support reuse. The following section will describe how this same connectivity semantics enables reuse through analogies.

18.4.2 From Substitutions to Analogies

The analogy menu specified in Figure 18.4 only uses four icons out of a much larger set of icons representing Cars and Trains. There are Cars and Trains with different headings as well as Streets and Tracks representing different topologies. For a Train to move properly on all kinds of Tracks, all of these icons are available to AgentSheets. A mechanism that would merely substitute the Car and Street icons for the Train and Track icons to create a set of analogous rewrite rules would not be very useful because it would only match a very small subset of all relevant rules. How does the analogy system establish the more general mapping between all these different but related items?

Analogy mechanisms need to have access to some minimal semantic information establishing more general correspondence (Chee 1993; Goldstone, Medin, and Gentner 1991; Medin, Goldstone, and Gentner 1993). It is no trivial matter for a computer system to substitute correctly *at all the necessary levels* required to render the resulting code useful and usable without further editing by a human. Lewis (1988) proposes a concept called *pupstitution* to decrease the brittleness inherent in straight copy-and-paste techniques.

In the AgentSheets substrate, systematicity in analogy (Perrone and Repenning 1998) is facilitated by connectivity semantics. Structural and behavioral similarity between the base and target objects defines systematicity. Analogies are made by specifying which relationship should be transferred. Cars and Trains are objects that can be as simple or complex as a user desires—they may have a single applicable behavior or many. However, when the user specifies that Cars move like Trains, it is this specific behavior that is transferred. For this to occur with a high degree of systematicity, and therefore effectiveness to the user, the Street and Track objects must be structurally similar.

AgentSheets assures this in two ways. Structure is created by the base icons created for the gallery. Syntactic transformations are applied by the system at the user's request that will automatically create meaningful variations to illustrate intersections and curves, as well as directional orientation (Repenning 1995). This creates the visual variations necessary to place the Agents on the AgentSheets worksheet and saves the user many hours of

18.7

Agent depictions are also transformed semantically. Semantics capture input/output information representing the implied connectivity of a depiction.

18.8

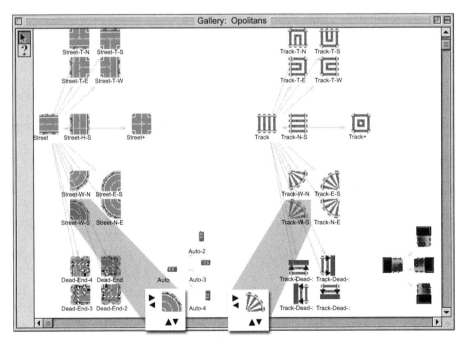

Icons are transformed syntactically and semantically. Users only define the basic root icons, such as the horizontal Street segment, which then get transformed into icons such as curves in terms of appearance and meaning. The semantic information is used to match up icons for analogies.

work on the icon depictions. Icons are then annotated by the user with semantic information such as connectivity (Figure 18.7), which is potential behavior. Connectivity defines input and output ports of each icon. For instance, a horizontal Street segment icon has inputs/outputs to its left and right. Transforming the annotated Track creates an entire family of Track icons (Figure 18.8, right), which essentially act as throughputs for objects that move on them.

This semantic and syntactic connectivity information about an icon is used to support pupstitution in PBAE. By specifying the connectivity of an icon (Figure 18.8, left) and then transforming it, the *move* GRR now acquires a useful dimension of complexity. After the analogy is made, Cars have a rule set isomorphic to the Train rule set, that is, Cars know how to move on all kinds of Streets (Figure 18.9). The system uses the semantic information available to ensure a high systematicity between the base and target; thus, the correct mapping between Tracks and Streets is made without the user's intervention.

The general insight is that a little semantics is necessary to enable meaningful analogies. On the one hand, this means that users will have to provide some additional up-front information to annotate their designs with minimalist semantics. On the other hand, this kind of semantic annotation dramatically improves the reusability of behavior. In the case of

FIGURE **18.9**

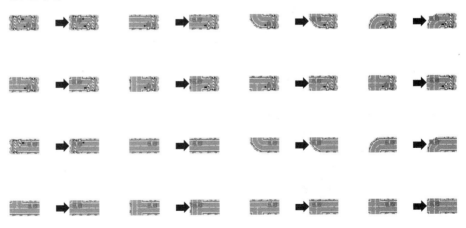

Only the first few out of a set of 256 rules created by AgentSheets' "Semantic rewrite rule" system to define the "Cars follow Streets like Trains follow Tracks" behavior.

AgentSheets, users only need to provide semantics information to the base agents. For instance, they need to specify the connectivity of a Street agent that they have defined. AgentSheets can automatically transform agents representing flow conductors such as streets, wires, or pipes syntactically (by applying geometric transformations to the agent bitmap) as well as semantically (by applying topological transformations to the agent's connectivity).

18.4.3 Reuse through Inheritance

In object-oriented programming, inheritance can serve the role of a reuse mechanism. An object subclass not only inherits the behavior of the super-class but can even overwrite and extend this behavior. How would inheritance have worked for our trains and cars example? One easy way to get analogous behavior is to make Car a type of, or subclass of, Train and Street a subclass of Track. While this approach will produce the desired behavior because of inheritance, it is ontologically unsound, and changing the object hierarchy in this way produces a misleading model based on weak design.

To correct this problem, it is expected that the end-user become a bit more of a programmer. In the class hierarchy, Cars become siblings of Trains and Streets become siblings of Tracks by creating two abstract super-classes: Moving Object and Movement Guiding Object (Figure 18.10).

FIGURE **18.10**

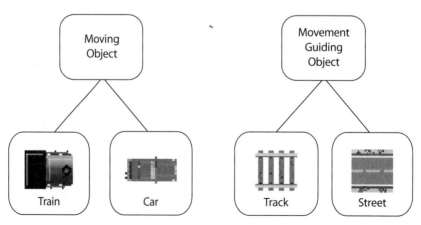

Reusing through inheritance.

To enable both Trains and Cars to move, a generalized GRR needs to be expressed in terms of Moving Object and Movement Guiding Object. While this new class hierarchy may be ontologically sound, it introduces serious problems:

- *Need for abstractions:* Abstractions are nontrivial for end users to make and are hard to represent visually. This is especially true in the case where objects are represented by user-defined icons. How would abstract objects embodying Moving Objects and Movement Guiding Objects look and who would have to draw them?

- *Overgeneralization:* If city traffic is run with this new representation in place, Trains can now move on Streets and Cars will now move on Tracks, which, although theoretically possible, should not be allowed to happen in the urban planning domain application. To get around this real-life constraint, the behavior of Trains and Cars would need to be specialized again to prevent these unwanted combinations of Moving Objects and Movement Guiding Objects.

Inheritance is a powerful means of generalization that could increase the usefulness of PBE. However, the tension between inheritance and PBE with respect to representational concreteness is hard to resolve. Inheritance is pulling toward the need to introduce and manipulate abstract representations, whereas PBE is pulling toward the need to provide highly concrete representations that can be manipulated by end users.

18.5 Conclusion

In PBE, the representation that the user sees at the GUI level may indeed be vastly different from the representation a user is faced with at the program level. In PBE systems, special representations are often used to make the transition between the two levels easier for an end user. These representational features enable programming by analogous examples, which in turn simplifies program reuse.

Our work with PBAE is at an early but promising stage. The combination of *some* semantic information with structural information has allowed reuse of complex behaviors in the context of interactive simulations. Of course, the more similarity between behavior the user has created and wants to reuse and the target behavior makes for a better analogy and minimal editing. We are continuing work on PBAE to allow for greater differentiation by a user trying to determine appropriate analogical matches. For instance, Cars moving on Streets and Electricity moving through Wires also share similarity, but Electricity can go both directions at an intersection. Therefore, an analogy made between the two creates accident-prone Cars. Next steps will also explore the use of PBAE in nonsimulation application domains.

Acknowledgements

The authors wish to acknowledge Clayton Lewis, Braden Craig, and the members of the Center of LifeLong Learning & Design at the University of Colorado. The research was supported by the National Science Foundation under grants No. DMI-9761360, RED 925–3425, and Supplement to RED 925–3425. AgentSheets research and AgentSheets Inc. are supported by the National Science Foundation (REC 9804930, REC-9631396, and CDA-940860).

References

Chee, Y. S. 1993. Applying Gentner's theory of analogy to the teaching of computer programming. *International Journal of Man Machine Studies,* 38: 347–368.

Cypher, A., and D. C. Smith. 1995. KidSim: End user programming of simulations. In *Proceedings of the 1995 Conference of Human Factors in Computing Systems* (Denver, Colo.). New York, NY: ACM Press.

Goldstone, R. L., D. L. Medin, and D. Gentner. 1991. Relational similarity and the nonindependence of features in similarity judgments. *Cognitive Psychology* 23: 222–262.

Lange, B. M. 1989. Some strategies of reuse in an object-oriented programming environment. In *CHI'89* (Houston, Tex.). New York, NY: ACM Press.

Lewis, C. 1988. Some learnability results for analogical generalization. Technical Report No. CU-CS-384–88, University of Colorado, Computer Science Department.

Lieberman, H. 1987. An example-based environment for beginning programmers. In *Artificial Intelligence and Education,* ed. R. W. Lawler and M. Yazdani. Norwood, N.J.: Ablex.

Medin, D. L., R. L. Goldstone, and D. Gentner. 1993. Respects for similarity. *Psychological Review* 100, no. 2: 254–278.

Microsoft Corporation, *Getting Results with Microsoft Word 98 Macintosh Edition* (Redmond, Wash.: Microsoft Corporation, 1987-1998), 227.

Nardi, B. 1993. *A small matter of programming*. Cambridge, Mass.: MIT Press.

Perrone, C., and A. Repenning. 1998. Graphical rewrite rule analogies: Avoiding the inherit or copy & paste reuse dilemma. In *Proceedings of the 1998 IEEE Symposium of Visual Languages* (Nova Scotia, Canada). Los Alamitos, Calif.: IEEE Computer Society Press.

Repenning, A. 1993. Agentsheets: A tool for building domain-oriented visual programming environments. In *INTERCHI'93: Conference on Human Factors in Computing Systems* (Amsterdam). New York, NY: ACM Press.

———. 1994a. Bending icons: syntactic and semantic transformation of icons. In *Proceedings of the 1994 IEEE Symposium on Visual Languages* (St. Louis, Mo.). Los Alamitos, Calif.: IEEE Computer Society Press.

———. 1994b. Programming substrates to create interactive learning environments. *Journal of Interactive Learning Environments* 4, no. 1 (*Special Issue on End-User Environments*): 45–74.

———. 1995. Bending the rules: Steps toward semantically enriched graphical rewrite rules. In *Proceedings of Visual Languages* (Darmstadt, Germany). Los Alamitos, Calif.: IEEE Computer Society Press.

Repenning, A., and T. Sumner. 1995. Agentsheets: A medium for creating domain-oriented visual languages. *IEEE Computer* 28, no. 3: 17–25.

Roschelle, J., C. DiGiano, M. Koutlis, A. Repenning, J. Phillips, N. Jackiw, and D. Suthers. 1999. Developing educational software components. *IEEE Computer* 32, no. 9: 50–58.

CHAPTER 19

Visual Generalization in Programming by Example

ROBERT ST. AMANT

North Carolina State University

HENRY LIEBERMAN

Massachusetts Institute of Technology

RICHARD POTTER

Japan Science and Technology Corporation

LUKE ZETTLEMOYER

North Carolina State University

Abstract

In programming-by-example (PBE; also sometimes called programming by demonstration) systems, the system records actions performed by a user in the interface and produces a generalized program that can be used later in analogous examples. A key issue is how to describe the actions and objects selected by the user, which determines what kind of generalizations will be possible. When the user selects a graphical object on the screen, most PBE systems describe the object using properties of the underlying application data. For example, if the user selects a link on a Web page, the PBE system might represent the selection based on the link's HTML properties.

In this chapter, we explore a different, and radical, approach—using visual properties of the interaction elements themselves, such as size, shape, color, and appearance of graphical objects—to describe user intentions. Only recently has the speed of image processing made feasible real-time analysis of screen images by a PBE system. We have not yet fully realized the goal of a complete PBE system using visual generalization, but we feel the approach is important enough to warrant presenting the idea.

Visual information can supplement information available from other sources and opens up the possibility of new kinds of generalizations not possible from the application data alone. In addition, these generalizations can map more closely to the intentions of users, especially beginning users, who rely on the same visual information when making selections. Finally, visual generalization can sometimes remove one of the worst stumbling blocks preventing the use of PBE with commercial applications—that is, reliance on application program interfaces (APIs). When necessary, PBE systems can work exclusively from the visual appearance of applications and do not need explicit cooperation from the API.

19.1 If You Can See It, You Should Be Able to Program It

Every PBE system has what Halbert (1993) calls the "data description problem": when users select an object on the screen, what do they mean by it? Depending on how you describe an object, it could result in very different effects the next time you run the procedure recorded and generalized by the system. During a demonstration to a PBE system, if you select an icon for a file "foo.bar" in a desktop file system, did you mean (1) just that specific file and no other? (2) Any file whose name is "foo.bar"? (3) Any icon that happened to be found at the location where you clicked?

Most systems deal with this issue by mapping the selection onto the application's data model (a set of files, email messages, circles and boxes in a drawing, etc.). They then permit generalizations on the properties of that data (file names, message senders, etc.). But sometimes the user's intuitive description of an object might depend on the actual visual properties of the screen elements themselves—regardless of whether these properties are explicitly represented in the application's command set. Our proposal is to use these visual properties to permit PBE systems to do "visual generalization."

For an example of why visual generalization might prove useful, suppose we want to write a program to save all the links on a Web page that have not been followed by the user at a certain point in time (Figure 19.1). If the Netscape browser happened to have an operation "Move to Next Unfollowed Link" available as a menu option or in its API, we might be able to automate the activity using a macro recorder such as Quickeys. But, unfortunately, Netscape does not have this operation (nor does it even have a Move to the Next Link operation). Even if we had access to the HTML source

FIGURE **19.1**

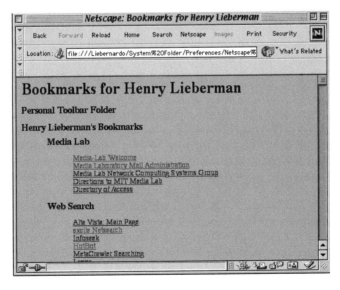

Can we write a program to save all the unfollowed links?

of the page, we still wouldn't know which links had been followed by the user. This is a general problem for PBE systems in interfacing to almost all applications. Procedures that seem easy for a user to carry out manually using the operations of the user interface are not always easy for an external agent program to carry out by using the application's API.

This example shows the conceptual gap between a user's view of an application and its underlying programmable functionality. Bridging this gap can be extremely difficulty for a PBE system—its representation of user actions may be a complete mismatch for the user's actual intentions. But perhaps we are looking at this problem from the wrong perspective. From the user's point of view, the functionality of an interactive application is defined by its user interface. The interface has been carefully developed to cover specific tasks; to communicate through appropriate abstractions; and to accommodate the user's cognitive, perceptual, and physical abilities. A PBE system might gain significant benefits if it could work in the same medium as a user, if it could process the visual environment with all its information. This is the key insight we explore in this chapter.

19.2   What Does Visual Generalization Buy Us?

Let's imagine a PBE system that incorporates techniques to process a visual interactive environment, to extract information potentially relevant to the user's intentions. What does the system gain from these capabilities?

- *Integration into existing environments:* Historically, most PBE systems have been built on top of isolated research systems, rather than commercial applications. Some have been promising but have not been adopted because of the difficulty of integration. A visual PBE system, independent of source code and API constraints, could potentially reach an unlimited audience.

- *Consistency:* Independence of an application's source code or API also gives a PBE system flexibility. Similar applications often have similar appearance and behavior; for example, users switch between Web browsers with little difficulty. A visual PBE system could take advantage of functional and visual consistency to operate across similar applications with little or no modification.

- *New sources of information:* Most important, some kinds of visual information may be difficult or impossible to obtain through other means.

Furthermore, this information is generally closely related to the user's understanding of an application.

These are all benefits to the developers of a PBE system, but they apply equally well to the users of a PBE system. In the Netscape example, a visual PBE system would be able to run on top of the existing browser, without requiring the use of a substitute research system. Because Netscape has the convention of displaying the followed links in red and the unfollowed links in blue, a user might specify the "Save the Next Unfollowed Link" action in visual terms as "Move to the next line of blue text, then invoke the Save Link As operation." This specification exploits a new, visual source of information. Finally, the general consistency between browsers should allow the same system to work with both Netscape and Microsoft Internet Explorer, a much trickier proposition for API-based systems.

Providing a visual processing capability raises some novel challenges for a PBE system:

- *Image processing:* How can a system extract visual information at the image-processing level in practice? This processing must happen in an interactive system, interleaved with user actions and observation of the system, which raises significant efficiency issues. This an issue of the basic technical feasibility of a visual approach to PBE. Our experience with VisMap (described later) shows that real-time analysis of the screen is feasible on today's high-end machines.

- *Information management:* How can a system process low-level visual data to infer high-level information relevant to user intentions? For example, a visual object under the mouse pointer might be represented as a rectangle, a generic window region, or a window region specialized for some purpose, such as illustration. A text box with a number in it might be an element of a fill-in form, a table in a text document, or a cell in a spreadsheet. This concern is also important for generalization from low-level events to the abstractions they implement: is the user simply clicking on a rectangle or performing a confirmation action?

- *Brittleness:* How can a system deal gracefully with visual variations that are beyond the scope of a solution? In the Netscape example of collecting unfollowed links, users may, in fact, change the colors that Netscape uses to display followed versus unfollowed links, thereby perhaps obsoleting a previously recorded procedure. A link may in fact extend over more than a single line of text, so that the mapping between lines and links is not exact. Similar blue text might appear in a GIF image and be inadvertently captured by the procedure. And, if the program is visually parsing the screen, links that do not appear because they are below the current scrolling position will not be included. Out of sight, out of mind! The latter problem might be cured by programming a loop that scrolled through the page as the user would. Most of these problems are put in a novel light if we observe that they can be difficult even for a human to solve. Almost everyone has been fooled now and then by advertising graphics that camouflage themselves as legitimate interface objects; without further information (such as might be provided by an API call), a visual PBE system cannot hope to do better.

19.3 Low-Level Visual Generalization

Potter's work on pixel-based data access pioneered the approach of treating the screen image as the source for generating descriptions for generalization. The TRIGGERS system (Potter 1993) performs exact pattern matching on screen pixels to infer information that is otherwise unavailable to an external system. A "trigger" is a condition-action pair. For example, triggers are defined for such tasks as surrounding a text field with a rounded rectangle in a drawing program, shortening lines so that they intersect an arbitrary shape, and converting text to a bold typeface. The user defines a trigger by stepping through a sequence of actions in an application, adding annotations for the TRIGGERS system when appropriate. Once a set of triggers has been defined, the user can activate them, iteratively and exhaustively, to carry out their actions.

Several strategies can be used to process visual pixel information so that it can be used to generalize computer programs. The strategy used by TRIGGERS is to compute locations of exact patterns within the screen image. For example, suppose a user records a mouse macro that modifies a URL to display the next higher directory in a Web browser (Figure 19.2). Running the macro can automate this process, but only for the one specific URL because the mouse locations are recorded with fixed coordinates. However, this macro can be generalized by using pixel pattern matching on the screen image. The pattern to use is what a user would look for if doing the task manually: the pixel pattern of a slash character. Finding the second to the last occurrence of this pattern gives a location from which the macro can begin the macro's mouse drag, which generalizes the macro so that it will work with most URLs.

FIGURE **19.2**

The generalizing pixel pattern:

Steps in a mouse macro to move a browser up one directory, and selecting a pixel pattern that can generalize the macro.

Even though this macro program affects data such as characters, strings, URLs, and Web pages, the program's internal data is only low-level pixel patterns and screen coordinates. It is the *use* within the rich GUI context that gives higher-level meaning to the low-level data. The fact that a low-level program can map so simply to a much higher-level meaning attests to how conveniently the visual information of a GUI is organized for productive work. Potter (1993) gives more examples.

The advantage of this strategy is that the low-level data and operators of the programming system can map to many high-level meanings, even ones not originally envisioned by the programming system developer. The disadvantage is that high-level internal processing of the information is difficult, since the outside context is required for most interpretation.

Another system that performs data access at the pixel level is Yamamoto's (1998) AutoMouse, which can search the screen for rectangular pixel patterns and click anywhere within the pattern. Copies of the patterns can be arranged on a document and connected to form simple visual programs. Each pattern can have different mouse and keyboard actions associated with it.

19.4 High-Level Visual Generalization

Zettlemoyer and St. Amant's (1999) VisMap is in some ways a conceptual successor to TRIGGERS. VisMap is a programmable set of sensors, effectors, and skeleton controllers for visual interaction with off-the-shelf applications. Sensor modules take pixel-level input from the display, run the data through image-processing algorithms, and build a structured representation of visible interface objects. Effector modules generate mouse and keyboard gestures to manipulate these objects. VisMap is designed as a programmable user model, an artificial user with which developers can explore the characteristics of a user interface.

VisMap is not, by itself, a PBE system. But it does demonstrate that visual generalization is practical in an interface, and we hope to apply its approach in a full PBE system. VisMap translates the pixel information to data types that have more meaning outside the GUI context. For example, building on VisMap we have developed VisSolitaire, a simple visual application that plays Microsoft Windows Solitaire. VisMap translates the pixel information to data types that represent the state of a generic game of Solitaire. This state provides input to an AI planning system that plays a reasonable game of solitaire, from the starting deal to a win or loss. It does not use an API or otherwise have any cooperation from Microsoft Solitaire.

VisSolitaire's control cycle alternates between screen parsing and generalized action. VisSolitaire processes the screen image to identify cards and their positions. When the cards are located, a visual grammar characterizes them based on relative location and visual properties. In this way the system can identify the stacks of cards that form the stock, tableau, and

FIGURE **19.3**

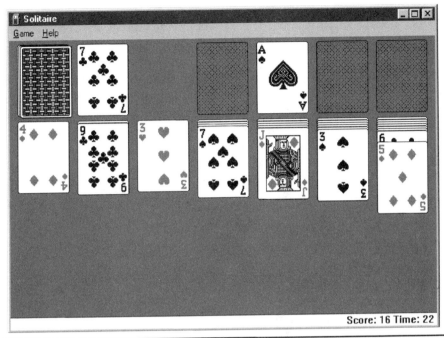

Visual Processing Results

Stock:	Tableau:	Foundation:
(:BACK)	(0 :BEHIND)(4 :DIAMONDS)	(:BLANK)
(7:CLUBS)	(1 :BEHIND)(9 :CLUBS)	(:ACE :SPADES)
	(0 :BEHIND)(3 :HEARTS)	(:BLANK)
	(4 :BEHIND)(:JACK :DIAMONDS)	(:BLANK)
	(5 :BEHIND)(3 :SPADES)	

VisSolitaire source data and visual processing results.

foundation, as well as classify each card based on visual identification of its suit and rank, as shown in Figure 19.3.

A bottom-up pattern recognition process is interleaved with a top-down interpretation of the visual patterns. Key to the effectiveness of the system is the loose coupling between these two components. The strategic, game-playing module represents its actions in general terms, such as "Move any ace that is on top of a tableau pile to an empty foundation slot." The visual processing component maps this command to the specific state of the Solitaire application: "Move the ace of spades to the second foundation slot." VisSolitaire, like a human solitaire player, relies on the layout of the cards to guide its actions, rather than the visual representations of the cards alone. VisMap's recognition of cards is one illustration of an application-specific visual recognition procedure that can be used in visual generalization.

To make a visual recognition approach work for PBE in general, we may have to define visual grammars that describe the meaning of particular interface elements or the visual language of particular applications. For example, if we understand that the format of a monthly calendar is a grid of boxes, each box representing the date and lines within the boxes representing particular appointments, we can infer the properties of a Now Up-to-Date Appointment object.

It is also possible that other properties of the appointment object (e.g., the duration of the appointment) are not represented in the visual display, so we may not be able to infer them from the screen representation alone. Developing the application display format grammars is time-consuming work for expert developers, not for end users. However, the effort for a particular application can be amortized over all the uses of that application. The model of the application need not be complete; it may only capture those aspects of the application data of current interest.

One way to utilize the results of this kind of processing in a PBE system is to adopt a similar approach to Tatlin (Leiberman 1998), which infers user actions by polling applications for their state periodically and compares successive states to determine user actions. Tatlin used the examinability of the application data models for the spreadsheet Excel and calendar program Now Up-to-Date via the Applescript interprocess communication language. In the scenario in Figure 19.4, a user copies information from a calendar and pastes it into a spreadsheet. Tatlin "sees" that the data pasted into the spreadsheet are the same as were selected in the calendar and infers the transfer operation. If we developed descriptions of the visual interface of the calendar and the spreadsheet, we could do the same simply by analyzing the screen image, even without access to the underlying application data.

Research by others gives further evidence of the potential of visual generalization. Lakin (1987) built several programming environments in an object-oriented graphical editor, vmacs. He used a recognition procedure on the visual relations between objects to attach semantics to sketched objects, which implemented a kind of visual generalization. Notably, the

FIGURE **19.4**

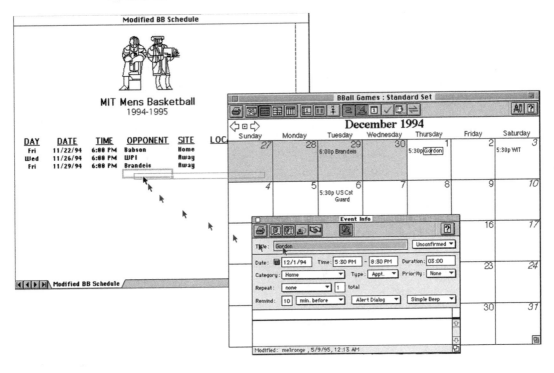

Tatlin inferring copying data from a calendar to a spreadsheet.

grammars used to drive the recognition procedure were themselves represented visually in vmacs itself, as and by the same kind of visual objects. Kurlander (1988) used a kind of visual generalization to automate search-and-replace procedures. But while Lakin and Kurlander were able to access the visual properties of objects directly in their own home grown graphical editors, we are proposing to extract the same kind of visual properties directly from pixel-level analysis of the screen.

19.5 Introducing Novel Generalizations: Generalizing on Grids

Visual generalization opens up the possibility of having different kinds of generalizations than are possible by generalizing from the properties of the underlying application data. As an example of a kind of useful generalization not possible with data-based approaches, consider that it might be possible to convey the general notion of a *grid,* so that procedures might be iterated throughout the elements of a grid (Figure 19.5).

The idea of a grid can be expressed purely with visual relations: "You start at one object, then move right until you find the next, and so on, until there are no more objects to the right. Then return to the object in the beginning of the row, move down one object, then start moving to the right again. Keep doing each row until you can't move down anymore."

Once you have the "idea" of a grid, you can apply it in a wide variety of applications. The same program could work whether operating on daily schedules in a calendar, program, icons in a folder window, or tables in Netscape, among other things.

FIGURE **19.5**

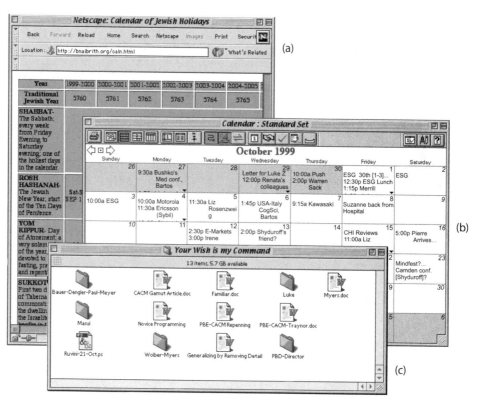

Examples of grids in (a) Netscape, (b) a calendar, and (c) the Finder.

For this to work, the definition of "move to the next object to the left" and "move to the next object down" may need to be redefined for each application. But given the ability to do so, we can make real the user's perception that all grids are basically the same, despite the artificial barriers that separately programmed applications place against this generalization.

19.6 Conclusion

We can ask several questions when exploring a new perspective such as that offered by a visual generalization approach. For example, *how can it contribute in a way that other existing perspectives are unable to?* Existing techniques such as Apple Events and OLE Automation can sometimes provide powerful perspectives from which to build programs. Adding a new perspective to a system can increase the user interface complexity significantly. If there is a large overlap in the range of information, then the new form of the information must provide some advantage—as can be demonstrated with TRIGGERS and VisMap.

What new challenges are raised by the new perspective, and what tools can address the challenges? TRIGGERS has the challenge of accurately specifying pixel patterns and distances that are cryptic when viewed out of context. It addresses this challenge using the Desktop Blanket, a technique for allowing direct manipulation widgets to float above the screen pixels of the display. VisMap has the challenge of inferring high-level features from low-level pixel data. It addresses this challenge using a two-stage translation process. The first stage works bottom-up and identifies low-level features. The second stage works top-down and infers high-level features from the low-level features.

Can complete solutions be built within the perspective? Such solutions may indicate the potential for an elegant special-purpose system. Working from one perspective, it has potential to have a simple elegant interface. Triggers show a small set of functionality that can automate nontrivial tasks. More work has to be done, however, to show that a significant user group can make use of this functionality.

How can we integrate the perspective with other perspectives? The TRIGGERS-IV system described in Potter (1999) addresses these issues by showing how the Desktop Blanket can be added to a conventional programming language. VisMap already has a textual interface that can easily be integrated with textual programming languages that use other techniques.

Our current intuitions about the design of a visual generalization system for PBE lean toward a broad-based approach that applies pixel-level operators, as in TRIGGERS, where appropriate, but also generates higher-level information inferred from the pixel data, as in VisMap. If the user knows what a particular piece of information looks like on the screen but does not know how to describe it, then a low-level pixel-based approach may be the best choice. If displayed information needed by a program is not provided by formal techniques and its visual appearance is complicated, then a high-level pixel-based approach may be the best solution. If the program needs efficient access to large data structures in an application, then the user can choose a technique such as OLE Automation or Apple Events, provided the application provides the necessary support.

Other issues for complete integration in applications include the granularity of event protocols, styles of interaction with the user, and parallelism considerations (Lieberman 1998). Event granularity determines the level of abstraction at which a visual system interacts with an interface. For example, should mouse movements be included in the information exchanged? If not all mouse movements, then which ones are important? Issues of parallelism can enter the picture when the system and the user both try to manipulate the same interface object.

We believe that the opportunities and challenges of visual generalization will be a fruitful new direction for PBE in the future. It might turn out that when it comes to graphical interfaces, beauty may indeed be only skin deep.

References

Halbert, D. 1993. Programming by demonstration in the desktop metaphor. In *Watch what I do: Programming by demonstration,* ed. A. Cypher. Cambridge, Mass.: MIT Press.

Kurlander, D., and E. Bier. 1988. Graphical search and replace. In *Proceedings of ACM SIGGRAPH '88.* (Atlanta, Ga.). New York, NY ACM SIGGRAPH.

Lakin, F. 1987. Visual grammars for visual languages. In *AAAI-87: The Conference of the American Association for Artificial Intelligence* (Seattle, Wash., July 12–17). Los Altos, Calif.: AAAI Press.

Lieberman, H. 1998. Integrating user interface agents with conventional applications. *Knowledge-Based Systems* 11, no. 1 (September): 15–24.

Potter, R. 1993. Triggers: Guiding automation with pixels to achieve data access. In *Watch what I do: Programming by demonstration,* ed. A. Cypher. Cambridge, Mass.: MIT Press.

———. 1999. *Pixel data access: Interprocess communication in the user interface for end-user programming and graphical macros.* Ph.D. diss. University of Maryland.

Yamamoto, K. 1998. A programming method of using GUI as API. *Transactions of Information Processing Society of Japan* (December): 26–33 (in Japanese).

Zettlemoyer, L., and R. St. Amant. 1999. A visual medium for programmatic control of interactive applications. In *Proceedings of ACM CHI'99 Human Factors in Computing Systems.* (Pittsburgh, Pa.). New York, NY ACM Press.

Index

2D CAD system, 143–145
    EBP, 143–144
    Pygmalion, 345
    See also CAD systems

A

abstraction-hungry systems, 251
abstractions
    creating, 246
    effects within task domain, 268
    hidden dependencies, 247
    inferred, 268
    invisible, 247
    need for, 367
    over context, 246, 254
    over time, 246
    PBE and, 246
    relationships between, 247
    user identification/naming, 251
actions
    additional user communication and, 103
    by example, defining, 240–241
    choosing most likely, 219–221
    classes, 276
    defined, 275
    executing, 101–102
    list of, 100
    PBAE, 356
    repetitive sequences of, 284
    sequence automation, 281
    suggesting, 100–101
    text editing, 216
    utility estimation, 101
    See also training dialogues
Adaptive Programming Environment (APE)
    action sequence automation, 281

Apprentice, 277–278
Assistant, 278–279
correct suggestions, 291
defined, 272, 274
definition of terms, 275
example 1, 279–281
example 2, 281, 282
example 3, 281–284
example 4, 284, 285
experimental results, 290–293
function illustration, 275
goal, 272, 274
illustrative examples, 279–284
integration into programming environment,
    293
learning time, 291–293
lessons learned, 293
loop detection, 274
machine-learning algorithm, 272
Observer, 275, 276–277
overview, 274–279
software agents, 274
use of, 290–293
AgentSheets, 11
    Agent depictions, 364
    Agent placement on worksheet, 363–365
    automatic agent transformation, 366
    bitmap generation, 361
    defined, 354, 356
    "Semantic rewrite rule" system, 365
    semantics information, 366
    substrate, 363
    syntactic agent transformation, 362
ambiguity removal, 148–149
analogical representation, 13, 14–15
analogies
    creating, 359
    defined, 352, 353

analogies (*continued*)
matching icons for, 364
mechanisms, 363
with PBE, 351–368
as representation level bridge, 353
semantics and, 365
from substitutions to, 363–366
use of, 352
See also programming by analogous
examples (PBAE)
animated programming
data structure, 22
defined, 22
See also ToonTalk
Apple Data Detectors, 229
action programming, 240
choosing, 240
illustrated, 229
regular expression recognizers, 240
Apple Events, 383
AppleScript, 240, 299, 313–318
application behavior change, 317
control structures, 313
data description, 314, 318
data types, 313
defined, 313
errors, 317
examinability, 315
extensions, 313
high-level event architectures, 313–314
implementation deficiencies, 316–317
implementations, 318
incomplete specified objects, 317
interaction/high-level command mismatch,
314
lack of recordable applications, 317
language deficiencies, 314–316
language elements, 313
as macro recorder, 299
persistence of objects/references, 315–316
recordable applications, 313
recording, 302
recording implementation, 318
recordings not matching actions, 316–317
scriptable applications, 313
shortcomings, 299, 300
shortcomings, learning from, 317–318
single-user assumption, 314
spatial relations representation, 315

speed, 315
syntax, 316, 317
timing, 315
undo support inconsistencies, 316
weaknesses, 313–318
application programming interfaces (APIs), 64,
65, 138
Apprentice, 277–278
activity, 277
C4.5 use, 291
detecting repetitive tasks, 284–286
learning, 277
learning situation patterns, 286
loop detection, 284–286
repetitive action sequence detection, 284
repetitive code detection, 286
repetitive error correction detection, 286
role illustration, 275
What-set, 277, 278
When-set, 277, 278
See also Adaptive Programming
Environment (APE)
arranging files, 301–304
after two demonstrations, 302
completion, 303
Familiar events, 301
prediction, 302, 303
user actions, 301
See also Familiar
artificial intelligence (AI) algorithms, 46
for demonstrational interfaces, 46
Gamut system, 52–53
sophisticated, 52–54
unproven, 49
Assistant, 278–279
functioning of, 278–279
known situation detection, 280
loop automation, 286
repetitive sequence of actions automation,
284
role illustration, 275
suggestion time, 293
suggestions, 278, 280
What-set, 278
When-set, 278
window, 279, 290
See also Adaptive Programming
Environment (APE)
AutoMouse, 378

B

Backus-Naur Form (BNF), 230–231
  pattern expressed in, 231
  syntax, 230, 231
  use difficulties, 231
behaviors
  complex demonstration, 167
  context-triggered, 330–333
  creating, 172
  feedback, 172
  hidden states and, 173
  hints, 170–171
  object representation of, 169
  predetermining, 52
  selecting, 170–171
blocks
  defined, 180
  specifying, 185
  See also Format Editor
bookmarks, 73–74
bounding choices, 170
brain representations, 12
  analogical, 13, 14–15
  Bruner's approach, 15–16
  Fregean, 13, 14
  Sloman's approach, 13–15
Bruner, Jerome, 15
Bruner's approach, 15–16
  child use of mentalities, 16
  Creator and, 16
  knowledge representation methods, 15
  See also brain representations

C

C4.5 algorithm, 289
  Apprentice use of, 291
  What-set, 289
  When-set, 289, 291
C32, 48
CAD systems
  2D, 143–145
  ambiguity removal, 148–149
  APPLY command, 156
  commands, 139, 156
  determinism, 148–149
  dimensional-driven, 140

as "editors," 145
  ENTER command, 156
  expressiveness, 149–155
  first-generation, 138
  fully integrated, 155–156
  geometrical entities in, 140
  interfaces, 139
  LOAD command, 156
  mouse-click position, 148
  parametric, 136, 141–142
  part family models, 138
  part libraries, portability, 142
  primitives, 140
  procedural, 141
  shape drawing, 141
  variational, 140–141
  WRITE/READ command, 156
CAD users, 136
  constraints and, 139
  expert, 146
CAD-LIB approach, 142
CAP, 273
cellular phones
  CDMA, 204–206
  display, 205
  jog dial, 205, 206
  POBox on, 204–206
  text input, 199
Celsius-Fahrenheit converter, 324–326
  Celsius indicator, 325
  Fahrenheit indicator, 325
  linear proportions, 339
  questions, 326
  thermometers, 324, 325
  See also stimulus-response systems
characterization
  defined, 94
  valuation of, 100
Chimera, 251
  defined, 170
  modes, 327–328
Cima
  defined, 171
  domain knowledge, 224
  hints, 224
  inference techniques, 242
  SMARTedit vs., 224
  user interface, 242
ClipBoard, 273

closeness of mapping, 247
Cognitive Dimensions of Notations, 247, 249, 267–268
collections, 92–93
    access, 92
    defined, 92
    in position specification, 92
    See also HyQL
Comic-Strip Program Representation Language. *See* C-SPRL
competence areas, 107
complex parameters, 340
composition by example (CBE), 191–207
    defined, 192
    introduction to, 192–193
computer-aided design (CAD)
    applications, PBE and, 4
    as dialogue language, 183
    end-user programming facilities in, 138
    explicit PBD solutions, 155–159
    modeling, 138
    naming in, 145–149
    part families, 137–138
    PBD requirements, 142–143
    solution, 143–155
    specificity, 145
    structured tasks in, 139
    as suitable PBD area, 137–140
    See also CAD systems; CAD users
concept learning
    algorithms, 289–290
    inductive, 289
constant object descriptor, 337
context-free grammars, 239–240
contexts
    abstractions over, 246
    defined, 94
    defining, 100
    dynamic management of, 146
    identification of, 103
    valuation, 100
context-triggered behaviors, 330–333
control structures
    AppleScript, 313
    block, 150–151
    branch contexts, 150
    loop, 150
    PBD, definition, 151–155

    REDOing, 157
    subroutines, 150
    support, 150–151
    UNDOing, 157
converting images, 309–311
    defined, 309
    illustrated, 310
    See also Familiar
C-SPRL, 123–131
    branching construct, 128
    categories, subcategories, members, 124–125
    commands, 127
    defined, 124
    do-all construct, 129
    editing representations, 128
    editor menu options, 129
    panel icons, 128
    program representation, 125
    sample queries, 131
    symbols, 127
    use summary, 128
    user tests, 130
CSV (Comma Separated Value) file format, 178

D

data extraction, 70–71
    by heuristics, 71
    by partial matching, 70–71
    message of failure, 82
    robustness, 72
data warehouse technologies, 176
debugging
    on examples, 157–158
    repetitive tasks, 281, 282
decision-tree algorithms, 53, 288
    C4.5, 289
    low error rate, 288
    use in CAP, 289
DEMO system, 326
    DEMO II guidewires, 168
    in stimulus mode, 330
    video-recorder-like mode palette, 327
Demonstration Interfaces group
    defined, 47

systems, 47–49
demonstrational interfaces, 45–58
   AI algorithms for, 46
   defined, 46
   inferencing, 46
   introduction to, 46–47
demonstrational systems
   C32, 48
   feedback, 54–57
   Gamut, 49
   Gilt, 48
   Gold, 48
   heuristics, 47
   Jade, 48
   Katie, 49
   Lapidary, 48
   level of intelligence, 49–54
   Marquise, 48–49
   Peridot, 47–48
   Pursuit, 48
   sophisticated AI algorithms, 52–54
   Topaz, 49
   Tourmaline, 48
   Turquoise, 49
dimensional-driven systems, 140
domain knowledge, 106
domain-independent systems, 297–319
   platform requirements, 311–312
   See also Familiar
DropZones, 229, 230
   action selection, 240
   illustrated, 230
dynamic context management, 146, 157
Dynamic Macro system, 193–197
   adding comment characters in, 195
   adding comment lines in, 196
   advantages, 196–197
   applications, 195
   defined, 192–194
   functioning of, 194
   implementation, 197
   keyboard macros, 194
   power, 197
   recording/invoking commands, 194
   REPEAT command, 194, 195, 196
   SMARTedit vs., 224
   use illustration, 195
   use of, 193

users and, 197
   See also text editing

E

Eager, 53, 273–274
   consecutive occurrence detection, 273
   defined, 273
   domain-independent principle, 299
   macro invocation, 323
   suggestions, 273
   user studies, 54
EBP system, 136
   as 2D system, 143–144
   as complete programming environment,
     157–159
   debugging on examples, 157–158
   defined, 136–137, 143
   design, 142
   display calculator, 144
   entity orientation, 149
   instances, 155
   model definitions, 143
   new features, 158–159
   parts-portable program libraries, 158
   in PLUS project, 158
   program generation, 158–159
   REDOing control structure, 157
   sessions, 156
   snapshot, 144
   true explicit PBD solutions, 155–159
   UNDOing control structure, 157
   variables, 156
   Visit menu, 157
Editing by Example (EBE) system, 193
   inferring regular expressions, 250
   SMARTedit vs., 224
Emacs
   "dabbrev" function, 193
   keystroke sequences, 192
   Lisp codes, 192
E-Mail Grammar, 233–235
   Categories view, 240
   defined, 233
   examples view, 239
   Host, 236, 237, 238
   Person, 234, 235

E-Mail Grammar (*continued*)
    recursive grammar rules, 236–238
    rule definition sets, 238–239
    top-down definition, 234–235
    See also Grammex
empirical learning systems, 336
encapsulation principle, 150
end-user programming, 8, 352
error rate, 287–288
event trace, 301
examinability, 241
Example-Based Programming in Parametrics.
      See EBP system
explanation-based learning systems, 336
explicit examples, 166
    defined, 166
    product creation with, 166
    users, 166
expression
    CAD system, 149–155
    evaluator, 249
    HyQL, 92
    PBD, 210
    SMARTedit, 223

F

Familiar, 274, 298–319
    for arranging files, 301–304
    Begin recording command, 298, 301
    consistency requirement, 312
    controllability requirement, 312
    for converting images, 309–310
    defined, 298
    domain independence, 298
    End task command, 301
    errors and, 304–305
    examinability requirement, 312
    feedback, 304
    Finder, 306, 309
    help balloon, 306
    History window, 303, 309
    incorrect parameter, changing, 308, 309
    incorrect predictions, examining/changing,
      305
    introduction to, 298–300
    iteration execution, 303–304

iterative pattern detection, 306
    iterative task completion, 303
    menu, 300
    on Eager platform, 299
    predictions, 304, 306
    Predictions window, 302, 303, 304
    purpose, 300
    recordability requirement, 312
    requirements, 311–312
    software, 298
    sort criteria, 300
    for sorting files, 306–309
    Stop recording command, 301
    summary, 318–319
    user interface requirement, 312
    users and applications requirement, 311–
      312
    windows, 302
feedback
    behavior code, 172
    demonstrational systems, 54–57
    Familiar, 304
    stimulus-response systems, 340–342
    user need for, 172
focus hints, 170–171
    defined, 170
    examples, 169, 170, 171
format designation, 175–190
Format Editor
    adjustment, 182
    copy and paste, 184–185
    defined, 178
    format files, 178
    format rules extraction, 187
    formats, 187–189
    formatting rules, 182–183
    iteration specification, 180–182, 186
    iterative mode, 185
    process, 179
    Sheet window, 179, 180, 183, 185
    Table Data window, 179, 180, 183
    user interface, 179–182
    window configuration, 179–180
    window status, 183, 184
    See also reporting tool
format files, 178
    defined, 178
    Report Generator and, 183

formatting rules, 178
    deterministic extraction, 190
    extracting, 182–183, 187
    information, 182–183
    pseudo-expression of, 187
Fregean representation, 13, 14
fully integrated PBD systems, 155–156
fuzzy logic, 173

G

Gamut, 52–53
    board game creation, 329
    build/test mode distinction elimination, 328
    complex parameters, 340
    context identification, 332
    decision tree algorithm, 53
    defined, 49, 52
    feedback, 57
    generalization, 336
    guide objects, 334–335
    information gathering techniques, 164
    interaction techniques, 53
    margins, 168
    metrics, 52
    mouse operation icons, 330
    nonconstant descriptors, 338
    philosophy, 333–334
    stimulus mode and, 328
    See also demonstrational systems
gap programming, 193
gardeners, 229–230
Garnet, 137
generalizations
    by removing detail, 21–43
    Gamut, 336
    inheritance for, 367
    low, 288
    novel, 381–383
    object descriptor problem, 337–338
    on grids, 381–383
    overgeneralization, 367
    Pavlov, 336
    of regular expressions, 253
    robots, 22, 29, 35
    stimulus-response PBD, 336
    use choice of, 243

visual, 371–384
Geographic Information Systems. *See* GIS
    software
Geometer's Sketchpad, 169
ghost marks, 335
Gilt, 48
GIS software, 115–132
    architecture for nonspecialist users, 123
    database query language, 122
    difficulty in using, 118–120
    end users and, 115–132
    heuristics, 119
    interface, user interactions with, 122
    introduction to, 116
    for nonspecialists, 132
    origination of, 120
    PBD approach to, 3–4, 116, 121–122, 123–131
    program representation language, 121
    queries, 120–121
    selection, 117
    surrogate users for, 118
    use obstacles, 118–119
    use of, 116
    user actions, 121
    user improvement, 120–121
    See also PBD GIS
goals
    APE, 272, 274
    general-purpose programming, 166
    PBD, 54, 167, 340
    SMARTedit, 218
    Stagecast Creator, 9
Gold, 48
grammar(s)
    of arbitrary complexity, 239
    by example, programming, 231–232
    categories, 238
    context-free, 239–240
    defining, for email addresses, 233–235
    definition complexity, 232
    end user difficulty, 231
    formalism, 239
    induction, 241–242
    recursive rule definition, 236–238
    top-down definition style, 235
    writing as text, 230–231
Grammars by Example. *See* Grammex

Grammex, 4, 228, 232
    Categories view, 239
    defined, 232
    Edit mode, 233
    as front end, 242
    grammar formalism, 239
    Grammar Window, 238
    incremental/iterative approach, 240
    inferring regular expressions, 251
    overview window, 232
    Parse mode, 233
    pop-up menus, 242
    rule windows, 232
    top-down definition, 234–235
"Grand Canyon" gap, 12, 13
graphical rewrite rules (GRRs), 356, 360
    defined, 356
    semantic, 362
    uses, 356
grids, 381–383
    examples, 382
    expression, 382
    "idea," 382
    See also visual generalizations
guesses
    Scrapbook, 81
    SmallBrowse, 81
    SMARTedit, 221
guide objects, 334–335

H

handwriting recognition systems, 199
heading pattern, 69
heuristics
    defined, 47
    demonstrational system, 47
    designing, 57
    GIS software, 119
    rule-based, 52
    TELS, 223
    ToonTalk, 27
    Topaz, 50
    Web page data extraction with, 71
high-level events, 313–314
    data description, 314
    interaction/high-level command mismatch,
      314

    See also AppleScript
high-level visual generalization, 378–381
hints
    behaviors, 170–171
    Cima, 224
    defined, 167
    extra channels, 167
    focus, 170–171
    giving, 167–171
    special objects, 167–170
human-computer interface (HCI), 49
HyQL, 91–96
    collections, 92–93
    defined, 91–92
    expressiveness, 92
    extraction refinement process, 95
    purpose, 92
    queries, 93
    as target language, 91
HyQL scripts, 93
    characterization, 94
    context, 94
    extraction refinement process, 95
    landmark, 94
    subtree, 95

I

IDHYS, 289–290
    defined, 289
    earlier version, 290
    hypothesis space search, 289
    What-set, 291
ILA, 111
image processing, 375
images, 189
inductive learning, 165
inference algorithm, 255–258
InferenceBear, 53
    Elements, Events & Transitions (EET), 57
    linear equation support, 53
    linear proportions, 339–340
    philosophy, 333–334
inferencing
    in demonstrational interfaces, 46
    from multiple examples, 52–54
    no, 50
    passive watcher, 165–166

rule-based, 50–52
systems with, 46–47
user intent problem, 63–64
InfoBox
    defined, 109
    illustrated sample, 110
    InfoBeans, 109
InfoBroker, 89–90
    database maintenance, 91
    defined, 89
information extraction trainer (IET), 91, 96
information management, 375
Information Manifold (IM), 110, 111
inheritance
    as generalization means, 367
    PBE tension between, 367
    reuse through, 366–367
instance-based algorithms, 288
InstantText system, 199–200
intelligent interfaces
    defined, 46
    "slippery slope," 54
interface builders, 324
    modes, 327
    stimulus-response demonstration
        augmenting, 324
interfaces
    Cima, 242
    demonstrational, 45–58
    "direct-manipulation," 2
    Format Editor, 179–182
    Grammex, 232
    HCI, 49
    IET, 96
    intelligent, 46, 54
    interactive specification of, 347–349
    passive watcher, 165–166
    PBD, 165, 173
    predictive, 273
    SMARTedit, 212–215
    SWYN, 251–255
    triggering responses in, 328
    X-MOTIF, 143
Interlisp, 277
Internet Scrapbook, 63, 65–73
    application domain, 81
    copying HTML data to, 84
    defined, 63, 66
    ease of use, 66

evaluation, 71–73
heading pattern, 69
heuristics, 67, 71
matching pattern generation, 67–70
overview, 66–67
page created by user, 67
page updated by system, 67
partial matching, 70–71
PBE process in, 68
preinstallation, 82
research area, 82
tag pattern, 69–70
TrIAs vs., 83
user selection in Web browsers, 67
Web page data extraction, 70–71
wrong guesses, 81
interprocess communication, 313
iteration
    execution, 303–304
    implication, 187
    pattern examples, 181
    specifying, 180–182, 186

J

Jade, 48

K

Katie, 49
keyboard macros
    automatic execution of, 194
    defined, 194
    disadvantages, 194
    recording/invoking commands, 194
    See also Dynamic Macro system
KidSim, 137
knowledge
    domain, 106
    procedural, 105
    structural, 105
    visual/semantic, 105–106

L

landmarks
    candidates, finding, 101

landmarks (*continued*)
  candidates, suggestion of, 104
  defined, 94
  defining, 100
  identification of, 103
  integrating, into wrapper, 104
languages
  "best," 247
  natural, 241
  PBD, 171
  power of, 171
  program representation, 121, 124–132
  stimulus-response, 326
Lapidary, 48
learning
  agents, 96
  Apprentice, 277, 286
  concept, 289–290
  empirical systems, 336
  inductive, 165
  interface agents, 273
  macros, 216
  procedure, 213
  SMARTedit, 213, 221–223
  time, 291–293
learning user habits, 286–290
  algorithms, 288–290
  difficulty, 287–288
  low error rate, 287–288
  low generalization, 288
  low prediction time, 287
  low training time, 287
  requirements, 287–288
  user-intelligible situation patterns, 287
Letizia, 83
LIKE system, 136, 145
  architecture, 147
  context management, 146–147
  in execution phase, 146
  in recording phase, 146
  results, 143
  tasks, 146
linear proportions, 339–340
  InferenceBear, 339–340
  Pavlov, 339
loops
  detecting, 284–286
  detecting, with APE, 274
  example, 152

  initiation, 153
  interactive definition of, 154
  recurrence relation evaluation, 155
  Repeat . . . until, 151
  structure, 150
  While, 151
low-level visual generalization, 376–378

M

macro recorders, 298–299
  AppleScript as, 299
  limitations, 299
  recording, 322–323
macros, 2
  invoking, 213–214
  keyboard, 194
  learning, 216
  Microsoft Word, 354
  recording, 212, 354–355
  SMARTedit, 212–214, 216
Macros by Example, 137
Marquise, 326
  defined, 48–49
  feedback, 55–56
  feedback window, 56
  ghost marks, 335
  video-recorder-like mode palette, 327
  See also demonstrational systems
Merge robots, 36–39
  about to train, 38
  joining, 39
  training, 37, 38
  See also robots; ToonTalk
MetaMouse, 53
Microsoft Word macros, 354
mission-critical forms, 189
Mondrian system
  defined, 57, 272
  recording, 323

N

naming
  abstractions, 251
  in CAD, 145–149
  problem of, 145–148

navigation, 92
negative examples, 254
no-inferencing approach, 50
Norman, Don, 12
novice programmers
    defined, 8
    gap, 12
    main problem of, 12

O

object descriptors, 337–338
    constant, 337
    Gamut, 338
    nonconstant, 337
    Pavlov, 337–338
    problem, 337–338
objects
    demonstrated, 337
    guide, 334–335
    intended run-time, 337
    invisible objects, 173
    iterative, 180
    pointing out, 167
    reacting asynchronously to events, 347–349
    representing common behaviors, 169
    for representing state, 168
    secondary area for drawing, 168
    special, creating, 167–170
    speed and direction indication, 169
    transferring relationship between, 359
    widgets, 169–170
Observer, 276–277
    defined, 276
    role illustration, 275
    See also Adaptive Programming
        Environment (APE)
OLE Automation, 383
OpenSesame!, 273
overgeneralization, 367

P

parametrics, 136, 141–142
    defined, 137, 141
    imperative program, 141
    part family models, 142

Pro-Engineer system, 141
    See also CAD systems
parsers, 229
part family, 137–138, 142
partial matching, 70–71
parts libraries, 142
passive watcher, 165–166
    advantages, 166
    defined, 165
    inferencing, 165–166
Pavlov system, 324, 345–349
    arcade game development, 331, 332
    context demonstration, 331
    defined, 346
    design evolution, 346
    dialogue, 341
    driving simulator built in, 335, 347
    Editor, 342
    example, 346–347
    generalization, 336
    global-time frame, 349
    for interactive specification of interfaces,
        347–349
    introduction to, 346
    linear proportions, 339
    nonconstant descriptors, 337–338
    operation recording, 349
    physical/logical operations and, 330
    Real Time Response mode, 334
    response demonstration, 334
    at run-time, 349
    Score, 348
    single time-line view, 348, 349
    stimulus-response scheme, 332
    stimulus-response score, 342
    timeline, 334
    video-recorder-like mode palette, 327
PBD GIS, 123–131
    Edit mode, 123
    Record mode, 123, 124
    user interface, 123, 124
    See also GIS software
PBE-based text editing systems, 193
pen-based computers
    handwriting recognition support, 200
    POBox for, 202–204
    RKC support, 200
Peridot, 137
    defined, 47–48

Peridot (*continued*)
   feedback, 54
   onscreen virtual mouse, 328
   program example in, 54–55
   question-and-answer dialogues, 54
   rule-based inferencing, 50
   See also demonstrational systems
Playground project, 40
PLUS project, 142, 158
POBox system, 193, 197–207
   architecture, 200–202
   defined, 193, 197
   display on Palm Pilot, 203–204
   filtering step, 201
   illustrated architecture, 201
   Japanese input mode of, 203
   on cellular phone, 204–206
   for pen-based computers, 202–204
   running on Windows95, 202
   selection step, 201
   server on Internet, 206–207
   startup display, 202
   text input techniques, 197–200
   use of, 193
predication time, 287
predictive interfaces, 273
premature commitment, 247
probabilistic algorithm, 256–258
problems
   inferring user intent, 63–64
   internal data access, 64, 65
   naming, 145–148
   PBE, 63–64
   representation, 340
   reuse, 353–354
   trainable information agents, 105
   TrIA, 105–109
   user intent, 63–64
procedural expression, 260
procedural knowledge, 105
procedure calls, 41
ProDeGE+, 137
Pro-Engineer system, 141
program representation languages, 121
   block-stacking metaphor, 132
   C-SPRL, 124–131
   Pursuit, 124

programming
   animated, 22
   APE integration into, 293
   by stimulus-response demonstration, 323
   by teaching, 221
   as cognitively challenging task, 42–43
   domain-independent, 297–319
   end-user, 8, 352
   environments, 4
   example-based, 148
   gap, 193
   grammars by example, 231–232
   GRRs and, 362
   parametrics, 137
   PBE replacement of, 2
   through reuse, 362–363
   timing and, 5
   widgets, 169
   without textual programming language,
      9–11
programming by analogous examples (PBAE),
      356–360
   actions, 356
   cars moving like trains example, 357–360
   defined, 352, 353
   pupstitution support in, 365
   reuse support, 358
   situations, 356
   syntactic rewrite rules and, 360–363
   user perspective, 356–360
programming by demonstration (PBD). *See*
      programming by example (PBE)
programming by example (PBE)
   abstractions and, 246
   analogous examples, 351–368
   animation system, 5
   automation, 4
   CAD and, 4, 135–160
   children and, 3, 5
   closeness of mapping, 247
   commercial environments, 5
   commercial platforms, 298
   component, adding, 64
   control structure definition, 151–155
   conventional software vs., 3
   defined, 2, 8, 164, 242, 272
   in domain terms, 11
   ease of use, 10

effectiveness, 207
example, 26–40
expressiveness, 149–155
for format designation, 175–190
fully integrated systems, 155–156
future directions, 5–6
general control structures, 150–151
generalization problem, 2
as general-purpose programming tool,
    164
GISs and, 3–4, 116, 121–122
goal, 54, 167, 340
growing use of, 4–5
GUI level, 353
heuristic inference, 242
interfaces, 165, 173
Internet Scrapbook process, 68
languages, 171, 173
limitations, 272, 319
machine-learning techniques, 164
macro invocation, 323–324
misconception, 166
operations recorded by, 12
personal solutions, 6
potential, 6, 173
premature commitment, 247
program level, 353
program representation, 121
programming environments and, 4
recorded program problem, 10
representation chasm, 353
representation problem, 340
reuse, 352–353
special-purpose, 42
Stagecast Creator, 8, 9
stimulus-response, 321–343
text editing systems, 193–197
text input systems, 197–207
underlying problems, 63–64
usability factors, 247–248
for user convenience, 4
visibility, 155, 247, 248–249
visual generalization in, 371–384
for Web-browsing tasks, 61–84
who is programming with, 166–167
programming environment, 171–172
    EBP system, 157–159
    importance of, 171–172

PBE and, 4
requirements, 172
VisualWorks Smalltalk, 274
pupstitution
    defined, 363
    support, 365
Pursuit, 251
    defined, 48
    feedback, 54–55
    program representation language, 124
    storyboard, 341
    See also demonstrational systems
Pygmalion system, 145
    conditionals, 41
    iconic representations, 41
    support, 40
    weakness, 42

Q

queries
    GIS software, 120–121
    sample (C-SPRL), 131
    schemes, 90

R

Real Time Response mode, 334
reconstructed reports, 176, 177
reconstruction, 176
recordable applications, 313
recursive grammar rules
    definition of, 236–238
    through multiple examples, 237
REDOing control structure, 157
regular expressions, 245–268
    defining set of phone numbers, 258
    display form, 249
    generalization of, 253
    heuristics for inferring repeated sections of,
        257
    improvement, 249
    induction by heuristic graph reduction, 256
    inference, heuristic algorithm, 255–258
    inferring from text examples, 249–250
    integrated facility for, 265–267

regular expressions (*continued*)
modification of, 266–267
notation, 249
PBE systems for inferring, 250–251
recognizers, 240
refining, 252, 266
repeated elements, 256
specialization of, 254
user creation of, 252
user interface for, 251–255
visual notation for, 258–265
See also SWYN
Repeat . . . until loops, 151
REPEAT command, 153
repetitive tasks
action sequences, 284
APE correct suggestion of, 291
in application debugging, 281, 282
in application testing, 279–281
code, 286
detecting, 284–286
error corrections, 286
loops, 284–286
Report Generator
defined, 178
process example, 183–187
See also reporting tool
reporting tool
defined, 176
evaluation, 187–190
for format designation, 175–190
Format Editor, 178
format-making phase, 178
functions, 177
phases, 178
process example, 183–187
reconstruction support, 176
Report Generator, 178
report-generation phase, 178
system configuration, 178–179
system overview, 178–179
user interface, 177
reports
for decision making, 176
formats, 176, 187–190
generating, 178, 183, 189
images, 189
increment calculation, 181

mission-critical forms, 189
planning and decision making, 189
reconstructed table, 176, 177
unification of repeatedly occurring data, 182
responses
defined, 334
demonstrating, 334
parameter descriptors, 338–339
triggering, 328
See also stimulus-response systems
reuse
PBAE, 356
PBE, 352–353
problem examples, 353–354
programming through, 362–363
through inheritance, 366–367
rewrite rules
graphical (GRRs), 356, 360, 362
semantic, 360–363
syntactic, 360–363
robots
actions recorded by, 30
defined, 22
doubling numbers, 28
generalizing, 22, 29, 35
Merge, 36–39
programmer's actions, 30
Sort, 31–34
testing, 29
thought bubbles, 35
training, 24, 25, 30
training, for base case of recursion, 36
truck loaded with, 25
See also ToonTalk
Roman-Kanji conversion (RKC), 197–199
rule-based inferencing, 50–52
example, 50
heuristics, 52
Peridot system, 50
predetermined behaviors, 52
rule changing, 52
Tourmaline, 52
rules
definitions, managing sets of, 238–239
formatting, 178, 182–183
grammar, automatic induction of, 241
recursive grammar, 236–238

S

scriptable applications, 313
ScriptAgent
    defined, 240
    using, 240–241
search engines, 173–174
search-and-replace operation, 248
secondary notation, 247, 251
    defined, 247
    example of, 251
See What You Need. *See* SWYN
Selection Recognition Agent, 240
semantic rewrite rules, 360–363
semistructured information, 228
SgmlQL, 112
Sheet window
    copy and paste with, 184–185
    defined, 185
    as drawing program, 185
    editing on, 186
    editing scheme, 180
    empty sheet display, 183
    example report image in, 185
    illustrated, 184, 185
    text strings, 180
    See also Format Editor
situations, 356
Sketchpad, 137
Sloman, Aaron, 13
Sloman approach, 13–15
    analogical, 13, 14–15
    Fregean, 13, 14
    predicate calculus statements, 13
    representation structure, 13
    representation types, 13
    See also brain representations
*A Small Matter of Programming: Perspectives on
    End-user Computing*, 137
SmallBrowse, 63, 73–81
    accuracy warning curves, 80
    anchor text, finding, 79–80
    application domain, 81
    C-URL, 79
    defined, 63, 74
    example task, 75–76
    hyperlink prediction accuracy, 81
    informational experiments, 80–81

newest URL, finding, 79–80
    overview, 74–80
    p-links, 75, 76, 79
    p-links prediction, 76–80
    recording a history, 76
    R-URL, 76, 79
    screen snapshot, 75
    S-URL, 76
    target market, 83–84
    tip help, 80
    URL determination from history, 78–79
    WBI vs., 83
    Web browsing on, 77
    wrong guesses, 81
SmallStar, 57, 137
Smalltalk, 278
    hierarchy of action classes, 276
    programming environment, 272, 274
    users, 290
SMARTedit, 209–225, 251
    Action nodes, 218
    adaptive orientation, 214
    as assistant, 221, 222
    Cima system vs., 224
    comparison with other systems, 223–224
    correcting, 214
    current application state capture, 220
    defined, 210
    deleting HTML comment, 212–213
    different users and, 222
    Dynamic Macro vs., 224
    EBE vs., 224
    expressiveness, 223
    function hypotheses, 219–220
    functions, 216, 218
    goal, 218
    guesses, 221
    improvement plan, 221–223
    Insert functions, 216
    interaction with user/teacher, 222
    learning process, 222
    locations in text file, 218
    machine learning technique, 223
    macros, invoking, 213–214
    macros, learning, 216
    macros, recording, 212
    Move functions, 216, 218
    next steps for, 221–223

SMARTedit (*continued*)
    other directions for, 223
    procedure learning, 213
    Programs, 218
    robust implementation of, 222
    role in learning process, 221
    smarts behind, 215–219
    space of programs, 216, 217
    Start recording button, 212
    Step through macro button, 213–214, 215
    suffix search functions, 219
    TELS system vs., 223–224
    testing, 220
    user effort, reducing, 216
    user errors and, 222
    user interface, 212–215
    version space, 216, 218
    version space algebra, 211, 225
    See also macros; text editing
software agents, 88
Sort robot, 31–34
    defined, 31
    finishing training of, 34
    sort boxes with one hole, 36
    Sort process, 33
    testing, 33
    training, 32
    See also robots; ToonTalk examples
sorting files, 306–309
    illustrated, 307
    incorrect parameter, changing, 308, 309
    iterative pattern detection, 306
    user actions, 306
    See also Familiar
special objects. *See* objects
Stagecast Creator, 8, 210
    analogical representations, 42
    Bruner's mentalities and, 16
    conclusion, 18
    creation illustrations, 17, 18
    defined, 9
    empirical evidence, 16–18
    enduring user interest, 17
    goal, 9
    implementation, 16–17
    syntax, 10
    teacher/parent use of, 16
    theoretical foundations, 11–13

stimuli
    context-triggered behaviors, 330–333
    demonstrating, 328–334
    physical and logical operations, 329–330
    structured text as, 333
    system events as, 333–334
    time as, 333
    Web page, 342
stimulus-response syntax, 326–335
    challenge, 326
    context-triggered behaviors, 330–333
    defined, 326
    demonstration aids, 334–335
    "Initial View" mode, 327
    physical and logical operations, 329–330
    response demonstration, 334
    stimuli demonstration, 328–334
    "Stimulus" mode, 327
    structured text as stimulus, 333
    system events as stimuli, 333–334
    time as stimulus, 333
    video-recorder-like mode palette, 327
stimulus-response systems, 321–343
    augmenting interface builders, 324
    complex parameters, 340
    example, 324–326
    feedback and editing, 340–342
    generalization, 336
    introduction to, 322
    linear proportions, 339–340
    macro invocation, 323–324
    macro recording, 322–323
    object descriptor problem, 337–338
    as programming language, 326
    response parameter descriptors, 338–339
    score, 341–342
    semantics, 336–340
storyboards, 341
structural knowledge, 105
subroutines, 150
suffix search functions, 219
surrogate users, 117
SWYN, 245–268
    defined, 249
    future versions, 255, 267
    initial interface state, 252
    interface, 251–255, 266
    negative examples, 254
    probabilistic algorithm, 256–258, 267

search-and-replace mode, 252
selection sets, 252–254
usability improvements, 251–252
visual expression support, 266
visual integration with data, 265–266
visual notation, 258–265
See also regular expressions
syntactic rewrite rules, 360–363
beyond, 360–363
meaning, 361
transformation, 362
See also rewrite rules

T

Table Data window, 179
tag pattern, 69
task library, 100
Tatlin, 380, 381
Tegic T9 system, 200
TELS system, 193
heuristic rules, 223
inferring regular expressions, 250–251
SMARTedit vs., 223–224
test trace, 290–291
text
by example, 227–243
composition, 192
formatting, 178
recognition agents, 228–230
writing grammars as, 230–231
text editing
Dynamic Macro, 193–197
functions, 216
Insert functions, 216
locations in text file, 218
Move functions, 216, 218
as sequence of changes, 215
with SMARTedit, 209–225
system comparison, 223–224
systems, 193–197
task, repetition, 209–225
user actions, 216
text input
fast, on handheld machines, 199
handwriting recognition systems, 199
Japanese, 197
method structures, 198

on CDMA phone, 206
on cellular phone, 199
on handheld computers, 199
systems, 197–207
techniques, 197–200
user provision for, 201
word dictionary, 199–200
textual programming language
as barrier, 9
programming without, 9–11
time
abstraction over, 246
predication, 287
as stimulus, 333
training, 287
Tinker system, 232
conditional test in, 41
support, 40
user questions, 41
ToonTalk, 210
animated programming, 22
birds, 22, 41
city, 24
clauses, 41
computer science equivalent terms, 23
data structure, 22
defined, 22
Dusty the Vacuum, 42
fundamental idea behind, 25
introduction to, 24–26
Magic Wand, 37, 42
nested conditionals and, 41
nests, 22, 41
object behavior in, 25
power/simplicity of, 41
program creation/generalization, 22
program development in, 40
scales, 37
users, 24
See also robots
ToonTalk examples, 26–40
card game, 27–40
doubling-numbers, 26–28
Sort robot, 31–34
Topaz
defined, 49
feedback, 56–57
heuristic, 50
inferencing and, 50

Topaz (*continued*)
    object generalization dialog box, 51
    See also demonstrational systems
Tourmaline
    defined, 48
    rules, 52
    See also demonstrational systems
trace
    event, 301
    test, 290–291
    train, 290
train trace, 290
trainable information assistants (TrIAs), 82–83,
       87–112
    action execution, 101–102
    action suggestion, 100–101
    application scenarios, 89–91, 109–110
    "Can I stop?" question, 105
    communication problem, 105–109
    cooperative problem solving, 111
    defined, 82–83
    exchange of roles, 109
    HyQL query language, 91–96
    image-processing capabilities, 108
    InfoBroker, 89–90
    instantiations of, 90, 110
    interactive session, 83
    introduction to, 88–89
    lessons learned, 104–105
    problems, 105
    query schemes, 90
    related work, 110–112
    Scrapbook vs., 83
    structural correctness, 102
    task library, 100
    training dialogue, 96–104
    user interaction and, 111
    for Web, 87–112
    "What to do next?" decision, 105
    wrappers, 94
training agents
    defined, 228
    for text by example recognition, 227–243
    text recognition, 228–230
training dialogues, 96–104
    actions, executing, 101–102
    actions, suggesting, 100–101
    cycle, 97

    illustrated sample, 99
    information types during, 105–106
    initiation of, 97
    invoking, 96
    sample, 102–104
    start of, 97
    terminating, 102
    in TrIA scenarios, 107
training time, 287
TRIGGERS system, 376, 383
    defined, 376
    pixel-level operators, 384
    strategy, 376
    TRIGGERS-IV, 383
Turquoise, 49

U

UNDOing control structure, 157
UNTIL command, 153
usability factors, 247–248
users
    agent communication problem, 105–109
    CAD, 135–160
    complex behavior demonstration, 167
    Dynamic Macro system and, 197
    explicit examples, 166
    feedback, 172
    generalizations, choosing, 243
    GIS software and, 118–122
    habits, learning, 286–290
    intent problem, 63–64
    operations, capturing, 65
    PBAE perspective, 356–360
    in PBD, 166–167
    SMARTedit interaction with, 222
    surrogate, 117
    text input and, 201
    ToonTalk, 24
    in trainer role, 107
    Web information access, 65–66

V

variational systems, 140–141
    defined, 140

geometry, 140
  user input, 140–141
  weaknesses, 141
  See also CAD systems
version space, 216
  Action, 218
  advantages, 219
  algebra, 211, 225
  defined, 216
  discriminating power, 221
  Location, 218
  See also SMARTedit
video-recorder-like mode palette, 327
viscosity, 247
visibility
  defined, 247
  improvement, 249–250
  test case, 248–249
VisMap, 375, 383
  card recognition, 380
  defined, 378
  pixel information translation, 378
  as programmable user model, 378
  textual interface, 383
VisSolitaire
  control cycle, 378
  defined, 378
  source data, 379
  visual processing results, 379
Visual Basic. *See* interface builders
visual before-after rules, 8
  AgentSheets, 11
  defined, 10
  defining, 10
  effects, 11
  interactive, visual process, 10, 11
  reading, 10–11
visual declarative expression, 260, 262
visual generalizations, 371–384
  benefits, 374–375
  brittleness, 375–376
  challenges, 375–376
  characteristics of, 372
  consistency, 374
  defined, 373
  event granularity, 384
  high-level, 378–381
  image processing, 375

information management, 375
  integration into existing environments, 374
  low-level, 376–378
  new information sources, 374–375
  novel, 381–383
  summary, 383–384
  usefulness example, 373–374
visual gesture language, 120
visual notation, 258–265
  alternatives, 259
  design, 258
  discussion, 264–265
  evaluation, 259–261
  experiment, 259–261
  method, 261–263
  performance of first/later tasks, 264
  procedural, 259, 260
  results, 263–264
  visual declarative, 259, 260, 262
  See also regular expressions
visual/semantic knowledge, 105–106

W

W3QL, 112
WBI, 83
Web browsers, 229
  APIs, 65
  user selection in, 67
  Web data copied from, 66, 84
Web browsing, 61–84
  as good PBE domain, 64–65
  history, 78
  on SmallBrowse, 77
  PBE and, 62–84
  as repetitive task, 62
  scroll operations, 73
task automation, 62
Web pages
  bookmarks, 73–74
  chronologically ordered articles, 72
  data extraction from, 70–71
  modification irregularities, 69
  stimuli, 342
WebSQL, 112
WebWatcher, 273

What-set
  Apprentice and, 277, 278
  Assistant and, 278
  C4.5 algorithm, 289
  IDHYS, 291
  learning, 289
  situation patterns, 287
  See also Adaptive Programming
    Environment (APE)
When-set
  Apprentice and, 277, 278
  Assistant and, 278
  C4.5 algorithm, 289, 291
  learning, 289
  situation patterns, 287
  See also Adaptive Programming
    Environment (APE)
While loops, 151
widgets, 169–170
  defined, 169
  programming, 169
  timer, 170
  used too heavily, 169

    See also objects
word dictionary, 199–200
wrappers
  accepting, 100
  class valuation, 98
  construction of, 94–96
  current, 103
  final version of, 104
  generation and assessment, 98–100
  generation approaches, 111
  induction methods, 111
  landmark integration into, 104
  producing, 96
  quality, 101
  rejection of, 104
  robustness, 100
WYSIWYC Spreadsheet, 137

X

XML parse trees, 112
X-MOTIF interface, 143

About the Authors

Alan Blackwell is a University Lecturer in computer science at Cambridge University and a Research Fellow of Darwin College. He completed a Ph.D. in psychology at the MRC Applied Psychology Unit in Cambridge, supervised by Thomas Green. That project investigated usability in visual languages—specifically the question of metaphor in diagrams. Prior to this, he completed a research MSc in artificial intelligence at Victoria University of Wellington, supervised by Peter Andreae, in the field of qualitative spatial reasoning. His first degree, in electrical engineering, was at Auckland University. He has worked for twelve years as a software engineer for companies including Arthur D. Little Cambridge Consultants and Hitachi Europe Advanced Software Centre.

His main research project at present investigates "new paradigms for visual interaction," especially the question of what alternatives there are to the use of metaphor when users must directly manipulate abstractions. To date, this question has been addressed in the contexts of music typesetting, word processor macros, domestic central heating controls, design sketching, predictive test entry, and home area networking. His research approach employs both cognitive science and experimental psychology methods as well as ethnographic observation, interviews, and implementation of prototype systems in collaboration with other researchers in Cambridge and elsewhere. He is active in the organization of international research communities devoted to the psychology of programming, diagrammatic reasoning, and visual languages. A selection of publications, and further details of Alan Blackwell's work, can be found at *http://www.cl.cam.ac.uk/ ~afb21/.*

Allen Cypher's main interest is end-user programming—giving all computer users capabilities that have traditionally belonged to programmers. He worked as a Senior Scientist in Apple's Research Labs for nine years. Together with David C. Smith, he developed Stagecast Creator. Prior to Creator, he developed a system called Eager, which was one of the first intelligent agents. He is the editor of *Watch What I Do: Programming by Demonstration,* which was published in 1993 by MIT Press. He received a B.A. in mathematics from Princeton University and a Ph.D. in computer science from Yale University. (*www.acypher.com*)

Dietmar Dengler is a Senior Researcher at the Intelligent User Interfaces Department of the German Research Center for Artificial Intelligence (DFKI) and currently works in the field of intelligent information assistant systems. He holds a Ph.D. in computer science from Saarland University for work on adaptive deductive planning.

Pedro Domingos is an Assistant Professor in the Department of Computer Science and Engineering at the University of Washington in Seattle. He received a Ph.D. in information and computer science from the University of California at Irvine. His research interests are in machine learning and data mining. He is the author of over sixty technical publications in the fields of scaling up machine-learning algorithms, multistrategy learning, model ensembles, probabilistic learning, model selection, programming by demonstration, data integration, anytime reasoning, computer graphics, and others. He is on the editorial boards of JAIR and IDA, has served on numerous program committees, and is the recipient of an NSF CAREER award, a Fulbright scholarship, an IBM Faculty Award, and best paper awards at KDD-98 and KDD-99. (*http://www.cs.washington.edu/homes/pedrod*)

Christophe Dony is "Maître de Conférences" at the Montpellier-II University and is member of the LIRMM research laboratory (*http://www.lirmm.fr*). He received a Ph.D. degree in computer science from Paris-VI University in 1989. From 1989 to 1992, he was a Research Scientist in a joint team, "Rank-Xerox-France and Paris-VI University." He joined the Montpellier-II University in 1992 and received a French "Habilitation" degree in computer science in 1998. Christophe Dony has worked and published on various aspects of object orientation (languages, programming, environments) including exception handling and debugging, study of reflective languages, study of classless prototype-based languages, algorithms for automatic-inheritance hierarchies construction or reorganization, tools for programming environments, and programmers assistance. (*http:// www.lirmm.fr/~dony*)

Patrick Girard is a professor at the University of Poitiers (France). He is a member of the Laboratory of Applied Computer Science (LISI, for Laboratoire d'Informatique Scientifique et Industrielle) at the Mechanical and Aerotechnical Engineering School (ENSMA for École Nationale Supérieure de Mécanique et d'Aérotechnique), Futuroscope, France. He received a Ph.D. in computer science at Poitiers in 1992 for his work on example-based programming in computer-aided design (CAD). End-user programming remains the main topic of interest of the HCI group he animates at LISI, with over thirty papers and five Ph.D.s in this area (three achieved and two in progress). The LISI web site is *http://www.lisi.ensma.fr.*

ToonTalk was designed and built by **Ken Kahn** (*KenKahn@ToonTalk.com*) who, after earning a doctorate in computer science and AI from MIT, spent twenty years as a researcher in programming languages, computer animation, and programming systems for children. He has been a faculty member at MIT, University of Stockholm, and Uppsala University. For over eight years, he was a researcher at Xerox PARC. In 1992, Ken founded Animated Programs, whose mission is to make computer programming child's play. ToonTalk's URL is *www.toontalk.com* and Ken's Kahn's URL is *www.toontalk .com/English/kenkahn.htm.*

Tessa Lau is a Ph.D. candidate at the University of Washington. She received her Masters degree at the University of Washington in 1997 and her B.S. at Cornell University in 1995. Her interests include artificial intelligence, human-computer interfaces, customizable environments, and everything feline. (*http://www.cs.washington.edu/homes/tlau/*)

Henry Lieberman has been a Research Scientist at the MIT Media Laboratory since 1987. His interests are in the intersection of artificial intelligence and the human interface. He is a member of the Software Agents group, which is concerned with making intelligent software that assists users in interactive interfaces. His current projects involve intelligent agents for the Web that learn by "watching what you do." He has also built an interactive graphic editor that learns from examples and from annotation on images and video. He worked with graphic designer Muriel Cooper in developing systems that supported intelligent visual design. Other projects involve reversible debugging and visualization for programming environments and new graphic metaphors for information visualization and navigation. From 1972–87, he was a researcher at the MIT Artificial Intelligence Laboratory. He started with Seymour Papert in the group that originally developed the educational language Logo, and he wrote the first bitmap and color graphics systems for Logo. He also worked with Carl Hewitt on actors, an early object-oriented, parallel language, and he developed the notion of prototypes and the first real-time garbage collection algorithm. He holds a doctoral-equivalent degree from the University of Paris-VI and was a Visiting Professor there in 1989–90. He has published over fifty papers on a wide variety of research topics. (*http://lieber.www.media.mit.edu/people/lieber/*)

Toshiyuki Masui is a researcher at Sony Computer Science Laboratories, Inc. Previously he spent ten years at Sharp Corporation and at Sony developing various systems for improving the efficiency of using computers, including the POBox system described in this book. The POBox is used as the standard text input method for many of Sony's products, like cellular phones and PDA's. Masui has a doctorate in computer science from University of Tokyo.

Tetsuya Masuishi joined Hitachi in 1983. He has designed many software products including electronic commerce software, application frameworks, and an example-based report generator. He is currently a director at the Advanced Middleware Development Department at Business Solution Systems Development Division, Hitachi. He was a Visiting Research Affiliate at the MIT Media Laboratory in 1990–91.

Richard G. McDaniel is a researcher at the Siemens Technology-To-Business Center where he is designing programming-by-demonstration languages for new domains. His latest work is a tool for building industrial automation applications. He received his Ph.D. in computer science at Carnegie Mellon University, where he developed Gamut, a programming-by-demonstration tool for creating games. He also developed tools for programming user interfaces as a member of the Amulet project. He received his B.Sc. at the University of Virginia and has worked as an intern at Microsoft where he prototyped and developed elements of the OLE 2.0 system. (Email: *richm@ttb.siemens.com*; Web: *http://www.cs.cmu.edu/afs/cs.cmu.edu/user/richm/public/www/whois-richm.html*)

Brad A. Myers is a Senior Research Scientist in the Human-Computer Interaction Institute in the School of Computer Science at Carnegie Mellon University, where he is the principal investigator for various research projects including Silver Multi-Media Authoring, Natural Programming, the Pebbles Hand-Held Computer Project, User Interface Software, and Demonstrational Interfaces. He is the author or editor of over 200 publications, including the books *Creating User Interfaces by Demonstration* and *Languages for Developing User Interfaces,* and he is on the editorial board of five journals. He has been a consultant on user interface design and implementation to about forty companies, and he regularly teaches courses on user interface software. Myers received a Ph.D. in computer science at the University of Toronto where he developed the Peridot UIMS. He received the MS and B.Sc. degrees from the Massachusetts Institute of Technology, during which time he was a research intern at Xerox PARC. From 1980 until 1983, he worked at PERQ Systems Corporation. His research interests include user interface development systems, user interfaces, hand-held computers, programming by example, programming languages for kids, visual programming, interaction techniques, window management, and programming environments. He belongs to SIGCHI, ACM, IEEE Computer Society, IEEE, and Computer Professionals for Social Responsibility. (*http:// www.cs.cmu.edu/~bam*)

Bonnie A. Nardi is an anthropologist at Agilent Labs in Palo Alto, California. She has lived and studied in Papua New Guinea and Western Samoa, and has investigated the technological habits of spreadsheet users, brain surgeons, reference librarians, and American teenagers, among others. She is currently developing a software system called "ContactMap" based on her research on social networks in the workplace. Bonnie Nardi is the author of *A Small Matter of Programming: Perspectives on End User Computing,* MIT Press, 1993, and the editor of *Context and Consciousness: Activity Theory and Human-Computer Interaction,* MIT Press, 1996. With Vicki O'Day, she wrote *Information Ecologies: Using Technology with Heart,* MIT Press, 1999. (*http://www.best.com/~nardi/default.html*)

Gordon W. Paynter is a researcher for the Department of Computer Science at the University of Waikato in New Zealand. His research interests include programming by demonstration, machine learning, digital libraries, and text mining. He received his Ph.D. from Waikato for work on "Automating iterative tasks with programming by demonstration." (*http:// www.cs.waikato.ac.nz/~paynter/*)

Corrina Perrone-Smith earned a joint degree in international business and computer science from the University of Colorado. She began her professional career creating artificial intelligence software systems for the defense industry. She also holds professional certifications in massage therapy (1990) and Ashtanga Yoga instruction (1991). She maintained both a private bodywork and yoga instruction practice and consulted for several years until a collision with a Mack truck in 1996. She has received international honors for her work in computer science focusing on the Internet in Education and Computer-Mediated Communications. She now works as a public relations professional and occasional Web consultant. (*http:// www.cs.colorado.edu/~corrina/*)

Richard Potter is currently a PRESTO Researcher at the Japan Science and Technology Corporation (JST). His research interests are tools and techniques that make programming practical for a wider range of users in more diverse situations. He received a B.S. in computer engineering from Clemson University and a Ph.D. in computer science from the University of Maryland, where he was a member of the Human-Computer Interaction Laboratory. (*http://www.cs.umd.edu/hcil/members/rpotter/*)

Alexander Repenning is the CEO and President of AgentSheets Inc., and a Research Assistant Professor and member of the Center for Lifelong Learning and Design at the University of Colorado in Boulder. He has worked in research and development at Asea Brown Boveri, Xerox PARC, Apple Computer, and Hewlett Packard. Repenning is the creator of the AgentSheets simulation and game-authoring tool. His research interests include end-user programming, visual programming, computers in education, human-computer interaction, and artificial intelligence. Repenning received his Ph.D. in computer science from the University of Colorado in 1993. (Email: *alexander@agentsheet.com*; Web: *http://www.agentsheets .com*)

Jean-David Ruvini received his M.Sc. degree and his Ph.D. degree in computer science from Montpellier-II University in 1996 and 2000 respectively. His research interests center on adaptive systems and include machine learning (shift of bias and multiple bias learning), programming by example (programming by demonstration), and predictive and adaptive interfaces. (*http://www.lirmm.fr/~ruvini*)

David Canfield Smith received a B.A. in mathematics from Oberlin College in 1967 and a Ph.D. in computer science from Stanford University in 1975. His Ph.D. work contained two new ideas: icons and programming by demonstration. After a brief stop at SRI in Doug Englebart's Augmentation

Research Center, Dave joined the Xerox Corporation's "Star" computer project in Palo Alto, remaining with it for seven years. He was one of the principal designers of the Star user interface, the ancestor of the Macintosh, inventing for it the concepts of icons (from his Ph.D. work), the desktop metaphor, dialog boxes, and generic commands (such as Move, Copy, Delete, Undo). Today all major personal computers have adopted these ideas, and more than 200 million people use them every day. After joining and/or founding three start-up companies in five years, Dave joined Apple Computer in 1988, where he worked with Alan Kay on educational software. The Creator product (called KidSim and Cocoa at Apple) is the culmination of that work. Dave is the co-inventor of Creator with Allen Cypher. In 1997, Dave, Allen, Larry Tesler, and a few others from Apple started Stagecast Software to bring this idea to the market. In 1999, Stagecast released its first product, available at *www.stagecast.com.* The unifying goal of Dave's work for the past thirty years has been to make computers more accessible to ordinary people. His outside interests include skiing, hiking, camping, traveling, photography, the Boy Scouts, and kids.

Robert St. Amant is an Assistant Professor in the Department of Computer Science at North Carolina State University. He received a Ph.D. in Computer Science from the University of Massachusetts, Amherst, in 1996. His current interests include planning agents in the user interface, cognitively plausible interface agents, and assistants for information visualization and navigation. (*http://www.csc.ncsu.edu/faculty/stamant*)

Atsushi Sugiura received B.E. and M.E. degrees in electric engineering from the University of Osaka in 1988 and 1990. He then joined NEC Corporation, where he is currently an Assistant Research Manager at the C&C Media Research Laboratories. From 1998 to 1999 he was a visiting scientist at the Department of Computer Science and Engineering, University of Washington. His research interests include human computer interaction, visual programming, programming by demonstration, and intelligent software agents. (*http://www.cs.washington.edu/homes/sugiura/*)

Nobuo Takahashi joined Hitachi in 1974. He has developed many software products especially with human-computer interaction, such as a user interface software platform and a time-sharing system for mainframe computers. He is currently working with a report generator for personal computers with example-based design interface at Software Division, Hitachi. He is a member of the Information Processing Society of Japan.

Larry Tesler is the CEO of Stagecast Software, Inc., an e-simulation company in Redwood City, California. Prior to the founding of Stagecast, Tesler served as VP and Chief Scientist of Apple Computer, where he nurtured innovations such as the Lisa user interface, MacApp, HyperCard, QuickTime, and the Apple Classroom of Tomorrow. At Xerox PARC, he contributed a number of ideas and techniques that have become common in graphical user interfaces. At the Stanford Artificial Intelligence Laboratory, he conducted research on document markup languages, cognitive modeling, and natural language understanding. During his career, Tesler has been involved in the design of several computer languages, including PUB, Smalltalk, Object Pascal, and AppleScript. Among his publications are invited articles on programming languages and networked computing in special issues of *Scientific American*. (*http://www.nomodes.com/*)

Carol Traynor is Assistant Professor in the Computer Science Department at St. Anselm College in Manchester, NH, where she teaches courses in human-computer interaction and computer science. Her research work focuses on end-user programming for non-technical end users of highly technical software, such as Geographic Information Systems. Traynor is a member of the Human-Computer Interaction Research Group at the University of Massachusetts Lowell, where she is currently engaged in further evaluation of the graphical query language C-SPRL.

Daniel S. Weld is Thomas J. Cable / WRF Professor of Computer Science and Engineering at the University of Washington. After formative education at Phillips Academy, he received bachelor's degrees in both computer science and biochemistry at Yale University in 1982. He landed a Ph.D. from the MIT Artificial Intelligence Lab in 1988 and received a Presidential Young Investigator's award in 1989 and an Office of Naval Research Young Investigator's award in 1990. Weld is on the editorial board of *Artificial Intelligence,* was a founding editor and member of the advisory board for the *Journal of AI Research,* was guest editor for *Computational Intelligence,* is guest editor for a special issue of *Artificial Intelligence* on Intelligent Internet Systems, edited the AAAI report on the Role of Intelligent Systems in the National Information Infrastructure, and was Program Chair for AAAI-96. Weld has published two books and scads of technical papers.

Dr. Weld is an active entrepreneur with several patents and technology licenses. In May 1996, he co-founded Netbot Incorporated, creator of Jango Shopping Search and now part of Excite. In October 1998, Weld co-founded AdRelevance, a revolutionary monitoring service for Internet advertising, which is now part of Media Metrix. In June 1999, Weld co-founded Nimble

Technology, which is developing advanced data integration products. In June 2000, Weld co-founded Asta networks, whose service minimizes the risk of Internet denial of service attacks. (*http://www.cs.washington.edu/homes/weld/weld.html*)

Marian G. Williams is Associate Professor of Computer Science at the University of Massachusetts Lowell. Her research interests center on tools and techniques that can be used in the participatory design of interactive experiences for users who don't have sophisticated computing backgrounds. She has worked with users from many walks of life, including astrophysicists, environmentalists, and public school teachers. Williams is the Director of UMass Lowell's Human-Computer Interaction Research Group and the coordinator of the Graduate Certificate Program in Human-Computer Interaction. When she's not teaching, advising graduate students, or doing research, Williams can be found playing Celtic fiddle (badly). (*http://www.cs.uml.edu/~williams*)

Ian H. Witten is a Professor of Computer Science at the University of Waikato. He directs the New Zealand Digital Library research project. His research interests include information retrieval, machine learning, text compression, and programming by demonstration. He received an M.A. in Mathematics from Cambridge University, England; an M.Sc. in Computer Science from the University of Calgary, Canada; and a Ph.D. in Electrical Engineering from Essex University, England. He is a fellow of the ACM and of the Royal Society of New Zealand. He has published widely on digital libraries, machine learning, text compression, hypertext, speech synthesis and signal processing, and computer typography. He has written several books, the latest being *Managing Gigabytes* (1999) and *Data Mining* (2000), both from Morgan Kaufmann. (*http://www.cs.waikato.ac.nz/~ihw/*)

David Wolber is an Associate Professor at the University of San Francisco. His research interests include user interface development, end-user programming, and Web-based tools. He designed and developed both the DEMO and Pavlov Programming-By-Demonstration systems, and he is currently developing an associative thinking agent. Wolber earned his Ph.D. from the University of California, Davis. He currently teaches software engineering and object-oriented development and is a consultant for Iris Financial in San Francisco. (*http://web.usfca.edu/~wolberd/index.html*)

Steve Wolfman is a Ph.D. student in computer science at the University of Washington. He received his B.S.E. from Duke University in 1997 and his

M.S. from the University of Washington in 1999. For the last few years he has worked on artificial intelligence, focusing on planning systems and collaborative agents. He is currently working on extending the user interface for SMARTedit to be adaptive and proactive. In his spare time, he also volunteers at the Seattle Animal Shelter walking, training, and bathing dogs (and attendant responsibilities). (*http://www.cs.washington.edu/homes/wolf/*)

David Wright is currently the Product Manager for Java Foundation Classes and JavaBeans at Sun Microsystems, Inc. Before joining Sun, David worked at Apple Computer, Inc., where he co-invented and co-developed Apple Location Manager and Apple Data Detectors. He also worked on the setup assistant that now ships on all new Macs and the setup assistant for Mac OS X Server. His last year at Apple was in Developer Relations as the Carbon Technology Manager, where he worked with developers to port their applications to Mac OS X.

Luke Zettlemoyer is currently the Director of Advanced Technologies at LiveWire Logic, Inc., in Raleigh, NC. His research interests include user interface agents, machine learning, dialogue systems, and programming by demonstration. He received a B.S. in applied math and a B.S. in computer science in 2000 from North Carolina State University.